THE GALLANT DEAD

THE GALLANT DEAD

Union and Confederate Generals
Killed in the Civil War

Derek Smith

STACKPOLE
BOOKS

Published by
STACKPOLE BOOKS
5067 Ritter Road
Mechanicsburg, PA 17055
www.stackpolebooks.com

Printed in the United States of America

10 9 8 7 6 5 4 3 2 1

FIRST EDITION

Library of Congress Cataloging-in-Publication Data

Smith, Derek, 1956 Nov. 3-
    The gallant dead : Union and Confederate generals killed in the Civil War / Derek Smith.
        p. cm.
    Includes bibliographical references and index.
    ISBN 0-8117-0132-8
    1. Generals—United States—Biography. 2. Generals—Confederate States of America—Biography. 3. United States. Army—Biography. 4. Confederate States of America. Army—Biography. 5. United States—History—Civil War, 1861–1865—Biography. 6. United States—History—Civil War, 1861–1865—Registers of dead. 7. United States—History—Civil War, 1861–1865—Campaigns. I. Title.

E467.S615 2005
973.7'4'0922—dc22
                                                                    2004029681

TABLE OF CONTENTS

INTRODUCTION

This is a book about leadership, honor, courage and death, all for conflicting causes.

Of the more than 400 Confederate generals in the Civil War, 78 were killed in battle or mortally wounded. By comparison, the Union armies fielded 583 generals, of whom 45 died of combat injuries.

This is the true story of those 123 Yankee and Rebel commanders.

The generals who died for the Confederacy were a diverse group who were outlived, albeit briefly, by their new nation's five years of existence. Like all who joined in the 1860–61 secession, they were branded traitors in the North and heralded as patriots of a second American Revolution in the South. Those who wore blue were defending the Union and, in the end, their priceless sacrifice was the red-blended mortar that helped cement the nation.

Some bore scars from Seminole or Mexican bullets, from running fights with Indian warriors on the western frontier or from personal duels.

Many were honed to bayonet sharpness on the drill fields of West Point or in the Mexican War, which would be the proving ground for numerous officers in blue or gray in the Civil War. Others were civilian soldiers when the war struck, serving in their state militias from Maine to Texas. There were a multitude of politicians, judges and lawyers, and a few were teachers and farmers or, in the South, gentlemen planters. Others were railroad engineers or merchants.

A few soon-to-be Rebels strode the halls of Congress in Washington before the rebirth of nations made them legislators in the first Confederate capital of Montgomery and later Richmond, the cannon bursts over Fort Sumter punctuating their transfer of allegiances.

Some had endured the pain of families torn apart by the war. Benjamin Helm was a brother-in-law of President Abraham Lincoln when he donned the gray. Archibald Gracie's family was one of New York City's most affluent, yet he sided with the Confederacy.

The Terrill family of Virginia lost two sons who were generals—William wore blue; his younger brother James joined the rebellion.

For the Union, the "Fighting McCooks" of Ohio were hardest hit, two general sons, Robert and Daniel, slain while their father, a Yankee major, also was killed in battle.

Even more basic, most of the commanders on both sides were husbands and fathers whose families were no less grief-stricken than those of the other approximately 650,000 soldiers killed in battle, or the many thousands of others who succumbed to illness or disease. Widows and fatherless children knew no rank, the loved ones of an Iowa private shot down at Corinth mourning just as deeply as the six daughters orphaned when Confederate general Felix Zollicoffer fell.

The oldest and highest ranking to die on either side was fifty-nine-year-old Confederate general Albert Sidney Johnston, slain at Shiloh. Among the Federals, Maj. Gen. Joseph K. F. Mansfield at fifty-eight was the senior casualty, killed at Antietam, while Maj. Gen. James B. McPherson, commander of the U.S. Army of the Tennessee, was the most prominent loss to the Union.

The youngest casualty was Edmund Kirby, a twenty-three-year-old New Yorker who fought as a Union artillery lieutenant at Chancellorsville. Severely wounded, he died almost a month later on the day he was promoted brigadier general. Among the Confederates, John Herbert Kelly was one of three twenty-four-year-old generals to die, an Alabamian mortally wounded in a cavalry clash near Franklin, Tennessee, in 1864.

All of these generals were trusted to lead and died in the effort. Sometimes their lives bought victory, but more often, especially in the case of the Confederates, their blood was spilled in defeat.

It is beyond the scope of this work to offer in-depth descriptions of the campaigns and battles in which these men fell. Likewise, the reader will have to look elsewhere for detailed biographies, with Ezra Warner's *Generals in Blue, Generals in Gray* and Bruce Allardice's *More Generals in Gray* being good places to start. My focus is on the circumstances of each of their deaths, including what was going on in their lives at the time, their careers, the battle conditions, and their likely frame of mind on their last day alive.

In some cases it was possible to pinpoint an individual soldier who killed a general; in others, a regiment or brigade, or a corps if scant information was available. Sadly for the Confederacy, in the deaths of Stonewall Jackson and Brig. Gen. Micah Jenkins, the men who pulled the trigger were their own.

CHAPTER 1

First to Fall—1861

CONFEDERATE BRIGADIER GENERAL
ROBERT SELDEN GARNETT
Corrick's Ford, Virginia, July 13, 1861

Eight days before the battle of First Bull Run, death claimed its first Confederate general in the rugged mountain country of western Virginia. Brig. Gen. Robert S. Garnett had worn the stars of command for little more than a month when he and his men faced the enemy at Corrick's Ford on July 13, 1861. Three days later the North rejoiced in his end and the defeat of his army, front page headlines in the *New York Times* proclaiming, "The Entire Army of General Garnett Routed" and "Another Important Victory in Western Virginia."[1]

The war was young and bloodshed on faraway battlefields was titillating as the Union girded to crush the rebellion. Garnett was West Point class of 1841 and had been an infantry officer in the U.S. Army for almost two decades before resigning his commission to join the Confederacy. "He was, therefore, twenty years an officer, nineteen of which saw him an honorable soldier, serving his country's flag," the *Times* stated, saying without words that his last year had been as a traitor.[2]

Garnett, forty-one, was born in Essex County, Virginia, and twice had been brevetted for bravery in the Mexican War. He was a cousin of Maj. Richard B. Garnett, himself soon to be a brigadier general who would die in Confederate service. The cousins had graduated together from the U.S. Military Academy. Robert Garnett was already somewhat of a tragic figure, being widowed after one year of marriage. He and Marianne Nelson of

New York had wed in 1857 but she and their infant son had died of bilious fever the following year. When Virginia seceded and Garnett resigned his major's commission in the U.S. 9th Infantry, he served as adjutant to Brig. Gen. Robert E. Lee before himself being promoted to Confederate brigadier. Within days of his promotion, Garnett was assigned to command Rebel forces in northwestern Virginia. On his staff was aide-de-camp William E. Starke who would himself become a brigadier general little more than a year later before falling at Antietam.[3]

Garnett had few troops, mostly green volunteers from Virginia, the Carolinas, Georgia, and Tennesee, and soon found himself threatened by larger Federal forces under Maj. Gen. George B. McClellan and Brig. Gen. William S. Rosecrans. In unfamiliar country, he tried vainly to raise more troops from the mountain counties and sent pleas to Lee for more men. Lee complied promptly, but these reinforcements would be too late to help.[4]

A friend later recalled Garnett's words on the night before he left Richmond for this command: "They have not given me an adequate force. I can do nothing. They have sent me to my death."[5]

The Southerners were forced to abandon positions at Rich Mountain and Laurel Hill as Garnett tried to withdraw toward the Shenandoah Valley with the Yanks hotly pursuing him. The retreat devolved into a series of sharp skirmishes along steep ridges and on rough mountain roads that were little more than cart paths, made all the more treacherous by rainy weather. Slowed by their wagon train, the Confederates reached Corrick's Ford on the Cheat River in what is now Tucker County, West Virginia, late Saturday morning, July 13, 1861.[6] But the river was rain swollen and some of Garnett's wagons bogged down at the ford, costing more critical time as the wet and muddy Rebels tried to free them.

After finally crossing, Garnett's rearguard, the 23rd Virginia Infantry under Col. W. B. Taliaferro, took position on the opposite bank to oppose Union infantry and artillery commanded by Brig. Gen. Thomas A. Morris of Indiana that had caught up to them due to the delay. Throughout the retreat, the Virginians had been alternating with the 1st Regiment of Georgia Volunteers in guarding the rear.

Pressing Taliaferro was Col. Ebenezer Dumont's 7th Indiana Infantry, but with cheers for Jefferson Davis, the Rebels opened fire on the bluecoats hidden in the leafy greenery across the river.

Bolstered by some artillery, the Virginians twice drove back the enemy, but suffered about thirty casualties before retreating, their ammunition running low. At another ford about half a mile from Corrick's, Taliaferro was met by Garnett who ordered him to post his best riflemen as skirmishers on a bluff overlooking the crossing. "This is a good place behind this drift-wood to post skirmishers," the general remarked.[7]

The Federals came up and rifles again echoed through the mountains. With his sharpshooters behind cover, Garnett and an aide, Sam M. Gaines, were the only Confederates visible and attracted enemy fire. Gaines ducked as balls whistled by, and he quickly drew a scolding from Garnett. Gaines recalled that "When I told him I had felt on my face the wind from several bullets, and that I could not help but stoop, he changed his tone and talked to me in a fatherly way as to the proper bearing of a soldier under fire."[8]

Minutes later, with the bluecoats now within about fifty yards of them, Garnett turned in the saddle and gave the order for the skirmishers to retire. Suddenly, a Union bullet plunged into his back at almost the same instant as one of his sharpshooters, Pvt. Sampson Phillips of the 23rd Virginia, was killed at his side.[9]

As Garnett toppled from his horse, Gaines dismounted and tried to lift the general onto his own horse. He was struggling to do so when he saw the Yankees nearing the ford. Gaines then grabbed the reins of Garnett's mount, climbed back into his own saddle and galloped to safety, leaving the dying general behind. Garnett survived only a few minutes, becoming the first general officer on either side to die in combat in the war. A sergeant named Burlingame in Dumont's command was credited with killing him. At least one account states that Garnett fell into the water when he was shot, his body being recovered by the Federals amid the hasty Rebel retreat from the field. Morris also captured a cannon and about forty wagons.[10]

McClellan sent a victorious dispatch the day after the battle: "Garnett and forces routed; his baggage and one gun taken; his army demoralized; Garnett killed. We have annihilated the enemy in Western Virginia. . . . Our success is complete and secession is killed in this country."[11]

Placed in a crude wooden casket by his enemies, Garnett's body was taken by train to Grafton, Virginia, arriving on July 15. That same day McClellan sent a note to the commander of Confederate forces near Staunton regarding the disposition of prisoners. In the dispatch he mentioned Garnett's demise: "You will, ere this, no doubt, be informed of the unhappy fate of General Garnett, who fell while acting the part of a gallant soldier. His remains are now at Grafton, preserved in ice, where they will await the instructions of his relatives, should they desire to remove them to his home."[12]

Garnett "was killed while attempting to rally his retreating forces," the *New York Times* said in its July 16 coverage. "Gen. Garnett was killed by an Indiana soldier in a regular battle."[13]

Garnett's remains and his personal effects were later returned to his family by old Army friends. He was buried temporarily in Baltimore's Green Mount Cemetery before being moved in August 1865 to his wife's family plot in Greenwood Cemetery, Brooklyn, New York.[14]

Years after the war, Confederate veteran and historian Robert White wrote of Garnett: "Thus fell, sharing the post of greatest danger in a disastrous retreat which he could not avoid, the first distinguished martyr of the Confederacy."[15]

CONFEDERATE BRIGADIER GENERAL BARNARD E. BEE
First Bull Run, July 21, 1861

Brig. Gen. Barnard E. Bee would die at Bull Run, but not before ensuring immortality for another general who fought there—along with everlasting controversy.

The war was in its opening months in July 1861 when a Union army of 39,000 under Brig. Gen. Irvin McDowell marched south from Washington, D.C., menacing Southern forces in north-central Virginia. Although the Confederacy was still absorbing the defeat and death of Robert Garnett, McDowell still faced about 21,000 rebels led by Brig. Gen. P. G. T. Beauregard, who were eager for a fight. These graycoats were positioned south of a tranquil stream called Bull Run near Manassas Junction, a key railroad center. Realizing he would need help to stop McDowell, Beauregard sent for reinforcements from Confederate general Joseph E. Johnston's army in the Shenandoah Valley.

Bee, thirty-seven, was one of Johnston's three brigade commanders, the others being Col. Francis Bartow of Georgia and Brig. Gen. Thomas J. Jackson. Bee was a native South Carolinian whose father had been secretary of state for the Republic of Texas. An 1845 graduate of West Point, he was a Mexican War veteran, but had resigned his captaincy in the 10th U.S. Infantry to join the Confederacy. He had been appointed a Rebel brigadier just over a month before his death.

Despite being confronted by another Union force in the Shenandoah, Johnston complied with Beauregard's request. Jackson's brigade and units from Bee's and Bartow's commands were sent by rail to Manassas, arriving on July 19–20. When his men prepared to board the train, Bee found there was not enough room for his entire brigade. Reaching Manassas about noon on July 20, he put his 4th Alabama, 2nd Mississippi, and two companies of the 11th Mississippi on the cars. Beauregard posted Bee and Bartow to support his right.

Beauregard planned to attack McDowell the next day, but McDowell had plans of his own and beat him to the punch. The Federals made two diversionary attacks before dawn on July 21 before launching a main assault against the Rebels' extreme left flank. This was the weakest point of the Southern line, guarded only by the brigade of Col. Nathan G. "Shanks" Evans. Greatly outnumbered, Evans fought desperately to hang on as Beauregard ordered Bee and Bartow to go to his aid. It was late morning when they joined Evans, but the Rebels here were still outmanned more than two-to-one by the Federals.

When he arrived and took in the panoramic view of the battle there, Bee remarked, "Here is the battlefield, and we are in for it!" Earlier he had been angry, believing that his move to reinforce Evans had taken him out of the expected fight on Beauregard's right.[16] Now he pressed his men forward in a battle line to Matthews Hill to bolster Evans.

By about noon, the Confederates here had been forced to retreat to Henry Hill several hundred yards to the south. Bee, who had assumed command of the Rebels in this sector, frantically pushed Col. Wade Hampton's Legion into action to try and stem the Federals, but with little effect. In another instance the general placed his hat on his sword point to wave a battery into position.

Jackson's brigade, meanwhile, had arrived on Henry Hill about 11:30 A.M. and did not immediately join in the fighting. Instead, Jackson ordered his Virginians to lie down just behind the crest, even as the brigades of Bartow and Evans retreated in disorder, while Bee's 4th Alabama fought like a veteran unit. It was not enough, however.

"Bee rode up and down his lines encouraging his troops by everything that was dear to them to stand up and repel the tide which threatened them with destruction," related a correspondent for the *Charleston Mercury*.[17]

Jackson's men then saw a horseman riding up the slope toward their line—Bee. "He was an officer, all alone, and as he came closer, erect and full of fire, his jet-black eyes and long hair, and his blue uniform of a general officer made him the cynosure of all," recalled D. B. Conrad, a surgeon with the 2nd Virginia in Jackson's Brigade. Bee asked one of the men what troops they were and was directed to Jackson.[18]

Bee and Jackson knew each other to some degree. Bee had graduated from West Point a year earlier than Jackson. Both had served in Mexico and with Joe Johnston. In this crisis—with the Rebel flank melting and a multitude of Yankees bearing down on him—Bee might have wondered why Jackson did not come to his aid, although Jackson's reputation as a fierce fighter had yet to be forged in Southern legend. Henry Kyd Douglas, an orderly sergeant in Jackson's brigade who later would be assigned to Jackson's staff, described the first meeting between Bee and Jackson on Henry Hill:

"General Bee, his brigade being crushed, rode up to him [Jackson] and with the mortification of an heroic soldier reported that the enemy was beating him back.

"'Very well, General,' replied Jackson.

"'But how do you expect to stop them?'

"'We'll give them the bayonet!' was the brief answer."[19]

Conrad, who gave a similar account of the conference, wrote that, "With a salute, General Bee wheeled his horse and disappeared down the hill, where he immortalized himself."[20]

Jackson, in his battle report, wrote of this brief conference with Bee: "Subsequently ascertaining that General Bee . . . was hard pressed, I marched to his assistance, notifying him at the same time that I was advancing to his support; but, before arriving within cannon range of the enemy, I met General Bee's forces falling back. I continued to advance with the understanding that he would form in my rear. . . . General Bee, with his rallied troops, soon marched to my support."[21]

After leaving Jackson, Bee found about the only organized unit left in his brigade, a portion of the 4th Alabama, which he gathered for an attack on the oncoming Federals. The remainder of the commands of Bee, Bartow, and Evans were either casualties or milling in confusion behind Henry Hill and the nearby Robinson House. Maj. William M. Robins of the 4th wrote that the Alabamians were "inspired by the lion like bearing of that heroic officer" when Bee asked if they were able to make a bayonet charge. According to Robins, Bee shouted to them, "Yonder stands Jackson like a stone wall. Let us go to his assistance."[22]

Thomas L. Preston, one of Johnston's staff officers, provides another account of the events, writing that Johnston and Beauregard had just reached this sector of the battlefield when they saw the Alabamians standing along an old fence, unsure of what to do in the absence of their killed or wounded officers. Col. States Rights Gist of Bee's staff was placed in charge of these men, leading them back toward the fighting. Just then, Bee rode up to Johnston, "dropped the reins of his bridle, and in a voice tremulous with emotion, the tears rolling down his cheeks, said, "General, my command is defeated and scattered, and I am alone." Johnston replied, according to Preston, "I know it is not your fault, General Bee; but don't despair, the day is not lost yet."[23]

The generals conversed briefly before Johnston noticed some South Carolina troops lying along a fence line and ordered Bee to rally them back into the battle. Preston went with Bee, who appealed to the Carolinians to "sustain the reputation of their State, and, pointing to General Jackson's brigade . . . exclaimed, 'Look, there is Jackson with his Virginians standing like a stone wall against the enemy.' The men were aroused by these appeals, and, falling into line, were led toward the front. . . ."[24]

Minutes later, at the head of the Alabamians (and the Carolinians, if Preston is correct), Bee charged into the teeth of the Federal assault and was desperately wounded in the stomach, his counterattack quickly crushed. Most accounts state that he rode into this last action, but a few contend that he was dismounted. One of Jackson's Virginians claimed that Bee was unscathed when he rode among the survivors of this assault as they fell back, and then turned and deliberately rode alone into the enemy fire.[25]

The wording of Bee's "stone wall" exclamation varies from source to source, the battle chaos obscuring forever what was actually said or heard. Douglas related that Bee yelled to his men, "Look! There is Jackson's brigade standing behind you like a stone wall!"[26]

Beauregard later wrote that Bee called out, "Look at Jackson's brigade! It stands there like a stone wall!" Col. James Chesnut of Beauregard's staff told his wife three days after the battle that Jackson's command "stood so stock still under fire that they are called a stone wall!" while the *Charleston Mercury*'s version was "There is Jackson standing like a stone wall. Let us determine to die here, and we will conquer. Follow me."[27]

Jefferson Davis was riding to the battlefield when he met the ambulance bearing Bee, who "had been mortally wounded after his patriotism had been illustrated by conspicuous exhibitions of skill, daring, and fortitude." Davis stopped the wagon, which was carrying other wounded as well, raised the cover and spoke briefly to Bee. Maj. W. H. C. Whiting of Johnston's staff led the remains of Bee's brigade through the rest of the battle.[28]

Bee was carried to his headquarters in a cabin near the rail junction while Jackson anchored the Confederate line at Henry Hill with the remnants of the commands of Bee, Hampton, Evans, and Bartow, the latter killed. Jackson's stand, and the time bought by these shattered brigades, allowed more time for reinforcements from Johnston's army to arrive by train and help shift the battle tide by late afternoon. McDowell's force, which had victory in hand a few hours earlier, fled in rout, and the Rebels had won the first major clash of the war.

Word of Jackson's exploits quickly spread among the Confederates, as did Bee's "stone wall" remark, and Jackson and his brigade soon had an immortal nickname. But was Bee calling Jackson a coward or a staunch warrior when he yelled that the Virginians were standing "as a stone wall"? Bee did not live to explain, dying on the morning of July 22. Capt. John D. Imboden, who commanded a battery under Bee, was with the general in his last moments. Imboden had been incensed during the battle because he felt his unit had been overly exposed to capture and blamed the general. Word of Imboden's ire had reached Bee during the night and despite his wound, the general had sent couriers searching for Imboden on the battlefield, to bring him to Bee's bedside.

A messenger had finally roused Imboden that morning, "summoning me to the side of my gallant commander," Imboden recalled. Bee wanted to tell Imboden that he had sent word for the captain's battery to withdraw, but that the enemy had pushed back his brigade, the courier never reaching Imboden. The Carolinian never got the chance. Imboden rode to Bee's headquarters where he found the stricken general unconcious. "In a few minutes, while I was holding his hand, he died," Imboden remembered. "I was grieved deeply not to have seen him sooner."[29]

The controversy over his stone wall remark endures however. In his memoirs, Confederate colonel John C. Haskell wrote that Maj. Thomas Rhett, who was Johnston's chief of staff, and James Hill, Bee's brother-in-law and aide-de-camp, agreed Bee was criticizing Jackson for his inaction. Rhett, who was a West Point classmate of Bee and Jackson, was with Bee from shortly after he was shot until the general died. Hill was with Bee when he fell on the battlefield. Based on Haskell's account, Rhett and Hill said Bee on his deathbed was angered by Jackson's conduct, and that their contention was supported by statements made by Whiting.

"He [Rhett] has told me often . . . that Bee said that his and Bartow's brigades were hard pressed and that Jackson refused to move to their relief and in a passionate expression of anger he [Bee] denounced him for standing like a stone wall and allowing them to be sacrificed," Haskell wrote. Hill, according to Haskell, told much the same story, stating that Bee "was angry and excited when the fight was going on and bitterly denounced Jackson for refusing to move."[30]

Bee was among the 2,000 Confederate casualties lamented across the South. "This victory . . . was dearly won by the death of many officers and men of inestimable value, belonging to all grades of our society," Beauregard said in his official report. "In the death of General Barnard E. Bee the Confederacy has sustained an irreparable loss, for, with great personal bravery and coolness, he possessed the qualities of an accomplished soldier and an able, reliable commander."[31]

The South had achieved a hallmark triumph, but Davis bewailed the body count, especially Bee and Bartow. "The victory, though decisive and important . . . had been dearly bought by the sacrifice of the lives of many of our bravest and best, who at the first call of their country had rushed to its defense," he wrote.[32]

A train bearing Bee and Bartow chugged into Richmond on the night of July 23 and was met by an honor guard, band, and hearses for the slain officers. Their bodies lay in state in the Capitol overnight before being sent home to their respective states. Bee was buried in Charleston's Magnolia Cemetery while the fame of Stonewall Jackson and the Stonewall Brigade flourished. After the war, Bee was reinterred next to his parents in the yard of St. Paul's Episcopal Church in Pendleton, South Carolina.

The answer to the "Stonewall" question lies with him.

UNION BRIGADIER GENERAL NATHANIEL LYON
Wilson's Creek, Missouri, August 10, 1861

Amid the battlefield carnage of Wilson's Creek on August 10, 1861, Confederate soldiers found the body of a red-bearded Union brigadier general lying under the boughs of a small blackjack oak. Bloodied by three wounds, the officer was Nathaniel Lyon, the first U.S. general to die in battle in the Civil War, and also the first to be killed in combat since the War of 1812. A Yankee all the way, the maverick Lyon "more than any other man saved Missouri for the Union in 1861," wrote noted historian Ezra Warner.[33]

The state was a tinderbox of raw emotion and gunpowder in the summer of 1861 as North and South vied for its allegiance, and the forty-three-year-old Lyon was a short-lived but central figure in the drama.

Although the war's first major battle had been fought at Bull Run in Virginia, Wilson's Creek would surpass it in fierce intensity a few weeks later and result in Lyon's death.

Lyon had grown up in rural Connecticut and graduated from West Point in 1841, ranked eleventh in his class. He fought in the Seminole and Mexican wars and later was posted in California and Kansas. On the Civil War's eve, he commanded the U.S. arsenal in St. Louis and soon became an aggressive leader of the Union cause in Missouri. His seizure of Camp Jackson, a pro-Confederate Missouri militia bivouac near St. Louis, resulted in his promotion from captain to brigadier in May 1861. Lyon spent the next two months trying to force pockets of Southern sympathizers out of the state to ensure that a pro-Union state government controlled Missouri.

"Gen. Lyon is the right man in the right place," the *New York Herald* said on July 8. "He has a strong physical constitution, a high order of intellect, and an energy which knows no bounds. The government has only to give him the means and the liberty to act."[34]

He was to meet his sternest test in early August. An enemy force of more than 12,000, led by Confederate brigadier general Ben McCulloch and major general Sterling Price of the Missouri State Guard, was encamped at Wilson's Creek, about twelve miles southwest of Springfield. Lyon's Army of the West numbered only about 7,000 troops, but Lyon was undaunted, making plans to attack the rebels on August 10. McCulloch and Price also had decided on an offensive that day, but later changed their minds due to threatening weather. Leaving some men to guard the town, Lyon split his remaining soldiers into two assault columns, one led by him and the other by Col. Franz Sigel. "On the way to the field I frequently rode near him," a *Herald* correspondent wrote. "He seemed like one bewildered, and often when addressed failed to give any recognition, and seemed totally unaware that he was spoken to."[35]

Lyon's column of about 4,200 men opened the battle around 5 A.M., driving rebel cavalry off Oak Hill, known since that day as "Bloody Hill." But Confederate artillery stymied the Union advance long enough for Price to form his infantry for a counterstrike.

Sigel, meanwhile, had used his cannon to make some early gains further south, his shelling driving the Confederates there from their camps. McCulloch sent reinforcements to this sector, however, and by about 9 A.M., Sigel's small force had been routed. Sigel's defeat enabled the Rebels to concentrate on Lyon as the combat intensified on Bloody Hill.

On the crest, Lyon's men had parried Confederate thrusts throughout the early morning. At one point, as Lyon was riding with his entourage of aides and orderlies, he saw a group of horsemen ride out from the Confederate line. Recognizing one of the riders as General Price, Lyon started toward the group, ordering his staff to "draw pistols and follow," recalled Maj. William Wherry, an aide-de-camp. At Wherry's urging, Lyon held back, not wanting to expose himself needlessly to fire from the enemy fire.[36]

Price, who weighed about 250 pounds, was wounded in the side during the fighting, remarked to a staff officer, "That isn't fair; if I were as slim as Lyon, that fellow would have missed me entirely."[37]

Lyon would not be slim enough, however. He was near a battery of the 2nd U.S. Artillery under Capt. James Totten, leading his horse and trying to keep his disordered men in line when he was wounded in the leg and head, his mount being killed. "He [Lyon] walked slowly a few paces to the rear and said, 'I fear the day is lost,'" reported Maj. John Schofield, Lyon's adjutant general. "But upon being encouraged that our troops could again be rallied, that the disorder was only temporary, he passed over to the right . . . where our line seemed to be giving way, obtained another horse, and swinging his hat in the air, led forward the troops, who promptly rallied around him."[38]

Union brigadier general
Nathaniel Lyon.
LIBRARY OF CONGRESS

Totten met Lyon about this time and described the encounter: "He [Lyon] was wounded . . . in the leg, and I observed blood trickling from his head. I offered him some brandy . . . in my canteen, but he declined, and slowly rode to the right and front."[39]

Lt. Col. George Andrews of the 1st Missouri Infantry was in the midst of the battle when he encountered Lyon and asked him if he had heard any news of Sigel's progress. "To this inquiry he shook his head," Andrews wrote. "I now noticed he appeared to be suffering, and found he had just received a shot in his leg."[40]

Union major Samuel Sturgis also encountered Lyon about this time and noticed blood on the general's hat. "It is nothing, Major, nothing but a wound in the head," Lyon told him, remounting his horse.[41]

It was now about 9:30 A.M., and the troops Schofield described were the 2nd Kansas, just getting into action, and two companies of the 1st Iowa. Lyon was out in front, shouting, "Come on my brave boys, I will lead you," when a musket ball smacked into the left side of his chest, his third wound of the day. "He slowly dismounted, and as he fell into the arms of his faithful orderly, [Ed] Lehmann, he exclaimed, 'Lehmann, I am killed,' and almost immediately expired," Wherry remembered.[42]

A *New York Herald* account said that someone asked the stricken general if he was hurt, to which Lyon replied, "No, not much," but Lyon soon "expired without a struggle." "A few moments later he was carried from the field dead," Schofield noted. "His death was known at the time to but very few, and those few seemed to fight with redoubled valor."[43]

Lt. Gustavus Schreyer of the 2nd Kansas and two of his soldiers carried Lyon to the rear, followed by Lehmann, "bearing the hat and loudly bemoaning the death of his chief." Wherry covered Lyon's face with his coat and Surgeon F. M. Cornyn, soon "pronounced life extinct." Maj. John Halderman of the 1st Kansas reported that Lyon and Col. R. B. Mitchell had been at the head of the 2nd Kansas's column moving forward when "they were fired upon by the enemy from an ambuscade," Mitchell also falling severely wounded. Major Sturgis assumed overall command upon Lyon's death, Wherry and had the general's corpse carried to a field hospital where it was placed in a wagon and covered. "Strict orders were given that under no circumstances was the body to be removed till the army returned to Springfield," Wherry related.[44]

The Yankees were able to stave off one last massive Confederate attack. It was about 11 A.M. when the Rebels recoiled from this effort and Sturgis, his survivors exhausted and with little ammunition, ordered a withdrawal. As the Federals retreated toward Springfield, the Southerners were too disorganized and spent to mount a pursuit. With the battle over, the foes counted their losses—1,200 to 1,300 Union and 1,000 to 1,200 Confederate.

Wherry and others soon realized, however, that Lyon's body had been left behind. The wagon holding his remains had been needed to evacuate some of the wounded and the general had been removed and left at the field hospital. A cavalry company and wagon were quickly dispatched to retrieve the corpse, but soon discovered that the Confederates had possession of the body. The Yankees had "made a hasty retreat," remembered R. G. Childress of the 3rd Texas. "They left their dying chieftain to the mercy of a victorious but magnanimous enemy."[45]

Col. W. O. Coleman of Price's Missourians claimed that a Rebel lieutenant, not realizing the body was that of Lyon, knelt to cut a button off his uniform. As he did so, a wounded Yankee lying under a nearby tree called out, "Don't do that, that's General Lyon." As Coleman watched, "In less than a minute's time a hundred men or more got around him and his horse, cutting souvenir buttons off Lyon's coat and hairs from his horse's tail."[46]

The body was taken to the farmhouse of John Ray, which the Southerners were using as a field hospital, and laid out in the front bedroom. Under a truce flag the next day, an escort of the Missouri State Guard returned Lyon's remains to Springfield, where it was taken to the general's former headquarters in the home of John S. Phelps, a future state governor.

Lyon's staff attended to the remains. Lyon had befriended Mrs. Phelps while he was in Springfield and when Sturgis made plans to withdraw toward Rolla on August 12, the general's staff contacted the governor's wife, who was staying at the family's country home outside of town. They requested that Lyon be buried on the Phelps's farm until it could be removed. Mrs. Phelps consented.

When the army retreated, the general's body was left in the care of Union surgeons and turned over to Mrs. Phelps on August 13. Lyon was temporarily buried in the Phelps's garden on Springfield's outskirts the same day. "In death his features wore the same troubled and puzzled expression that had been fixed upon them for the past week," related the *New York Herald* reporter who had ridden with Lyon just before the battle.[47]

The Confederates had their own accounts of Lyon's fall. J. N. Boyd of the 1st Arkansas Mounted Riflemen was wounded in the battle, but recalled seeing a "Federal officer on a gray horse not far to the right of Totten's Battery. Several of our boys who had Mississippi rifles captured from the enemy at Neosho took shots at him. The dead bodies of General Lyon and his horse were found not far from the position held by Totten's Battery." W. H. King, a rebel captain in the 3rd Missouri, had seen the colonel of his brigade shot dead almost at his feet, noting that this officer and Lyon were killed no more than one hundred yards apart and "where the dead lay thickest." King related that Lyon was "a very able and capable man, who would doubtless have reached the highest rank in the Federal service if he had lived."[48]

Arkansas, Texas, and Missouri units all claimed the honor of killing Lyon. Some of the Johnnies admitted that his death likely turned the combat tide for them. "General Lyon was killed gallantly leading his men to what he and they supposed was victory, but which proved (it may be because they were deprived of his enthusiastic leadership) disastrous defeat," recalled Confederate brigadier general N. B. Pearce who led the Arkansas militia. "In the light of the present day, even, it is difficult to measure the vast results had Lyon lived and the battle gone against us."[49]

Word of Lyon's death amid the heavy Union casualties rocked the North. "The loss of our brave little army was severe," the *New York Times* said on August 15. "Its heroic leader, Gen. Lyon, fell in the engagement. He died just where the country would have predicted of him—leading a charge at the head of his column." The *New York Herald* added: "The loss of such a General as Lyon is not easily repaired; and had sufficient reinforcements been sent to him in time, not only would he have been still alive, in all human probability, but the victory would have been unmistakably his also. . . . He was a gallant soldier, and died bravely as a soldier should, in front of his men."[50]

From St. Louis on August 25, Maj. Gen. John Fremont, commander of the U.S. Department of the West, issued general orders to the troops regarding Lyon's fall: "The general commanding laments, in sympathy with the country, the loss of the indomitable General Nathaniel Lyon. . . . Let all emulate his prowess and undying devotion to his duty." Sturgis recalled that "Wherever the battle most fiercely raged, there was General Lyon to be found."[51]

Sixteen days after his death, members of Lyon's family put the general's corpse on a train that left Rolla bound for Connecticut. He was buried on September 4, 1861, in a cemetery near the village of Phoenixville.

On Christmas Eve 1861, the U.S. Congress approved a resolution recognizing Lyon's "gallant and patriotic services" and thanking the soldiers of his command for the "victory" at Wilson's Creek. "The country to whose service he devoted his life will guard and preserve his fame as a part of its own glory." Sturgis offered a fitting epitaph for Lyon: "Thus gloriously fell as brave a soldier as ever drew a sword, a man whose honesty of purpose was proverbial, a noble patriot, and one who held his life as nothing when his country demanded it of him."[52]

CHAPTER 2

Death in the West—
Early 1862

CONFEDERATE BRIGADIER GENERAL
FELIX K. ZOLLICOFFER
Mill Springs, January 19, 1862

In the cold, wet dawn of January 19, 1862, Brig. Gen. Felix K. Zollicoffer's command closed in on the enemy's camps at Logan's Crossroads in Kentucky. He had precipitated the coming battle that would cost him his life and ruin the career of another Rebel general.

Zollicoffer, forty-nine, was a Tennessean who had been a three-term U.S. congressman, journalist and a state politician before the conflict. His only military experience had been one year of service in the Seminole Wars as a lieutenant of volunteers.[1] When the war came, Zollicoffer was a widower with six daughters; his wife, Louisa, had died several years earlier. (Tragically, the Zollicoffers had also lost a total of five infant sons.) His political influence apparently secured him a general's commission in the Provisional Confederate States Army in July 1861, and he was assigned to eastern Tennessee.

Zollicoffer's main objective was to guard Cumberland Gap, but he aspired to accomplish more. After establishing winter quarters at Mill Springs, he moved his force to the Kentucky side of the Cumberland River in an effort to bolster Confederate influence in the region around Somerset, Kentucky. This unauthorized action came before the arrival of his surprised superior officer, Maj. Gen. George B. Crittenden, who ordered Zollicoffer back across the river. Zollicoffer did not comply.

When Crittenden reached the field, he found his little army of about 6,000 dug in on the Kentucky side at Beech Grove with the river at its back and a Union force under Brig. Gen. George H. Thomas nearby. Thomas and about 4,400 troops were at Logan's Crossroads, about ten miles from Beech Grove, and were expecting reinforcements. Crittenden called a council of war on the night of January 18, and it was decided to attack Thomas the next day, the Confederates realizing that they must strike him before he was strengthened if they were to have a chance of victory.

The Rebels left their camps around midnight with Zollicoffer's brigade of Tennessee and Mississippi troops in the lead behind a cavalry screen. Unknown to Crittenden and Zollicoffer, Thomas had already received some reinforcements, meaning that he now outnumbered his attackers.

In a misty predawn rain the Confederates encountered Union pickets about a mile from the crossroads and pushed them back. Moving further ahead, the Rebels met increasing resistance from Thomas's infantry and artillery, prompting Zollicoffer to deploy his men on both sides of the road before resuming his advance. The Confederates entered some woods as the battle heightened, and Zollicoffer received word from Col. Sidney Stanton of the 25th Tennessee that some of the Rebel units were mistakenly firing into each other. Zollicoffer reached the 19th Tennessee of Col. D. H. Cummings and ordered it to cease fire, believing the men were shooting at their comrades.

With at least two staff officers, Zollicoffer then rode further forward to try to determine the enemy's location. But in the rain and gloom, he bypassed his own line and went up a hill where the Federals were stationed in some strength. He advanced "as if to give an order to the lines of the enemy, within bayonet reach . . . his fatal mistake," Crittenden wrote.[2]

He blundered into a Union regiment, the 4th Kentucky Infantry of Col. Speed S. Fry that was posted in some woods. Fry recalled that he was near the right of his regiment when he saw an unidentified officer on a white horse riding slowly down the road and only about twenty paces from his men. Zollicoffer's uniform was covered by a long mackintosh, or rubber overcoat, but he was wearing what appeared to be Union uniform pants.

"His near approach . . . his calm manner, my close proximity to him, indeed everything I saw led me to believe he was a Federal officer belonging to one of the regiments just arriving," Fry recalled. "So thoroughly was I convinced that he was one of our men, I did not hesitate to ride up to his side so closely that our knees touched. He was calm, self-possessed and dignified in manner. He said to me 'We must not shoot our own men,' to which I responded, 'Of course not; I would not do so intentionally.'"[3]

Confederate brigadier general
Felix K. Zollicoffer.
LIBRARY OF CONGRESS

Fry then rode a short distance from Zollicoffer, more convinced than ever that he had been talking with another Union officer. Events suddenly took a quick turn. Another horseman appeared from behind a large tree near Zollicoffer, leveled a pistol and fired at a surprised Fry. The ball missed the colonel but inflicted a flesh wound to his horse, the rider ducking back behind the tree as Fry drew his Colt revolver to retaliate. "Not until this time was I aware that I had been in conversation with an [enemy] officer," he related. "In an instant the thought flashed across my mind that the officer with whom I had met and conversed had attempted to draw me into the snare of death . . . or capture . . . and, feeling thus, I aimed at him [Zollicoffer] and fired."[4]

Another account states that one of the Yankees recognized Zollicoffer despite his rain gear and shouted, "There's Zollicoffer! Kill him!" One of Zollicoffer's aides immediately shot and killed the Federal. Apparently hoping to mislead the enemy, Zollicoffer rode to within a few feet of Fry and said, "You are not going to fight your friends, are you?" and pointed to a Mississippi regiment in the distance.[5]

Whatever the conversation, Fry fired, as did some of his Kentuckians, and Zollicoffer collapsed dead from his horse. A rebel soldier dropped his musket and was trying to lift the stricken general when Capt. James A. Vaughan of Fry's regiment shot and killed him.[6]

The Federal musketry also mortally wounded Maj. Henry Fogg and Lt. Evan B. Shields of Zollicoffer's staff, and clipped the left ear of the general's mount.

But debate over who actually killed Zollicoffer exists to this day. General Thomas reported that Zollicoffer was killed by Fry's revolver shot while the Confederates contended that he died from four bullets of the Union volley, being hit twice in the head and in the chest and thigh. The Southern version is based on the account of Dr. D. B. Cliffe, one of Zollicoffer's surgeons, who remained behind after the battle to aid the wounded. Zollicoffer's body was recovered by the Yankees, and Cliffe apparently examined it as it was being "prepared for the casket."[7]

At least one account states that Zollicoffer was able to ride so close to the Kentuckians before being detected because they were looking for a new brigade commander, and Zollicoffer approached them from the flank where they did not expect any Rebels.

With Zollicoffer's end, the Confederate command structure failed, as did many of the old flintlocks carried by the rebels and rendered useless in the rain. Crittenden's left flank caved in and the graybacks began a disorganized retreat toward Beech Grove, abandoning much of their artillery and baggage trains. Closely harassed by Thomas, Crittenden withdrew across the Cumberland on the night of January 19–20.

Soldiers of the 10th Indiana, meanwhile, found themselves in possession of documents found on Zollicoffer's body. "In justice to the enemy I must say they exhibited a courage and determination worthy of a better cause," Col. M. D. Manson of the 10th related in a January 27 report. "General Zollicoffer, who commanded a part of their forces, fell while leading on his men, his body pierced by three bullets. . . . All the papers and plans of the late General Zollicoffer have fallen into my hands, which I will have preserved for the future use of the Government."[8]

Some of the Federals ripped away patches of Zollicoffer's uniform and buttons or cut snippets of his hair for souvenirs before officers restored order. Fry retained Zollicoffer's sword and a note found in one of the dead general's pockets. For years after the war, rumors circulated that Zollicoffer's corpse had been defiled by the Yankees. Fry eventually defended himself, stating that his men took the general's body to the rear as soon as they could and placed it in a tent. Zollicoffer's muddy, bloody uniform was removed and his body washed before being dressed in clothes from Fry's wardrobe. The body was then shipped through the rival lines to Nashville with a stop to transfer it from a wooden coffin, the best the bluecoats could find, to a more stylish metal casket.[9]

In Nashville, Zollicoffer lay in state at the capitol for a day or so while mobs of grieving admirers filed past. "I am pained to make report of the death of Brigadier General F. K. Zollicoffer, who fell while gallantly leading his brigade against the foe," Crittenden wrote in a January 29 report. "In his fall the country has sustained a great loss. In counsel he has always shown wisdom, and in battle braved dangers, while coolly directing the movements of his troops." Crittenden also said, "To myself, to the army, and to the country the fall of General Zollicoffer was a severe loss."[10] The general's now orphaned children were raised by Virginia, the eldest daughter, and her husband's family, as well as the second oldest, Ann Maria.

The battle of Mill Springs, also known as Logan's Crossroads or Fishing Creek, was a small affair—Confederate losses of about 440 and Union 230—compared to larger and bloodier Civil War engagements, but its impact was far reaching. Crittenden absorbed the blame, the defeat basically wrecking his military career. More importantly, the debacle meant the Confederacy had lost control of eastern Kentucky in the war's early critical stages. Zollicoffer, however, was beyond further criticism, being laid to rest in Nashville's City Cemetery.

"He was a man of unblemished moral character, amiable and modest in deportment, but quick to resent an insult," one Confederate historian wrote. "He was untiring in application to his duties. . . . Many public honors were paid to his memory in the South."[11]

Among the tributes to Zollicoffer was the poetry of Harry Linden Flash:

> First in the fight and first in the arms
> Of the white-winged angel of glory,
> With the heart of the South at the feet of God
> And his wounds to tell the story.[12]

CONFEDERATE BRIGADIER GENERALS BEN MCCULLOCH, JAMES M. MCINTOSH, AND WILLIAM Y. SLACK
Pea Ridge, March 7, 1862

Hard-as-nails Brig. Gen. Ben McCulloch was wearing velvet when a Union skirmisher drew a bead on him in the Arkansas brush at Pea Ridge on March 7, 1862. The Rebels girding for this battle faced a Federal army led by Gen. Samuel R. Curtis with control of Missouri and Arkansas likely hanging in the balance. McCulloch, fifty, was already combat proven—winning the battle of Wilson's Creek in August 1861—and was a star of the Confederate military west of the Mississippi. His life prior to secession was a frontier adventure no fiction could match. A neighbor of Davy Crockett on the Tennessee frontier, McCulloch had journeyed to Texas where he fought in the battle of San Jacinto during the war for Texas independence.

He later was a surveyor and Indian fighter who saw combat in the Mexican War and prospected for gold in California before returning to Texas and serving six years as a U.S. marshal. His younger brother, Henry, also would become a Confederate general and survive the war.[13]

In the first weeks of 1862, McCulloch and his Rebel force joined with Maj. Gen. Sterling Price in the Boston Mountains of northwestern Arkansas. Price and his pro-South Missouri State Guard had been driven out of Missouri by Curtis and his 10,000-man U.S. Army of the Southwest, and Curtis intended to keep him out. When Price linked with McCulloch, Curtis halted his advance and settled into positions at Pea Ridge about forty miles north of the mountains.

On March 2, Confederate major general Earl Van Dorn arrived in the Rebel camp. Van Dorn was the newly appointed commander of all Confederate troops west of the Mississippi, and quickly named the force of Price and McCulloch the Army of the West. Van Dorn was intent on retaking Missouri and issued orders for an immediate advance. Taking care of Curtis was the first order of business and the Rebel army of some 16,500 marched north in a blizzard on March 4. Price led one division of the army with McCulloch in command of the other, both under Van Dorn. The Southern ranks included about 800 Cherokee warriors under Brig. Gen. Albert Pike.

Commanding McCulloch's cavalry was Brig. Gen. James M. McIntosh, a thirty-three-year-old Floridian whose father, an army colonel, had been killed in the Mexican War. Graduating last in the West Point class of 1849, McIntosh had seen action with the U.S. 1st Cavalry on the frontier before casting his fortunes with the Confederacy in 1861. He was serving as colonel of the 2nd Arkansas Mounted Rifles when he was promoted to brigadier in January 1862. McIntosh's brother, John, was a Union general.[14]

Learning of Van Dorn's approach, Curtis entrenched along Little Sugar Creek on the Telegraph Road near Elkhorn Tavern on Pea Ridge. Nearing the enemy positions on the night of March 6, Van Dorn decided on a daring plan of action: he would march around the Union right flank and attack Curtis from the rear. Throughout the night and into the next morning, the Rebels struggled on their flank march through the backcountry. Price reached the Telegraph Road behind Curtis about midmorning, but McCulloch's division fell so far behind that Van Dorn ordered McCulloch to make his attack from west of the tavern. Curtis, meanwhile, had discovered the enemy movement and remarkably had turned most of his army north to face Price. He then attacked both segments of Van Dorn's

*Confederate brigadier general
Ben McCulloch.*
LIBRARY OF CONGRESS

divided army. McCulloch's command was assailed near the hamlet of Leetown by the Union divisions of Cols. Peter J. Osterhaus and Jefferson C. Davis, the combat raging in cornfields and woods.

McCulloch, who disdained the gray uniform of a Confederate general, preferring instead to wear a suit of black velvet, rode ahead of his troops in preparation for an advance. "He spoke a few words in passing," recalled J. M. Bailey, a color bearer for the 16th Arkansas Infantry. "He was carrying, as was his custom, a short breech-loading rifle and his field glass." McCulloch then rode alone through some trees.[15]

As had been his habit as a Texas ranger, McCulloch apparently wanted to scout the enemy himself. From a fence at the edge of a field on the Oberson Farm, a company of Union skirmishers from the 36th Illinois saw him riding toward them, about forty yards distant.

A volley from them tore the air and a bullet ripped into McCulloch's breast. Dr. Paul C. Yates, surgeon for a Missouri regiment, had been in the rear organizing ambulances and was returning to General Price when he saw McCulloch fall. "Just as I was passing McCulloch's command I saw him ride out in front, giving a command to the troops . . . when suddenly I saw his body first bend forward, then backward, and the next moment fall from his horse . . . in such a manner that I knew he was dead," Yates wrote.[16]

The Federals, including Osterhaus, congratulated Pvt. Peter Pelican of Company B, 36th Illinois, for firing the fatal shot.[17]

Bailey later described seeing McCulloch's body "lying in some thick woods, full length on his back, with a bullet hole showing plainly in the right breast of his coat. I recall vividly the quiet, peaceful expression his face bore in death. A bit of white cotton patching, powder-stained . . . was sticking in the hole made by the bullet in his coat. . . . His horse, gun, field glass and watch were gone." Based on Bailey's account, a lieutenant in his regiment, Benjamin Pixlee, covered McCulloch's body with his overcoat while telling Bailey that they must not inform the men of the general's death. About this time, another regiment of Arkansas infantry hustled past and some of their officers asked who was killed. Pixlee told them it was an orderly sergeant, Bailey wrote.[18]

McIntosh assumed command of McCulloch's wing and ordered a general attack, but was shot through the heart by an enemy sharpshooter shortly after McCulloch fell and in the same sector. Some accounts say another unit of the 36th Illinois claimed McIntosh's life with a volley while he was at the head of a regiment of Texas cavalry. The loss of these generals and the arrival of Union reinforcements resulted in the retreat of McCulloch's division. "McCulloch and McIntosh led their troops in person and both fell," reported Osterhaus.[19]

Price's Rebels, meanwhile were engaged in a bloody fight with the Union division of Col. Eugene A. Carr. Yet even in battle, these Southerners were curious about what was going on with their other attack force. "We had not heard a gun or a yell from McCulloch's men since nine or ten o'clock in the morning," remembered W. L. Truman, a Missouri cannoneer, "but later in the night we learned that McCulloch and McIntosh were killed early in the morning. The other officers were puzzled on the subject of rank, and could not decide who should take command."[20]

Dr. Yates had ridden to Price and told him of McCulloch's death, Price asking him, "Is this official?" When Yates replied that he had seen it, Price "seemed much affected." Minutes later a courier arrived and handed Price a dispatch. After reading it, he told Yates, "It is Gen. McIntosh that is killed." To which the physician answered, "Then it is both, I know Gen. McCulloch is dead."[21]

The sharpest combat of the day occurred around the tavern before Price drove back Carr's Yankees. The battle waned by sunset but flared again on March 8, with both sides intent on possessing the high ground around Elkhorn Tavern. Van Dorn had concentrated his battered army in a defensive position there during the night. In the early morning, Curtis bludgeoned the Confederates with accurate artillery fire, forcing them to fall back. Curtis then attacked with his entire army.

Exhausted from their long march, little food and the previous day's combat, the Rebels caved in, their units scattering in almost every direction. While losses were almost equal: 1,500 Confederate; 1,400 Union, Curtis' victory at Pea Ridge would mean that the Confederates would never again be able to mount a serious threat to reclaim Missouri

The bodies of McCulloch and McIntosh were taken by wagon to Fort Smith, Arkansas, where they were buried in what is now the National Cemetery. In a funeral procession, their flag-cloaked coffins were carried side-by-side in a hearse drawn by six white horses ornamented in black and led by three black-clothed slaves. Soldiers with reversed arms escorted the generals through a "a silent multitude gathered from the whole countryside, standing with uncovered heads and moist eyes." McCulloch was later reinterred in the State Cemetery in Austin, Texas.[22]

"No successes can repair the loss of the gallant dead who fell on this well-fought field," reported Van Dorn. "McCulloch was the first to fall. I had found him, in the frequent conferences I had with him, a sagacious, prudent counselor, and a bolder soldier never died for his country."[23]

Van Dorn wrote of McIntosh: "He was alert, daring, and devoted to his duty. His kindness of disposition, with his reckless bravery, had attached the troops strongly to him. . . . After leading a brilliant charge of cavalry and carrying the enemy's battery he rushed into the thickest of the fight again at the head of his old regiment and was shot through the heart."[24]

Of the lost generals, Van Dorn continued: "The value of these two officers was best proven by the effect of their fall upon the troops. So long as brave deeds are admired by our people, the names of McCulloch and McIntosh will be remembered and loved."[25]

Van Dorn's chief of staff, Col. Dabney H. Maury, however, was less than complimentary of the manner in which McCulloch and McIntosh met their deaths:

> The remarkable fatality which befell [them] was fairly attributed to the same indiscipline. McCulloch was killed by a sharpshooter while riding alone to reconnoitre [*sic*] the ground in front of his army—where he ought not to have been. McIntosh . . . yielded to a gallant impulse and placed himself at the head of a regiment of Texas horse, which was moving to charge a Federal battery. He was one of the few killed in the charge, and was entirely out of his proper place when he fell.[26]

McIntosh was a "typical cavalier, unacquainted with fear, magnetic to a degree rarely if ever surpassed," related J. N. Boyd of the 1st Arkansas Mounted Riflemen, adding that McIntosh was "a model soldier, a born leader, and men followed where he led without question or hesitation. He was to McCulloch what Jackson was to Lee, and when they gave up their lives . . . the army and the Confederacy suffered an irreparable loss."[27]

In a battle report General Curtis referred to the slain enemy commanders: "The fall of Generals McCulloch, McIntosh and other officers of the enemy, who fell early in the day, aided us in our final success at this most critical point; and the steady courage of officers and men in our lines chilled and broke down the hordes of Indians, cavalry, and infantry that were arrayed against us."[28]

Unmentioned by Curtis was a Confederate officer who had been desperately wounded in the battle and who would die before his official promotion to brigadier general. However, William Y. Slack was a forty-five-year-old brigadier in the Missouri State Guard, and Confederate battle reports of Pea Ridge refer to him as a general. A native Kentuckian, Slack had been a lawyer before the war, but had seen action under Price in Mexico. Siding with the South, he was in combat at Carthage and wounded in the left hip at Springfield, Missouri. He had recovered sufficiently to lead the 2nd Brigade of Missouri Volunteers under Price at Pea Ridge.[29]

As part of Price's advance that morning, Slack had sent his infantry forward to occupy Sugar Mountain, also known as Trott's Hill. The Missourians had just deployed in battle line near the summit when they came under musket fire. Minutes later, a rifle ball plunged into Slack's hip in almost the same spot as his previous injury. With no choice but to be taken from the field, Slack ordered his senior officer, Col. Thomas H. Rosser, to assume command of the brigade.

After his meeting with Price and on his way to attend to his wounded brother, Dr. Yates encountered two soldiers carrying an officer. "I went to them, and they had Gen. Slack, wounded in the groin, which proved fatal," Yates remembered.[30]

Slack was carried to a house near the battlefield and appeared to improve for a few days after the battle. "General Slack, after gallantly maintaining a long-continued and successful attack, was shot through the body; but I hope his distinguished services will be restored to his country," Van Dorn wrote on March 27, unaware that the worst had already happened.[31]

Due to the threat of being captured, Slack was moved about seven miles east to another house at Moore's Mill. His condition deteriorated quickly here, and he died early on the morning of March 21. The

Missourians grieved for Slack, "whom his men idolized and whom the whole army held in honor," Missouri colonel Thomas Snead recalled.[32]

Unaware of his death, Slack's promotion to Confederate brigadier was confirmed by the Senate in faraway Richmond, and he was promoted to rank from April 12, 1862. The new general, meanwhile, was lying in a grave at Moore's Mill. His body would be moved to the Confederate Cemetery in Fayetteville, Arkansas, in 1880. Writing on the day after Slack's death, Sterling Price described him as one of "my best and bravest officers."[33]

The "noble General Slack fell" at Pea Ridge, recalled W. J. Ervin of the 3rd Missouri Infantry years later. Ervin also recognized how the loss of the other generals as well as the battle upended Confederate fortunes: "And here it was that our hopes were blighted when the pride of the West, Gen. Benjamin McCulloch, went down, together with General McIntosh, the fall of which dissipated our last hopes for the recovery of Missouri."[34]

CHAPTER 3

Johnston:
The Eagle's Fall at Shiloh

**CONFEDERATE GENERAL ALBERT SIDNEY JOHNSTON
AND CONFEDERATE BRIGADIER GENERAL
ADLEY H. GLADDEN; UNION BRIGADIER GENERAL
W. H. L. WALLACE**
Shiloh, April 6–7, 1862
Like a rattlesnake fresh out of hibernation, the Confederate Army of the
Mississippi coiled to strike its adversary in the Tennessee woods around
Shiloh meeting house on April 6, 1862.

Gen. Albert Sidney Johnston's 44,000 Rebels had come up from
Corinth, Mississippi, to smite the U.S. Army of the Tennessee before they
could gain any more ground after victories at Forts Henry and Donelson in
February. Union major general Ulysses S. Grant's army was camped on the
west bank of the Tennessee River, preparing for a thrust at the Southerners
at Corinth. Unknown to Grant and his men, Johnston and his second-in-
command, P. G. T. Beauregard, had marched their men the twenty-two
miles from Corinth and were poised for a massive, early morning surprise
attack against the bluecoats. "I will water my horse in the Tennessee River
tomorrow night, or die in the attempt," Johnston is said to have remarked
as his army prepared to fight.[1]

Johnston, fifty-nine, was one of the Confederacy's most prominent and
wizened military commanders. The tall, erect Kentuckian with the thick
mustache was an 1826 graduate of West Point and saw action in the Black
Hawk War before resigning from the army in 1834. Johnston went to Texas
and fought in the war for Texas independence, serving as a general and later

secretary of war for the new republic. He was under fire in the Mexican War and rejoined the U.S. Army in 1849, being posted on the Texas frontier as colonel of the 2nd Cavalry. Johnston led the Utah expedition against the Mormons in 1857 for which he was brevetted a brigadier general. Resigning his commission after Texas seceded, Johnston was made a full general in the Confederate army to rank from May 30, 1861, and was put in command of all Rebel troops west of the Alleghenies.[2] The fall of Forts Donelson and Henry, however, unleashed a firestorm of criticism for Johnston's strategy in the west. President Jefferson Davis, however, defended Johnston, stating, "if Johnston is not a general . . . we have no general."[3]

As the sun rose at Shiloh, Johnston was ready to prove that Davis's faith in him was not misplaced. Beauregard had devised a plan calling for Maj. Gen. William Hardee's corps to attack in a long battle line strung between Owl and Snake Creeks. Following Hardee was the corps of Maj. Gen. Braxton Bragg, with the army's reserves under Leonidas Polk and John Breckinridge set to go in where they were needed.

Hardee's corps churned forward through the dark woods about 5 A.M., steamrolling two Federal divisions, many of the Yankees still in their tents or cooking their breakfast when the Rebels burst upon them.

Among the Southerners in Bragg's attack was Brig. Gen. Adley H. Gladden, a fifty-one-year-old South Carolinian with a reputation as a hard fighter who had been severely wounded while serving as colonel of the Palmetto Regiment in the Mexican War. Gladden had been a cotton broker and the postmaster of Columbia, South Carolina, before secession, and was living in New Orleans when the war flared. At Shiloh, he led a brigade of Alabama and Louisiana troops in Brig. Gen. J. M. Withers's division.

Gladden's brigade had moved out of camp, marching in Bragg's battle line, and had soon come in sight of Union troops aligned in their front. Behind these bluecoats, who belonged to Brig. Gen. Benjamin M. Prentiss's division, the Rebels could see the Federals' camps. When the Southerners advanced within 200 yards of the blue line, the Yankee infantry met them with a wave of musketry. A few Union cannons also opened on Gladden's ranks, the Rebels taking casualties as a battery attached to his brigade rolled into position.

The enemy guns were silenced, but not before Gladden, who was leading a charge around 8:15 A.M., was struck by a cannonball fragment that nearly took off his left arm. The general was "gloriously sustaining the reputation won in Mexico at the head of the immortal Palmetto Regiment" when he was mortally wounded, reported Col. Z. C. Deas of the 22nd Alabama. Col. Daniel W. Adams of the 1st Louisiana took command of the

*Confederate general
Albert Sidney Johnston.*
LIBRARY OF CONGRESS

brigade and led an assault that drove the Federals through their bivouac as
Prentiss fell back to try to regroup his reeling soldiers.[4]

Gladden's arm, meanwhile, was amputated on the battlefield, and he
was taken to Beauregard's headquarters near Corinth. But the Carolinian
could not rally, lingering until April 12 when he succumbed to his injuries.
"In his death our country has sustained a serious loss," reported one of his
regimental commanders, Col. J. Q. Loomis of the 25th Alabama. "He was
one of nature's noblemen—a good soldier, an accomplished gentleman, and
a true patriot. Long will his name live in the memory of those whom he so
gallantly led against our enemy's forces."[5]

Beauregard, in an April 11 report, described Gladden as a "gallant and
able soldier and captain" who was "conspicuous to his whole corps and the
army for courage and capacity."[6]

Years after the war, Beauregard wrote: "We early lost the services of the
gallant Gladden, a man of soldierly aptitudes and experience, who, after a
marked influence upon the issue in his quarter of the field, fell mortally
wounded."[7]

With the first grumble of cannon and musketry that morning, Albert
Sidney Johnston headed toward the sound of the guns. "General Johnston
rode straight to the front, and we were soon where the bullets were singing

around us and where we could see the Federal tents," remembered Lt. George W. Baylor, one of his aides.[8]

By late morning the Federals had been pushed back some distance, but their stubborn fighting in pockets had delayed the Confederate onslaught long enough for them to form a patchwork defensive line several miles long.

Astride his bay, Fire Eater, Johnston rode all over the battlefield throughout the morning and early afternoon, directing and encouraging his troops. In his hands he twirled a little tin cup that he had picked up when the Confederates overran one Federal camp. After one heavy charge he passed a group of wounded men from both sides and ordered his surgeon, Dr. David W. Yandell, to go and assist all of them. "They were our enemies, but are fellow sufferers now," Johnston said, according to Baylor's account.[9]

About 2 P.M., Johnston was following the advance of Brig. Gen. John Bowen's brigade in Breckinridge's division, trying to find and turn the left of the Union line. The Yankees battling them in this sector belonged to Grant's 4th Division under Brig. Gen. Stephen A. Hurlbut, the foes blasting at each other across a narrow wooded valley. The close-range musketry was hot and heavy, but the Federals could not be dislodged. "They are offering stubborn resistance here," Johnston told some of his men. "I shall have to put the bayonet to them."[10]

As Breckinridge prepared to attack, Johnston rode slowly down the line, hatless, fingering his cup and with his sword in its scabbard. "His presence was full of inspiration," wrote his son and aide-de-camp, Col. William P. Johnston. "His voice was persuasive, encouraging, and compelling. His words were few; he said "Men, they are stubborn; we must use the bayonet." When he reached the center of the line, he turned. "I will lead you!" he cried, and moved toward the enemy. A sheet of flame and a mighty roar burst from the Federal stronghold. The Confederate line withered; but there was not an instant's pause. The crest was gained. The enemy were in flight."[11]

After the assault, Johnston dispatched his staff officers, including Tennessee governor Isham G. Harris, who was serving as a volunteer aide, to carry orders to various commanders.

The general had weathered the early hours of the fighting with only minor wounds. A spent bullet had hit him in the right thigh while a shell fragment had nicked him in the right side. Another slug had sliced through his left boot sole and others had ripped his uniform. Fire Eater had been wounded two to four times, depending on various accounts.

Harris was riding back to Johnston, who was sitting on his horse near a large oak tree, when he saw the general sway in the saddle. "By the chance of war, a minie-ball . . . did its fatal work," William Johnston wrote.[12]

Reaching the commander's side and seeing him very pale, Harris asked if he was wounded. Johnston answered "in a very deliberate and emphatic tone: 'Yes, and, I fear, seriously.' These were his last words," his son related.[13]

Harris and Capt. Leigh Wickham of Johnston's staff led Fire Eater to a ravine behind a hill and lifted the general from his saddle while trying to locate his wound. Harris noticed blood on Johnston's right pants leg, but assumed he had been hit in the body and was desperately looking for some injury on the general's torso. Johnston's brother-in-law and aide, Col. William Preston, returned from delivering orders to discover Johnston dying. "I found the general lying on the ground and near his head Governor Harris . . . and only one or two other persons," Preston reported. "He had neither escort nor surgeon near him. His horse was wounded and bleeding. He breathed for a few minutes after my arrival, but did not recognize me. I searched but found no wound upon his body. I attempted to revive him, but he expired without pain a few moments after."[14]

Lieutenant Baylor also had been away when Johnston was wounded. He reined in before a group of officers clustered around the prone general among some tall oaks in the ravine. "As I dismounted I saw that a stream of blood had run from the General's body some six or eight feet off and ended in a dark pool," Baylor recalled.[15]

Colonel Johnston wrote that when Preston lifted his father's head and "addressed him with passionate grief, he smiled faintly, but uttered no word. His life rapidly ebbed away, and in a few moments he was dead."[16]

Baylor stated that Preston was cradling Johnston's head, but that he was cramped with the position of his body and asked the lieutenant to relieve him, which he did. "As I looked upon his noble face I thought of the dauntless warrior who had ridden out of camp that morning so full of life and hope, his face alight with the excitement of approaching battle," Baylor related. "Leaning over him, I asked: 'General, do you know me?' My tears were falling in his face, and his frame quivered for a moment, then he opened his eyes, looked me full in the face, seeming to comprehend, and closed them again. He died as a soldier must like to die: at the moment of victory and surrounded by loving comrades in arms." It was about 2:30 P.M., and "there was not a dry eye in that sad group," Baylor said. Preston sobbed aloud, excusing himself to the others: "Pardon me, gentlemen, you all know how I loved him."[17]

Another account states that Johnston was given brandy but soon lost consciousness. When one of the staff officers tried to revive him by pouring whiskey down his throat, the liquid dribbled out of his mouth.[18]

A closer examination showed that the artery in Johnston's right leg had been sliced by a gunshot between the knee and his boot top, Baylor writing that the "wound seemed to have been inflicted by a navy revolver or buck-shot." William Johnston later related that his father might have lived under different circumstances: "His wound was not necessarily fatal. General Johnston's own knowledge of military surgery was adequate for its control by an extemporized tourniquet, had he been aware or regardful of its nature." Baylor agreed, stating that Johnston's decision to leave Dr. Yandell with the wounded soldiers cost the general his life. "A simple tourniquet or a silk handkerchief twisted with a stick would have stopped the hemmorhage and have saved his life," he wrote.[19]

Yandell had issued tourniquets to Johnston and his staff officers but, tragically, no one had the presence of mind to use them. "His staff seemed dazed with the great calamity, and there was no surgeon near to apply the simple bandage," said Baylor.[20]

With the battle rippling in full fury, General Beauregard, who had been ill, rose from his sick bed to lead the Confederates. The group with Johnston's body, meanwhile, wrapped it in a blanket—to conceal it from the troops—and draped it on Fire Eater, even though the wounded horse could barely walk. They sadly escorted the general back to the field headquarters he had set up that morning on the Corinth Road.

"At this moment of supreme interest it was our misfortune to lose the commanding general," General Hardee later wrote. "This disaster caused a lull in the attack . . . and precious hours were wasted. It is, in my opinion, the candid belief of intelligent men that, but for this calamity, we would have achieved before sunset a triumph signal not only in the annals of this war, but memorable in future history."[21]

General Polk, commander of the Confederate 1st Corps, had attended West Point with Johnston and learned of his death about 3 P.M. "His loss was deeply felt," Polk wrote. "It was an event which deprived the army of his clear, practical judgment and determined character. . . . He was a true soldier, high-toned, eminently honorable, and just. Considerate of the rights and feelings of others, magnanimous, and brave. His military capacity was also of a high order, and his devotion to the cause of the South unsurpassed by that of any of her many noble sons who have offered up their lives on her altar. I knew him well from boyhood—none knew him better—and I take pleasure in laying on his tomb . . . this testimonial of my appreciation of his character as a soldier, a patriot, and a man."[22]

━━ ≡✦≡ ━━

Among the Federals trying to hold their lines was Brig. Gen. W. H. L. Wallace, a forty-year-old Ohioan who commanded Grant's 2nd Division. Many of his men had been finishing breakfast or washing dishes when the

Confederate wave hit. In the face of the massive enemy onslaught, Wallace was forced to pull back to the position held by Brig. Gen. Benjamin Prentiss's division. This area, a portion of a shallow old wagon road where the Yankees made a determined stand, would be immortalized as the "Hornets' Nest."

Still, the Federals could only hold so long against repeated Rebel charges, and Prentiss finally had to surrender after six hours of defense. Hammered by Confederate artillery, this pocket of Yankee resistance crumbled about 5:30 P.M.

Wallace was attempting to withdraw his units from this hopeless situation when he was seriously wounded in the head. Lt. Cyrus Dickey, Wallace's brother-in-law, was riding with the general when he was hit. Dickey and an orderly managed to carry the general about a quarter of a mile to the rear, but with Rebels closing in on them and believing Wallace dead, they left him to make their escape. Wallace was one of hundreds of wounded soldiers who lay in the woods and fields that night as a cold rain pelted them, someone throwing a blanket over him.

Despite Johnston's death, the battle tore through the rest of that Sunday, and Grant's jumbled units retreated even further to a defensive line closer to the Tennessee River. The Confederates had shoved them back about three miles, but these Yankees were done backpedaling. On high ground and bolstered by artillery, they fought off more Rebel assaults before nightfall forced some semblance of a cease-fire.

The battle was still much in doubt that evening when Beauregard sent a telegram to Confederate adjutant general Samuel Cooper: "Losses on both sides heavy, including our commander-in-chief General A. S. Johnston, who fell gallantly leading his troops into the thickest of the fight."[23]

As Beauregard wrote, members of Johnston's staff were preparing to embark with his body to Corinth and then to New Orleans. Beauregard recalled that Johnston died "after having shown the highest qualities of the commander and a personal intrepidity that inspired all around him."[24]

Beauregard later came under harsh criticism for failing to capitalize on Johnston's success from earlier in the day, with some of the blame coming from William Johnston, the general's son, who wrote, "The determinate purpose to capture Grant that day was lost sight of. The strong arm was withdrawn, and the bow remained unbent. . . . The hand that launched the thunder-bolt of war was cold."[25]

Johnston's body, meanwhile, was returned to the home of Col. William Inge, which had been the general's headquarters in Corinth. Mrs. Inge wrapped Johnston in a Confederate flag, the body lying in state in the parlor for several hours while "his comrades came with tear dimmed eyes to look upon all that was mortal, the pulseless form of him they loved so well."[26]

By the morning of April 7, Grant had been reinforced by the 20,000 troops of Brig. Gen. Don Carlos Buell's Army of the Ohio and was ready to seize the offensive against the now outnumbered and exhausted Rebels. Grant ordered a wholesale advance that forced the Confederates back over the bloody ground they had won the previous day. Beauregard ordered his fought-out army to withdraw to Corinth that afternoon.

As the armies counted their losses in the days afterward, citizens of New Orleans gathered for the arrival of Johnston's body, en route to Texas for burial, as well as other casualties from local units that fought at Shiloh. George Cable, a Mississippi cavalryman, recalled that the general's bier "passed slowly up St. Charles [S]treet behind the muffled drums, while on their [the residents'] quivering hearts was written as with a knife the death-roll of that last battle." New Orleans joined the rest of the Confederacy in mourning Johnston, "the great chevalier."[27]

An autopsy pointed to a startling revelation: Johnston had bled to death from a .577-caliber minié bullet fired from a British-made Enfield rifle that entered the back of his right calf just below the knee and hit an artery. The angle of entry raised the possibility that Johnston was shot by one of his own men deployed behind him. A number of Confederates carried Enfields at Shiloh, but the weapon was scarce in the Union ranks. The findings were never widely circulated.[28]

Nowhere was the sorrow over Johnston's fall as great as in Richmond. The capital had received reports of his death on April 7, everyone from Jefferson Davis down hoping against hope that the news was false. Richmond was celebrating Shiloh as a great triumph, but when Davis stood before his Congress on April 8, this "glorious and decisive victory" as he called it, was terribly marred by confirmation of Johnston's death. Sobs almost drowned out Davis's words as he told the legislators that the general was dead. "I never shall forget how strong men wept," Louisiana senator Thomas J. Semmes recalled.[29]

"The last lingering hope has disappeared, and it is all but too true that General Albert Sidney Johnston is no more," Davis said. He then read a dispatch from Colonel Preston briefly detailing how Johnston died, before continuing: "My long and close friendship with this departed chieftain and patriot forbids me to trust myself in giving vent to the feelings which this sad intelligence has evoked. Without doing injustice to the living, it may safely be asserted that our loss is irreparable; and that among the shining hosts of the great and the good who now cluster around the banner of our country, there exists no purer spirit, no more heroic soul than that of the illustrious man whose death I join you in lamenting. . . . [L]ong and deeply will his country mourn his loss."[30]

In a post-battle dispatch to President Abraham Lincoln, Maj. Gen. John McClernand, commander of Grant's 1st Division, claimed that Johnston was killed within thirty yards of his headquarters tent, around which were left some 150 bodies, mostly Rebels. Writing to Grant, McClernand credited the 11th Illinois, 20th Illinois and 11th Iowa with not only capturing an enemy battery but with killing Johnston.[31]

Federals of Brig. Gen. Thomas J. Wood's 6th Division captured a field desk, apparently belonging to Johnston or one of his staff officers, containing papers with the organization of the Confederate army and a copy of an address Johnston circulated to his troops before the battle.

Shiloh cost the Union some 13,000 casualties compared to about 12,000 Confederate losses, but it was a clear-cut Northern victory, cementing Federal control of central and western Tennessee and clearing the way for the capture of the important railroad junction at Corinth.

Johnston's death might have been equally as costly. Davis reflected years later on the magnitude of his loss so early in the conflict: "Sidney Johnston fell in sight of victory; the hour he had waited for, the event he had planned for, had arrived. . . . In his fall the great pillar of the Southern Confederacy was crushed, and beneath its fragments the best hope of the Southwest lay buried. . . . Not for the first time did the fate of an army depend upon a single man, and the fortunes of a country hang, as in a balance, on the achievements of a single army."[32]

Writing after the war, Grant addressed the consequences of Johnston's fall at Shiloh:

> His wound . . . was not necessarily fatal, or even dangerous. But he was a man who would not abandon what he deemed an important trust in the face of danger, and consequently continued in the saddle, commanding, until so exhausted by the loss of blood that he had to be taken from his horse, and soon after died. The news was not long in reaching our side, and, I suppose, was quite an encouragement to the National soldiers. I had known Johnston slightly in the Mexican war and later as an officer in the regular army. He was a man of high

character and ability. His contemporaries at West Point, and officers generally who came to know him personally later, and who remained on our side, expected him to prove the most formidable man to meet that the Confederacy would produce.[33]

Grant also addressed the fact that Beauregard had come under withering criticism from many Southerners who believed he had let victory slip from their grasp after Johnston died. He wrote of Beauregard, "I do not believe his fallen chief could have done any better under the circumstances." Grant also stated that after studying Johnston's dispatches and orders from the Shiloh battle, he felt Johnston was "vacillating and undecided in his actions."[34]

From Corinth on April 10, Beauregard issued this message to his army:

Soldiers: Your late commander-in-chief, General A. S. Johnston, is dead. A fearless soldier, a sagacious captain, a reproachless man, has fallen; one who in his devotion to our cause shrank from no sacrifice; one who, animated by a sense of duty and sustained by a sublime courage, challenged danger and perished gallantly for his country whilst leading forward his brave columns to victory. His signal example of heroism and patriotism, if imitated, would make this army invincible. A grateful country will mourn his loss, revere his name, and cherish his manly virtues.[35]

Diarist Mary Boykin Chesnut deplored Johnston's death while criticizing Beauregard:

There is grief enough for Albert Sidney Johnston now; we begin to see what we have lost. We were pushing them into the river when General Johnston was wounded. Beauregard was lying in his tent, at the rear, in a green sickness—melancholy—but no matter what the name of the malady. He was too slow to move, and lost all the advantage gained by our dead hero. Without him there is no head to our Western army.[36]

Mrs. Chesnut also noted Gladden's loss in her journal: "Gladden, the hero of the Palmettos in Mexico, is killed. Shiloh has been a dreadful blow to us."[37]

Among the Union dead was General Wallace, who had fallen only a few miles from where his wife was waiting for him behind the Union lines.

"Will" Wallace had grown up in Illinois and was admitted to the state bar in 1846, fighting as a volunteer in the Mexican War. He was practicing law when the Civil War erupted and was appointed colonel of the 11th Illinois. Wallace's conduct in commanding a brigade in the siege and capture of Fort Donelson resulted in his promotion to brigadier general of volunteer in March 1862. He was unrelated to Maj. Gen. Lew Wallace, who commanded Grant's 3rd Division.[38]

Without her husband's knowledge, Ann Dickey Wallace had traveled south to be near him. She had arrived at Pittsburg Landing on the Tennessee River aboard the steamboat *Minehaha* on the morning of April 6, hearing the distant gunfire. An Illinois captain volunteered to ride ahead and determine what was going on before Mrs. Wallace embarked to try to find her husband at his headquarters. The officer soon returned with news that Wallace had already taken his command into battle and it was decided that Ann should wait on the boat. Her frustration and anxiety must have been intense, because her father, two of her brothers, two of Will's brothers and several more distant relatives were also in the Union ranks and involved in the fighting.[39]

She remained on the steamboat, assisting the wounded brought aboard and wondering about her Will's fate. Late in the day, Cyrus Dickey came aboard and told her the awful news. Grieving for her supposedly dead husband, she spent much of the night caring for the suffering men aboard.

As the Federals counterattacked the next morning, Ann learned about 10 A.M. that her husband had been found alive on the battlefield. The general was brought to a boat on the river where Ann rushed to him. Any flicker of hope she had for his recovery must have gone out when she saw the severe nature of his injury.

Wallace was taken to the William Cherry mansion, Grant's former headquarters in Savannah, Tennessee Over the next two days he faded in and out of consciousness, speaking briefly to Ann as his condition worsened. He finally succumbed on the night of April 10. Wallace was buried in a private cemetery near Ottawa, Illinois.

Gladden was buried in Mobile's Magnolia Cemetery, while Johnston was laid to rest in the State Cemetery in Austin, Texas, carrying with him the distinction of being the highest ranking general on either side to die in the war.

CHAPTER 4

A Deadly Virginia Summer—1862

CONFEDERATE BRIGADIER GENERAL
ROBERT H. HATTON
Fair Oaks Station, May 31, 1862

When former U.S. congressman Robert H. Hatton was promoted Confederate brigadier general on May 23, 1862, he would have only eight days to enjoy his new rank. There was little time for anything other than battle for the Rebel army of Gen. Joseph E. Johnston arrayed to defend Richmond. Blue and gray were in the lethal embrace of the Peninsular Campaign as Johnston tried to prevent the Union forces of Gen. George B. McClellan from taking the Rebel capital.

Hatton was a thirty-six-year-old Ohioan who had relocated to Tennessee to attend college and stayed there. He had been a teacher, lawyer and state representative, as well as an unsuccessful gubernatorial candidate in 1857. Two years later he was elected to Congress as a member of the Know-Nothing Party, but resigned in 1861 to become a Confederate colonel of Tennessee infantry. He had fought well in the western Virginia operations, serving with Robert E. Lee and Stonewall Jackson before joining Johnston's army on the Virginia peninsula.[1]

Hatton was in camp near Richmond on May 28, when he wrote letters to his wife, Sophie, as well as his parents. They would be his last words to them:

37

My Dear Wife: My brigade will move in an hour from its
encampment. . . . We go to attack the enemy on tomorrow
beyond the river. . . . May the God of right and justice smile upon
us in the hour of conflict! Would that I might bind to my heart
before the battle my wife and children! That pleasure may never
again be granted me. If so, farewell; and may the God of all mercy
be to you and ours a Guardian and Friend![2]

To his mother, Hatton wrote:

You have been to me all a mother ever was to a man—loving,
kind, unremitting in your efforts for my comfort and happiness. If
I should not return, be a mother to my wife and children. God
bless you, my own dear old mother![3]

The general's sentiments to his father were much the same:

A tenderer, more loving father never lived. To me you have
been the best of fathers. If I never return, let all your affection lavished in the past upon me be transferred to Sophie and her children. Let her never be alone, but be comforted and cheered by
the company of my parents.[4]

On May 31, Johnston's army was engaged in fighting at Fair Oaks Station where Hatton's Tennessee Brigade was assigned to Johnston's left wing,
commanded by Maj. Gen. G. W. Smith. Hatton's men were held in reserve
much of the day, but were finally ordered forward late in the afternoon to
reinforce the brigades of Brig. Gens. Wade Hampton and James J. Pettigrew.

The night before, Hatton had formed the brigade in close columns and
given a rousing pre-battle speech. "Just in our rear is our capital city, invested
by a vandal horde," he shouted at one point. "Shall it be sacked and plun-
dered?" In a deep bass, a colonel's voice rang out, "No, never!" the soldiers
snatching off their hats and joining in the refrain, "No, never!" Now as they
double-quicked toward the front, Jefferson Davis passed the Tennesseans as
"every boy saluted the chieftain of the Confederacy by making the welkin
ring with the 'Rebel yell,' recalled H. T. Childs of Hatton's command.[5]

Davis, Johnston, Lee, and other Confederate dignitaries were present
when Hatton's men reached the battlefield and formed for the attack. T. H.
Benton of the 14th Tennessee recalled: "I shall never forget what President
Davis said . . . which was: 'General Hatton, I want your Tennesseans to

charge those people. The North Carolinians have been charging them all day, and have driven them but three miles.' 'All right, Mr. President, if you say so,' replied General Hatton."[6]

"Mounted upon a splendid horse, which seemed almost inspired with the spirit of the rider, he passed along his line, encouraging the weak and securing the confidence of the most intrepid," George A. Howard, adjutant of Hatton's old regiment, the 7th Tennessee, recalled.[7]

Shouting "Forward, my brave boys! Forward!" Hatton led his brigade across a field and into a swampy area filled with fallen trees. Astride his horse, Old Ball, the general was just behind the brigade's center colors, "his hat off and waving us onward," wrote Childs, who described Hatton's assault as "the grandest, sublimest sight I ever witnessed."[8]

Watching the Tennesseans attack, Davis is said to have remarked, "That brigade moves in handsomely, but it will lose its commander."[9]

The terrain was so overgrown and the gun smoke so thick that officers could see only a few of their men at any given time, making coordinated movements all but impossible. The Tennesseans had just come under fire with Hatton and General Smith riding together when Hatton was shot, dying instantly. "We hadn't been in the fight very long before General Hatton was killed," related Benton.[10]

Darkness ended the battle, with the enemies drawn up close to each other in the thickets and the Tennesseans mourning Hatton's loss. "A whole community will assemble around the stricken widow of our general; and the mothers of the noble boys who fell by his side will mingle their tears with hers," wrote Lt. Col. John K. Howard of the 7th Tennessee.[11]

Hatton's remains were temporarily buried in Knoxville, Tennessee, and were returned to his adopted hometown of Lebanon in 1866 where he was laid to rest at Cedar Grove Cemetery. Thirty years after the war, Hatton's widow and two daughters received a priceless artifact from Fair Oaks Station. The day after Hatton's death, a Union colonel found a pistol in the mud of the battlefield. The weapon belonged to Hatton, and the officer sent it to his home in New York as a war trophy. Years later he returned it to the general's family.

CONFEDERATE BRIGADIER GENERAL TURNER ASHBY
Harrisonburg, Virginia, June 6, 1862

> Saw ye the veterans—
> Hearts that have never known
> Never a quail of fear,

Near a groan—
Sob mid the fight they win,
Tears their stern eyes within
Ashby, our Paladin,
Ashby is gone!
—From *Dirge For Ashby* by Margaret Junkin Preston[12]

Next to Jeb Stuart, no Confederate general was romanticized more as a gray Ivanhoe than cavalryman Turner Ashby. The war was barely a year old when Ashby was killed near Harrisonburg, Virginia, on June 6, 1862, but his reputation already had spread throughout the South, and he was immortalized in poem, song and eulogy. "Riding his black stallion, he looked like a knight of the olden time"; Henry Kyd Douglas recalled him "galloping over the field on his favorite war horse . . . he was fascinating, inspiring. Altogether he was the most picturesque horseman ever seen in the Shenandoah Valley."[13]

The thirty-three-year-old Ashby was a Virginian who as a boy had been schooled by his mother and private tutors on the family's Fauquier County estate. He had been a farmer and businessman before Virginia's secession and had no military training, yet his natural leadership and horse-manship aided his rise in the Confederate ranks. He was colonel of the 7th Virginia Cavalry when he was assigned command of Maj. Gen. T. J. "Stonewall" Jackson's cavalry in the spring of 1862, and fought superbly in Jackson's Shenandoah Valley Campaign.[14]

Ashby was promoted brigadier general on May 23, 1862, little more than two weeks before his death. At the time, he and Jackson were in the throes of the Shenandoah chess game against the Union forces of Maj. Gen. Nathaniel P. Banks. Jackson had maneuvered his outnumbered army brilliantly in attempting to oust the Federals from the valley and prevent them from sending reinforcements east to the army of Maj. Gen. George McClellan advancing on Richmond. Battles at Kernstown, McDowell, and Front Royal resulted in Jackson's seizure of Winchester on May 25, with Ashby and his cavalry playing a key role in Stonewall's success through their reconnaissance and tenacious fighting.

About a week after taking Winchester, Jackson learned that three Union forces were converging on him from different directions. A retreat of some fifty miles in only two days immortalized Jackson's infantry as "foot cavalry," but the Rebels still had to contend with their prime antagonist, a Federal army under Maj. Gen. John C. Fremont.

Ashby was riding the same horse upon which Jackson had been mounted at First Bull Run when the Confederates reached Harrisonburg on June 6. Jackson sent his sick and wounded to Staunton while the rest of his army moved off the Valley Turnpike toward Port Republic. Jackson stayed with his rearguard, including Ashby's cavalry, until about noon. The Rebels soon were pressured by the 1st New Jersey Cavalry under Col. Percy Wyndham, and Ashby retreated about two miles from town, halting on wooded Chestnut Ridge. Ashby was especially eager to engage Wyndham, since the English soldier of fortune had vowed to "bag" Ashby, the Confederates had heard.

Ashby set up an ambush, concealing some of his troopers in the woods and an adjacent grain field while putting others in plain view on the road. Seeing the graycoats in the road, Wyndham charged and was greeted by a deadly crossfire. The Federals were thrown into disorder and the colonel and some sixty of his men were captured.

Expecting the Union attack to be renewed, Ashby requested infantry and Maj. Gen. Richard Ewell sent him the 1st Maryland and the 58th Virginia.[15]

The cavalier was anxious to punish the enemy further, saying, "These people have pressed me long enough and I will make them stop it today!" Soon the Federals surged forward again, this time with infantry and cavalry. The 58th Virginia especially became engaged in a fierce fight with Ohio, West Virginia, and Pennsylvania infantry.[16]

The Confederate line began to crack and Ashby rode to the front to rally them for a charge. His horse was shot from under him, but he jumped from the saddle and ran forward, whipping his sword and yelling, "Charge men! For God's sake, Charge!" Moments later he was shot in the right side near the waist, the bullet emerging under his left arm as he pitched over dying.[17]

The Rebels managed to fight off the enemy thrust, but Ashby's loss was a heavy price to pay. "He never spoke," Douglas wrote of Ashby, "but calmly breathed his last in the arms of Lieutenant Jim Thom[a]son, who loved him as only a fearless young soldier can love his hero." Grieving soldiers wrapped the general's body in a blanket and carried it to the rear.[18]

Among prisoners taken by the Southerners was Lt. Col. Thomas L. Kane of the 13th Pennsylvania "Bucktails." Kane was slightly wounded, but told his captors how he had saved Ashby's life in the day's fighting, unaware that his words amounted to a eulogy for the slain general:

I have today saved the life of one of the most gallant soldiers in either army—General Ashby—a man I admire as much as you do. His figure is familiar to me for I have seen him often enough in our front. He was today within fifty yards of my skirmishers, sitting on his horse, unconscious of the danger he was in. I saw three of them raise their guns to fire, but I succeeded in stopping two of them and struck up the gun of the third as it went off. Ashby is too brave to die in that way.[19]

After learning of Ashby's death, Kane is said to have remarked, "Deal justly with the memory of Ashby. He must have been a noble fellow, a brave soldier, and a gentleman."[20]

Even in the midst of the campaign, Jackson's men were shocked and grief-stricken by Ashby's fall. "Among the killed was the redoubtable Ashby, which sad loss was deeply lamented by the entire army," recalled Lt. James Wood of the 37th Virginia Infantry. "No leader stood higher in the estimation of his comrades or had promise of a brighter future."[21]

Jackson was interviewing Wyndham at his headquarters when a messenger arrived with the news of Ashby's death. The usually impassive Stonewall dismissed Wyndham and locked himself alone in his room for several hours. "What transpired there, how he wrestled with his sorrow, no one will ever know," related Douglas. "If he found comfort in his grief at the sudden taking off of his invaluable ally, he never spoke of it to anyone."[22]

Ashby's men were devastated by his loss. "We camped for the night near Cross Keys," wrote cavalryman William Wilson. "There is a gloom throughout the whole camp and an awful stillness that can almost be heard. Few men like Turner Ashby have graced the annals of any people. Ages will roll away and another like [him] will not be."[23]

Until his death in 1892, Trooper Frederick Trullender of the 1st New Jersey Cavalry, claimed that he fired the bullet that killed Ashby. Some of his old saddle mates backed up his contention, but Confederate veterans argued that Wyndham's command had been driven from the field before Ashby fell and that Kane's Bucktails were responsible for his death. Yet any debate about who among the Yankees had slain the popular cavalryman was lost on the Rebel army this day as word spread of his demise.

Ashby's body was at first taken to the Frank Kemper house in Port Republic where Jackson and others came to pay their respects. A hearse bearing the dead general soon set out for Charlottesville while tearful soldiers of his command, as well as Union prisoners watched solemnly along the road. Douglas noted:

Uncontrollable was the grief of his troopers, a sad parting, as their knightly chief, covered by a military pall, was carried from their midst. He the invincible and, as they had learned to believe, the invulnerable, was wounded and conquered and dead. . . . Their captured foes . . . as if in sympathy for their bereavement and in respect for their great enemy, stood in respectful silence and many of them with uncovered heads.[24]

"Poor Ashby is dead," Jackson wrote to future Confederate brigadier John Imboden. "He fell gloriously. I know you will join with me in mourning the loss of our friend, one of the noblest men and soldiers in the Confederate army."[25] Stonewall continued his praise in an official report: "As a partisan officer, I never knew his superior. His daring was proverbial, his powers of endurance almost incredible, his tone of character heroic, and his sagacity almost intuitive in divining the purposes and movements of the enemy." Jefferson Davis would refer to Ashby as the "stainless, fearless cavalier."[26]

Despite Ashby's loss, Jackson won a decisive victory at Port Republic on June 9, securing control of the Shenandoah and further enhancing his legend.

In 1866, Ashby's remains were reinterred in the Stonewall Cemetery in Winchester, Virginia, during an impressive ceremony. He would share a grave with his brother Richard, who had been killed earlier in the war. "He was the idol of his men and the beloved of everyone who had the honor of knowing him intimately," Virginia captain Jed Hotchkiss wrote of the brigadier after the war. "His exploits have been embalmed in song and story, and his memory lives with that of Stonewall Jackson."[27]

> Weep, daughters of Virginia, weep!
> Weep for the gallant dead;
> For calmly in his last long sleep
> Lies Ashby's noble head.
> —From "Lines On General Turner Ashby"
> by E. V. Clemens[28]

CONFEDERATE BRIGADIER GENERAL RICHARD GRIFFITH
Savage Station, June 29, 1862

Brig. Gen. Richard Griffith was leading a Confederate brigade of Mississippians when he was killed at Savage Station during the Peninsular Campaign.

Griffith, forty-eight, was born near Philadelphia and graduated from Ohio University, but had moved to Vicksburg, Mississippi, after graduation to pursue a teaching career. He served in the 1st Mississippi Rifles during the Mexican War and formed a strong friendship with his commanding officer, Jefferson Davis. After the war he was a banker and U.S. marshal, and he served two terms as Mississippi state treasurer. When the Civil War came, he was elected colonel of the 12th Mississippi and promoted to brigadier in the Confederate army in November 1861. He was assigned command of a brigade of four Mississippi regiments in Virginia as part of Maj. Gen. John Magruder's division. Griffith's brigade was held in reserve during the battle of Seven Pines, but was heavily engaged in the Seven Days battles near Richmond.[29]

In this fighting, on June 29, 1862, Griffith and his command were among Magruder's Confederates pursuing Union forces that had abandoned positions on the Nine-Mile Road and were believed to be retreating along the York River Railroad. The Union army had begun a general withdrawal toward the James River. Late in the afternoon, Magruder smacked into elements of Maj. Gen. Edwin V. Sumner's II Corps which was serving as the Federals' rearguard along an evacuated trench line near the Savage Station depot.

"On reaching these fortifications a fire was opened upon us by the enemy's rear guard," reported Col. William Barksdale of the 13th Mississippi in Griffith's command. The brigade was immediately ordered into battle line, but Griffith fell, severely wounded in the thigh by an artillery round. At least one account states that the shell hit one of the railroad buildings and exploded near Griffith's men, a fragment hurtling through the air before hitting him.[30] Griffith's adjutant, Col. William Inge, scrambled from his horse to catch him as he fell. The general inquired about his injury, and when told it was likely fatal supposedly remarked, "If I only could have led my brigade through this battle, I would have died satisfied."[31]

The battle seethed for about two hours before nightfall calmed matters, and Sumner's men resumed their withdrawal after dark. Two of Griffith's staff officers bore the wounded general from the field and Barksdale took command. Griffith was taken into Richmond to the home of banker W. Pierce, but he was beyond medical care and died the same day.

"The enemy, having ascertained the general disposition of our troops— opened a brisk artillery fire upon the railroad and our center, unfortunately mortally wounding the gallant General Griffith," Magruder wrote in a report to Robert E. Lee.[32]

"While we were driving the enemy before us along the railroad track, he was struck by a shell from one of the enemy guns, fell from his horse and died in a few hours," recalled W. G. Johnson of the 18th Mississippi.

"A good man, a true patriot, and a gallant officer." His body was taken to Jackson, Mississippi, where he rests in Greenwood Cemetery.[33]

"Thus, at Savage station, fell this noble son of Mississippi on the threshold of what promised to be a brilliant career," wrote Confederate colonel Charles E. Hooker. Howell Cobb, another of Magruder's brigadiers, wrote of the "brave and lamented Griffith" in his action report.[34]

Years after the war, Jefferson Davis still mourned Griffith's death. "Our loss was small in numbers, but great in value," he wrote of Savage Station. "Among others who could ill be spared, here fell the gallant soldier, the useful citizen, the true friend and Christian gentleman, Brigadier-General Richard Griffith. He had served with distinction in foreign war, and, when the South was invaded, was among the first to take up arms in defense of our rights."[35]

CONFEDERATE BRIGADIER GENERAL CHARLES S. WINDER
Cedar Mountain, August 9, 1862

A near disaster at sea before the war had cast Charles S. Winder in the limelight long before he met his death in command of the Stonewall Brigade. Yet as he unknowingly rode to his end at Cedar Mountain on August 9, 1862, Winder was far from being in good graces with a number of his soldiers; in fact, some were threatening to kill him themselves.

Considered one of the most capable officers in the Confederate army, Winder was a thirty-four-year-old Marylander and an 1850 West Point graduate. As an army second lieutenant in 1854, he had attracted the attention of then Secretary of War Jefferson Davis for his bravery at sea. Winder had been aboard the steamship *San Francisco* carrying U.S. troops to Panama, when during a violent ocean storm, the steamer had been disabled and set adrift in heavy swells. A bark had come to the rescue, but could not accommodate all the soldiers. The commissioned officers left in order of their rank, with Winder alone staying with the enlisted men. They managed to keep the ship afloat until another vessel reached them and took them aboard. For his skill and daring, Winder was promoted to captain, supposedly the youngest at that time in the U.S. Army.

Casting his lot with the seceding states, Winder had taken part in the Fort Sumter bombardment. Afterwards, he was sent to Virginia where he was promoted brigadier in March 1862 and given command of the Stonewall Brigade. Winder led the brigade through the 1862 Shenandoah Valley Campaign and in the Seven Days fighting.[36]

In the summer of 1862, Jackson and three Confederate divisions were sent to north-central Virginia to counter the threat of Maj. Gen. John Pope operating in the area of Culpeper Court House. On August 7, Jackson believed he had an opportunity to defeat a portion of Pope's army before it could be reinforced, and his 22,000 men attacked the 12,000 Federals. But the advance was hampered by poor communication, bad roads, and hot, dry weather, and Jackson made little progress. He crossed the Rapidan River near Orange Court House on August 8, and by early the next day was closing in on the Union force under Maj. Gen. Nathaniel Banks near Cedar Mountain (also called Slaughter Mountain for a family living in the area) in Culpeper County.

Winder led Jackson's division while Jackson directed the entire force, and while these iron-willed generals had never seen eye to eye, their mutual respect outweighed their personal differences. Henry Kyd Douglas of Jackson's staff recalled that Winder had "a will as inflexible as that of Jackson himself. At first their relations were not very cordial and each certainly underrated the other; in many things, they were too much alike to fit exactly." Douglas also added that Winder "was the most brilliant of the many valuable officers Maryland gave to the Confederacy."[37]

A few days earlier, Winder, known as a stern disciplinarian, punished about thirty of his men for straggling, hanging some of them by their thumbs. He and Jackson had clashed about this severe penalty, as most of those who had been disciplined either deserted or vowed revenge on the Marylander. Adding to his problems, Winder had been feverish for several days. On the morning of the battle, Jackson recommended that he relinquish command until he was in better health. Winder refused, saying that he would not leave his men on the eve of a fight. Weak and pale, he climbed from an ambulance to mount a horse and lead his command.

When the battle opened with an artillery duel after 4 P.M. on August 9, Winder's division was on the left of Jackson's line. The brigadier dismounted near a gate on a dirt lane leading off the main road, and because of the heat, removed his tunic and rolled up his shirtsleeves. He was directing the Maryland battery of Capt. R. S. Andrews or gunners of the Rockbridge Artillery, based on various accounts. The gray cannoneers were being shelled themselves and a number had been hit, but Winder seemed oblivious to the explosions and casualties around him.

He was shouting an order with his hand to his mouth when he was mortally wounded, a Union shell fragment ripping his left side after first tearing through his left arm. His body quivering, Winder fell backward, his binoculars flying through the air as men ran to his aid. Terribly injured, he was rushed to the rear on a litter as other Rebel troops headed into the battle. "Hastening towards the front, I saw the bleeding, mangled form of the gallant Winder," a Virginian recalled.[38]

One of the general's aides, Lt. McHenry Howard, choked back tears when he saw the extent of Winder's wounds. "General, do you know me?" Howard asked, his voice trembling. Winder answered that he did and then mumbled a few words about his wife and children.[39]

Shortly after Winder fell, General Banks launched an attack with almost two divisions against the Confederate left and center. The yelling blue infantrymen barged through the wheat and corn, rolling over several Rebel brigades and threatening to rout Jackson's army. With his ranks crumbling, Jackson's war fury boiled over. He tried unsuccessfully to pull his sword, but it was rusted in its scabbard, having never before been drawn in battle. Undaunted, he unhooked it from his belt and waved the sheathed blade, riding about to rally his troops. Grabbing a Rebel flag from its bearer, he shouted, "Rally men! Remember Winder! Where's my Stonewall Brigade? Forward, men, forward!"[40]

The sight of Stonewall steeled the rattled Confederates, also who were bolstered by the timely arrival of Maj. Gen. A. P. Hill's fresh division. The outnumbered Federals were eventually pushed back, and by about 7 P.M. the fighting was over. At approximately the same time, so too was the life of General Winder.

In immense pain, he had been taken to a crude log farmhouse behind the Rebel lines. As he was being carried to the rear, he passed the Stonewall Brigade preparing to go into combat. Officers and men gazed at him in solemn silence, Winder asking how the battle was progressing. A chaplain knelt over him at one point, saying, "General, lift up your heart to God." Winder replied weakly, gasping "I do, I do lift it up to Him."[41]

Howard accompanied Winder to the rear. "He became quieter presently, and as I walked beside with his hand in mine, I could feel it growing colder," the lieutenant remembered.[42]

Winder died at the farmhouse about two hours later as Howard cradled him. "At sundown, with my arm around his neck and supporting his head, he expired, so quietly that I could scarcely mark the exact time of death," he related.[43]

"I can hardly think of the fall of Brigadier-General C. S. Winder without tearful eyes," Jackson said of his adversarial colleague, while Douglas wrote that in Winder's fall "the army was deprived of one of its most promising officers."[44]

The 2nd Maine Battery of Capt. James A. Hall was officially credited with firing the round that killed Winder. Hall's cannoneers and a Maryland battery were posted near the main road between two infantry brigades to silence the Rebel guns firing under Winder's direction. Under a truce flag after the battle, Confederate major general Jeb Stuart informed Brig. Gen. George Bayard of the Union cavalry that "the first discharge of our battery . . . killed the rebel General Winder," reported Maj. Davis Tillson, of the U.S. III Corps artillery.[45]

Pope proclaimed Cedar Mountain a Union triumph, but his force had left the field with losses of almost 2,400 compared to about 1,300 Confederate casualties. General Lee sent a congratulatory note to Jackson on August 12, closing with a brief tribute to Winder: "I mourn with you the loss of many gallant officers and men, and chief among them that noble and accomplished officer and patriot General C. S. Winder."[46]

Lee would later refer to "the courage, capacity, and conspicuous merit of this lamented officer."[47]

In his account of the action, Jackson described Winder as "an accomplished officer. Richly endowed with those qualities of mind and person which fit an officer for command, and which attract the admiration and excite the enthusiasm of troops, he was rapidly rising to the front rank of his profession, and his loss has been severely felt."[48]

Brig. Gen. William Taliaferro, who assumed division command when Winder fell, also praised his predecessor. "No one can estimate the loss his brigade, this division, the army has sustained in the early fall of Brigadier-General Winder," Taliaferro said in his battle report. "He was warmly loved by all who knew him as a man and had the full confidence of his command as a soldier."[49]

His coffin draped in the flags of Maryland and the Confederacy, Winder's body lay in state in the Virginia Senate chamber on August 18 before being taken to Hollywood Cemetery for burial. He was later reinterred at Wye House near Easton, Maryland. In describing Winder after the war, Jefferson Davis compared his exploits aboard the *San Francisco* with his conduct at Cedar Mountain: "He died manifesting the same spirit as on the wreck—that which holds life light when weighed against honor."[50]

CHAPTER 5

Phil Kearny and
Other Union Losses

UNION BRIGADIER GENERAL THOMAS WILLIAMS
Baton Rouge, Louisiana, August 5, 1862

In the foggy predawn of August 5, 1862, about 2,600 Rebel troops under Maj. Gen. John C. Breckinridge trudged toward the Union defenses at Baton Rouge, intent on retaking the Louisiana capital for the Confederacy. Facing them were approximately 2,500 bluecoats arrayed in a single battle line without earthworks and commanded by Brig. Gen. Thomas Williams, a stalwart New Yorker with an impeccable military background.

Williams, forty-seven, graduated from West Point in 1837. His family had been among the first settlers of Detroit, but had moved to Albany, New York, to escape the turmoil there during the War of 1812. Williams's father had been a militia general in the Black Hawk War, and his son served as a private under him. After West Point, Williams had seen action in the Seminole Wars, and became instructor at the Military Academy. During the Mexican War he was on Gen. Winfield Scott's staff, earning brevet promotions for gallantry, and later saw service on the frontier. When secession erupted, Williams was named major of the 5th U.S. Artillery, and appointed brigadier general of volunteers in late September 1861. Williams was in combat during Ambrose Burnside's North Carolina expedition a few weeks later, and then led a brigade in the offensive to capture New Orleans. Stationed at Baton Rouge after its capture in May 1862, Williams's brigade had also taken part in one of the failed efforts to seize Vicksburg.[1]

If Williams's record was exceptional, his reputation was less so; a New York officer described him as "a man of many idiosyncrasies, [who] outside of his staff was cordially disliked for his severe treatment of the men."[2]

The Rebels opened their attack on the Union forces at Baton Rouge about 3:45 A.M., pushing aside Federal units offering piecemeal resistance, but shelling from gunboats hampered their progress. Breckinridge had counted on the CSS *Arkansas* to neutralize the enemy vessels, but engine failure kept the ironclad out of action.

Williams's first battle line was driven back, but the general rallied his troops closer to the town and held on as the Confederates gradually lost steam. Williams decided to mount a counterattack. The 14th Maine was enduring a "perfect shower of bullets" when Williams rode up to the regiment's Col. Frank Nickerson and asked if the men could advance. The soldiers answered with three cheers.

The regiment plunged forward under heavy fire, but Williams did not live to see the result. A musket ball punched into Williams's chest, killing him instantly, and he fell from his horse. "Just in our rear General Williams fell in sight of our men," recalled Nickerson. "This did not dampen their ardor."[3]

In the minutes before he fell, Williams also had rallied the 21st Indiana, which had lost all of its field officers in the fighting. "Boys, your field officers are all gone; I will lead you," he shouted to them, and the men cheered in reply. "The sound had scarce died away when he fell," reported Col. Thomas W. Cahill of the 9th Connecticut, who assumed command.[4]

"The brave General Williams fell in front of the 6th Michigan toward the end of the conflict," reported Lt. Godfrey Weitzel of the U.S. engineers, "while giving his men a noble example of reckless and daring bravery."[5]

By about 10 A.M., the fighting was over, Breckinridge's offensive thwarted at a cost of about 500 Rebels. As smoke from the burning *Arkansas*—scuttled and torched by her crew—stained the sky on August 6, the Federals counted their losses at just under 400.

From his New Orleans headquarters on August 7, Union major general Benjamin Butler, commander of the Department of the Gulf, issued general orders regarding Williams's death, stating that the victory at Baton Rouge "is made sorrowful by the fall of our brave, gallant, and successful fellow-soldier."[6]

Butler continued:

His country mourns in sympathy with his wife and children. . . . We, his companions in arms, who had learned to love him, weep the true friend, the gallant gentleman, the brave soldier, the accomplished officer, the pure patriot and victorious hero, and the devoted Christian. All and more went out when Williams died. . . . The chivalric American gentleman, he gave up the vantage of the cover of the houses of the city—forming his lines in the open field—lest the women and children of his enemies should be hurt in the fight. . . . A brave soldier, he received the death-shot leading his men. A patriot hero, he was fighting the battle of his country and died as went up the cheer of victory. A Christian, he sleeps in the hope of the blessed Redeemer. His virtues we cannot exceed—his example we may emulate—and mourning his death, we pray "may our last end be like his."[7]

Butler also stated that Williams was decapitated by a cannonball, which varies from official reports from officers who were in the battle.[8]

Williams's body was placed in a casket and put aboard the transport *Lewis Whiteman*, which was also carrying wounded soldiers down river to New Orleans. On the morning of August 7, the *Whiteman* collided with the gunboat *Oneida* and sank. A few of the men were lost, as was Williams's coffin, which was discovered the next day floating near the shore on some wreckage. A trunk containing the general's belongings was later pulled from the water and ended up in the hands of an area planter who turned it over to Federal authorities, directing that the possessions be sent to Williams's family. The man had been moved when, in going through the trunk, he found a collection of seashells for the Williams's four small children.[9]

Williams's funeral was held on August 21 at St. George's Church in Newburgh, New York Bells pealed solemnly and a large crowd joined the procession. Afterward, the general's coffin was loaded aboard the steamer *Daniel Drew* for transport to Detroit, where he was buried in his family's lot at Elmwood Cemetery. "An extremely rigid disciplinarian, a thoroughly trained and most accomplished officer, and a man of the highest courage and honor, General Williams's death was long and deeply regretted in the department," a Union officer wrote.[10]

UNION BRIGADIER GENERAL ROBERT L. MCCOOK
Near Winchester, Tennessee, August 6, 1862

The controversial death of Brig. Gen. Robert L. McCook would involve Union and Confederate notables at the highest levels interested in the fate of McCook's killer. It also raised the question of whether the general died in a military action or was gunned down in a calculated act of murder.

McCook, thirty-four, was one of the "Fighting McCooks," fifteen men from the same family who fought for the Union. His brother Alexander was a Federal general as was a first cousin, Edward. Another brother, Daniel, would die of combat wounds the day after his promotion to brigadier.

Robert McCook was born in Lisbon (now New Lisbon), Ohio, and was a prewar attorney in Steubenville, Columbus, and Cincinnati. In 1861, he organized and became colonel of the 9th Ohio Infantry and tasted battle in western Virginia. He was wounded at Mill Springs in early 1862 and promoted brigadier general in March. He served in Tennessee and Mississippi and was ill when elements of Maj. Gen. Don Carlos Buell's army moved from Alabama into eastern Tennessee.[11]

On August 5, the day of his mortal wounding, McCook's 3rd brigade was on the march from Athens, Alabama, to Union lines near Winchester, Tennessee. McCook was bedridden due to his wound and severe dysentery, and was riding in an open wagon about three miles ahead of his main column. Clad only in his undergarments, McCook was not wearing any insignia of rank. The general was accompanied by Capt. Hunter Brooke of his staff, Maj. Henry Boynton of the 35th Ohio, and nine mounted soldiers serving as his escort.[12]

The soldiers were attacked about noon by what witnesses described as a band of mounted guerrillas, numbering 100 to 200, between Winchester and the town of Decherd, Tennessee. McCook's party had earlier stopped at the home of a man named Petit to inquire about possible campsites in the area. At the time of the strike, Boynton and one soldier, accompanied by a civilian, were about half a mile behind McCook's party while three other Federals from the escort had ridden ahead, both groups looking for a suitable camp ground for the brigade.

Brooke, unarmed, was in the wagon, attending to McCook when the Rebels struck. The wagon driver, an unidentified black teamster, managed to turn the vehicle about and started back toward the advance of McCook's brigade, but the Confederates quickly descended on the wagon. Its canvas top snagged on a tree branch, causing the vehicle to swerve against an embankment where it lodged. The enemy horsemen closed fast and opened fire, their first target being a Yankee sutler named Aug, who in his panic rode his mule into the path of the attackers. Unhurt, Aug fell from his mount and into some bushes. At least one account states that McCook himself seized the reins from the teamster and tried to dislodge the wagon. In the next few confused moments, at least three shots were fired into the wagon.

Col. Ferdinand Van Derveer of the 35th Ohio (who would succeed McCook in brigade command) wrote of the action:

> The general succeeded in turning his carriage, but not before the guerrillas were within range and firing. He was soon overtaken and surrounded, although his horses were running at the top of their speed. In reply to the oft-repeated cry of "Stop!" "Stop!" the general rose in his bed and exclaimed, "Don't shoot; the horses are running; we will stop as soon as possible." Notwithstanding this surrender those riding within a few feet by the . . . carriage fired, one ball passing through his hat and one inflicting a mortal wound in the abdomen.[13]

McCook was hit once in the left side just below the ribs. he was quickly surrounded by the Rebels, who also captured Brooke, two teamsters and two escort soldiers. The general was taken to a nearby house but there was little that could be done for him. Among the Confederates who came to his bedside was Capt. Frank B. Gurley. He and Capt. J. M. Hambrick commanded the two companies of Rebels who attacked McCook's party and Gurley was identified as the man who had shot the general. Gurley spoke with McCook, who apparently did not express any bitterness or anger toward the captain.

McCook died about noon the next day. Federal troops found his body in the house where the Rebels had left it. His last words were reported to be, "Tell Alech (alluding to his brother, Gen. Alexander McDowell McCook) and the rest, that I have tried to live like a man and do my duty."[14]

Gurley and Hambrick had been in the area recruiting for the Confederate cavalry, but since their men did not have uniforms or military identification, the Federals assumed they were guerrillas when they attacked. Gurley had been an officer of regular Confederate cavalry, but at the time of McCook's death was a partisan captain appointed by Gen. Edmund Kirby Smith.[15]

On August 7, Maj. Gen. George H. Thomas, McCook's division commander, issued general orders to McCook's soldiers announcing his death. Thomas stated that the general died "from wounds received from a party of guerrillas, who attacked him while proceeding in an ambulance."[16]

Thomas continued: "He was affable in his manners and a courteous gentleman. A brave officer and a congenial friend is lost to this division, and the country has been deprived of a general who was firm and devoted to its interests. Whilst we deplore his loss let us be steady in our efforts to maintain such discipline as will insure to our arms a just retribution upon the dastardly foe who could take advantage of his defenseless condition." Anger over McCook's death quickly inflamed his men, and the soldiers and the Northern press almost instantly claimed the general was "butchered" near the wagon or shot on his sick bed in cold blood.[17]

"The condition of General McCook could not but have been known to the attacking party, as he was on his bed, divested of all outer clothing, except a hat used as a shade, and the curtains of the carriage being raised on all sides," Van Derveer wrote in an August 9 report. "There are good reasons for supposing that the attack was planned solely for General McCook's capture or murder."[18]

"The Murder Of General McCook," read an August 9 headline in the *New York Times.* Outraged by "this cowardly assassination," a number of McCook's men primarily from the 9th Ohio went on a rampage through the countryside, burning property and shooting a Confederate lieutenant who was on furlough but suspected of being connected with the marauders. Several men "implicated in the murder were taken out and hung to trees by the infuriated soldiery," the *New York Herald* stated. McCook's body, meanwhile, was taken to Nashville and kept at the Commercial Hotel before being transported by train to Louisville on August 8. "The city is in a perfect uproar of excitement over the details of the death," wrote a *Times* correspondent in Nashville. "Amazement and revenge are pictured on every countenance." Rumors flew that several of the city's more prominent secessionists had been shot by Union sympathizers. "The death of General McCook will be remembered there, and a terrible retribution will fall upon the assassins of this brave and gallant soldier," the *Herald* said.[19]

Federal authorities soon identified Gurley as McCook's killer, making him one of the most wanted men in the country. Gurley was captured near Chattanooga in late October 1863 and transported to a military prison in Nashville. By now, Brooke, who had been in McCook's wagon, was acting judge advocate of the U.S. Department of the Cumberland. He persuaded Union secretary of war Edwin M. Stanton and judge advocate Joseph Holt to authorize an early trial for Gurley before a military commission.

Top-level Confederates, meanwhile, were working on Gurley's behalf. On December 28, Confederate secretary of war James A. Seddon wrote to Gen. Joseph Johnston, commander of the Army of Tennessee:

Information is received that . . . Gurley, a gallant partisan, acting under authority from General E. K. Smith, has been captured while sick in Alabama and is about to be tried by military commission at Nashville as a bushwhacker or unauthorized insurgent. He killed General R. L. McCook, and is thus the object of special spite. Make inquiry, and if satisfied of the facts take proper steps to warn against and prevent such outrage.[20]

By this time, other notable Rebel leaders, including Lt. Gen. W. J. Hardee and Maj. Gen. Nathan B. Forrest, had written to Union authorities to assist Gurley.

Maj. Gen. Ulysses S. Grant offered this reply to Hardee: "Captain Gurley being an officer in the Confederate Army does not preclude the possibility of his having committed a foul murder, for which he can be held fully amenable by the laws of war, and if found guilty punished with death. . . . He will receive a fair and impartial trial." Grant added that if acquitted, Gurley would be held as a prisoner of war.[21]

The commission found Gurley guilty of murder on January 11, 1864, and sentenced him to death by hanging. General Thomas approved the guilty verdict but suspended the execution sentence because of the "peculiar circumstances and excitement under which the crime was committed." He also recommended that the sentence be reduced to five years imprisonment.[22]

Holt, however, lobbied to have Gurley hanged, and sent trial records to President Abraham Lincoln, who approved the verdict, but delayed action on the death sentence.

Gurley remained in prison for the next year, but his journey was about to take another fascinating twist. Federal military bureaucracy resulted in his mistaken release in a prisoner exchange near Point Lookout, Maryland, in March 1865.

Gurley made his way home to Madison County, Alabama, staying with relatives until after the surrender of Robert E. Lee's army in Virginia. He then went to Huntsville, took the oath of allegiance and received his parole. After living without incident for several more months, Gurley believed he could lead a normal life. He ran for and was elected sheriff of Madison County in November 1865.

Gurley did not know, however, that Holt, with the approval of President Andrew Johnson, had issued orders in September to have Gurley arrested and the death sentence carried out. Shortly after his election,

Gurley was apprehended by federal authorities and imprisoned in Huntsville where his execution date was set for November 30. A number of his friends and associates then came to his aid, contacting Johnson directly and urging that he meet with a delegation from their ranks. The president agreed to this, knowing that some of Gurley's supporters were strong Unionists, and on November 28, he suspended the execution until further notice. Johnson might also have been swayed by the fact that news of Gurley's arrest and pending hanging had incensed some residents who were threatening violence. Johnson met with the delegation, and Gurley remained incarcerated as he awaited his fate.

In April 1866, Johnson consulted with General Grant about the case, and despite Holt's continued insistence that Gurley be hanged, Grant recommended that the case be dropped. Johnson agreed and a War Department order on April 17, 1866, ended the U.S. government's case against Gurley:

"Frank B. Gurley, citizen, sentenced by a military commission 'to be hanged by the neck until he is dead' upon the recommendation of Lieutenant-General Grant, is hereby released from confinement and will be placed upon his parole as a prisoner of war duly exchanged. By order of the President of the United States."[23]

When Gurley was freed, Robert McCook had been at rest in Cincinnati's Spring Grove Cemetery for more than three years. He had not lived to suffer the death of his father, Maj. Daniel McCook, killed in a clash with John Hunt Morgan's Rebel cavalry at Buffington Island, Ohio, in July 1863; or the fall of his brother, Daniel Jr., mortally wounded on the slopes of Kennesaw Mountain the following June, living only long enough to be promoted to brigadier.

Gurley died of natural causes in 1920.

UNION BRIGADIER GENERAL HENRY BOHLEN
Freeman's Ford, Virginia, August 22, 1862
August would also herald the death of the first foreign-born Union general in the war. Brig. Gen. Henry Bohlen, fifty-one, was a native of Bremen, Germany, who became a wealthy dealer of foreign wines and liquor after immigrating to the United States. A Mexican War veteran, he played a key role in organizing the 75th Pennsylvania Volunteers, a Philadelphia unit, and was named its colonel in September 1861.

Bohlen had served during the 1862 Shenandoah Valley Campaign, and had been promoted to brigadier general of volunteers. He had performed capably at Cross Keys and had covered the retreat of John Pope's Army of Virginia after Cedar Mountain.[24]

He led a brigade in Maj. Gen. Franz Siegel's I Corps, his command composed of regiments from Ohio, Pennsylvania, and West Virginia, with some Pennsylvania artillery. Losses in battle or to illness notwithstanding, it had already been a tragic year for Bohlen's brigade: fifty-one men of his old 75th Pennsylvania had drowned on April 15 while trying to cross the Shenandoah River on a partially burned boat.

After the battle of Cedar Mountain, Stonewall Jackson moved his men to the area of Gordonsville where he was joined by Maj. Gen. James Longstreet's corps as well as Robert E. Lee. On August 21, the Rebels moved toward the Rappahannock River. The rival armies then marched upriver—Pope's Federals on the north side and the Rebels on the south—in a series of inconclusive moves to gain the upper hand.

Jackson was on the march on August 22, leaving Brig. Gen. Isaac Trimble's brigade near Freeman's Ford to guard his wagon trains. Bohlen's brigade was sent on a reconnaissance across the ford, which is located near Remington, Virginia. That afternoon, Bohlen threatened the Confederate wagon trains but Trimble blocked him. Trimble was soon reinforced by Brig. Gen. John Bell Hood's division.

The Confederates attacked Bohlen with three brigades, pushing the outnumbered Yankees back toward the river. Bohlen tried to make a stand on hills near the ford, but was soon forced to retreat again. The Federals slogged back across the river, under the protection of Union artillery, but among their casualties was Bohlen, dropped from his saddle by a musket round. When Confederates found Bohlen's body on the field, he was still wearing a colonel's insignia on his uniform, not yet having been updated to his brigadier's star. "The Federals suffered considerable loss, General Bohlen himself being among the slain," a Southern historian wrote.[25]

The *New York Times* on August 26 reprinted an article from the *Philadelphia Press* about Bohlen's end: "And when the army was safely across the Rappahannock, still nearest the enemy, Bohlen's brigade were fighting continually, and unfortunately for the country and its cause . . . Bohlen was observed by a rebel sharpshooter, while riding across the field, directing the movements of his troops, and shot through the head."[26]

Robert E. Lee noted the clash in a report, stating, "After a short but spirited engagement the enemy was driven precipitately over the river with heavy loss."[27]

There were rumors that Bohlen was shot in the back, a victim of his own disgruntled men, but the evidence indicates that he was well liked by his troops and that he died from enemy fire.

Bohlen was buried in Philadelphia's Laurel Hill Cemetery, the *Press* pronouncing: "Thus fell one of Philadelphia's best, bravest and brightest children."[28]

UNION BRIGADIER GENERAL GEORGE W. TAYLOR
Second Bull Run Campaign, August 27, 1862

Five days after General Bohlen's death, another Union general was mortally wounded when his lone brigade stumbled upon Stonewall Jackson's command at Manassas Junction.

Brig. Gen. George W. Taylor, fifty-three, was a native of Hunterdon County, New Jersey, and graduated from a military academy in Middletown, Connecticut, in 1827. He joined the navy, but resigned in 1831 to become a farmer. After serving as an infantry officer in the Mexican War, he lived in California for a few years but returned to New Jersey where he was engaged in the iron business when the South seceded. Taylor was named colonel of the 3rd New Jersey Infantry, promoted to brigadier general in May 1862, and fought in the Seven Days Battles as part of Brig. Gen. Henry Slocum's division of the IV Corps.[29]

When a Confederate force threatened the Federal supply depot and railroad center at Manassas Junction in the last week of August, Taylor's brigade was the first to be dispatched to the scene. Composed of four New Jersey regiments, the brigade left camp near Alexandria about 4 A.M. on August 27 and was carried by train on the Orange & Alexandria Railroad to the railroad bridge over Bull Run, near the junction. With no artillery support, they crossed the bridge and about 8:30 A.M. came under severe cannon fire as well as cavalry thrusts.

Unknown to him, Taylor was facing Jackson, Jeb Stuart, and a nest of Confederates who had descended on Manassas. The Southerners were feasting and enjoying the captured Union supplies when Taylor's command approached. The Rebels trained two batteries on the outnumbered Yankees and also attacked with Maj. Gen. A. P. Hill's division. In danger of being cut off, Taylor ordered a retreat, but the artillery shelling soon turned the withdrawal into a rout. Taylor was seriously wounded in the left leg in the confusion.

Lt. Robert Kennedy of Taylor's staff was caught up in the exodus near the bridge when he saw soldiers carrying the wounded general. "About this time General Taylor, suffering from his wound, passed, borne upon a litter, and appealed to me to rally the men and for God's sake to prevent another Bull Run," Kennedy reported. "I promised to do all I could." The New Jersey men fell back over the bridge and the line was bolstered by the arrival of two Ohio regiments.[30]

"The general was severely wounded and turned over the command to me, informing me that the enemy was in large force compared to ours," reported Union colonel E. P. Scammon. He managed to hold his ground east of the run until he retreated about 3:30 P.M. Scammon was blunt in assessing the conduct of the brigade. "I am constrained to say that the behavior of the New Jersey brigade after General Taylor retired from the field was discreditable; they retreated rapidly and in disorder," the colonel said. "They declared that the general had ordered them to retire, and retire they did, most disgracefully," he added.[31]

Taylor, meanwhile, had been taken to Burke's Station by soldiers using a railroad handcar. There he was put on a train for the trip to Mansion House Hospital in Alexandria which belonged to the Corcoran family but had been converted into a medical facility for the military. . The train endured some Rebel fire en route, but managed to make it through. Stuart claimed that Confederates manning captured Federal artillery killed Taylor. He reported that Louis Terrill, a volunteer aide to cavalry Brig. Gen. Beverly Robertson "extemporized" lanyards and that volunteer infantry serving as cannoneers "turned the captured guns with marked effect upon the enemy. Their general (G. W. Taylor of New Jersey) was killed during this fire."[32]

Jackson described the action in which Taylor fell: "Soon after a considerable body of Federal infantry, under Brigadier-General Taylor, of New Jersey, came in sight, having, it is believed, that morning left Alexandria in the cars, and boldly pushed forward to recover the position and stores which had been lost the previous night. The advance was made with great spirit and determination and under a leader worthy of a better cause. . . . In this conflict the Federal commander, General Taylor, was mortally wounded."[33]

Taylor arrived in Alexandria about thirteen hours after his misfortune. On August 28, surgeons amputated his lower leg, but Taylor lost a considerable amount of blood even for such a procedure. He died about 4 A.M. on September 1,[34] and was buried in Rock Church Cemetery in his home county.

UNION MAJOR GENERALS PHILIP KEARNY AND ISAAC I. STEVENS
Chantilly, Virginia, September 1, 1862
Two days before his death, Maj. Gen. Philip Kearny told a battle-shaken young officer, "You must never be frightened of anything." His words

would prove to be a fitting epitaph for Kearny himself and Maj. Gen. Isaac I. Stevens (whose promotion to major general was posthumous), both killed at Chantilly.[35]

John Pope's Union army was in retreat after the battle of Second Bull Run. Determined to cut off the enemy's escape route after the battle, Stonewall Jackson sent his troops on a wide flank march. On September 1, his units collided with the divisions of Kearny and Stevens on the Little River Turnpike near Ox Hill.

Kearny led the 1st Division in the Army of the Potomac III Corps of Maj. Gen. Samuel P. Heintzelman. Stevens commanded the 1st Division of the U.S. IX Corps under Maj. Gen. Jesse Reno.

"He was short and rather stout, with a swarthy complexion and very bright dark eyes," Pope recalled of the forty-four-year-old Stevens. "He was a man of very superior abilities and of marked skill and courage."[36]

Born into an old Massachusetts family, Stevens graduated first in his West Point class of 1839, and was commissioned into the Corps of Engineers. In the Mexican War, he was seriously wounded at Mexico City and brevetted for gallantry. He resigned from the Army in 1853 to accept the governorship of Washington Territory. He clashed with the federal government, but served as governor and later the territory's member of the U.S. House of Representatives until 1861. Believed by some to have pro-slavery sympathies, Stevens was appointed colonel of the 79th New York Infantry in July 1861, and promoted to brigadier general less than two months later. He saw his first action along the South Carolina coast and came under some criticism for his conduct at the battle of Secessionville in June 1862. During the fighting, he made an unsuccessful assault under protest, his detractors accusing him of cowardice. He returned to Virginia in July and was assigned to the IX Corps.[37]

At Chantilly, Stevens formed his division and attacked about 4:30 P.M., dismounting and taking his post near the center of his advancing line. To help hold his units together, Stevens assigned officers of his staff to each of his regiments. Among these officers was his son and adjutant, Capt. Hazard Stevens, who was to attack with Stevens's old 79th. Much of the fighting would be done in a heavy thunderstorm.

The division moved across an open field in silence until the Federals were within seventy-five yards of a rail fence bordering some woods. The fence shielded brigades of North Carolinians and Virginians led by Brig. Gen. Lawrence O. Branch and Col. J. M. Brockenbrough, and they unleashed a terrific fire. The Yankees suffered heavily and the 79th's color

Union major general Philip Kearny.
LIBRARY OF CONGRESS

bearer went down, as did Captain Stevens, the latter wounded in the hip and arm.

Seeing his men waver, the general picked up the New Yorkers' flag, ran in front of them and shouted, "Follow me, my Highlanders!" The Federals surged forward, taking the fence and driving the Rebels from the edge of the trees. Stevens, however was dead "upon the broken fence, a rebel bullet through his brain, with the colors of the Highlanders still held firmly in his grasp."[38]

Pope added: "His conduct in the battle in which he lost his life, and in every other operation of the campaign, was marked by high intelligence and the coolest courage, and his death in the front of battle ended too soon a career which would have placed him among the foremost officers of the war."[39]

Kearny's men, meanwhile, had been on the march on the Warrenton Pike when a courier from Stevens arrived requesting assistance. "My God, I will support Stevens anywhere!" Kearny replied. Without orders, Kearny ordered Brig. Gen. David Birney's brigade to the action and followed with a battery of Rhode Island artillery commanded by Capt. George Randolph.[40]

The forty-seven-year-old Kearny was among the most dashing and combat-savvy officers in the Union army. A member of one of New York

City's wealthiest and most socially elite families, he was an 1833 graduate of Columbia University. A millionaire by inheritance, Kearny nevertheless had always wanted to be a soldier and was commissioned a second lieutenant in the 1st U.S. Dragoons in 1837. He went to France to study European cavalry tactics, but returned home in time to see action in the Mexican War, losing his left arm at the battle of Churubusco. Kearny resigned from the army in 1851, spending the next few years traveling around the globe or relaxing on his New Jersey estate. Returning to France in 1859, he served in Napoleon III's Imperial Guard, seeing much action in the Italian War. When the Civil War began, Kearny headed home and was among the first brigadier generals of volunteers appointed, commanding a New Jersey brigade. He was in battle during the Peninsular Campaign and was promoted major general as of July 4, 1862. The general also originated the "Kearny patch," predecessor of the Union army's corps badges.[41]

Birney's brigade reached the field about 5 P.M., with orders to support Reno's command, and almost immediately went into battle. Kearny, mounted on his favorite horse, a brown named "Bayard," arrived about 6:30 P.M. and in the wet, deepening gloom met with Birney. Stevens's division had retreated in some disorder by this time, leaving Birney's right flank exposed.

Kearny rode off to find troops to plug this gap, his reins in his teeth and his sword in his hand. In the murkiness it was difficult to distinguish friend from foe, musket flashes and lightning cracks marking the lines. He encountered the 21st Massachusetts which had been shattered in the day's earlier fighting, and ordered it to support Birney. The muskets of many of these soldiers had been rendered useless in the rain and their commander asked Kearny to allow them a few moments to clear their wet charges.

Kearny refused "with a hot sneer at our cowardice, and the threat that unless the regiment moved instantly . . . he would turn a battery upon us," one of the Massachusetts men recalled. Kearny then rode to Randolph's battery (Battery E, 1st Rhode Island Artillery) which was in action a few rods to the rear. An artillery officer soon galloped to the Massachusetts unit, offering compliments "coupled with the assurance that it [the battery] would play upon us unless the order given was instantly obeyed," wrote Lt. Charles Walcott of the 21st. The New Englanders tramped across open ground toward a cornfield near Birney's position. They came under musket fire and halted among the cornstalks.[42]

"Gen. Kearny was following us up closely . . . and tried to force us forward, saying that we were firing on our own men, and that there were no rebels near us," Walcott recalled. Skirmishers had captured two Confederates belonging to the 49th Georgia during the advance, and Walcott, who belonged to the brigade staff, brought them before Kearny to persuade him of the enemy's nearness. Incensed, Kearny raged, "—— —— you and your prisoners!" Alone, the general spurred away "apparently in an uncontrollable rage . . . [and] forced his horse through the deep, sticky mud of the cornfield" past the regiment's left. Walcott then described Kearny's last moments: "I watched him moving in the murky twilight through the corn, and, when less than twenty yards away, saw his horse suddenly rear and turn, and half-a-dozen muskets flashed around him; so died the intrepid soldier, Gen. Philip Kearny!"[43]

He found some troops in position in brush at the edge of a clearing. Too late, he realized they were Rebel skirmishers who opened fire. Confederate major general James Longstreet gave this account of Kearny's end:

> It was raining in the woods, and was so late in the day that a Federal was not easily distinguishable from a Confederate. Kearny did not seem to know that he was in the Confederate line, and our troops did not notice that he was a Federal. He began to inquire about some command, and in a moment or so the men saw that he was a Federal officer. At the same moment he realized where he was. He was called upon to surrender, but instead . . . wheeled his horse, lay flat on the animal's neck, clapped spurs into his sides and dashed off. Instantly a half-dozen shots rang out, and before he had gone thirty steps he fell. He had been in the army all his life, and we knew and respected him.[44]

Capt. James H. Haynes of the 55th Virginia in Brockenbrough's brigade of A. P. Hill's division claimed to be on the skirmish line "in the edge of a brushy place with a clearing in front. It was raining heavily and growing dark when Kearny rode suddenly upon the line, and asked what troops they were. Seeing his mistake, he turned and started across the open ground to escape, but was fired on and killed."[45]

A single bullet struck Kearny in the back near the belt line, traveling upward. Various accounts state that the round lodged near his heart or exited near the shoulder, but whatever the course, the wound was deadly. He fell from Bayard into the mud, thrashed briefly and died. The Rebels carried Kearny's body to the rear, General Hill recognizing him and exclaiming, "Poor Kearny! He deserved a better death than this." Birney, meanwhile, believed Kearny had been taken prisoner when he did not return and assumed command of the division, which helped hold the Union line until early the next morning. He later wrote that Kearny "fell a victim to his gallant daring."[46]

Confederate captain W. W. Blackford of Gen. Jeb Stuart's staff, was at Robert E. Lee's headquarters when word arrived that the body of a Federal general with only one arm had been found on the battlefield. Blackford accompanied Stuart and others to identify the remains, which they already believed to be Kearny. "The body, dressed in a plain undress uniform, had been laid in a house and proved to be, as supposed, that of Kearny," Blackford noted.[47]

The house was the formerly stately country home of Chantilly, which had now been ravaged by the battle. "[I]t was hardly habitable," recalled Alexander Hunter, a Rebel private in Kemper's Brigade, "the furniture was smashed to kindling wood, the windows dashed to pieces with the butt-end of the muskets, the plastering from the walls knocked off, and the rooms so defaced and defiled that it discounted a hog pen in filth." Chantilly now brimmed with casualties of both armies. "In this space lay many wounded and dead, among others General Phil Kearny, the most brilliant, chivalrous, dashing officer in the Yankee army," Hunter wrote. "He was killed in a charge and rode in the advance with his hat in the air and the bridle held in his teeth, for he had but one arm, the other he lost in the Mexican war. He was a brave ideal of a soldier. Most of our soldiers viewed his dead body."[48]

The Union rearguard withdrew from the field before dawn on September 2. Under a truce flag a few hours later, Kearny's body was sent through the lines with a note to Pope from Lee: "The body of General Philip Kearny was brought from the field last night, and he was reported dead. I send it forward under a flag of truce, thinking the possession of his remains may be a consolation to his family." Lee also included a letter of condolence for Kearny's widow, Agnes.[49]

Among the Union soldiers and in Washington, news of Kearny's death cast a pall over early reports that he had been only slightly wounded and captured, information that had also been relayed to the general's wife. Kearny and Stevens were the highest-ranking Union generals to die at that point in the war, and the fact that they fell on the same day increased the public shock and gloom.

In battle reports, Stonewall Jackson and A. P. Hill wrote that Kearny fell in front of Col. Edward Thomas's brigade of Georgians, but Hill added that Brockenbrough's Virginia brigade held the skirmish line. Henry Kyd Douglas, one of Jackson's staff officers, wrote that Kearny and Stonewall had known each other in the Mexican War. "No two men were unlike in all personal qualifications, yet both had that touch of martial genius which made them akin."[50]

A page one headline in the September 3 *New York Times* told of the deaths of Kearny and Stevens, an accompanying story stating that Stevens was "killed with a Minié ball, which entered his brain while he was leading his men into action, bearing the colors in his hand, the Color-Sergeant having been slain."[51]

"General Kearny rode forward alone to reconnoiter in his usual, gallant, not to say reckless, manner, and came upon a rebel regiment," General Heintzelman stated in his report. "In attempting to escape he was killed. The country has to mourn one of her most gallant defenders. . . . His name is identified with its [his division's] glory."[52]

Kearny's body was taken to Washington, arriving on the night of September 2, and was to be embalmed before being shipped home. Gen. George McClellan was said to have "wept bitterly" when first seeing the corpse. "Army officers here think this the greatest loss we have sustained during the war, and freely acknowledge that we had no abler General in the service," wrote a *Philadelphia Press* correspondent in Washington.[53]

Pope described Kearny and Stevens as "two officers of the highest capacity and distinction, whose death caused general lamentation in the army and country." He added, "The loss of these two officers was a heavy blow to the army, not so much because of their soldierly capacity as because of their well-known and unshakable fidelity to duty, and their entire loyalty to their comrades in arms." In an action report, Pope stated the generals were "both killed while gallantly leading their commands and in front of their line of battle. It is unnecessary for me to say one word of commendation of two officers who were so well and widely known to the country. Words cannot express my sense of the zeal, the gallantry, and the sympathy of that most earnest and accomplished soldier Major-General Kearny. In him the country has suffered a loss which it will be difficult, if not impossible, to repair. He died as he would wish to die, and as became his heroic character." Pope added that Stevens's "death will be deeply felt by the army and the country."[54]

Kearny was "always forgetful of his own safety," the *Times* said on September 4, adding that the "country has to deplore the loss of one of its most accomplished, experienced and enterprising officers. . . . Had his bravery been attempered with the slightest dash of personal prudence, a career so splendid and so promising would not have been so untimely ended." In the same editorial, the *Times* addressed Stevens's loss and the allegations of cowardice at Secessionville, stating that the accusations "must be forever canceled and silenced by the dauntless bravery of the man on his last battlefield. He fell a victim to his too zealous gallantry. The people have too few servants of skill and discretion and zeal to spare any without bitter regret. The two just lost are of the few, and must be mourned deeply and earnestly."[55]

Stevens was posthumously promoted major general in March 1863. He was buried in Island Cemetery, near his wife's home in Newport, Rhode Island.

On September 4, Birney issued general orders to the division noting Kearny's death "with deep sorrow." He continued: "The entire country will mourn the loss of this gallant, chivalric soldier, and no one of this division but will hold ever fresh his memory. Let us try to show our regard for him by ever sustaining the name that in his love for this division he gave it, viz, the 'Fighting Division.'" In addition to wearing black mourning bands, division officers were also allowed to keep pieces of scarlet cloth attached to their caps or to have the crowns of their hats made of scarlet in Kearny's memory.[56]

Other Confederate notables also mourned Kearny, among them Brig. Gen. George Pickett who had served with him in Mexico. Pickett was recuperating from an arm wound sustained at Gaines' Mill and wrote of Kearny's fall in a letter to his fianceé, Sally Corbell. "The news came, too, this morning of the death of Kearny, one of the most brilliant generals of the Federal Army, a man whose fame as a soldier is world-wide . . ." Pickett stated. "I wish we had taken him prisoner instead of shooting him. I hate to have such a man as Kearny killed. Marse Robert, who was his old friend, sent his body to Pope under a flag of truce. I am glad he did that— poor old Kearny!"[57]

Kearny's body was sent to his family's home near East Newark, New Jersey, where hundreds of mourners came to pay their respects. The funeral was held on September 6, the remains enclosed in a rosewood casket and conveyed in a hearse drawn by four gray horses. As bells tolled, the procession, including military units and "tens of thousands," made its way to New York City's Trinity Churchyard. "All along the line of march the stores were closed, flags innumerable hung at half-mast, and the streets were lined with a silent expectant people," the *New York Times* said.[58]

The family barred newspapermen from the funeral, but *Times* reporter Joseph Howard got the story anyway, disguising himself as a priest. The general was reinterred at Arlington National Cemetery in 1912. Of Kearny, Pope said that he "died as he himself would have wished to die, and as became his heroic character, at the head of his troops and in the front of the battle."[59]

Antietam's Terrible Toll

UNION MAJOR GENERALS JESSE L. RENO, JOSEPH K. F. MANSFIELD, AND ISRAEL B. RICHARDSON, AND BRIGADIER GENERAL ISAAC P. RODMAN

CONFEDERATE BRIGADIER GENERALS SAMUEL GARLAND JR., WILLIAM E. STARKE, LAWRENCE O. BRANCH, AND GEORGE B. ANDERSON

Maryland Campaign, 1862

Antietam, the bloodiest day of the Civil War, would claim six generals to join two others slain in combat at South Mountain three days earlier. Each side would lose four commanders among the thousands killed and maimed and scattered over the Maryland countryside.

When Robert E. Lee's army crossed the Potomac River into Maryland in September 1862, the Rebels hoped to move out of war-torn Virginia and fight Maj. Gen. George B. McClellan's Army of the Potomac in a battle likely to decide the Confederacy's independence.

In Maryland, Lee boldly divided his army, sending Stonewall Jackson to capture Harpers Ferry with its garrison of about 11,000 poorly supplied Federals. Maj. Gen. Daniel Harvey Hill's division was dispatched to Boonsboro near South Mountain, which Lee hoped to use as a natural defensive line to keep McClellan from pouncing on his scattered forces. McClellan pursued the Confederates to Frederick, Maryland, where fate presented him with a copy of Lee's Special Order No. 191 lost by the Rebels. The document revealed the disposition of the gray army and gave McClellan an opportunity to destroy the fragmented enemy.

McClellan pressed toward South Mountain, twelve miles away, where Hill was waiting. Hill's units were separated themselves with only two of his five infantry brigades and a handful of cavalry to defend the mountain passes at Fox's Gap, Turner's Gap, and Crampton's Gap. Hill arrived on the heights on Sunday morning, September 14, and deployed his men to cover these passes, sending the North Carolina brigade of Brig. Gen. Samuel Garland Jr. to guard Fox's Gap. McClellan, meanwhile, had sent his army's right wing under Maj. Gen. Ambrose Burnside to attack the Rebels at Turner's Gap and Fox's Gap. Burnside's wing consisted of the I Corps, led by Maj. Gen. Joseph Hooker, and Maj. Gen. Jesse L. Reno's IX Corps, some 25,000 troops in all, although Hooker was still on the march several hours away.

Facing this threat, Garland moved his less than 1,000 men into positions on the eastern slope guarding the Old Sharpsburg Road at Fox's Gap. Hill had ordered Garland to hold the road at all costs to protect Lee's large wagon train, which was near Boonsboro. According to Hill, Garland "went off in high spirits and I never saw him again. I never knew a truer, better, braver man."[1]

There were rumors that Garland had a death wish. His wife of five years, Elizabeth Meem Garland, and their only son, four-year-old Samuel, had died of influenza within three months of each other in the summer of 1861, and some believed that the general wanted nothing more than to join them in the afterlife. Garland, thirty-one, belonged to an old Virginia family, President James Madison being his great uncle. He graduated from Virginia Military Institute in 1849 and the University of Virginia law school two years later before settling into practice in Lynchburg, his hometown. As colonel of the 11th Virginia Infantry, he was wounded at Williamsburg and, after being promoted to brigadier in May 1862, was assigned to a brigade of North Carolinians in Hill's division. Garland was conspicuous in combat at Seven Pines, the Seven Days battles and Second Bull Run.[2]

At South Mountain he made his stand near the summit, posting his men on both sides of the road. Some of the Tarheels were stationed in an open field atop a ridge on the Daniel Wise farm. The rugged terrain meant that his regiments would fight independently and with little contact with each other.

About 9 A.M., skirmishers of Garland's 5th North Carolina were assailed by Union brigadier general Jacob Cox's Kanawha Division of Reno's corps, a force of about 3,000, infantry, artillery and cavalry, with

Col. Eliakim Scammon's Ohio brigade as his sword point. The Carolinians were soon also immersed in a firefight with the 23rd Ohio of Lt. Col. Rutherford B. Hayes, the future U.S. president. Scammon's Federals made a spirited attack on the left of Garland's position. Unseen Federals were on a thickly wooded rise in front of the Southerners and a regiment or so of Yankees had found cover behind a rail fence.

The musket fire was constant from these hidden bluecoats and Lt. Col. Thomas Ruffin Jr. of the 13th North Carolina was concerned about Garland being in the open while directing his men. He suggested that the general move to a safer position. "But with Garland, the post of danger was the post of honor," Hill related.[3]

Ruffin gave this account of Garland's last moments:

I said to him, "General, why do you stay here? You are in great danger." To which he replied: "I may as well be here as yourself."

I said: "No, it is my duty to be here with my regiment, but you could better superintend your brigade from a safer position."

A bullet then pierced Ruffin's hip, and he exclaimed to Garland that he had been shot, but the general had little time to react. "He turned and gave an order," Ruffin remembered. "In a moment I heard a groan, and looked and found him mortally wounded and writhing in pain."[4]

One account says that one of Garland's aides, Lt. Donald Halsey, was the first to reach the fallen general, who gasped, "I am killed, send for the senior colonel."[5]

The bullet had hit Garland in the center of the back, apparently as he turned to survey his line, tearing through his body and exiting above his right breast. He was dead moments later. Col. D. K. McRae of the 5th North Carolina took over the fallen general's command. Garland's Tarheels, demoralized by his fall and the pressure of the Union assaults, broke in disorder shortly afterward, yielding some 200 prisoners, Hill stated. By 10 a.m. the brigade was out of action for the rest of the day.

Rebel soldiers on the road between Boonsboro and South Mountain were disheartened to see the body of "the gallant General Garland" being borne to the rear, a Georgia officer noted.[6]

"General Garland is brought to his tent dead," the Reverend Alexander Betts, chaplain of the 30th North Carolina, wrote in his journal that day. "A few days ago I saw him under different circumstances that will make me admire him forever. His Brigade was crossing a stream on a narrow footway. His men began to plunge into the little stream, up to their knees. He knew it would be bad for them to march with wet feet. He drew up his fiery horse in the road in the water and stayed there till his entire command had passed, pointing to the narrow bridge and shouting to the men, compelling them to take time and go over in single file. That manly form now lies before me silent but 'speaking.'"[7]

Fighting continued throughout the day at Fox's Gap, Turner's Gap, and Crampton's Gap as the Confederates clung to their positions. On the Union side, General Reno reached Fox's Gap late in the day and rode forward to see what was hindering his progress. "A little before sunset Reno came up in person, anxious to know why the right could not get forward quite to the summit," recalled Brig. Gen. Jacob Cox.[8]

Reno, thirty-nine, was a native of Wheeling, (now West) Virginia, grew up in Pennsylvania, and graduated West Point in 1846, a class that also included, McClellan, Stonewall Jackson and George Pickett. Twice brevetted for gallantry in the Mexican War, he had been a West Point instructor and served on the Utah Expedition, among other assignments, before disunion. Commissioned a brigader general of volunteers in late 1861, he had participated in Burnside's expedition to the North Carolina coast. Promoted major general in summer 1862, he led the IX Corps at Second Bull Run and Chantilly before joining in the Maryland Campaign.[9]

Reno rode on, and about 7 P.M. reached the position held by Brig. Gen. Samuel Sturgis's division before venturing further on a personal reconnaissance. He was in the same area where Garland had been killed that morning. Now a Confederate sharpshooter drew a bead on Reno and he toppled with a bullet in his body.

"His side was partially turned to the enemy," wrote a *New York Times* correspondent, "when a minié ball entered and passed entirely through, coming out between the ribs on the right side and striking the palm of the hand." Several bluecoats carried him back to Sturgis's post. "He was conscious and requested to be carried to headquarters," the *Times* reporter stated.[10]

Cox recalled that "it seemed to me he had hardly gone before he was brought back upon a stretcher. . . . He had gone to the skirmish line to examine for himself the situation there and had been shot down by the enemy posted among the rocks and trees."[11]

When he arrived at Sturgis's camp, Reno called out to his brigadier: "Hallo, Sam, I'm dead!" His voice was so natural that Sturgis at first believed him to be joking. Sturgis replied that he hoped it was not as bad as it sounded. "Yes, yes, I'm dead—good by[e]!" Reno answered.[12]

The general was placed under a large oak tree and attended by his surgeon, Dr. Calvin Cutter. Minutes later, however, he was dead. Cox assumed temporary corps command and the fighting continued until night-fall, the Yankees going into action with cries of "Remember Reno!" The *Times* reported that "the wound was mortal, and about an hour after the fatal bullet struck, the gallant soldier and true patriot breathed his last."[13]

"The loss in killed and wounded here was considerable on both sides, and it was here that Major-General Reno, who had gone forward to observe the operations of his corps and to give such directions as were necessary, fell, pierced with a musket ball," McClellan wrote in an October 15 report. "The loss of this brave and distinguished officer tempered with sadness the exaltations of triumph. A gallant soldier, an able general, endeared to his troops and associates, his death is felt as an irreparable misfortune." McClellan would later write, "In General Reno the nation lost one of its best general officers. He was a skillful soldier, a brave and honest man."[14]

Burnside added: "I will not attempt . . . to express the deep sorrow which the death of the gallant Reno caused me. A long and intimate acquaintance, an extended service on the same field, and an intimate knowledge of his high and noble character had endeared him to me, as well as to all with whom he had served. No more valuable life than his has been lost during this contest for our country's preservation."[15]

The Confederate general Hill, whose troops killed Reno, reported: "The Yankees on their side lost General Reno, a renegade Virginian, who was killed by a happy shot from the Twenty-third North Carolina" The Tarheels, who had lost their general, Garland, hours earlier, were posted among rocks and had been "pouring a constant and destructive fire into the enemy," related the Rebel colonel McRae who had replaced Garland. "It was by the fire of this regiment that General Reno was killed."[16]

Reno "fell at the moment he was gallantly leading his command to a crowning victory," said cavalry Brig. Gen. Alfred Pleasonton who fought at South Mountain. "The clear judgment and determined courage of Reno rendered the triumphant results . . . second to none of the brilliant deeds accomplished on that field. At his loss a master-mind had passed away." The *New York Herald* stated, inaccurately, that Reno died of a head wound, adding that he fell defending the "flag he loved so well."[17]

Despite Reno's fall, the Rebels were driven out of the passes by early evening, but their blood at South Mountain had bought precious time for Lee's army to reunite. "This brilliant service, however, cost us the life of that pure, gallant, and accomplished Christian soldier, General Garland, who had no superiors and few equals in the service," General Hill recalled of the fight, later describing Garland as "the most fearless man I ever knew."[18]

The brigadier's cousin and aide, Lt. Maurice Garland, escorted Garland's body home to Lynchburg. His remains lay in state at the Lynchburg courthouse for a day before his funeral was held at St. Paul's Episcopal Church on September 19. Church bells tolled and the town's businesses were closed in respect for the native son. After a military procession to Presbyterian Cemetery, Garland was buried next to his wife and son in the Meem family plot. "Had he lived, his talents, pluck, energy, and purity of character must have put him in the first rank of his profession, whether in civil or military life," Hill said of him.[19]

On the same day as Garland's service, a few hundred miles away, General Reno was laid to rest. His body was taken to Boston, where his wife was living, and his funeral was held at Trinity Episcopal Church at noon on September 19. Massachusetts Governor John Andrew was among those in attendance and members of Reno's staff served as pallbearers. After the service, the casket was opened so the mourners could see the remains, which were adorned with flowers. Reno was dressed in a uniform tunic with a major general's stars on the shoulder straps, but was otherwise in civilian clothes. His body would be placed in a vault in the church cemetery, but was reinterred at Oak Hill Cemetery, Georgetown, D.C., in 1867.[20]

⚜

For two days after South Mountain, the foes sized each other up, filtering into positions near the tiny village of Sharpsburg, Maryland, and along opposite banks of the nearby Antietam Creek. At dawn on September 17, Maj. Gen. Joseph Hooker's corps opened the climatic battle by attacking the Confederate left, commanded by Jackson, north of the town.

In the fighting's early stages, the division of Brig. Gen. John R. Jones in Jackson's corps came under horrific shelling from Union artillery. A round exploded over Jones's head, incapacitating him to the point that he had to be taken from the field. Brig. Gen. William E. Starke of the 2nd Louisiana Brigade took over the division command.

Amid the tempest of what would be one of the most monumental battles of the war, Starke was called upon to step up, even though he was technically under arrest by Jackson. Starke, forty-eight, was a Virginian who had been a prosperous peacetime cotton broker in Mobile and New Orleans. He had served on Gen. Robert Garnett's staff in western Virginia and had seen much action in the Seven Days fighting where his son had been killed at Seven Pines. Promoted brigadier a month earlier, he fought at Second Bull Run and followed Jackson into Maryland. One of Starke's brothers, Peter, would also become a Confederate general and survive the war.

Starke and Jackson had clashed a few days earlier after the army had marched through Frederick. A few townspeople and merchants blamed the Rebels for looting and minor violence, accusing "foreign" soldiers among the Southerners in Jackson's ranks in particular. After meeting with a civilian delegation about the issue, Jackson ordered Starke to bring his brigade back to Frederick to try to determine if any of his Louisianians were guilty. Angered that his men were singled out, Starke refused to obey Jackson's order and Stonewall had him arrested, although he remained in command pending trial.[21]

When he replaced Jones, Starke turned over command of his brigade to Col. Leroy Stafford. A half hour later, Federal infantry of Brig. Gen. Abner Doubleday's division in Hooker's corps advanced on Starke's line, and he ordered his men forward to meet the threat. They moved out of the West Woods and across a clover field. Starke seized the flag of his Louisiana Tigers, even though he was leading the division, and rode ahead of his brigade as they attacked. The Rebels reached the west side of the Hagerstown Pike and engaged the Federals at volley range, some of the Confederates lying down to fire at the bluecoats through the rail and post fence along the road, the battle lines at one point being only about thirty yards apart.

Blue and gray unleashed their musketry with devastating results and among the casualties was Starke, hit almost at the same instant by several bullets and pitching from his horse near the turnpike fence. "[T]he gallant and generous Starke fell, pierced by three balls, and survived but a few moments," Jones wrote in his report. "His fall cast a gloom over the troops. They never for a moment faltered, but rushed upon the enemy and drove him back."[22]

"It was in this early part of the engagement that our brave and chivalric leader, Brigadier General William E. Starke, loved and honored by every man under his command, fell . . . and was carried from the field in a dying condition, surviving his wounds but an hour," wrote Col. Edmund Pendleton of the 15th Louisiana in Starke's brigade. Maj. H. J. Williams of the 5th Virginia wrote that Starke fell "while cheering his men in the discharge of their duty."[23]

Their general was mortally wounded, but the Louisianians had no time for anything other than biting cartridges and ramrod work as they pushed the bluecoats across the road and charged, a terrific fire dropping men at every step. At the cost of his life, Starke's counterattack blunted Doubleday, but the Rebels were quickly caught in a crossfire of artillery and musketry, the survivors falling back to regroup in the West Woods.

With the battle intensifying the first Union general to die was shot down near the East Woods. Sporting silver hair and a snowy beard, Maj. Gen. Joseph K. F. Mansfield had only been in command of the U.S. XII Corps for two days. He was personally leading a portion of Brig. Gen. Samuel Crawford's brigade in Hooker's support.

Mansfield, fifty-eight, had been in the Army for some forty years as an engineer, but this was his first combat assignment of the war, taking over command from Brig. Gen. Alpheus Williams. Some of his officers found him to be nervous and fussy. Mansfield was a member of one of Connecticut's oldest families, and had entered West Point when he was thirteen. He graduated from the Military Academy ranked second in the class of 1822. He had seen action in the Mexican War, and in May 1861 had been appointed brigadier general, assigned to the Washington defenses. He arrived at XII Corps headquarters the day after the South Mountain fight.[24]

Mansfield was facing some of John Hood's Confederates posted in the East Woods and had brought some reinforcements, the 128th Pennsylvania, to the field when he saw soldiers of his 10th Maine firing into the trees to their front. One of Hooker's staffers had told him that some I Corps troops remained in the woods and Mansfield rode down his line, shouting, "You are firing into our own men!" The soldiers yelled back in disagreement. "Thomas Wait and myself told him we were not firing at our own men for those that were firing at us from behind the trees had been firing at us from the first," related Sgt. E. J. Libby. Other Federals pointed at Rebels who had now stepped out from the trees and were aiming muskets at them and the general. "Yes, yes, you are right," Mansfield answered. In the next instant his horse was shot and Mansfield himself sagged with a bullet wound in the chest. He climbed from the saddle and was able to lead his horse toward the rear before he collapsed.[25]

"A rebel sharpshooter, seeing him mounted in front; within range of an excellent rifle, and evidently perceiving, also, from his venerable appearance, that he was a general officer, took deliberate aim and shot him down," the *New York Herald* said.[26] Men of the 127th Pennsylvania used their muskets to carry Mansfield toward the rear before someone fashioned a blanket into a makeshift litter. They finally reached an ambulance, which took him to a field hospital. There an excited physician gave him a drink of whiskey that almost choked him.

———— ≕✠≔ ————

Like sparked kindling, the battle roared down the lines to a normally peaceful spot that would haunt both sides ever after as Bloody Lane. Along this sunken road, a low-lying dirt path rutted by generations of farm wagons, was posted D. H. Hill's Rebel division, the center of Lee's army. In this natural trench, with farmer Henry Piper's large cornfield to their rear, were the brigades of Brig. Gens. George B. Anderson and Robert Rodes, both of Hill's command, along with elements of three other brigades including Garland's—about 2,500 men total.

A Southern historian described Anderson as "a magnificent specimen of manhood, full six feet, erect, broad-shouldered, round-limbed, with a deep, musical voice, and a smile wonderfully gentle and winning." The thirty-one-year-old general, no doubt, cherished thoughts of his pregnant wife back home as the battle heightened.[27]

Anderson was a North Carolinian, West Point class of 1852, and was known for great personal courage. He had served on the frontier with the 2nd U.S. Dragoons and had been commissioned colonel of the 4th North Carolina in the Confederate service. His reputation had largely been forged in the fighting around Williamsburg, Virginia, in June 1862. There, as Jefferson Davis watched, Anderson grabbed the colors of a Georgia regiment and led a charge on foot, planting the flag on the enemy breastworks. Davis appointed him a brigadier general shortly afterward. Anderson was wounded at Malvern Hill, but fought during the Seven Days and at South Mountain.[28]

About 9:30 A.M., Hill's men were attacked by Brig. Gen. William French's division of the U.S. II Corps charging across the fields of the William Roulette farm. The fighting was bitter and bloody as French's brigades were all but wrecked in vainly trying to oust Hill's Rebels. The II Corps division of Maj. Gen. Israel Richardson soon joined the fray with the remnants of French's units.

Anderson was holding his line against these renewed Federal attacks when he was wounded late in the morning. He was standing on a slight rise behind his men, and directing them in "cool and collected orders" when a musket ball hit him in the foot near the ankle. Amid heavy fire, some of the general's men were able to carry him to a field hospital where doctors examined the wound and pronounced it "severe, but not serious,"

*Union major general
Israel B. Richardson.*
LIBRARY OF CONGRESS

according to Anderson's adjutant, Maj. Seaton Gales. "No one dreamed that one of the truest and bravest men that ever lived had the wound of death upon him."[29]

With Anderson receiving medical treatment, the Sunken Road Rebels fell back early in the afternoon, finally driven out of the corpse-jammed lane by confused orders and reinforced Union assaults. Anderson was one of the more than 5,000 casualties on both sides who fell in this sector in some four hours of combat.

Richardson's Federals had figured prominently in finally smashing Hill's position, and some of his units plunged into the breach toward the Piper farm. The center of Lee's line was cracked and if the Yankees could take advantage, they could divide and likely destroy the Rebel army. Richardson was the man for the job.

Known to his men as "Fighting Dick," or "Greasy Dick," due to his combat courage, Richardson was a forty-six-year-old Vermonter with an imposing physical build. He was "tall and commanding, six feet in height, broad chested, powerful in sinew, with an eye like an eagle's, and a voice that rang out above the shrilling of trumpets," wrote one observer. "He was scarcely the man that even a chivalrous Southerner would select for a personal antagonist on the field." A *New York Herald* correspondent added that Richardson "probably never knew fear in his life, and went under fire with as much nonchalance as ordinary people go to breakfast."[30]

Richardson graduated West Point in 1841, one of twenty-three cadets in that class to become a Civil War general. He fought in the Seminole and Mexican Wars, but resigned from the service in 1855 to take up farming in Michigan. After secession, he recruited, organized, and was appointed colonel of the 2nd Michigan Infantry. His unit saw limited action at First Bull Run, but his coolness and discipline amid the Federal rout resulted in Richardson's promotion to brigadier in August 1861. Richardson commanded a division in the Peninsular Campaign and was appointed major general in July 1862.[31]

Near the Piper house, Richardson posted his men on the crest of a hill, but soon found himself under severe artillery fire with no guns to reply as the Rebels rallied. A section of horse artillery finally arrived and began banging away, being joined quickly by a battery of the 1st U.S. Artillery commanded by Capt. William M. Graham. The Federals in this position soon came under attack by Confederate infantry, which Graham was able to drive off. Two enemy batteries of rifled guns then began bombarding them, one with enfilading fire. Graham replied, but his cannon did not have the range to have any effect. He was conversing with Richardson about this dilemma when "General Richardson was mortally wounded by a ball of a spherical case from the battery enfilading mine," Graham reported.[32]

"The brave general was himself mortally wounded while personally directing its [the artillery] fire," McClellan wrote. Maj. Alford Chapman of the 57th New York Infantry had just reached the line when Richardson went down about 1 P.M. The general "was in the act of assigning me my position when he was badly wounded and carried from the field," Chapman wrote. Various accounts state that Richardson was wounded in the side, breast, and shoulder, all of which could be accurate in vague terms.[33] Brig. Gen. W. S. Hancock was put in division command after Richardson's fall.

"Gen. Richardson was everywhere conspicuous during the action up to the time he received a gunshot wound in the left breast," the *New York Times* reported. "While being removed from the field he said to the surgeon in attendance, 'Tell Gen. McClellan I have been in the front rank, doing the duty of a Colonel. I have done a hard day's work, and have worked all day. I am wounded, and he must detail some one to take my command.'"

The September 21 *New York Herald* said shrapnel hit Richardson in the shoulder, adding, the "wound was painful but not dangerous. It was sufficient, however, to deprive the General of the pleasure of commanding his men during the remainder of the action."[34]

After he was hit, Richardson was taken to the Phillip Pry house, a brick home serving as McClellan's headquarters. The wounded Hooker

*Confederate brigadier general
Lawrence O. Branch.*
LIBRARY OF CONGRESS

also was being attended to there. In a second-floor bedroom, surgeons examined Richardson and tried to stop the bleeding.

"No one but a soldier could understand our sorrow at seeing him carried off the field," one of his men recalled. The Confederates, meanwhile, patched their sparse line in their center and hung on desperately.[35]

For hours on this day, McClellan waited for Burnside's IX Corps to get into battle. Burnside had orders to attack Lee's right flank, but he had been held up since early morning by a few hundred Georgia riflemen contesting his crossing of a stone bridge over Antietam Creek. Burnside finally forced his way over the span (now famously called Burnside Bridge), and after some two hours of reforming his corps, advanced that afternoon, threatening to cut Lee's line of retreat.

With the battle outcome, as well as the existence of Lee's army, hanging in the balance, three brigades of Maj. Gen. A. P. Hill's Light Division began arriving on the field about 4 P.M. after a grueling eight-hour, seventeen-mile march from Harpers Ferry. Without waiting to realign or regroup, Hill threw his men immediately into the battle to stave off Burnside.

Among these Rebels was Hill's senior brigadier, Lawrence O. Branch, a forty-one-year-old North Carolinian, Princeton graduate, and former U.S. congressman who had, in his early life, been a tutor for Salmon P. Chase, President Lincoln's Secretary of the Treasury and chief justice of the U.S. Supreme Court. Branch himself had declined Cabinet posts in President

James Buchanan's administration. Promoted brigadier in November 1861, he fought at New Bern before his brigade was sent to Virginia and assigned to Hill's division, seeing action from the Seven Days battles hence.[36]

Despite being greatly outnumbered, Hill's counterattack stopped Burnside, and with the aid of massed Confederate cannons, the Yankees were beaten back to the heights near the bridge within an hour. (Hill later estimated that his three brigades did not number over 2,000 men, hundreds having dropped by the wayside on the forced march, but drove off the 15,000 of Burnside's corps with great credit to the artillery.)

Soon after the assault, Hill's three brigadiers—Branch, James J. Archer, and Maxcy Gregg—were consulting on the field, firing having ceased in their immediate front. But as Branch raised his field glasses, a Union sharpshooter's bullet zipped into the group. The ball struck Branch, ripping through his right cheek and out the rear of his head near the left ear. He tumbled dying into the arms of his staff officer, Maj. Joseph A. Engelhardt. At least one account states that the general was borne from the battlefield by his black servant, Wiley. Late in the afternoon, Col. James Lane of the 28th North Carolina had received orders to report to Branch, his brigadier. Lane was en route when he met Engelhardt and asked where he could find the general. In a shaky voice, the major replied: "He has just been shot; there he goes on that stretcher, dead, and you are in command of the brigade."[37]

"The Confederacy has to mourn the loss of a gallant soldier and accomplished gentleman who fell in this battle at the head of his brigade," Powell Hill wrote. "He was . . . one to whom I could have entrusted the command of the division, with all confidence." A North Carolina officer related that Branch's men "almost idolized him. He died as a soldier would wish to die, facing the enemy, in the discharge of his duty."[38]

One of the results of Hill's counterattack was the mortal wounding of another Union brigadier. Isaac P. Rodman, forty, was a Rhode Island Quaker and the oldest of sixteen children. Before the war, he was a prominent merchant in his hometown of South Kingstown, and also served in the state legislature. In 1861, he accepted a captaincy in the 2nd Rhode Island, but resigned in October to become colonel of the 4th Rhode Island. He participated in Burnside's North Carolina expedition and was promoted brigadier general of volunteers in April 1862. Illness, possibly typhoid fever, waylaid him at this point, however, and he went home to Rhode Island to recuperate. He rejoined the Army on the eve of the

Maryland Campaign and was given command of the Third Division, IX Corps, under Reno. Rodman saw combat at South Mountain before joining the rest of the Federal army along Antietam Creek. At home, his wife, Sally, cared for their five young children.[39]

As part of the attack against Lee's right flank, Rodman's command had crossed the Antietam at Snavely's Ford after much delay, to link with more of Burnside's troops. Other than some sniping and a roundabout march to cross the creek, Rodman's men were fresh. The brigadier and Col. Edward Harland of his 2nd Brigade were with the 8th Connecticut when they saw Confederate troops off to the south and nearing the corps' exposed flank about 3:30 P.M. These were some of A. P. Hill's men just reaching the battlefield.

Rodman sent an aide to warn the 16th Connecticut and the 4th Rhode Island about this threat, then rode through a cornfield and into an open field to alert his 1st Brigade, New Yorkers under Col. Harrison Fairchild. As he was riding across this meadow, he was shot from his horse by a Rebel sharpshooter. The chest wound would be mortal. Harland took over division command when Rodman fell.

⊷ ⊨✦⊨ ⊶

Nightfall brought an end to the struggle, with Lee defiantly holding his ground the next day, basically daring McClellan to attack. "Little Mac," however, had had enough and did not resume his assaults.

General Mansfield lingered through the night but died on September 18. "General Mansfield, a worthy and gallant veteran, was unfortunately mortally wounded while leading his corps into action," reported Maj. Gen. Edwin V. Sumner of the Union II Corps who also temporarily led Mansfield's corps after the latter's fall. In one of his campaign reports, McClellan described how Hooker's and Mansfield's commands had repulsed the Confederates, "the gallant and distinguished veteran Mansfield losing his life in the effort."[40]

Mansfield's body arrived in Baltimore on September 19 and was embalmed there. In March 1863, Mansfield was posthumously promoted to major general of volunteers to rank from July 18, 1862. He was buried at Indian Hill Cemetery in Middletown, Connecticut.

The Rebel army slipped back across the Potomac into Virginia during the night of September 18, ending the Maryland Campaign without the decisive victory Lee had hoped for. The approximately 23,000 total casualties at Antietam, including the killed, wounded, and missing remains a grim milestone in American history. Never before or since have American losses been as high on one day of battle in any conflict.

Amid the gray exodus, Starke's body was carried to Richmond, where he was buried next to his son at Hollywood Cemetery.

In misery, General Anderson was carried first to Shepherdstown, Maryland, then to Staunton and Richmond as Lee retreated. With his brother and aide-de-camp, Capt. R. Walker Anderson, also wounded at Antietam, the general was conveyed to Raleigh, North Carolina, arriving in late September. For two more weeks there, Anderson suffered with great pain before doctors decided to amputate his foot. The surgery was performed, but he did not recover, dying on October 16. Anderson's wife gave birth to their daughter the next day. "His death was regarded as a public calamity, not only by his companions-in-arms . . . but by the people of the State, who were proud of him as a North Carolinian," recalled A. M. Waddell, an officer in Anderson's brigade. With Anderson's burial set for Raleigh's Oakwood Cemetery, a large assemblage of mourners gathered for his funeral, "his mortal remains followed by sorrowing friends, a military escort and a large concourse of citizens" to the gravesite, Waddell remembered. "Thus in its early prime ended a life consecrated to duty and crowned with honor."[41]

Losing Garland and Anderson meant that D. H. Hill would have to replace two brigadiers after Antietam. He described Anderson as a "high-toned, honorable, conscientious Christian soldier, highly gifted, and lovely in all the qualities that adorn a man."[42] Walker Anderson, meanwhile, recovered from his Antietam wound, only to be killed at the Wilderness.

In the days after the battle, General Branch's family waited anxiously, like other relatives of soldiers in Lee's army, for word of their loved one. The Branches were going to church in Raleigh the following Sunday when they received a dispatch that Branch had been killed. "Oh such a shock it was," Branch's daughter, Susan, later wrote to her Aunt Sue. "We had not even heard that he was in the battle. All day Sunday we endured the suspense, not knowing whether it was a mere idle rumor coming from a straggler from the battle field, or whether it was a sad reality." That night another message arrived, stating that Branch was safe. For the next two days the Branches were left in awful limbo by contradictory reports about the general's fate.

A telegraph from Major Engelhardt on September 22 finally confirmed the worst outcome. "Pa was shot by a rifle ball through the head," Susan Branch wrote to her aunt the day after absorbing the horrible news. "Oh Aunt Sue, it is terrible, terrible to bear. What is home with out him, or what will it ever be? Ma says do come to see her, for it will be the greatest comfort in the world to us all to see you. . . . The thought is almost unbearable that he should be so cut off from a dependent family. I hope we will all be reunited once more in that land of rest, where there is neither trouble nor sorrow."[43]

Branch's remains arrived in Raleigh a few days later and were interred in the Old City Cemetery.

━━ ⚞✦⚟ ━━

Rodman finally succumbed on September 30. His body was returned to Providence, Rhode Island, on the morning of October 3, and lay in state at the State House until noon the next day. The funeral for the "brave and fearless soldier" was held that afternoon, attracting a great throng of mourners. He was buried in a family cemetery at Peace Dale, Rhode Island.[44]

Abraham Lincoln came to Sharpsburg for four days in early October, the army holding a grand review for him on October 4. At the time, the troops had just learned of Rodman's death, and Harland led the late general's division on parade. Burnside issued orders that same day announcing Rodman's demise: "one of the first to leave his home at his country's call, General Rodman, in . . . constant and unwearied service, now ended by his untimely death, has left a bright record of earnest patriotism, undimmed by any thought of self; that respected and esteemed in the various relations of his life, the army mourns his loss as a pure hearted patriot and a brave, devoted soldier, and his division will miss a leader who was always at the post of danger."[45]

A few days earlier, Burnside had issued General Orders No. 17 to the IX Corps regarding Reno's loss: "By the death of this distinguished officer, the country loses one of its most devoted patriots, the army one of its most thorough soldiers. In the long list of battles in which General Reno has fought . . . his name always appears with the brightest luster, and he has now bravely met a soldier's death while gallantly leading his men at . . . South Mountain. For his high character and the kindly qualities of his heart in private life, as well as for the military genius and personal daring which marked him as a soldier, his loss will be deplored by all who knew him, and the commanding general desires to add the tribute of a friend to the public mourning for the death of one of the country's best defenders."[46]

━━ ⚞✦⚟ ━━

Less than a week after the battle, General Richardson faced little chance of survival. "Gen. Richardson is severely, if not fatally, wounded in the shoulder by a shell," the *New York Times* reported on September 22. "His physician pronounces his case hopeless."[47] President Lincoln visited with Richardson at the Pry house during his Antietam trip. By this time, Richardson's wife, Frances, had arrived to help care for her husband.

The armies quickly moved on, but Sharpsburg and its environs would be a vast hospital for weeks afterward. In an October 29 report to Maj. Gen. Henry Halleck, McClellan wrote: "There are now several hundred of our wounded, including General Richardson, in the vicinity of Sharpsburg, that cannot possibly be moved at present."[48]

Just after the battle, Richardson received much attention from Union surgeons, but the multitude of wounded to be treated resulted in his doctors not seeing him on a regular basis. The general's sister visited him in October and although she saw slight improvement she felt that he was weak and despondent.[49]

Richardson soon developed pneumonia, but his doctors disagreed whether it was related to his injuries. They did, however, agree that he would not survive. Some members of his medical team argued that Richardson should be told of his grim prognosis, but his attending physician ruled that telling him would likely kill him.

At any rate, Richardson died at the Pry house on November 3, 1862, the sad news quickly traveling across the Union. The *New York Herald* on November 5 announced not only Richardson's death but also that of Maj. Gen. Ormsby M. Mitchel, an October 30 victim of yellow fever on the South Carolina coast: "Their loss will severely be felt by the army and the country."[50]

"A brief message comes by telegraph, announcing that Maj.-Gen. Israel B. Richardson died at Sharpsburgh on Monday night," stated a page five story in the November 6 *New York Times*. "So great a loss was seldom told in so few words. The nation is called to mourn one of its staunchest supporters, the army one of its most gallant leaders. His comrades in battle— and in few battles has our flag been borne where 'Fighting Dick' did not lead the van—will learn their loss with heavy hearts, and for his death alone the future historian will write the victory of Antietam dearly bought."[51]

Richardson "was no holiday soldier, and had no doubt that war is earnest business, in which men must shoot and be shot, and not a mere opportunity to wear fine clothes, and disport in the bravery of evening parades," the *Herald* stated. The general's body was returned to Pontiac for burial at Oak Hill Cemetery, having left the battlefield "only when the summons of death came," the *Times* said. "He never drew his sword without crowning her with honor, and only caused her grief when he died."[52]

CHAPTER 7

Bloody Mississippi and Perryville

CONFEDERATE BRIGADIER GENERAL LEWIS H. LITTLE
Iuka, Mississippi, September 19, 1862

Two days after Antietam, the war boiled over again, this time in Mississippi where a Rebel general from Maryland would be killed. The battle setting was the little northeastern Mississippi railroad town of Iuka where Confederate major general Sterling Price had assembled about 14,000 troops. Price was trying to coordinate his operations with Gen. Braxton Bragg who was launching an offensive into Kentucky. But Price soon found himself threatened by about 17,000 Federals in two forces under Maj. Gens. William S. Rosecrans and E. O. C. Ord, marching on Iuka from the south and west respectively.

If Price was to confront these Yankees, he would rely heavily on Brig. Gen. Henry H. Little, one of his division commanders, who had become almost like a son to him. Little, forty-five, was a Baltimore native and the son of a veteran Maryland congressman. Commissioned directly into the U.S. Army in 1839, he was brevetted for gallantry in the Mexican War, but resigned from the service in 1861 to join the rebellion. Attached to Price's staff, Little soon developed into one of his favorite officers. He had fought well at Pea Ridge and was promoted brigadier in April 1862, commanding a division after the Rebels evacuated Corinth.[1]

Price had occupied Iuka on September 14 after flushing out its small Federal garrison. Little, however, was weakened by illness and traveled much of the way by ambulance. Ord's 8,000 troops converged on the town four days later and were set to strike the Rebels. But Maj. Gen. Ulysses S. Grant, commander of the U.S. Army of the Tennessee, knew that Rosecrans would not reach there until the next day and told Ord not to attack until he heard Rosecrans's guns.[2]

On the afternoon of September 19, Rosecrans approached Iuka from the southwest on the Jacinto Road. Of his 9,000 troops, less than half would reach the field in time to fight, the units broken up by the march. About 4 P.M., Rosecrans's lead elements smacked into two brigades of Little's division strongly posted in a wooded ravine just south of town and commanded by Brig. Gen. Louis Hebert and Col. John D. Martin. The combat swelled back and forth as the Rebels swarmed out of the gully and captured an Ohio battery.

The Federals counterattacked, and were in turn driven back. Little, despite his weakness, personally led the 37th and 38th Mississippi infantry in the fighting. He had reached the front about 5 P.M. and immediately went into combat with the Mississippians after ordering the rest of his division to hasten to this danger point.

About forty-five minutes later, Little was called to a battlefield conference with Price, Hebert, and Col. J. W. Whitfield of the 1st Texas Legion at the base of a hill just east of the Jacinto Road, near the battle line of the dismounted 3rd Texas Cavalry.

Price had his back to the enemy when a Federal bullet whizzed under his outstretched arm. The minié struck Little in the forehead, killing him in the instantly. Col. Celsus Price, the general's son, eased Little to the ground, although some accounts state that Little collapsed into the arms of Sgt. T. J. Cellum of the 3rd Texas. Capt. Frank Von Phul, an aide-de-camp on Little's staff, wrote that, "the brave man, limp and lifeless, fell into the arms of a comrade."[3]

Sterling Price is said to have cried over Little's corpse before composing himself enough to order Hebert to take over Little's division. The battle sputtered out after dark with neither side gaining any real advantage. Rosecrans and Price both claimed victory at Iuka, each sustaining some 700 to 800 casualties. Ord, meanwhile, never got into action, and Grant blamed high winds blowing in the opposite direction that prevented him from hearing the battle just a few miles away.

"General Price returned sorrowfully to town, for he had lost his most trusted lieutenant—the very best division commander I have ever known—Henry Little," recalled Missouri colonel Thomas Snead, Price's adjutant.[4]

"It will thus be seen that our success was obtained at the sacrifice of many a brave officer and patriot soldier," Price wrote after the battle.

"Chief among them was Brig. Gen. Henry Little. . . . Than this brave Marylander no one could have fallen more dear to me or whose memory should be more fondly cherished by his countrymen. Than him, no more skillful officer or more devoted patriot has drawn his sword in this war of independence. He died in the day of his greatest usefulness, lamented by his friends, by the brigade of his love, by the division which he so ably commanded, and by the Army of the West, of which he had from the beginning been one of the chief ornaments."[5]

In his battle report, Hebert wrote of the effect Little's death had on his soldiers:

> The fall of the general was immediately known throughout the lines, but, far from creating consternation, panic, or confusion, every officer and every soldier seemed to become animated with new determination. The leader whom they had learned to love and esteem and in whom they had full confidence had fallen. The foe who had deprived them of him was in front and revenge was within their grasp. The First Division of the Army of the West will ever remember and venerate the name of Henry Little.[6]

The Reverend Jonathan Bannon of St. Louis, chaplain of the 1st Missouri Infantry, took charge of Little's body and had it conveyed to the small cottage in Iuka that had served as the brigadier's headquarters. Von Phul went to Price that night to determine his wishes regarding Little's body, but Price was too distraught to give him an answer, saying only, "My Little is gone; I've lost my Little," according to Von Phul. "He was almost crazed with grief, and I don't believe he knew what I was asking him."[7]

Little's officers later received word that the army was withdrawing from Iuka before dawn and that Price wanted Little's body buried as soon as possible. "The soldiers dug a grave in the little garden just to the rear of our headquarters, and a few minutes before midnight the saddest funeral train I ever witnessed . . . formed in line and moved to where the fresh earth had been rolled back," Von Phul remembered. The party of mourners carried candles "that flickered mournfully in the night air, and we gathered about the open grave as the rough coffin was lowered in the earth."[8]

Bannon conducted the brief ceremony, which Price was unable to attend due to his preparations to move his army. "It was just midnight as the last spadeful of earth was placed upon the grave and patted into shape," Von Phul related. "Our candles still flickered in the darkness, sending out weird shadows." A pine board with Little's name and rank was placed at the head of the grave before the men dispersed.[9]

Little's death "saddened every heart," recalled Confederate brigadier Dabney H. Maury who also fought at Iuka. "No more efficient soldier . . . ever fought for a good cause. . . . In camp he was diligent in instructing his officers in their duty and providing for the comfort and efficiency of his men, and on the battlefield he was as steady, cool and able a commander as I have seen. His eyes closed forever on the happiest spectacle he could behold, and the last throbs of his heart were amidst the victorious shouts of his charging brigade."[10]

Jefferson Davis called Little "an officer of extraordinary merit, distinguished on many fields" whose loss was "deeply felt by his Missouri brigade, as well as by the whole army, whose admiration he had so often attracted by gallantry and good conduct."[11]

Little's fellow Marylander, Brig. Gen. Bradley Johnson, wrote after the war that the "gloom among the troops caused by [Little's] death was one of the main causes for the abandonment of the field" by Price. Supporting this claim, Von Phul said that Snead told him that Price had wanted to fight the next day, but that Hebert and others contended their soldiers were too demoralized by Little's death. They then decided to retreat.[12]

There probably is some truth in these assertions, but Price also expected Rosecrans to concentrate his force and coordinate with Ord, which would have meant destruction of his army. Instead, the Rebels evacuated Iuka during the night. Price marched for Ripley, Mississippi, where he joined Confederate major general Earl Van Dorn and planed an attack on Union-held Corinth.

Little was later reinterred at Green Mount Cemetery in Baltimore, but the witching hour ceremony in the cottage garden was ingrained in Von Phul's memory to the end of his days: "That was the only midnight funeral I ever attended, and it is the most vivid recollection of my life."[13]

UNION BRIGADIER GENERAL PLEASANT A. HACKLEMAN
Corinth, Mississippi, October 3, 1862

The blood of more than 6,000 men would soak the Mississippi countryside at the battle of Corinth, including that of a Union brigadier from Indiana. The town, an important railroad center and the cornerstone of Federal defenses in northern Mississippi, had been evacuated by the Confederates in late May. But in early October, with Bragg's drive into Kentucky, the Southerners decided to try to retake the town. By October 2, Price and Van Dorn had about 22,000 Rebels menacing Corinth from the west.

Defending the town were about 23,000 Federals led by Maj. Gen. William S. Rosecrans.

Among Rosecrans's subordinates was Brig. Gen. Pleasant A. Hackleman, a forty-seven-year-old Indianian whose father had been an officer in the War of 1812. An attorney and judge before disunion, Hackleman had twice run unsuccessfully for Congress, but had been a delegate to the Republican National Convention, which nominated Lincoln for the presidency. Commissioned colonel of the 16th Indiana Infantry after First Bull Run, he had tasted battle at Ball's Bluff and been promoted brigadier general of volunteers in April 1862. In June he had been sent to Tennessee and assigned a brigade in Brig. Gen. Thomas Davies's division in the Army of West Tennessee. His command consisted of Illinois and Iowa units.[14]

The Union defenses consisted of two systems of earthen entrenchments, the outer constructed by the Rebels when they held Corinth, and the inner line erected by the Federals with batteries at key points. Hackleman, with the rest of Davies's division, was posted in the center of Rosecrans's position.

The Confederates opened their attack about 10 A.M. on October 3, Price's corps engaged with elements of Davies's units. A portion of the Union line dissolved under pressure and Hackleman and Brig. Gen. Richard Oglesby, another of Davies's brigade commanders, tried to stem the flood.

Col. Thomas Sweeny of the 52nd Illinois described what happened next: "It was while endeavoring to rally these men that Generals Hackleman and Oglesby were wounded. The former received his death-wound while thus rallying troops to sustain his gallant brigade." Hackleman was shot in the neck. Before he was carried to the rear, his last words were "I am dying, but I die for my country. If we are victorious, send my remains home; if not, bury me on the field," Sweeny reported. "No nobler sentiment was ever uttered by soldier or patriot." With Hackleman's fall, brigade command devolved upon Sweeny "and the fight continued with unabated fury."[15]

The Confederates pushed the Yankees away from the outer defenses and into the secondary line about two miles to the rear before darkness prevailed. After the battle sputtered out, Davies rode in to town to check on his wounded. He found Hackleman, Oglesby, and his other wounded brigade commander, Col. Silas Baldwin, being attended to in a room at the Tishomingo Hotel, which was crowded with casualties. "General Hackleman breathed his last while I was with him," Davies lamented. Oglesby would survive and Baldwin's injuries were minor. Rosecrans wrote that

Hackleman fell "bravely fighting at the head of his brigade . . . shot through the jugular vein."[16]

On October 4, the Confederates assaulted the interior defenses. There was terrible fighting around Batteries Powell and Robinette, but the Federals held. With almost 5,000 casualties in two days of battle, Van Dorn withdrew his army about noon. The struggle for Corinth was over, Hackleman among the approximately 2,350 Union losses.

"General Hackleman fell while gallantly leading his brigade," Maj. Gen. U. S. Grant reported to Maj. Gen. Henry Halleck on October 5, describing the Rebel repulse.[17]

In an October 8 dispatch, President Lincoln complimented Grant for the Corinth victory and added a personal note. "I congratulate you and all concerned in your recent battles and victories. How does it all sum up? I especially regret the death of General Hackleman, and am anxious to know the condition of General Oglesby, who is an intimate personal friend." Hackleman was buried in Rushville, Indiana. His death "cast a gloom over all who were under his command," wrote Col. Elliott Rice of the 7th Iowa Infantry. "His coolness, bravery, and eminent ability secured for him the entire confidence and esteem of all."[18]

UNION BRIGADIER GENERALS JAMES S. JACKSON AND WILLIAM R. TERRILL
Perryville, Kentucky, October 8, 1862

The night before the battle of Perryville in which they died, Union generals James S. Jackson and William R. Terrill, along with Col. George Webster, were discussing the odds of a soldier falling in combat.

"Their opinion was that men would never be frightened if they considered the doctrine of probabilities and how slight the chance was of any particular person being killed," recalled Col. Charles Denby of the 42nd Indiana. "Theory failed, as it has often done before; all three were killed in the next day's fight."[19]

The battle would be the climax of Confederate general Braxton Bragg's drive north from Tennessee into Kentucky in late summer 1862. Bragg's objectives were to weaken Union forces threatening Chattanooga and bring the Bluegrass State solidly to the Confederate side, and he had brought about 16,000 Rebels with him to do it. Yet Bragg would first have to deal with the U.S. Army of the Ohio, about 37,000 Yankees commanded by Maj. Gen. Don Carlos Buell.

Jackson, thirty-nine, commanded the 10th Division of Maj. Gen. A. M. McCook's 1st Corps in Buell's army. A native Kentuckian, he attended college in Kentucky and Pennsylvania, and had studied law at Transylvania University before being admitted to the bar in Greenupsburg, Kentucky, in 1845. During the Mexican War, Jackson served with a Kentucky cavalry unit he helped to recruit, but resigned after a duel with the regiment's colonel. Elected to Congress in 1860, he left his seat in December 1861 to become colonel of the 3rd Kentucky (U.S.) Cavalry. Jackson was appointed brigadier general of volunteers in July 1862, and shortly afterward given command of the Union Army of Kentucky's cavalry. A few weeks later, he was reassigned to lead an infantry division under McCook.[20]

Commanding Jackson's 33rd Brigade was Brig. Gen. William R. Terrill, a twenty-eight-year-old Virginian from a house divided. Terrill's younger brother, James, would become a Rebel brigadier and die in action at Bethesda Church in 1864. The Terrills were cousins of Confederate cavalry general Jeb Stuart. The son of a well-known state legislator and attorney, William was an 1853 West Point graduate who had served in Florida and Kansas, as well as at the Military Academy as a mathematics instructor before the war. When Virginia seceded, Terrill is said to have gone home to discuss with his father what he should do. Ultimately, and much to his father's bitter condemnation, he decided to fight for the Union if he did not have to serve in Virginia. Commissioned captain of the 5th U.S. Artillery, Terrill was assigned to duty in Washington before being sent to Kentucky. He was a division artillery commander in the Army of the Ohio and fought at Shiloh and Corinth before action in Kentucky, where he was promoted brigadier in early September 1862.[21]

At Perryville, Terrill's command consisted of untried regiments from Illinois and Ohio plus detachments of Kentucky and Tennessee troops and an eight-gun battery under Lt. Charles Parsons.

The rival armies had converged on the small community of Perryville by October 7, the Rebels occupying it and positions west of town. The weather was hot, and the creeks and riverbeds were mostly dry, making water an precious commodity for soldiers on both sides.

Combat flamed in earnest before dawn on October 8 along the Springfield Pike, but died out around midmorning with little gain. Bragg used the lull to shift units to the north—the foes generally facing east-west—in hope of striking the Union left flank. Bragg made his move about 2 P.M., sending Maj. Gen. Benjamin Cheatham's division to hit the flank. Cheatham's men swarmed ahead and smashed into the Federals of McCook's corps, who were moving into position along the Mackville Pike.

These Yankees were surprised when a strong force of Confederates appeared at the edge of some woods about ninety yards away. Terrill and

Parsons had been directing cannon fire in a different direction and quickly ordered their artillerists to fire at this mass of Rebels. Their Napoleons barked grapeshot, but the Confederates were too many and too close, so Terrill ordered his 123rd Illinois to charge with the bayonet. Enemy fire and a rail fence, however, broke up the Illini attack, however, and they fell back after triggering a volley. It was about 2:30 P.M. when a cannonball narrowly missed Jackson and crashed into the ground about a foot from him.

Terrill's greenhorns soon cracked under the strain of the enemy onslaught. "Being composed of entirely raw troops, Terrill's brigade in a few moments gave way in confusion," reported Maj. Gen. Charles Gilbert of the U.S. III Corps. "General Jackson, who was with this brigade, was killed at the first fire."[22]

Just before he was hit, Jackson remarked, "Well I'll be damned if this is not getting rather particular," reported Capt. Samuel M. Starling, Jackson's inspector general, who was near the general when he was wounded.[23]

Jackson was standing to the left of Parson's gunners about this time when two bullets ripped into the right side of his chest. Capt. Percival Oldershaw of Jackson's staff was nearby and "found him on his back, struggling to speak, but unable to do so. He died in a few moments." Starling added, "I am sure he breathed not once."[24]

A *New York Herald* correspondent, however, gave a slightly different account of Jackson's end. The general, "seeing his men wavering, advanced to the front line, and . . . cheered and urged them on. While thus gallantly displaying the true courage for which he [was] noted," a shard of shrapnel wounded Jackson in the right breast, knocking him from his horse. "It is said by those near him that he said only 'Oh, God!' and died without a struggle."[25]

Oldershaw reported that he and other members of Jackson's staff immediately carried his body off the hill and about fifty yards to the rear. While a volunteer aide rode to find an ambulance, Oldershaw went to Terrill and Webster to notify them of their commander's death. Before Jackson's corpse could be removed to safety, the Rebel assault swamped the Union line and "it was impossible to recover the body of the fallen general," Oldershaw stated. The Confederates, belonging to Cheatham's division and S. A. M. Wood's brigade, swarmed after Terrill's fleeing infantry, seizing Parson's guns in the pursuit. "Cheatham and Wood captured the enemy's battery . . . and among the pieces and amid the dead and dying was found the body of General James S. Jackson," reported Confederate major general William J. Hardee.[26]

McCook's remaining regiments withdrew slowly and formed a new line. In the confused fighting, Terrill was to assume division command after

Jackson's death but did not live to take charge. Attempting to reform his brigade about 4 P.M., he was hit by a shell fragment in the left shoulder.

Maj. James A. Connelly of the 123rd Illinois was one of the first to reach the stricken general. "I . . . raised him to a sitting position and saw that nearly his entire breast was torn away by the shell," Connelly remembered. "He recognized me and his first words were: 'Major, do you think it's fatal?'" Moments later Terrill exclaimed, "My poor wife, my poor wife!"[27]

"General Terrill did all in his power to steady his men, but in vain," General Gilbert related. "While still striving to rally his broken troops, he was mortally wounded." With McCook making a stand now, Bragg hurled a brigade at Brig. Gen. Phil Sheridan's Union division on the Springfield road. Sheridan's men not only repelled the assault, but drove the Rebels back into the town itself before withdrawing. The battle of Perryville was over.[28]

Terrill died in a field hospital about 11 P.M., although Connelly claimed that he survived until about 2 A.M. on October 9. Also dying was Webster, who led Jackson's 34th Brigade. The Confederates claimed Jackson's remains.

"Among the dead and wounded Federals lay one who, the prisoners told us, was Gen. James S. Jackson, the commander of one of McCook's divisions," wrote Col. Joseph Wheeler of Bragg's cavalry. Tennessee private Sam Watkins came across Jackson's body while bringing off wounded after the fighting. "I saw dead on the battlefield a Federal General by the name of Jackson," he recalled. "It was his brigade that fought us so obstinately at this place."[29]

When Buell brought up reinforcements during the night, Bragg decided to retreat, moving his outnumbered army out of Kentucky and back into eastern Tennessee. His casualties totaled more than 3,000 while Buell's losses were about 3,700, including the two generals. Kentucky remained in Union hands for the rest of the war.

Captain Starling and another Federal officer struck out at sunup on October 9, looking for Jackson's body on the battlefield. They found him just where he had been left, but the general's hat, boots and buttons were gone. The *New York Herald* reported that Jackson's "body was 'stripped entirely.'"[30]

"The nation is called upon to mourn the loss of such spirits as Jackson, Terrill . . . and others, who fell upon this bloody field," McCook wrote in his battle report, while Sheridan referred to the slain generals as "commanders of much promise."[31]

Buell admitted that Cheatham's assault and the loss of the generals were key to the army's early setback. "The suddenness and strength of the attack, and the fall of two of their gallant leaders, Jackson and Terrill, caused some of the new troops . . . to fall into disorder," Confederate major general Leonidas Polk noted in a report, stating that he "was killed amid the guns of one of that batteries that was taken."[32]

The bodies of Jackson, Terrill, and Webster were taken to Louisville where a funeral service for Jackson was held on the afternoon of October 11 at Christ Church. The Kentuckian left "no family to mourn his loss," the *New York Times* stated that day. "In manner he was brusque and over-bearing and, as a consequence was a party to numerous quarrels, which sometimes resulted in duels."[33]

The remains of Terrill and Webster were taken by mail boat to Cincinnati the next day while Jackson was temporarily buried in Cave Hill Cemetery. Jackson was later relocated to Riverside Cemetery, Hopkinsville, Kentucky, while Terrill was laid to rest at West Point. A popular story was that the Terrill brothers were interred in the same grave, which is untrue. James Terrill's body was recovered by Union troops and buried on the battlefield. In Bath County, Virginia, the Terrill family, symbolizing its brother-against-brother tragedy, erected a monument to the generals' memory, the inscription reading, "God Alone Knows Which One Was Right."[34]

CHAPTER 8

Fury at Fredericksburg

CONFEDERATE BRIGADIER GENERALS THOMAS R. R. COBB AND MAXCY GREGG

UNION BRIGADIER GENERALS GEORGE D. BAYARD AND CONRAD F. JACKSON
Fredericksburg, Virginia, December 13, 1862

On the frosty, foggy morning of December 13, 1862, Robert E. Lee's Confederate army was arrayed in defensive positions on the hills outside Fredericksburg, Virginia. Unseen in the milky shroud, thousands of Federals manueuvered into attack positions.

The thick mist dissipated about 11 A.M., raising a curtain on an awesome panorama of military might. Spread before the Rebels on the plains below was the U.S. Army of the Potomac, bayonets and brass winking in the sun, flags whipping over what seemed to be an endless belt of blue infantry with the church spires and modest buildings of the town framing the masses of soldiers.

A day earlier, the first of Maj. Gen. Ambrose Burnside's 120,000 Union troops crossed the Rappahannock River on pontoon bridges and occupied Fredericksburg after vicious street fighting. Now they were preparing to attack the Confederates, who were holding the low range of irregular hills southwest of town. Lee's army of about 78,000 was deployed in two wings, the left commanded by Lt. Gen. James Longstreet and the right by Stonewall Jackson. Probably the most formidable point in these defenses was a four-foot-high stone wall bordering a sunken portion of the Telegraph Road, which ran along the base of Marye's Heights, a shallow ridge in Longstreet's line.

Among the Southerners behind this wall was a Georgia brigade under thirty-nine-year-old Brig. Gen. Thomas R. R. Cobb, the younger brother of Brig. Gen. Howell Cobb, who had been one of the South's leading voices for secession. These Georgians both had been Confederate congressmen, with Thomas resigning to organize and lead Cobb's Legion. A University of Georgia graduate, Cobb had been one of the state's most prominent lawyers prior to the rebellion. He also had hand-written much of the original Confederate Constitution.[1]

Cobb had tasted action in the Seven Days battles, at Second Bull Run, and in the Maryland Campaign, and had been promoted brigadier about six weeks before the armies met at Fredericksburg. Throughout the war he had written regularly to his wife, and he continued this habit while the Rebels dug in and shivered at Fredericksburg.

"We have had two nights of intense cold," he penned on December 8. "The snow lies on the ground unmelted, and what is worse, the commissary department has failed to furnish any rations for two days, except some flour. The river is frozen over here, and in two days more the Yankees will not need pontoon bridges."[2]

Burnside's army was divided into four grand divisions, and one of these, commanded by Maj. Gen. Edwin V. Sumner, was aimed at Marye's Heights. The Union attacks began about noon on December 13, and the first wave of blue infantry rolled toward the stone wall and Longstreet's artillery, which shredded the tightly-ranked columns as they came on.

Waving his hat in the air, Cobb exhorted his men, who took aim and waited for the Yankees to get closer. In the heat of combat, he probably did not recall his last letter to his wife, written three days earlier:

> I do not now anticipate a battle at this place, at least for some time. Do not be uneasy about my being "rash." The . . . reputation cannot drag me into folly. God helping me, I will do my duty when called upon, trusting the consequences to Him. I go on picket again to-morrow, and hence cannot write regularly.[3]

At a distance of 150 to 200 yards, the Confederates triggered a volley that cut down scores of oncoming Federals, but there were thousands more behind them. The Yankees made a series of piecemeal attacks against the stone wall, but the Rebel artillery and musketry were lethally efficient, the smoky slope in front of them soon layered with blue-clad bodies.

Cobb knew he occupied a prime defensive sector. Before the battle, a messenger had come to him with orders about what to do if the troops on his left were forced to retreat. The general had scoffed at the notion of any withdrawal, remarking, "Well! If they wait for me to fall back, they will wait a long time."[4]

Cobb's brigade chaplain, Rev. R. K. Porter, gave this account of the enemy attacks:

> As they threw column after column against him he would calmly hold his men, with but a scattering musket shot until you could count the Yankee buttons, then as steadily as on dress parade he could be heard "Ready! aim! fire!" and it was a simultaneous roar. Before it the advancing horde would go down like wax.[5]

Few positions in the war were so strongly held or so hopelessly assailed, and yet Cobb would not live to savor his successful defense.

There are two versions of how Cobb was mortally wounded. Some say that he was standing in the road when an enemy artillery shell smashed through the nearby Stephens house, a small wooden building where Cobb had established his headquarters. The round crashed through the home and exploded, hurling a fragment that hit Cobb and killed two other soldiers. At least one version is that the enemy gun was posted on Federal Hill in the yard of a house where Cobb's parents were married.[6]

In contrast, Brig. Gen. Joseph Kershaw related that Cobb was wounded by an enemy marksman. Kershaw, who took command of this portion of the Rebel line after Cobb fell, recalled a stinging fire from Union sharpshooters posted in a few buildings on his left flank, and wrote in his report, "General Cobb, I learn, was killed by a shot from that quarter."[7]

Col. E. P. Alexander, Longstreet's artillery chief, reported that after the repulse of a U.S. division, the battle calmed for about twenty minutes, during which time the rival sharpshooters and artillery "exchanged compliments." Cobb was hit by a sniper's bullet during this lull, and he crumpled in the road under a locust tree in the yard of the Stephens house, Alexander related. "The fatal shot came from a house some hundred and fifty yards in front and to the left, and which was occupied by the Federal skirmishers," he said. "It was during this interval that a ball from a sharpshooter mortally wounded the gallant and Christian patriot." A company of the 2nd South Carolina dislodged these Yankees by "pouring a constant fire upon the windows," Alexander recalled.[8]

However it was sustained, the general's wound was severe. The projectile had ripped his left thigh, shattering bone and slicing the femoral artery.

Cobb's staff desperately tried to stem his heavy bleeding with a makeshift tourniquet before he was hurried to a field hospital in the rear, all the while shouting to his command to hold its ground. Cobb was treated at the Wiet house, which the Rebels were using as a field hospital, but he was in great pain and rapidly weakened due to blood loss that could not be controlled.

Chaplain Porter rode to the hospital and "there on a common stretcher, I met my best and noblest friend, broken, dying, though I did not dream then of fatal results. . . . As his head lay on my arm I constantly bathed his pale face. 'Porter, it is very painful,' he said again and again. Stimulants were administered and everything possible done, but he suddenly sunk into insensibility, and then for the first time I believed his life in danger." Cobb died about 2 P.M., and Porter remarked that, "He could not be aroused, and soon the glorious light went out forever."[9]

Col. Robert McMillan of the 24th Georgia assumed brigade command after Cobb was shot, but Kershaw was soon on the scene, as the Federal attacks continued until sundown.

"Brigadier General T. R. R. Cobb fell, mortally wounded, in the heat of the battle of the 13th," Longstreet reported. "He defended his position with great gallantry and ability. In him we have lost one of our most promising officers and statesmen."[10]

"The country and the army have to mourn the loss," of Cobb, wrote Maj. Gen. Lafayette McLaws, the Georgian's division commander. Cobb "fell while in position with his brigade, and was borne from the field while his men were repulsing the first assaults of the enemy. . . . His devotion to his duties, his aptitude for the profession of arms, and his control over his men I have never seen surpassed. Our country has lost a pure and able defender of her rights both in the council and the field."[11]

* ⚔ *

Even as Cobb's final drama unfolded, the intense combat continued along the lines several miles to the southeast where another Union assault was underway. Two enemy generals would die in the effort.

Burnside's Left Grand Division, commanded by Maj. Gen. William B. Franklin, had been trying to get untracked against Stonewall Jackson's positions since about 8:30 A.M. But the Federals had been bedeviled by two guns of Maj. John Pelham's horse artillery that had incredibly held up Franklin's advance for several hours.

Jackson had some 35,000 Confederates strung along the forested ridges of Prospect Hill, and while Franklin had nearly twice as many men, he decided to commit only one division to make the attack. About 1 P.M., these three brigades, about 3,800 Pennsylvanians led by Maj. Gen. George Meade, pressed across the Richmond Stage Road and against the Confederate line held by Maj. Gen. A. P. Hill's Light Division. A heavy bombardment by Union guns preceded the assault. To reach the ridge crest, Meade's men advanced across half a mile of open ground, crossed the Richmond, Fredericksburg & Potomac Railroad, and charged uphill.

Under Rebel cannon fire, the Federals aimed at a sliver of trees extending past the rail line toward the river. The terrain here was swampy and, other than a few skirmishers, the Confederates had left it unprotected. What the Yankees had found was a 600-yard gap between the Rebel brigades of Brig. Gens. James J. Archer and James H. Lane and they piled into it. (Hill was possibly preoccupied when he deployed his troops. His firstborn, three-year-old daughter Netty, had died a few days earlier.)[12]

Directly in the path of the charging Pennsylvanians was the unsuspecting South Carolina brigade of Brig. Gen. Maxcy Gregg, which was in reserve behind Jackson's main line. With their muskets stacked in the military road along the ridge, many of the Carolinians were resting or eating their midday rations when the Federals burst upon them.

Gregg was a forty-eight-year-old South Carolinian who was a prewar attorney and had been an officer in the Mexican War. Commissioned a brigadier general in December 1861, Gregg had seen action in the Peninsular Campaign, Cedar Mountain, Second Bull Run, and the Maryland Campaign.

"General Gregg was one of the most courteous and gallant gentlemen that I had ever known," Dr. Hunter McGuire of Jackson's staff recalled. Even though his men were in the rear, some of his fellow officers felt Gregg had been exposing himself somewhat unnecessarily to enemy fire earlier in the day. Knowing that Gregg was nearly deaf, Col. A. S. Pendleton, one of Stonewall's aides, rode to him and shouted that the Yankees were shooting at him. Gregg replied, "Yes sir, thank you. They have been doing so all day."[13] Now with Meade's men boiling up out of the trees, some of the Rebels grabbed their rifles and opened a ragged fire, but Gregg immediately tried to stop them, apparently believing they were firing on their own retreating skirmishers. He then realized the oncoming soldiers were Federals, but by this time the bluecoats were too close to repel.

On horseback, Gregg was frantically trying to rally his disorganized men when a minié plunged into his spine, mortally wounding him and knocking him from the saddle. In short order the Yankees mashed his brigade and seized a portion of the road as the Carolinians scattered toward the rear.

A. P. Hill, described Gregg's fall: "The advancing columns of the enemy had also encountered an obstacle in the military road, which they little expected. Gregg's brigade of South Carolinians stood in the way. Taken somewhat by surprise, Orr's Rifles was thrown into confusion, mistaking the advancing enemy for our own troops falling back. It was at this moment that. . . . Gregg, himself fearful of harming our friends, fell in front of the Rifles, mortally wounded. A more chivalrous gentleman and gallant soldier never adorned the service which he so loved."[14]

Not all of Meade's men had been able to reach the gap in the Rebel line; Brig. Gen. Conrad F. Jackson's Pennsylvanians banged into Archer's Confederates and could not make much headway. Jackson, forty-nine, belonged to one of the oldest families in his native Berks County, Pennsylvania. After some militia experience as a young man, he fought in the Mexican War and worked with the U.S. Revenue Service. He was employed by the Reading Railroad and living in Pittsburgh when hostilities flared. Based on his continued militia service, Jackson was appointed colonel of the 9th Pennsylvania Reserves (also known as the 38th Pennsylvania Infantry) in 1861, and fought in the Peninsular Campaign and at Second Bull Run, having been promoted brigadier general of volunteers in July 1862.

Despite his military record, Jackson's aversion to war was much stronger than many others in uniform. He belonged to a religious sect called the Society of Friends which abhorred all violence. Nevertheless, he fought because he felt the need to serve his country despite his beliefs. Missing the Antietam Campaign due to illness, he returned to duty in time for Fredericksburg.[15]

On this terrible winter day, Jackson's white horse was shot from under him while he was encouraging the 5th Pennsylvania Reserves. He drew his sword and was standing on the railroad track, which bisected his line of attack, when an officer from Meade's staff, Lt. Arthur Dehon, approached him with an order from Meade. They almost immediately attracted Rebel fire and Dehon was killed by a bullet to the chest. Another enemy volley not only wounded a few members of Jackson's staff, who were mounted, but also Jackson himself, who crumpled to the ground with a head wound. He died moments later. The "fatal shot entered the right temple, near the eye of the General, and passed through his head and out behind the left ear," the *Philadelphia Inquirer* reported. The *New York Herald* added that Jackson was "killed by a musket ball to the head while endeavoring to rally his men." At least one other account states that Jackson was sitting on the railroad track when he was slain.[16]

When Jackson fell, Col. Joseph W. Fisher took over brigade command. "In the death of General Jackson, who fell while encouraging and sustaining his men, this brigade has lost a brave and good leader," wrote Lt. Col. Robert Anderson of Jackson's command. "To his example and conduct, and that of his aides . . . is owing, in a great measure, the steadiness and perseverance with which the troops fought."[17]

Meade had made a daring and successful attack, but he was in the middle of a Rebel beehive, greatly outnumbered and needing reinforcements to hold his ground. None were forthcoming from Franklin, however, and the Pennsylvanians soon were in the crosshairs of a counterattack by two Confederate divisions.

Despite his terrible wound, Gregg remained full of fight as these graybacks rushed past him. "The old hero, unable to speak, unable to stand alone, raised himself to his full height by a small tree, and, with cap in hand, waved them forward," one Southerner recalled. As he was rushed to the rear on a litter, Gregg is said to have raised his hat in salute to other Rebs rushing to plug the hole punched by the Yanks.[18] Overwhelmed, Meade's units crumbled, scrambling off the slopes and back to their lines with losses of some 1,800. Elements of another Federal division were hurled back also. Because of the Union army's retreat after the battle and the exposed nature of the ground where they fell, the bodies of General Jackson and Dehon were not recovered until two days later under a truce flag. Colonel Anderson reported that "the brigade was forced to fall back, leaving General Jackson dead upon the field."[19]

Given some whiskey and blankets, Gregg was taken by ambulance to the nearby Yerby home where surgeons vainly tried to save him. Realizing that he would not live, Gregg dictated a dispatch to the governor of his state. "I am severely wounded," he wrote, "but the troops under my command have acted as they always have done, and I hope we have gained a glorious victory. If I am to die now, I give my life cheerfully for the independence of South Carolina, and I trust you will live to see our cause triumph completely."[20]

By nightfall, Burnside's army had sustained some 12,600 casualties, two-thirds of which had been sustained in front of Cobb's stone wall. Lee's lost about 5,300. Only two Federal cavalrymen were killed in the battle, but one of them was a talented young commander whose loss added to the sting of the wholesale Confederate victory.

Brig. Gen. George D. Bayard led the cavalry brigade of about 3,500 men attached to Franklin's Left Grant Division. Bayard was born in New York State, but grew up in Iowa. He graduated West Point in 1856 as a cavalry lieutenant and served on the frontier. He was blamed for igniting an uprising of Kiowas and Comanches by killing Kiowa Chief Big Pawnee in 1859. Appointed colonel of the 1st Pennsylvania Cavalry when the war came, he served in Washington's defenses along the Rappahannock River, and in the Shenandoah Valley where he fought at Port Republic. His promotion to brigadier general of volunteers in April 1862 included his appointment as chief of cavalry for the III Corps. Bayard saw action at Cedar Mountain and in the Second Bull Run Campaign. At Fredericksburg on December 13, he was five days away from his twenty-seventh birthday and was engaged to be married to the daughter of a West Point professor.[21]

Franklin's headquarters was in a grove of magnificent trees at "Mansfield," the stately stone mansion of the Bernard family overlooking the Rappahannock. The house itself was used as a Union hospital. During the fighting, some Confederate artillery shells hurtled into this rear area where Bayard was awaiting orders. Despite the bombardment, the brigadier "was as calm and collected as he would be at dress parade," one observer noted. "He was frequently urged by his aides and others present not to expose himself so recklessly."[22]

Shortly thereafter, one of these shells did its lethal work on Bayard, who had been sitting at the base of a large tree. The cavalryman was with his friend, Capt. H. G. Gibson, who commanded a battery of flying artillery, when a round shot whipped into them. The cannonball sliced Gibson's sword belt without injuring him before hitting Bayard in the right thigh, "shattering the hip terribly," one account said. Franklin, who was about ten feet away, was unhurt.[23]

Bayard was taken into the Bernard home where surgeons examined the mutilated hip and leg. "He was as cool and collected after being hit as before, saying that 'they had him this time,' and seemed to know at once that his wound was mortal," the *Herald* said. Bayard at first balked at the amputation recommended by the doctors, saying that he preferred death to losing a limb, but soon relented and the operation was performed. All quickly realized that recovery still was not possible. The general was "apprised of the hopelessness of his case, and his heroic firmness under the . . . trying circumstances is most affecting," the *Herald* stated. "A feeling of deep gloom prevails among his friends, and few will soon forget the bravery and high-toned sentiments of the gallant and unfortunate young general." The physicians and his staff did all they could to "mitigate his sufferings. He did not seem to suffer much pain, but occupied his last hours in writing to his friends."[24]

As the battle sputtered out in the deepening cold and darkness, Stonewall Jackson sent an aide, Capt. James P. Smith, to express his "regards and sympathy" to Gregg. Smith rode to the Yerby house where he "found

General Gregg on a bed in the center of a large room, surrounded by surgeons and other officers. I conveyed my message to him personally. He was much affected and desired me to thank General Jackson for his thoughtful remembrance."[25]

Jackson also dispatched Dr. McGuire to Gregg's bedside with a message of condolence, the physician already having seen firsthand that the general's wound was mortal. McGuire returned to Yerby's and with Gregg "slowly getting worse" delivered Stonewall's compliments. "I had hardly gotten out of the room into the hall when I met General Jackson, who must have ridden very close behind me to have reached there so soon," McGuire recalled. "He . . . asked about General Gregg, and went into the room to see him. No one else was in the room. What passed between these two officers no one will ever know."[26]

Before daylight on December 14, Jackson again went to see the fading Gregg, and Smith, who accompanied him, described the touching scene:

> There was an affecting interview between Jackson and Gregg, a large man, who was suffering greatly and failing rapidly. Gregg wished to explain and express regret for an endorsement he had written . . . which he feared was offensive to General Jackson. Jackson did not know to what Gregg referred and soon interrupted the sufferer to say that it had given him no offense whatever, and then, with Gregg's hand in his, he added, "The doctors tell me that you have not long to live. Let me ask you to dismiss this matter from your mind and turn your thoughts to God and to the world to which you go." Both were much moved. General Gregg with tears said: "I thank you; I thank you very much." Silently we rode away, and as the sun rose, General Jackson was again on the hill near Hamilton's Crossing[27]

Henry Kyd Douglas wrote that Jackson was with Gregg to "soothe his dying pillow and join in his last prayer." Also beside Gregg's deathbed was his longtime servant William Rose, to whom the general gave his watch. Gregg died on December 15, his body later returned to his hometown of Columbia, South Carolina, for burial at Elmwood Cemetery. In a torrential rain that night, Burnside retreated across the Rappahannock.[28]

❖

General Bayard lingered through the night but died about noon on December 14. "His death has cast a gloom over the whole army, as he was generally known and respected as a brave man and good general," the *Her-*

ald said. He was "much endeared to us by his social qualities and his rare merits as a cavalry leader," recalled Maj. Gen. William F. Smith, the Union VI Corps commander at Fredericksburg. "Many generals could have better been spared from the service."[29]

Bayard was already dead by the time news of his wounding appeared on page one of the *New York Times*'s December 15 edition. "Gen. Bayard was struck in the hip by a solid shot, while conversing with Gen. Franklin and his Staff, and cannot survive," read the report. "His right leg has been amputated, but the operation will only serve to prolong his life a short time." The *Herald* the same day had a brief account of Bayard's wounding, erroneously stating that he was knocked "clean out of the saddle" by a cannonball. "Poor Bayard, he never dreamt of danger in the thickest of the battle, and never lost his courage, even when his leg was amputated," the *Herald* correspondent wrote. "The surgeons say that he cannot survive many days, and that the operation . . . can only prolong his agony a short while."[30]

Confederate major general D. H. Hill credited a Whitworth gun in Capt. Robert Hardaway's battery of his division with firing the shot that killed Bayard, "as no other of our guns could carry so far as to the point where he was struck."[31]

Franklin wrote of the deaths of Bayard and Conrad Jackson in a January 3 report:

> Brigadier-General Bayard . . . was killed by a piece of shell while at my headquarters, where he remained at my request. . . . The loss of this gallant young general is a severe blow to his arm of the service, and in him the country has lost one of its most dashing and gallant cavalry officers. . . . Brigadier-General Jackson, of Meade's division, was killed while leading his troops into action. He had already shown distinguished gallantry on the day of his death, and his brigade, under his command, had defended the construction of the bridges on the previous day.

Lee mentioned the enemy generals' deaths in reports to Confederate Secretary of War James A. Seddon on December 15–16.[32]

Bayard was buried in Princeton, New Jersey, while Jackson was laid to rest at Allegheny Cemetery in Pittsburgh.

From his camp near Fredericksburg five days after the battle, Lee wrote lengthy letters about both of his slain generals, one to South Carolina

Governor Francis W. Pickens about Gregg and the other to Cobb's brother, Gen. Howell Cobb. Lee penned to Pickens:

> While South Carolina is mourning the loss of the gallant and distinguished son, General Maxcy Gregg, permit me to join in your sorrow for his death. From my first acquaintance when you sent him with his gallant regiment to the defense of our frontier in Virginia, I have admired his disinterested patriotism and his unselfish devotion. He has always been at the post of duty and of danger, and his services in this army have been of inestimable value, and his loss is deeply lamented. In its greatest triumphs and its bloodiest battles he has borne a distinguished part. On the Chickahominy, on the plains of Manassas, at Harper's Ferry, Sharpsburg, and Shepherdstown he led his brigade with distinguished skill and dauntless valor. On the wooded heights of Fredericksburg he fell, in front of his brigade, in close conflict with the advancing foe. The death of such a man is a costly sacrifice, for it is to men of his high integrity and commanding intellect that the country must look to give character to her councils, that she may be respected and honored by all nations. Among those of his State who will proudly read the history of his deeds, may many be found to imitate his noble example.[33]

Lee's words to Howell Cobb were no less praiseworthy of the fallen Georgian:

> General: I beg leave to express my sympathy in your great sorrow. Your noble and gallant brother has met a soldier's death, and God grant that this army and our country may never be called upon again to mourn so great a sacrifice. Of his merits, his lofty intellect, his genius, his accomplishments, his professional fame, and above all his true Christian character, I need not speak to you, who knew him so intimately and well. But as a patriot and soldier, his death has left a gap in the army which his military aptitude and skill renders it hard to fill. In the battle of Fredericksburg he won an immortal name for himself and his brigade. Hour after hour he held his position in front of our batteries, while division after division of the enemy was hurled against him. He announced the determination of himself and his men to not leave their post until the enemy was beaten back, and, with unshaken courage and

fortitude, he kept his promise. May God give consolation to this effected family, and may the name and fame of the Christian statesman and soldier be cherished as a bright example and holy remembrance.[34]

Lee echoed his thoughts in a report to Adj. Gen. Samuel Cooper: "We have again to deplore the loss of valuable lives. In Brigadier-Generals Gregg and Cobb, the Confederacy has lost two of its noblest citizens and the army two of its bravest and most distinguished officers. The country consents to the sacrifice of such men as these, and the gallant soldiers who fell with them, only to secure the inestimable blessing they died to obtain."[35]

After Cobb's death, Chaplain Porter had the body returned to camp and dressed for burial. Some Fredericksburg women provided a linen shirt, and a coarse coffin was constructed. Porter accompanied the general's remains to Richmond where Confederate treasury secretary C. G. Memminger "wept over him as a brother."[36]

Cobb's body was eventually returned to Georgia for burial at Oconee Hill Cemetery in Athens. "He was the noblest man I ever knew," Porter wrote to Howell Cobb. "My heart was his as no other man can ever have it forever. He needed no dying testimony."[37]

A feisty veteran of the 18th Georgia in Cobb's Brigade, however, spoke much more bluntly a half century after Fredericksburg, the decades not dimming his combat ire. George Todd recalled that on the day after the battle he "walked along the silent ranks of dead Irishmen (Meagher's Brigade) U.S.A., lying in line of battle in front of the rifles of the 18th Georgia at Marye's Hill . . . and yet they all were not worth the life of General Cobb, whom they killed at that place."[38]

CHAPTER 9

Stones River and Port Gibson

CONFEDERATE BRIGADIER GENERALS JAMES E. RAINS AND ROGER W. HANSON

UNION BRIGADIER GENERALS EDWARD N. KIRK AND JOSHUA W. SILL

Stones River, December 31, 1862–January 2, 1863

In the cold and rainy last week of December 1862, Union and Confederate armies in central Tennessee braced for what would be one of the most terrible but overlooked battles of the war. During two days of combat along the banks of Stones River at Murfreesboro, the enemies would count the loss of a combined 26,000 men, more than the total casualties of both sides at Antietam, Fredericksburg, or Cold Harbor. The fact that substantially fewer troops were engaged at Stones River makes the toll even more appalling. Two Union brigadiers and two Confederate generals were among the thousands spilling their blood.

On the day after Christmas 1862, U.S. major general William S. Rosecrans put his Army of the Cumberland on roads south out of Nashville. The target of his 44,000 troops was Gen. Braxton Bragg's Confederate Army of Tennessee which was in winter quarters at Murfreesboro, some thirty miles distant. Bragg had only 34,000 men to meet Rosecrans, but he was determined to make a stand as the Confederacy grimly clung to any toehold it could retain in Tennessee at this point in the war.

Bragg deployed his army on both sides of the serpentine river north and west of Murfreesboro, and skirmishing heightened as Rosecrans cautiously inched down the Nashville Pike through the mud and rain. Bragg expected a wholesale assault on December 30, but when it did not come, he plotted a surprise of his own. Before sunrise the next day, most of the Confederate army pounced on Rosecrans's right flank with Lt. Gen. William Hardee's corps as the spearhead. Rosecrans himself had planned to attack the enemy right that drizzly morning, but Bragg beat him to the punch, the Rebels attacking the Federal wing commanded by Maj. Gen. Alexander McCook. Masses of yelling Confederates emerged from the gloom about 6:30 A.M., storming the Union lines, including those manned by the division of Brig. Gen. R. W. Johnson. The brigades of Brig. Gens. Edward N. Kirk and August Willich, whom McCook described as "two of the best and most experienced brigadiers in the army," suddenly found themselves in a hopelessly desperate firefight.[1]

Kirk was a thirty-four-year-old Ohioan who had been a schoolteacher and lawyer before hostilities. He was key in raising the 34th Illinois Infantry and was commissioned its colonel in 1861. Kirk led a brigade at Shiloh, where he was wounded, and was promoted brigadier general of volunteers little more than a month before Stones River.[2]

The imposing Rebel assault, however, was too much to bear, even for these veteran officers, and their positions were overrun, forcing them to fall back. Willich's horse was killed and he was captured. Kirk, meanwhile, was severely wounded in the hip early in the action, the bullet lodging near his spine. McCook reported that their brigades, "deprived of their immediate commanders . . . gave way in confusion."[3]

Kirk was near Capt. W. P. Edgarton's Ohio battery when he was shot. Edgarton recalled that Kirk was "dangerously wounded in a desperate attempt to rally his broken regiments to support my battery, riding almost upon the bayonets of the enemy." Another Federal officer wrote, "The lines of General Kirk soon yielded to an assault which no troops in the world could have withstood."[4]

Union surgeon F. G. Hickman was at his post at a field hospital in the rear when an ambulance clattered to a halt. Inside was the wounded Kirk, who would not allow anyone to remove him from the wagon because of the enemy's quick advance. "Boys, get out of here as soon as possible, or you will all be captured," the general exclaimed before the ambulance trundled away, Hickman related.[5]

When he fell, Kirk was replaced in command by Col. J. B. Dodge of the 30th Indiana. "This brigade met with a serious loss, in the person of

General Kirk, early in the engagement," Dodge later reported. "He fell at the head of his brigade, trying manfully to resist and repel the overwhelming force thrown against it." Edgarton had more praise for Kirk: "I had learned highly to respect General Kirk as a fine gentleman and accomplished soldier. I reverenced him for his heroic courage in the presence of the enemy."[6]

The *New York Herald* gave this account of Kirk's wounding: "Gen. Kirk acted in the most gallant manner. He rode up to Edgarton's battery, shook the Captain by the hand and said a few words of commendation to him. As he turned away and was urging his men into line he was struck by a shot in the side and carried from the field. His brigade was cut to pieces in a few moments, but fought admirably. His losses are heavy."[7]

A great force of Confederates advanced out of the woods on the opposite side of a cotton field, attacking Brig. Gen. Joshua W. Sill's 1st Brigade of Phil Sheridan's 3rd Division in McCook's wing. Sill was an Ohioan who had turned thirty-one less than a month earlier. He had graduated third in the West Point class of 1853, whose members also included Sheridan, James McPherson, John Schofield, and John Bell Hood. Sill had served as an instructor at the Military Academy before resigning his commission in January 1861 to become a mathematics professor at Brooklyn Collegiate and Polytechnic Institute. He was in battle at Rich Mountain and was appointed colonel of the 33rd Ohio Infantry in August 1861. By early winter he was leading a brigade in the U.S. Department of Ohio, and was promoted brigadier general of volunteers in July 1862.[8]

The night before the battle of Murfreesboro, Sill had stopped by Sheridan's tent to visit with his old classmate. When he left, he mistakenly picked up Sheridan's coat instead of his own. Hours later, about 2 A.M., Sill reported enemy activity in his area.

The Southerners attacked Sheridan about 7:15 A.M., surging across the field in Sill's front and coming under musketry and the artillery fire of three batteries. The Rebels weathered the terrible fire and came on, only to waver and break as they neared the Union line.

As they fell back, Sill's men charged and drove them even further, the brigadier wearing Sheridan's coat. Sill did not live to savor this triumph, however. "In this charge the gallant Sill was killed, a rifle ball passing through his upper lip and penetrating the brain," Sheridan wrote.[9]

Sill's successor in brigade command, Col. Nicholas Greusel of the 36th Illinois, offered another account of the brigadier's death. Greusel reported

Confederate brigadier general James E. Rains.
LIBRARY OF CONGRESS

that "while directing the movements of the brigade, our brave General Sill was struck in the face by a musket ball and instantly killed." Capt. Henry Hescock, the division's artillery chief, added that Sill's death occurred while the 1st Brigade was defending one of his batteries. "The brave general fell dead between the guns," Hescock stated.[10]

The remnants of McCook's wing were forced back to a new line along the turnpike. Much of the fighting now centered on a patch of woods called the Round Forest, which anchored the Federal position along the pike.

Among Hardee's commanders in the attack was twenty-nine-year-old Brig. Gen. James E. Rains, who had put his Yale Law School degree to use as an attorney in his native Nashville where he and his wife, Ida, raised their daughter before the hostilities. As colonel of the 11th Tennessee, he had seen combat in and around Cumberland Gap and had been appointed brigadier general in November. Rains's brigade was assigned to Maj. Gen. John P. McCown's Division at Stones River.[11]

The previous spring, Rains, then a colonel, had been the darling of Nashville where he and his Tennesseans had been presented a Confederate flag by the women of the city. Rains had delivered an eloquent address, vowing that "We'll come back in glory or we'll come not again." At Stones River, Rains would deliver on his promise.[12]

Rains's brigade, on the extreme left of Bragg's entire army, was ordered forward to attack some enemy guns that were causing bloody problems for three other advancing Confederate brigades. "The sound of cannon and the rattle of small arms were as inspiring to General Rains as the first sounds of ballroom music to the lover of the dance," recalled Joseph Hutcheson of the 3rd Georgia Battalion in Rains's command.[13]

When they attacked toward the turnpike around 11 A.M., Rains and his men immediately encountered stubborn resistance from Federal infantry posted in a cedar thicket. "Here the struggle of the day took place," recalled Col. Robert Vance of the 29th North Carolina, one of Rains's units. "The enemy, sheltering themselves behind the trunks of the thickly standing trees and the large rocks . . . stubbornly contested the ground inch by inch. Our brave boys . . . advanced through a very tempest of leaden hail. . . . Here the enemy's batteries, on an eminence half mile beyond, began to play on us."[14]

Rains exhorted his men, shouting "Forward my brave boys, forward!" A minié ball hit him inthe chest a moment later, killing him. "The leaden hail was terrible," Hutcheson remembered. "In this cedar wood our gallant Rains was right at the front, encouraging his men onward by the most daring example and patriotic words, when pierced by a bullet which sent that knightly soul back to the God who gave it."[15]

"The men stood to their places amid this storm of shot and shell and grape and canister until it was ascertained that their ammunition was exhausted," Vance related. "Just at this moment, too, General Rains was seen to fall, and the news, running like wild-fire along the whole line, produced a temporary confusion." General McCown added, "Every moment I expected to see General Rains take these batteries. I was doomed to disappointment. I was informed that General Rains fell, shot through the heart, at the moment the enemy was routed."[16]

With Rains dead, Vance, who was the brigade's senior colonel, took over. His men were out of ammunition and suffering a hell of musketry and artillery, causing Vance to order a withdrawal. "His gallantry and daring exposure of himself was certainly not surpassed upon the field. Peace to his ashes," Vance later wrote of Rains. "Unfortunately, this brave officer and accomplished gentleman [Rains] fell . . . and his brigade recoiled in confusion," Hardee wrote.[17]

When he was shot, Rains was among the Confederates attacking Johnson's Union division in which Colonel Dodge was leading the brigade of the wounded Kirk. Ironically, these Yankees may have killed Rains. Dodge had his men in two lines firing into the oncoming mass of Rebels, including Rains. "The fire the enemy received from us, although well directed and as effective as a fire from two ranks generally is, produced no visible effect on him as he moved his heavy column forward upon a double-quick," Dodge reported. "General Rains, who commanded a part of their column, fell dead or mortally wounded at this point."[18]

Union colonel William H. Gibson of the 49th Ohio Infantry, however, credited his brigade, also in Johnson's division, with Rains' death: "It was before our fire that General Rains, of the rebel army, was killed, and a vast number of subordinate officers and men killed and wounded. Every rod of ground over which we retired was marked by the blood of the foe."[19]

The combat savagery rampaged into the afternoon. Rosecrans had sustained grievous losses, but so had Bragg, and the Union line was stable enough to repel more assaults.

The exhausted armies spent a cold and cheerless New Year's Day caring for the thousands of wounded and studying the positions of each other across the body-strewn hills, thickets, and fields. When neither side retreated, it was only a matter of time before they collided again.

Joseph Hutcheson, the Georgian in Rains's brigade, had been wounded in the arm and spent some of January 1 in Murfreesboro "where confusion reined supreme." The town brimmed with countless prisoners as well as the wounded and dying. Hutcheson and some of his comrades also saw "the long black casket containing the body of our beloved General Rains, which cast a deep gloom over our spirits. His presence in battle had been equal to a regiment."[20]

In the Confederate camps, there was controversy as to which unit should be credited with killing the Yankee General Sill. The 2nd Arkansas in Brig. Gen. S. R. Liddell's brigade and the 17th Tennessee of Brig. Gen. Bushrod Johnson's brigade, both in Patrick Cleburne's division, each claimed the distinction of having killed Sill near a house that was serving as a Union hospital. The Tennesseans were backed by their Lt. Col. Watt Floyd, who claimed the regiment captured the hospital some thirty minutes before other Confederates reached the scene, killing Sill in the process.

The general's body was found near a fence beside a lane about seventy-five yards behind the hospital "and it appears exceedingly probable that he was killed by the Seventeenth Regiment firing from the fence," Floyd wrote in his battle report. "This is the impression prevailing in the Seventeenth." He added that "Until other facts are developed in . . . this matter, I am disposed to think that no regiment can establish a claim in its own favor."[21]

Col. D. C. Govan of the 2nd Arkansas reported that Sill's body was brought to the hospital about 11 A.M., and that the general fell a short distance away "near the fence or lane. My regiment passed, still fighting, immediately over the ground where he was killed." An Arkansas private took the general's gloves and turned them over to his company captain, and Govan stated that the soldier confessed he would have taken Sill's uniform as well "but it was too large for him." Liddell, meanwhile, reported that Govan's men were ordered "to fire at officers on horses near the building," resulting in Sill's death. "I was informed by prisoners that the Federal General Sill was killed by my division while endeavoring to rally his defeated troops," added the Rebel general McCown.[22]

Sill had enraged the Confederates due to alleged depredations imposed on local civilians days before the battle, and Bragg did not mince words about Sill in one of his action reports: "The body of Brigadier-General Sill, one of their division [actually brigade] commanders, was found where he had fallen, and was sent to town and decently interred, though he had forfeited all claim to such consideration by the acts of cruelty, barbarity, and atrocity but a few days before committed under his authority on the women, children, and old men living near the road on which he had made a reconnaissance."[23]

* * *

The battle rekindled on Friday, January 2, when Bragg ordered Maj. Gen. John Breckinridge to attack a Union hill position on the river's east side that threatened the Confederate right flank. The Federals here were a reinforced division commanded by Brig. Gen. Samuel Beatty of Gen. Thomas Crittenden's corps.

In the afternoon, Breckinridge formed his division of about 4,500 men into two battle lines—the brigades of Brig. Gens. Gideon Pillow and Roger W. Hanson in the first wave. In a chill rain, these Rebels fixed bayonets with orders to fire a volley before relying on cold steel.

Breckinridge opposed the attack because even if he managed to take the enemy position, Yankee artillery west of the river would likely sweep him from the ridge. Indeed, Hanson called the plan "murderous" and was so incensed that he wanted to kill Bragg. Hanson was known to his men by several nicknames, including "Old Flintlock," due to his military record and strict discipline; "Bench-leg," because of his limp from a prewar duel; and "Old Roger." His command was the 1st Kentucky, which would enter wartime legend as the Orphan Brigade. Hanson, thirty-five, had been a Kentucky lawyer and legislator who had unsuccessfully run for Congress in 1857 after serving as a lieutenant of Kentucky volunteers in the Mexican War. He had been captured at Fort Donelson where he was serving as colonel of the 2nd Kentucky, and not exchanged until late 1862. He had been promoted to brigadier just over two weeks before Stones River.[24]

Pillow and Hanson were followed by the brigades of Brigs. William Preston and Daniel Adams, the latter commanded by Col. Randall Gibson since Adams had been wounded earlier in the battle. The Rebels would have to cross 600 to 700 yards of open ground that gently ascended to the Federal positions. Seeing the Rebels forming for this assault, Crittenden ordered his artillery chief, Capt. John Mendenhall, to mass about sixty cannons on the heights above the river's west bank to support the Federals on the eastside hill. Forming his men for the assault, Hanson's earlier anger looked to have dissipated and an uncharacteristic fatalism seemed to engulf him. "I believe this will be my last!" he remarked.[25]

The Confederate attack began about 4 P.M. as the rebels swept up the slope in the face of heavy musketry and artillery. Breckinridge, meanwhile, had ridden forward to observe the assault and was stirred by the sight of Hanson's charge. "Look at old Hanson!" he exclaimed. As his men closed with the Yankees, Hanson was wounded in the left hip by a piece of rifled artillery shell and fell near a fence. Colonel Gibson had, moments earlier, ridden forward to speak with Hanson. "I had scarcely reached him when he was struck, and, I observed, so seriously wounded as to disable him from conferring with me," Gibson related. "General Hanson had hardly fallen, however, when his line began to show symptoms of yielding, and after a few moments many of his men were falling to the rear."[26]

Breckinridge rode to Hanson's aid, W. B. Pickett, one of Hardee's staff officers, recalling how Breckinridge knelt beside the fallen brigadier and tried to stem the blood gushing from his leg, all while enemy shells were bursting overhead and nearby. "It was a sight indelibly pressed on my memory, the dying hero, his distinguished friend and commander kneeling by his side holding back the lifeblood . . . with tears of affection," Pickett wrote. "All this under the fiercest fire of artillery that can be conceived made it ever memorable."[27]

Presently, Hanson's brother-in-law and staff officer, Capt. Charles Helm, arrived with an ambulance, tears dribbling down his face. Hanson was loaded into the vehicle in short order and Breckinridge resumed his focus on the assault, which met with initial success. The Southerners overpowered Beatty's men, driving them off the crest and across the river into the shallows at McFadden's Ford. The yipping Rebels pursued, but Mendenhall's gunners were waiting, most of his artillery posted only about 100 yards from the crossing. A murderous barrage butchered the Confederates, destroying their charge and sending the survivors scampering to safety. The Yankees counterattacked and reclaimed the gory hill that had been Breckinridge's target. Hanson's brigade alone suffered about 400 casualties while battle reports of Bragg, Hardee, and Breckinridge list the division's loss on this day from 1,200 to 1,700 in an hour of combat. The setback compelled Bragg to prepare for a retreat from Murfreesboro.

As he was being borne to the rear, Hanson passed Lt. Gen. Leonidas Polk and other officers who expressed their sympathy about his injury which, though serious, was not believed to be fatal. Hanson "was cheerful and to the hope expressed by the bishop-general that he would soon recover, replied that it was a serious wound, but added that it was glorious to die for one's country," a Confederate historian wrote.[28]

Behind the line he was treated by Dr. John Scott, surgeon of the 2nd Kentucky, who gave the general a stimulant. Hanson "did not utter a groan or speak a complaining word," the physician recalled. At Hanson's request, Scott left him to attend to other wounded and the general's ambulance plodded on into Murfreesboro, accompanied by Capt. Steve Chipley, who had been among the first to reach the fallen Hanson.[29]

Hanson was taken to the Haynes family home where Breckinridge's wife, Mary, cut off his boot and tore strips from her dress to use for bandages. A distraught Virginia Hanson worked with Mrs. Breckinridge to try to make her husband as comfortable as possible. Dr. David Yandell, who had been on the staff of Albert Sidney Johnston at Shiloh, examined Hanson and decided that he was too weak to survive the leg's amputation. "Well, do your best for me, doctor," the general told Yandell. "I would like to live to see the war through. I feel that we are right, and ought to succeed." Still, "the shock to his system was too great for the skill of the surgeon," and the general's loss of blood was too much to overcome.[30]

Late that bitterly cold night, Breckinridge left a council of war with Bragg and rode to check on "Old Flintlock," who was fading. Hanson summoned the strength to tell Breckinridge, "General, Dr. Yandell does not think I will live, nor do I; but I have this satisfaction, I shall die in a just cause, having done my duty."[31]

With Virginia at his side, Hanson died about 5 A.M. on Sunday, January 4, a few hours after Bragg had retreated from Murfreesboro in a downpour. "Here in the presence of his heartbroken wife, and sorrowing friends his life gradually ebbed away and took its flight to the realms above," recalled Sgt. Lot Young of the Orphan Brigade.[32]

Hanson was among about 2,000 badly wounded Confederates whom Bragg left behind with what medical staff he could afford them. Each side had lost about 13,000, which meant that the bloodied Federals were in no mood or condition to pursue the Rebels. Hanson "fell in the pride of his manhood in the thickest of the fight, nobly doing his duty," reported Col. Robert Trabue of the 4th Kentucky, who assumed brigade command when the general was wounded. Breckinridge lamented his slain brigadier in a report, stating that Hanson "received a mortal wound at the moment the enemy began to give way. Endeared to his friends by his private virtues, and to his command by the vigilance with which he guarded its interest . . . he was, by the universal testimony of his military associates, one of the finest officers that adorned the service of the Confederate States."[33]

The Orphan Brigade earned its nickname at Stones River, according to some accounts. After the charge, Breckinridge is said to have wept over the losses of his Kentuckians, calling them "my poor orphans." The name stuck. "Many brave men and able officers fell in the attack," recalled General Hardee, adding that Hanson was "a spirited and intrepid officer." Pickett, of Hardee's staff wrote, "Hanson's death was a great loss to the Southern cause. He was an able, conscientious, intrepid officer. Had he lived, he would have attained high rank."[34]

"We have fought one of the greatest battles of the war, and are victorious," Rosecrans penned to U.S. secretary of war Edwin Stanton on January 5. The Rebels' "loss has been very heavy. Generals Rains and Hanson killed." In another battle report the same day, Col. William B. Hazen of the 41st Ohio Infantry related that the "famous rebel General Roger W. Hanson was killed" in his sector where the bodies of a number of Southerners, horses and three caissons were found.[35]

The Rebel sergeant Young was apparently among a number of Orphans who believed Bragg had intentionally sent their brigade into a death trap, claiming Bragg disliked the Kentuckians because of the split loyalties of their state. Young wrote that Hanson was "a splendid soldier and his loss grieved me very much. Many another gallant Kentuckian, some of our finest . . . were left on the field, a sacrifice to stupidity and revenge. . . . Among the first of these was the gallant and illustrious Hanson, whose coolness and bearing were unsurpassed and whose loss was irreparable. He with Breckinridge understood and was fully sensible of—as indicated by the very seriousness of his countenance—the unwisdom of this [attack]." Young added that Bragg's decision to make the assault caused Hanson's death, "the loss of such a magnificent soldier and gentleman—uselessly and foolishly."[36]

Rosecrans granted permission on January 6 for the bodies of Rains and Hanson to be taken to Union-held Nashville for private burial by friends, but with no military honors. Rains, however, was initially buried at Murfreesboro. In 1888, his remains were moved to Mount Olivet Cemetery in Nashville. Hanson was ultimately laid to rest in the City Cemetery of Lexington, Kentucky. "Among the gallant dead the nation is called to mourn, none could have fallen more honored or regretted," Bragg said of his slain generals in a February 23 dispatch to Adj. Gen. Samuel Cooper. "They yielded their lives in the heroic discharge of duty and leave their honored names as a rich legacy to their descendants."[37]

—◄ ═╬═ ►—

The slain Sill and the seriously wounded General Kirk were lamented in the Union ranks. "In General Sill we all feel that we have lost an able commander and a kind friend," related Greusel, "though but a short time with us, he had endeared himself to the whole command by his quiet, unassuming disposition, combining gentleness with strict discipline, courageous in action almost to a fault. We all feel that the brigade and the service have lost an officer hard to be replaced."[38]

A few hours before his death, Sill had checked on one of his staff members who had been seriously wounded in the skirmishing on December 30. A Union soldier who was present recalled the moment: "Just before leaving [the general] stood for a while leaning on his sword, wrapt in deep thought, and I imagined a shade of sadness on his fine face," the Yankee related. "The next morning, when he was killed almost instantly at the opening of the battle, I wondered whether some sad presentment of his fate was not passing through his mind as he stood the evening before, gazing silently upon his wounded aide."[39]

"The nation is again called to mourn the loss of gallant spirits who fell upon this sanguinary field," reported General McCook, adding that Sill "was noble, conscientious in the discharge of his duty, and brave to a fault. He had no ambition save to serve his country. He died a Christian soldier, in the act of repulsing the enemy."[40]

The *New York Herald* reported that Sill was killed "by a bullet through his left eye. He fell in the front of his command, and his body was left on the field. Sill was one of the best men in the service, and his place will be with difficulty filled." Sill rests in Grand View Cemetery at Chillicothe, Ohio, his hometown.[41]

Sheridan recalled after the war: "Sill's modesty and courage were exceeded only by a capacity that had already been demonstrated . . . and his untimely death . . . abruptly closed a career which, had it been prolonged a little more, not only would have shed additional lustre on his name, but would have been of marked benefit to his country."[42]

Kirk, meanwhile, had been taken to his home in Sterling, Illinois, to try to recover but to no avail. His struggle lasted almost seven months before he died at the Fremont House in Chicago on July 21, 1863. Kirk was interred in Chicago's Rosehill Cemetery.[43]

CONFEDERATE BRIGADIER GENERAL
EDWARD D. TRACY
Port Gibson, Mississippi, May 1, 1863

When his exhausted brigade trudged into the Confederate lines at Port Gibson, Mississippi, on the night of April 30, 1863, Brig. Gen. Edward D. Tracy's Alabamans had covered more than forty miles in about twenty-seven hours. It would be a force march to Tracy's death.

These Confederates were among about 8,000 Rebels hastily assembled in a frantic attempt to stop Union major general U. S. Grant's army of 24,000 that was threatening Vicksburg from the south. The Federals had been vainly trying for months to capture the Confederate bastion on the Mississippi River, but Grant's four previous operations north of the city had ended in failure. In late March 1863, however, Grant had struck south into Louisiana along the west bank of the Mississippi, bent on assailing Vicksburg from a different direction. On April 30, his troops crossed the river into Mississippi at Bruinsburg, down river from the city. Confederate forces in the Mississippi interior were scattered and few in number, but Rebel brigadier John Bowen cobbled together what men he could to face Grant. Bowen, with Tracy's command of 1,500 and the brigade of Brig. William Baldwin, concentrated a few miles west of the town of Port Gibson.

A Georgian, Tracy, twenty-nine, had been a lawyer and politician in Huntsville, Alabama, before the rebellion. Fighting with the 4th and later the 19th Alabama, he was in combat at Shiloh and in eastern Tennessee before being commissioned brigadier general in August 1862. Tracy and his brigade of five Alabama regiments had been posted in the Vicksburg sector since earlier in the year.[44]

When they reached Port Gibson after dark on April 30, Tracy's worn-out men had outmarched their ordnance train and had scant ammunition. Sleeping on their muskets and having had little to eat, his soldiers were awakened by artillery fire about 2 A.M. on May 1. After sending a regiment and two guns to reinforce another area of the Confederate line, Tracy posted the rest of his brigade along a ridge before daylight with a battery under Capt. J. W. Johnston in the center. Tracy was guarding the Bruinsburg road on the right of Bowen's position. The terrain was basically a series of vine-choked ravines, ridges, and thickets that Bowen hoped would disrupt the enemy and help the Rebels make up for their inferior numbers.

Tracy's men came under fire about 7 A.M. when they were attacked by Brig. Gen. Peter J. Osterhaus's Union division. Johnston's cannoneers and the 30th Alabama Infantry bore the initial brunt of the action. "The contest here soon became warm and bloody," reported Col. Isham Garrott of the 20th Alabama. "The battery was in range of the enemy's sharpshooters, and in a short time a number of officers, men, and horses had been killed or wounded."[45]

Tracy was hit in the chest by a musket round shortly before 8 A.M. while directing his men north of the A. K. Shaifer house. He "fell near the front line, pierced through the breast, and instantly died without uttering a word," stated Garrott, who assumed brigade command.[46]

Despite Tracy's death and heavy casualties, his troops clung to their hilltop. Bowen was aided by the broken, overgrown nature of the battlefield, and the fighting stormed throughout the day and into the night before Grant's manpower forced the Rebels to retreat. The Southerners had stood their ground for about eighteen hours, inflicting about 900 casualties while losing slightly less, including Tracy and some 270 of his Alabamians.

"Among the slain whom the country deplores I regret to mention Brig. Gen. E. D. Tracy, a brave and skillful officer, who fell where it is the soldier's pride to fall—at the post of duty and of danger," wrote Lt. Gen. John Pemberton, commander of Rebel troops in Mississippi and eastern Louisiana, in his August 25 campaign report. Bowen related, "Among our gallant dead is numbered . . . Tracy, who fell early in the fight, but after giving signal proof of his ability as an officer and bravery as a man."[47]

Tracy's remains, meanwhile, were conveyed to his hometown of Macon, Georgia, for burial. On May 3, Grant sent word of the triumph to Union major general William T. Sherman and noted Tracy's death amid the glory of Port Gibson. In little more than two weeks his army would at last be at the gates of Vicksburg.

CHAPTER 10

Stonewall and Chancellorsville

CONFEDERATE LIEUTENANT GENERAL THOMAS J. "STONEWALL" JACKSON AND BRIGADIER GENERAL ELISHA F. "BULL" PAXTON

UNION MAJOR GENERALS HIRAM G. BERRY AND AMIEL W. WHIPPLE AND BRIGADIER GENERAL EDMUND KIRBY

Chancellorsville, May 1–4, 1863

Stonewall Jackson smelled blood.

In the battle-ravaged Virginia woods at Chancellorsville on the night of May 2, 1863, Jackson and an escort party rode into no-man's-land to scout the enemy. It had been a day of startling triumph for the Army of Northern Virginia, and Jackson had been the blacksmith, his flank march the anvil blow against the Union right wing that staggered Maj. Gen. Joseph Hooker's Army of the Potomac. Jackson found the Federals in the darkness that night, but history twisted on the trigger finger of a jumpy Rebel infantryman from North Carolina. In a flash of musketry from his own men, believing they were under attack by Yankee cavalry, Stonewall fell with a wound that would ultimately lead to his death eight days later.

No loss of the war demoralized the Confederacy more than that of thirty-nine-year-old Lt. Gen. Thomas J. "Stonewall" Jackson who had earned his nickname at First Bull Run, and by late spring 1863 was second only to Robert E. Lee as the South's most lionized warrior.

Jackson was born on January 21, 1824, in Clarksburg, Virginia (now West Virginia), and graduated from West Point in 1846. He was twice brevetted during the Mexican War, but resigned his commission in 1852 to become an instructor at Virginia Military Institute. Later siding with the Confederacy, he was initially assigned as a colonel of Virginia militia before being promoted a Confederate brigadier in June 1861. His Virginia brigade helped save the day for the Rebels at First Bull Run, thus burning the name of Stonewall into the vocabularies of the warring states. Renowned for his religious beliefs, peculiarities, and ungainly appearance as much as his zest for merciless marching and the bayonet, Jackson would become Lee's most relied-upon lieutenant. Promoted to major general in October 1861, Jackson conducted a masterful campaign against three Union armies in the Shenandoah Valley in 1862. While his performance in the Seven Days fighting was lackluster, he played a vital role in the Confederate victory at Second Bull Run in August 1862. In the Maryland Campaign Jackson captured Harpers Ferry and its garrison of 12,000 Federals before absorbing the first blow of the Union attack at Antietam. Jackson was made lieutenant general in October 1862 and led Lee's right wing at Fredericksburg.[1]

The stage was set for Chancellorsville, simultaneously the zenith of his military career and the beginning of his life's final chapter. The campaign had opened with sparkling promise for "Fighting Joe" Hooker and his Union army of some 130,000. The enemies had faced each other across the Rappahannock for most of the winter before Hooker began a spring offensive in late April. He sent a good portion of his infantry across the river with the intent of getting behind Lee's army of 60,000 at Fredericksburg. By April 30, Hooker was concentrated at Chancellorsville, a country crossroads a few miles west of Fredericksburg in a region of dense forests and thick undergrowth known as the Wilderness. On May 1, Hooker moved east toward Fredericksburg with about 70,000 soldiers and Lee, outflanked, had to rush troops west of town to meet this threat. There was hard fighting on a ridge at Zoan Church and the Federals were driven back to Chancellorsville where Hooker dug in for the night.

With the coolness of riverboat gamblers, Lee and Jackson then concocted one of the most daring plans of the war. They decided to divide their forces further—a rear guard already having been left at Fredericksburg—to seize the momentum from the enemy. The chess king of this new move would be Jackson who would lead his 30,000 men on a twelve-mile flank march around Hooker to hit the Union army from behind or in the flank on May 2. The risks were high; Lee would be outnumbered almost seven to one during the ten or so hours it would take Jackson to reach his

*Confederate major general
Stonewall Jackson, 1862.*
VIRGINIA MILITARY INSTITUTE ARCHIVES

point of attack. If the Federals sensed the intended surprise, the divided
Rebel forces could be gobbled up one at a time. It was a game of bluff or
destruction.

Jackson's column was on the march before dawn, and during the day was
indeed detected and engaged by the Yankees. But since these Rebels were
moving south on their circuitous route at that point, Hooker believed Lee's
army was retreating. By late afternoon, however, Jackson was poised for
attack on the unsuspecting right flank of Hooker's line. His men poured out
of the forest, yipping the Rebel yell and crushing several of Hooker's divisions—some of the Yankees still had their arms stacked while cooking supper.
The Southerners rolled up about half of the Union line before sundown.

With nightfall the fighting died out, leaving both sides equally disorganized. Divisions, brigades, and regiments had become separated and intermingled in the brambly woods, and no one could say for sure where the
rival lines were in the darkness.

Inflamed by the successes of the day, Jackson had no intention of letting
the night prevent him from continuing his assault, despite the confusion
and worn condition of his troops. There were also rumors that the Yankees
were massing to make an attack down the Orange Turnpike, which
bisected the battleground.

Jackson rode ahead about 8 P.M. to investigate and find a route that
would allow him to position troops in the enemy's rear. With him were his
aide-de-camp and brother-in-law, Lt. J.G. Morrison, Capt. R. E. Wilbourn

of the Signal Corps, Capt. James K. Boswell of the engineers, and five or six couriers.

Jackson's party had advanced a short distance down the road when it drew scattered Union fire from in front and to the right. Stonewall and the others wheeled to the left off the road and made for the rear. Some dog-tired North Carolinians of Brig. Gen. James Lane's brigade in A. P. Hill's division of Jackson's corps suddenly saw shadowy riders coming toward them through the smoke-streaked trees. "Yankee cavalry!" someone yelled and the Tarheels leveled their muskets and fired at the intruders, emptying some saddles and dropping some horses at almost point-blank range.

Stonewall was hit in the left arm and right hand, his frightened horse, Little Sorrel, swerving into heavy brush, knocking off the general's cap and scraping his face. As Jackson lost his balance in the saddle, Wilbourn managed to reach the general, stop his horse, and steady the general. Four others in the entourage, including Boswell, were killed or mortally wounded, and two more were injured, their bodies and those of several horses littering the landscape.

Morrison jumped from his spooked mount, which was running toward the enemy lines, and shouted to the Confederate infantry, "Cease firing! You are firing into your own men!" A North Carolina colonel, however, yelled, "Who gave that order? It's a lie! Pour it into them." Morrison found the officer and convinced him of the mistake.[2]

Standing by Jackson, who was still mounted, Wilbourn saw the general "was bleeding profusely, the blood streaming down so as to fill his gauntlets." He and another Signal Corps soldier, W. T. Wynn, were momentarily alone with Jackson, the only ones left from his party.[3]

After they determined that Jackson's arm was broken, Stonewall, weakened by blood loss, murmured "you had better take me down" and was assisted to the ground by the two men. They assisted him to the side of the road and laid him under a small tree while Wilbourn supported his head. The captain ordered Wynn to go for Dr. Hunter McGuire, the corps' medical director, and an ambulance, adding strict instructions that he was not to reveal the news to anyone other than McGuire or another physician. As Wynn departed, Wilbourne tried to determine the extent of Jackson's wounds. He removed the general's fieldglasses and a haversack and used a pen knife to "cut away the sleeves of the [I]ndia rubber overall [rubber overcoat], dress-coat and two shirts from the bleeding arm."[4]

While Wilbourn was engaged in this, A. P. Hill arrived with members of his staff and dismounted to help. He expressed his regret to Jackson about his injury and removed his commander's gloves, as well as his sword and belt, to make him more comfortable. Stonewall did take a swallow of whiskey, or brandy, which seemed to refresh him. With no sign of Wynn, Hill dispatched Capt. Benjamin W. Leigh of his staff to find a physician and ambulance.

The group with Jackson faced an immediate dilemma. "It seemed impossible to move him without making his wounds bleed afresh, but it was absolutely necessary to do so, as the enemy were not more than a hundred and fifty yards distant and might advance at any moment," Wilbourn related.[5]

Hill, meanwhile, cradled Jackson's head and used handkerchiefs to try to stop the bleeding. Leigh soon returned with Dr. Richard Barr, an assistant surgeon in Dorsey Pender's brigade, and two litter bearers. Barr administered a tourniquet on the arm, but nothing more could be done until Jackson was moved to a hospital. Proof of their danger came within minutes when the Confederates captured two Union soldiers only a few yards from where Jackson lay. Now, Hill eased from under Stonewall and, with pistol drawn, mounted his horse to return to his troops and prepare them for the possible enemy attack. Before leaving, he promised Jackson that he would "keep his accident from the knowledge of the troops" for which Stonewall thanked him.[6]

Capt. James P. Smith, another aide-de-camp on Jackson's staff, and Morrison had joined Jackson's party by now, Morrison exclaiming, "Let us take the General up in our arms and carry him off!" Jackson, hearing this, replied faintly, "No, if you can help me up I can walk." The men assisted him to his feet and started toward the Confederate lines. Leaning on Leigh, Jackson "slowly dragged himself along . . . the blood from his wounded arm flowing profusely over Captain Leigh's uniform," Wilbourn remembered.[7]

As they trudged toward safety, they encountered some of Hill's soldiers moving toward the front, the officers using several horses to conceal the stricken general from them. Jackson had not walked twenty paces before he exhausted himself and was placed on the stretcher. They had scarcely begun to move again when Union artillery opened a furious fire and "a hurricane of shell and canister swept down the road," Wilbourn stated.[8]

One of the litter bearers was wounded, and the men were forced to lay the stretcher on the road, Smith and Leigh shielding Jackson with their bodies as shells screamed overhead, shearing off tree branches. (Morrison also claimed to have been present although accounts by Leigh and Smith do not mention him.) The litter bearers were so frightened that they fled.

At one point, Smith had to hold Jackson down as he tried to get up, telling him, "Sir, you must lie still; it will cost you your life if you rise!"[9] Wilbourn, meanwhile, had ridden to try to find Dr. McGuire.

Leigh and Smith were alone with Jackson now, the road crowded with soldiers and horses minutes earlier now empty. When the cannon fire changed direction, Smith and Leigh helped the general stand and assisted him into the sheltering trees where Jackson sank to the ground from exhaustion. The litter was soon brought and Leigh impressed several soldiers to help carry the general, the party now moving through the woods for better cover. They had gone a short distance when one of the bearers tripped on a vine and fell, causing the litter to careen. Jackson "fell to the ground [on the wounded arm] with a groan of deep pain," Smith recalled. He scrambled to check on the general, who "opened his eyes and wearily said, "Never mind me, captain, never mind me." Leigh added, "For the first time he groaned piteously; he must have suffered agonies."[10]

Jackson was helped to his feet and was approached by General Pender shortly afterward. "Oh, General, I hope you are not seriously wounded," Pender said, based on Smith's account. "I will have to retire my troops to reform them, they are so much broken by this fire." At this, Jackson "rallying his strength, with firm voice said, 'You must hold your ground, General Pender; you must hold your ground, sir!' and so uttered his last command on the field," Smith related.[11]

The general was then placed back on the litter and carried through the underbrush and along the road despite the enemy shelling. Finally they located an ambulance and Jackson was driven to Melzi Chancellor's house where Dr. McGuire met them, having been located by Wilbourn. As McGuire knelt beside him, Stonewall told him, calmly but weakly, "I am badly injured, Doctor; I fear I am dying." "His clothes were saturated with blood," McGuire recalled. "His calmness amid the dangers which surrounded him and at the supposed presence of death, and his uniform politeness . . . were remarkable."[12]

Jackson, his face pale, was given whiskey and morphine for his extreme pain as McGuire accompanied him in the ambulance to the corps field hospital. Also in the wagon was Col. Stapleton Crutchfield, Jackson's artillery chief, who had been severely wounded in the leg. When told that his general was seriously injured, Crutchfield could not restrain himself, crying, "Oh, my God." At one point as the wagon rumbled along, Crutchfield groaned loudly and Jackson asked that the ambulance be stopped to try to ease the colonel's suffering.[13]

Various accounts lay the blame for Stonewall's mortal wounding on Lane's 7th, 18th, or 37th North Carolina, but it is unlikely that it will ever be known which regiment was actually responsible for the shooting. The 18th North Carolina bore much of the criticism, although the entire brigade shouldered culpability. Smith said Jackson was little more than ten yards from the Confederates when they fired. "General Lane got scared, fired into our own men, and achieved the unenviable reputation of wounding severely Lieutenant-General Jackson," a Virginia lieutenant wrote in his battle report.[14]

A tent for Jackson had been prepared and warmed at the II Corps field hospital near the Wilderness Tavern when the general arrived. Covered in blankets, he was given water and a drink of whiskey as a stimulant. It was well after midnight on Sunday morning before McGuire, Dr. Harvey Black and other physicians were able to thoroughly examine the general. They found that he had been shot three times—a round ball had entered the middle of his right palm while another had passed around his left wrist and torn through the left hand. The most destructive ball, however, had hit Jackson in the left arm midway between the shoulder and elbow, splintering the large bone and causing a great loss of blood.

About 2 A.M., McGuire told Jackson that amputation likely would be necessary and the general replied, "Yes, certainly, Dr. McGuire, do for me whatever you think best." Chloroform was administered, and as Jackson fell under its influence, the pain subsiding, he exclaimed, "What an infinite blessing," repeating the last word several times before falling unconscious.[15]

The surgeons first extracted the ball from his hand. They then performed the amputation about two inches below the shoulder. "Throughout the whole of the operation, and until all the dressings were applied, he continued insensible," McGuire remembered.[16]

Another of Jackson's aides, Maj. Sandy Pendleton, arrived about 3:30 A.M., after the surgery was completed, and asked to see the general. McGuire reluctantly agreed after Pendleton told him the fate of the army might be at stake. Jackson was somewhat alert when Pendleton entered the tent, asking him several quick questions about the progress of the battle before he weakened. At one point, Jackson roused and said he had heard wonderful music: "I believe it was the sawing of the bone."[17]

Captain Smith sat with the sleeping general through the rest of the night before he stirred about 9 A.M. on Sunday to the sound of cannon fire, Jeb Stuart leading Jackson's corps in his absence.

Lee learned of Jackson's wounding before daybreak, Wilbourn delivering the news based on Pendleton's orders. Wilbourn rode to Lee's headquarters and found the commander sleeping on a cot beneath a blanket strung over him for shelter. He recalled:

When I told General Lee about it, he made me sit by him on his bed, while he raised up, resting on his elbow, and he was very much affected by the news. When I told him that the wounding was by our own troops, he seemed ready to burst into tears, and gave a moan. After a short silence he said, "Ah! Captain, don't let us say anything more about it, it is too painful to talk about," and seemed to give way to grief. It was the saddest night I ever passed in my life; and when I saw this great man so much moved, and look as if he could weep, my cup of sadness was filled to overflowing."[18]

Jackson at some point that early morning sent Lee a dispatch about his misfortune. Lee replied to his most valued lieutenant:

General: I have just received your note, informing me that you were wounded. I cannot express my regret at the occurrence. Could I have directed events, I should have chosen for the good of the country to be disabled in your stead. I congratulate you upon the victory, which is due to your skill and energy.[19]

In the tent that afternoon, Smith read the message to Jackson, who "turned his face away and said, 'General Lee is very kind, but he should give the praise to God.'"[20]

The Confederate high command was still reeling from Jackson's calamity when Brig. Gen. Elisha F. "Bull" Paxton, commander of the Stonewall Brigade, was killed that Sunday morning after apparently having a premonition of his death.

Paxton, thirty-five, was in Isaac Trimble's division, temporarily being led by Brig. Gen. R. E. Colston. A Virginian and an attorney before the war, Paxton had given up his practice in 1859 due to failing eyesight. When the war came he fought with the 27th Virginia Infantry and saw combat at First Bull Run before serving on Jackson's staff. On Jackson's recommendation he was promoted to brigadier in November 1862 and given command of the Stonewall Brigade. Paxton led the brigade at Fredericksburg but was not in action in Chancellorsville's early stages, having been assigned to hold a road junction.[21]

Paxton's brigade was posted in line during the night of May 2 and received orders to advance early the next morning. Paxton, however, believed he would not survive the battle, confessing his feelings in a late night talk with Capt. Henry Kyd Douglas of Jackson's staff.

"He did not seem morbid or superstitious but he spoke with earnest conviction," Douglas recalled. Paxton told Douglas where to find his personal papers and asked him to write to his wife, Elizabeth, after his death. He also asked Douglas to make sure that his body was sent home to Lexington. Paxton would carry a picture of his wife and a Bible into action with him.[22]

"I was never so impressed by a conversation in my life," Douglas wrote later. "Paxton was not an emotional man but one of strong mind, cool action, and great force of character. He was the last man to give way to a superstition. When he finished I had no doubt of his sincerity and of his awful prescience."[23]

In likely his final letter to Elizabeth, written during the last week of April, Paxton described the uncertainty facing him:

> The future, as you say, darling, is dark enough. Though sound in health and strength, I feel that life to many of us hangs upon a slender thread. Whenever God wills it that mine pass from me, I feel that I can say in calm resignation, "Into thy hands I commend my spirit."[24]

The Confederates were poised to strike at daybreak on Sunday, May 3. In the dawn's dim light, cannon fire and the snapping of muskets could already be heard when Douglas found Paxton, sitting against a tree and reading his Bible while waiting for his brigade to go into action. "As I approached he closed it, greeted me cheerfully, and we conversed for a little while on indifferent subjects," Douglas related.[25]

Paxton then returned to the night's conversation, saying that upon his death, the brigade command should go to Col. J. H. S. Funk. Before they parted, Paxton asked Douglas to assist Funk in leading his troops. The Stonewall Brigade went into combat a short time later, and Douglas never saw Paxton alive again. Lt. Randolph Barton of Paxton's staff recalled years later that Paxton was wearing a new uniform that had arrived a day or so earlier from Richmond. Writing to Paxton's son John more than twenty years after the war, Barton described how the coat bore the insignia of a brigadier but then stated, "Perhaps the wreath was not on the collar, only the stars—one of your father's characteristics being aversion to display."[26]

In battle line and under fire, Paxton's men moved forward across the Plank Road, and crossed some hastily constructed breastworks that had been abandoned by the Yankees. The Southerners reformed their ranks, which had been thrown into disarray in the thick undergrowth, and pressed forward again, firing as they went, Paxton now leading his men on foot.

To Paxton's son, Barton described how he was at the general's side when Paxton was shot:

> Suddenly I heard the unmistakable blow of a ball, my first thought being that it had struck a tree near us, but in an instant

your father reeled and fell. He at once raised himself, with his arms extended, and as I bent over him to lift him I understood him to say, "Tie up my arm," and then, as I thought, he died.[27]

Paxton had been struck in the chest by a minié ball, and some of his men carried him to the rear. He died within the hour. Barton himself was seriously wounded shortly thereafter, and while being taken to a field hospital, passed Paxton's body, which had been placed in an ambulance. "Here General Paxton fell while gallantly leading his troops to victory and glory," related Colonel Funk of the 5th Virginia, who took over the brigade as Paxton had requested.[28]

Word of Paxton's fall was sent to Jackson who, despite his own injuries, was visibly upset and "spoke in serious and tender strain of the genius and virtues of that officer," related physician R. L. Dabney. Paxton would be temporarily buried on the grounds of the Thomas Chandler plantation.[29]

Douglas also learned of Paxton's death and discussed it during a visit with Jackson late in the day, adding that Jackson "spoke most feelingly of the deaths of Paxton and Boswell," the latter killed in Stonewall's entourage. Douglas fulfilled his promise to write to Paxton's widow the next day.[30]

Elizabeth Paxton was left with three young children, and Douglas tried to soothe her grief in his promised letter to her:

> Beloved and esteemed by officers and men, his loss is deeply
> mourned, and the brigade mingle their tears with those of his
> family. I have for some time thought that the General expected
> the first battle in which he led his brigade would be his last,
> and . . . he was preparing his mind and soul for the occasion.[31]

He described how he saw Paxton reading his Bible that morning, "preparing himself like a Christian soldier for the contest." After the battle Lee wrote that Paxton "fell while leading his brigade with conspicuous courage," but in the concern over Jackson's well being, Paxton's loss was basically obscured in the battle smoke.[32]

The battle reached a crescendo on Sunday with the enemies blazing away at each other through the tangled underbrush before the Rebels gained an advantage by massing artillery on an elevated clearing known as Hazel Grove. Hooker gave more ground and the Confederates also held off a thrust by the Union VI Corps, which was threatening them after slicing through the thin Rebel defenses at Fredericksburg.

Douglas found Jackson "not only cheerful but talkative" and appeared to be in "excellent condition." Stonewall asked about the battle and various troop movements and losses, including Paxton. He also wanted to know about the performance of the Stonewall Brigade, and Douglas told him how they had made a successful charge shouting "Remember Jackson!" For an instant the war passion again flushed Jackson's face before his eyes moistened and in a trembling voice he replied, "They are a noble set of men. The name of Stonewall belongs to that brigade, not to me."[33]

Jackson had complained of pain in his side earlier in the day, possibly caused by his fall from the litter, but he felt better by nightfall "and in all respects he seemed to be doing well," Dr. McGuire noted.[34]

The combat flamed anew on Monday, May 4, but by now Hooker had been forced into a defensive pocket with his back to the Rappahannock. Taking no chances with Jackson, however, Lee sent word to McGuire that morning to have Stonewall moved as soon as his health would allow, due to the threat of Union forces capturing the field hospital. Some Rebel troops were detached to guard the facility. Learning of the threat of capture, Jackson said, "I am not afraid of them; I have always been kind to their wounded, and I am sure they will be kind to me."[35]

Lee sent a similar warning that evening, and preparations were made to transfer Jackson the next morning. Early on Tuesday, Jackson was put into an ambulance for the day-long trip to the Thomas Chandler plantation, "Fairfield," at Guinea's Station (also commonly called Guiney's Station). During the twenty-seven-mile trip, engineer troops preceded the ambulance, removing obstructions in the country roads to make the passage less bumpy, and clearing other vehicles from the road. "The rough teamsters sometimes refused to move their loaded wagons out of the way for an ambulance until told that it contained Jackson, and then, with all possible speed, they gave the way and stood with hats off and weeping as we went by," McGuire wrote. Along the route, civilians ran out to the ambulance "bringing all the poor delicacies they had, and with tearful eyes they blessed him and prayed for his recovery." Jackson was cheerful during the trip, talking about the battle and the performance of his officers.[36]

Located about eighteen miles south of Fredericksburg, Guinea's Station was on the Richmond, Fredericksburg & Potomac Railroad and was being used as a Confederate supply depot. The Chandlers offered to allow Jackson to stay in the main house, but McGuire and the general's staff chose to use the one-story frame office on the plantation grounds. Jackson could rest comfortably there and, if all went well, eventually be taken to Richmond by train for further treatment and recovery. Jackson had bread and tea that night and slept well after the journey.

He was still settling into his new quarters on Wednesday, May 6, when Hooker pulled his army back across the Rappahannock. Lee, with much credit due to Stonewall, had won his greatest victory of the war. Hooker had lost some 17,000 compared to Lee's 12,800 but even this greatest hour of triumph for the Confederacy was diluted by concern for Jackson. At Chandler's, however, doctors believed Stonewall to be "doing remarkably well," his wounds appearing to heal nicely, McGuire noted.[37]

"Our base foe will exult in the disaster to Jackson," the *Richmond Enquirer* said on May 7, "yet the accursed bullet that brought him down was never moulded [*sic*] by a Yankee. Through a cruel mistake, in the confusion, the hero received 2 balls from some of his own men, who would all have died for him."[38]

Mary Anna Jackson and infant daughter Julia joined her husband at the Chandler plantation on May 7. It had been little more than two weeks earlier at Guinea's Station, on a rainy April 20, that Jackson had reunited with Anna after more than a year apart and had seen his five-month-old daughter for the first time. They had come on a train from Richmond and he had been there to meet them as troops cheered the little family. This time, however, the arrival of wife and daughter was under much more somber circumstances—Jackson was worsening. The general had developed pneumonia, which McGuire and the other physicians attributed to his fall from the litter. Just before she went in to see her wounded husband for the first time, Mrs. Jackson was informed of General Paxton's death, a shock since Paxton had been a friend and neighbor from the Jacksons' time in Lexington at VMI. The news was no better when she entered the room where Jackson lay in a four-poster bed, his servant, Jim Lewis, at his bedside. McGuire told her of his turn for the worst.

Nevertheless, Jackson was cheered to see Anna and the baby, but soon noticed his wife's sadness and tried to comfort her. "I know you would gladly give your life for me, but I am perfectly resigned," he said to her softly. "Do not be sad. I hope I may yet recover."[39]

"Against our hopes, notwithstanding the skill and care of wise and watchful surgeons, watched day and night by wife and friends, amid the prayers and tears of all the Southern land, thinking not of himself, but of the cause he loved, and for the troops who had followed him so well and given him so great a name, our chief sank, day by day," wrote Captain Smith.[40]

Lee was almost disbelieving when he learned that Jackson was in decline and remarked, "Surely General Jackson must recover. God will not take him from us now that we need him so much. Surely he will be spared to us in answer to the many prayers which are offered for him."[41]

Lee also told Jackson's chaplain, B. Tucker Lacy, "Give [Jackson] my affectionate regards, and tell him to make haste and get well, and come back to me as soon as he can. He has lost his left arm, but I have lost my right."[42]

The doctors dressed his wounds again on Friday, May 8, but Jackson was having trouble breathing and complained of exhaustion. Other physicians were called from Richmond on Saturday, but there was little anyone could do. McGuire wrote that "all that human skill could devise was done to stay the hand of death. He suffered no pain to-day, and his breathing was less difficult, but he was evidently hourly growing weaker."[43]

Anna and Julia were with him that day, Jackson caressing and playing with the baby for some time and calling her his "little comforter." McGuire wrote that at one point Jackson raised his bandaged hand above his head, closed his eyes and prayed silently. He then told McGuire, "I see from the number of physicians that you think my condition dangerous, but I thank God, if it is His will, that I am ready to go."[44]

That night, Anna read to him from Psalms and then she and her brother, Lieutenant Morrison, led those in the bedroom in a hymn. "The singing had a quieting effect, and he seemed to rest in perfect peace," Mrs. Jackson later recalled.[45]

Despite all efforts, Jackson continued to wane and by Sunday, May 10, the doctors had lost all hope. Near sunrise, Anna told her husband that his recovery was unlikely and that he should prepare for the worst. "He was silent for a moment," McGuire recalled, "and then said: 'It will be infinite gain to be [sent] to Heaven.'[46]

Through the early morning Jackson's strength sagged, so much so that about 11 A.M., Anna knelt by his bedside, saying that he would soon "be with his Savior." Jackson replied, "Oh, no; you are frightened, my child, death is not so near; I may yet get well." Anna fell across the bed, sobbing that the physicians had told her there was no hope for him. When McGuire told him that was the case, Jackson "turned his eyes toward the ceiling and gazed for a moment or two as if in intense thought, then replied: 'Very good, very good, it is all right,' McGuire remembered. "He then tried to comfort his almost heart-broken wife, and told her that he had a great deal to say to her, but he was too weak."[47]

For the last time he saw his baby, playing with her and calling her affectionate names until he lapsed into unconsciousness again. When he roused again, Jackson was aware that it was Sunday and when Pendleton came into the room about 1 P.M., the general asked "who was preaching at headquarters." Pendleton told him the entire army was praying for him, and

Jackson answered, "Thank God, they are very kind," and added, "It is the Lord's Day; my wish is fulfilled. I have always desired to die on Sunday."[48]

"His mind now began to fail and wander, and he frequently talked as if in command upon the field, giving orders in his old way; then the scene shifted and he was at the mess-table, in conversation with . . . his staff; now with his wife and child; now at prayers," McGuire related. During one of the brief intervals when Jackson regained his wits, McGuire offered him brandy and water, but Stonewall declined, saying, "It will only delay my departure, and do no good; I want to preserve my mind . . . to the last."[49]

With his last energy Jackson rode back into combat in a delirium shortly after 3 P.M. "He was virtually dying on the field, amid the trophies and ruins of his last victory," said Douglas. "His spirit was riding on the whirlwind of the conflict."[50]

"Order A. P. Hill to prepare for action!" Jackson cried. "Pass the infantry to the front rapidly! Tell Major Hawks ——." The order was left unfinished. "Presently a smile of ineffable sweetness spread . . . over his pale face, and he cried quietly and with an expression as if of relief, 'Let us cross over the river and rest under the shade of the trees,'" McGuire remembered, "and then, without pain or the least struggle, his spirit passed from earth to the God who gave it."[51]

At Fredericksburg that Sunday, Lee wrote of Jackson's loss to Secretary of War James Seddon:

> It becomes my melancholy duty to announce to you the death of General Jackson. He expired at 3:15 P.M. to-day. His body will be conveyed to Richmond in the train to-morrow, under charge of Major Pendleton, assistant adjutant-general. Please direct an escort of honor to meet it at the depot, and that suitable arrangements be made for its disposition.[52]

The awful tidings spread quickly by telegraph and word of mouth. "That evening the news went abroad, and a great sob swept over the Army of Northern Virginia; it was the heart-break of the Southern Confederacy," wrote Douglas.[53]

In General Orders No. 61, issued on May 11, Lee officially told his troops the awful news:

> With deep grief the commanding General announces to the army the death of Lieut-General T. J. Jackson. . . . The daring, skill, and energy of this great and good soldier, by the decree of an all-wise

Providence, are now lost to us. But while we mourn his death, we feel that his spirit still lives, and will inspire the whole army with his indomitable courage and unshaken confidence in God as our hope and our strength. Let his name be a watchword to his corps, who have followed him to victory on so many fields. Let officers and soldiers emulate his invincible determination to do everything in the defence of our beloved country.[54]

Among the most distraught was Jackson's servant Jim Lewis whose "grief was almost inconsolable."[55] Jefferson Davis recognized the magnitude of Jackson's death and expressed it in writing to Lee the same day:

> Dear General: A national calamity has befallen us, and I sympa-
> thize with the sorrow you feel and the embarrassment you must
> experience. The announcement of the death of General Jackson
> following frequent assurances that he was doing very well, and
> though the loss was one which would have been deeply felt under
> any circumstances, the shock was increased by its suddenness.
> There is sincere mourning here, and it will extend throughout the
> land as the intelligence is received.
>   Your friend,
>   Jefferson Davis[56]

That Sunday night, members of Jackson's staff clothed his body in a civilian suit obtained by Lewis, the general's uniform being too bloodied and torn to use. Placed in a simple wooden coffin decorated with flowers, the remains were carried from the office to the Chandler's main house. Douglas, meanwhile, rode to Lee's headquarters with a special request. The Stonewall Brigade's officers had chosen him to ask the commander if the brigade, or a portion of it, could accompany their late general to the capital.

Douglas remembered that Lee listened to him patiently before replying in a gentle, sad tone:

> I am sure no one can feel the loss of General Jackson more
> deeply than I do, for no one has the same reason. I can appreciate
> the feelings of his old brigade; they have reason to mourn for him,
> for he was proud of them. I should be glad to grant any request
> they might make to show their regard for him, and I am sorry
> the situation of affairs will not justify me in letting them go to
> Richmond or even Lexington. But it cannot be. Those people

over the river are again showing signs of movement and I cannot leave my Headquarters long enough to ride to the depot and pay my dear friend the poor tribute of seeing his body placed upon the cars. . . . He never neglected a duty while living and he would not rest the easier in his grave if his old brigade had left the presence of the enemy to see him buried. Tell them, Captain, how I sympathize with them. Tell them that deeply as we lament the death of their General yet, if his spirit remains behind to inspire his corps and the whole army, perhaps in the end his death may be as great a gain to us as it is to himself.[57]

"Words have no power to express the emotion which the death of Jackson has aroused in the public mind," said the *Richmond Dispatch*. "The heart of our whole people bleeds over the fallen hero, whom they loved so well because he so loved their cause. . . . The affections of every household in the nation were twined about this great and unselfish warrior. . . . He has fallen, and a nation weeps, but not as those without hope. No grave more glorious can a soldier ask than the lap of victory; no future brighter than that which awaits one who united with the soldier the saint!"[58]

Virginia governor John Letcher sent a special car to Guinea's Station that Sunday night, and the general's remains were loaded aboard on Monday morning, May 11. Among the funeral party were Anna and Julia, Dr. McGuire, Pendleton, and Morrison and Smith from Jackson's staff. The body arrived in Richmond to tolling church bells and flags at half staff about 4 P.M. that day. It had been expected at noon, and a huge crowd had descended on the depot, only to learn that the train was late—at every station, mourners had come to pay their respects, delaying the trip. When the train finally huffed to a stop at the corner of Fourth and Broad streets, where a military procession was waiting, the throng of mourners was even larger than before. "It seemed as if every man felt himself an orphan," said the *Richmond Enquirer*. "It would be impossible to measure the depth of love felt by the people for the great and good man whom they were now come forth to mourn. . . . The streets, for some distance in the vicinity of the train, were literally blocked up with people."[59]

Shrouded in a Confederate flag, Jackson's casket was carried out of its car and placed in a hearse drawn by two white horses adorned with sable plumes. With an armory band's dirge as accompaniment, the marchers proceeded to Capitol Square where the coffin was passed along a line of soldiers into the Governor's Mansion. "The bells were tolled till sundown, till which time hundreds of people remained on the square," reported the

Richmond Dispatch. "We have never before seen such an exhibition of heart-felt and general sorrow . . . as has been evinced by all since the announce-ment of the death of Stonewall Jackson."[60]

The general's body was embalmed on the night of May 11 and placed in a metal coffin. It was carried the next day to the Capitol amid an impressive and mournful parade through the crowded streets. "Long before the appointed hour for the procession to move a dense crowd had congre-gated on the Square to pay the last sad tribute of respect to one whom all delighted to honor," the *Dispatch* said the next day.[61]

Eight generals and a Rebel commodore served as mounted pallbearers. Jefferson Davis and Vice President Alexander Stephens followed the hearse in a carriage and the Confederate Cabinet and other dignitaries trailed on foot. Also in the cavalcade were Stonewall Brigade veterans, in Richmond recov-ering from wounds. A military band's doleful "Death March," the boom of minute guns, and the slow, somber pealing of church bells accented all, everything and everyone cloaked in sweltering morning heat. Jackson lay in state at the Capitol the rest of the day where "the throng pressed through in a continuous stream for a first and last view of the great general, whom they had learned to honor without seeing and love without knowing."[62]

The coffin had a glass plate in the lid so that the general's face could be seen, and also bore a silver plate which included the inscription, "All the incidents connected with these interesting, but melancholy ceremonies, were marked by a deep feeling of sorrow. Eyes unused to weep were suf-fused with tears, and the great popular heart pulsated with emotions of grief too deep for utterance."[63]

Watching tearful women kiss the casket, a well-dressed gentleman said, "Weep not; all is for the best. Though Jackson has been taken from the head of his corps, his spirit is now pleading our cause at the bar of God."[64]

Mrs. Jackson, meanwhile, spent much of the day in a darkened room at the Governor's Mansion where she was comforted by her oldest brother, a few friends, and a minister who offered scriptural solace.

Escorted by an honor guard, Jackson's body was removed from the Capitol on the morning of May 13 and, after a stop at the Governor's Mansion, was taken to the Virginia Central Railroad station to be sent to Lexington for burial. Jackson's body was accompanied by Anna and the baby, Governor Letcher, and members of Jackson's staff, among others.[65]

⊷ ⊱✦⊰ ⊷

The Federals, meanwhile had picked up snippets here and there about Jackson. President Abraham Lincoln wrote to Hooker on May 6, wonder-ing about the state of the Federal army: "We have . . . the contents of Richmond papers of the 5th. . . . The substance is, General Lee's dispatch . . . claiming that he had beaten you, and that you were then retreating across the Rappahannock . . . and that General Paxton was killed, Stonewall Jackson severely wounded."[66]

The Yankees were aware of Jackson's end on May 12 when they acquired Richmond newspapers announcing the news. In the Union lines across the river from Fredericksburg, the Federals heard Confederate military bands playing dirges in the town.

The *New York Times* ran a page one headline and brief army dispatch about Stonewall's death, along with a reprint of the May 7 *Richmond Enquirer* article.

Hooker was trying to save his career when he finally replied to Lincoln on May 13, mentioning Jackson's death: "I know that you are impatient, and I know that I am, but my impatience must not be indulged at the expense of dearest interests. . . . Jackson is dead and Lee beats McClellan in his untruthful bulletins."[67]

Disguised as a Rebel cavalryman, a Federal scout named Clifford had ridden some 100 miles on May 9, bumping into enemy patrols, engaging the Southerners in casual conversation about Jackson's injuries. That night he sent off a dispatch to U.S. major general Henry Slocum which described Confederate movements and Jackson: "Stonewall Jackson lost his right [actually his left] arm Sunday night. Will come through soon as my horse gets rested."[68]

In a May 20 report, Union major general Dan Sickles, commander of the U.S. III Corps, lamented the loss of two generals and other officers in his ranks, but found solace in the Rebels' casualty lists:

> It is a consolation to know that they and their noble associates among the dead did not fall unrevenged, for in the loss of Jackson and [A. P.] Hill [who was wounded but would recover], and the flower of the rebel army . . . the enemy learned to respect the prowess [of the III Corps].[69]

Jackson's casket, transferred from the train to a packet boat at Lynchburg, arrived in Lexington on the night of May 14, and VMI cadets who had participated in General Paxton's funeral two days earlier now prepared to honor an even greater warrior. Stonewall lay in state that night in one of his lecture rooms on the campus. Jackson's funeral was held the next morning at the town's Presbyterian Church, where he had been a deacon, the accompanying cortege smaller than that in Richmond, but no less moving. Jackson and Paxton were buried in what is now Jackson Memorial Cemetery in Lexington.

Lee had endured more than four months of fighting, including the Gettysburg Campaign, by the time he sent a detailed report of Chancellorsville to Adj. Gen. Samuel Cooper in September 1863, noting Jackson's loss:

> I do not propose here to speak of the character of this illustrious man, since removed from the scene of his eminent usefulness by the hand of an inscrutable, but all-wise Providence. I nevertheless desire to pay the tribute of my admiration to the matchless energy and skill that marked this last act of his life, forming, as it did, a worthy conclusion of that long series of splendid achievements which won for him the everlasting love and gratitude of his country.[70]

Jefferson Davis summed up Stonewall thusly in a postwar account:

> Our loss was much less in killed and wounded than that of the enemy, but of the number was one, a host in himself. . . . Of this great captain, General Lee in his anguish at his death, justly said, "I have lost my right arm." As an executive officer he had no superior, and war has seldom shown an equal. Too devoted to the cause he served to have any personal motive, he shared the toils, privations, and dangers of his troops . . . He was the complement of Lee; united, they had achieved such results that the public felt secure under their shield. To us his place was never filled.[71]

THE UNION GENERALS

Overlooked even today in just about any study of Chancellorsville is the fact that three Union commanders, including two major generals, were killed in the battle.

Maj. Gen. Hiram G. Berry, thirty-eight, was a Maine native whose father had fought in the War of 1812 and whose grandfather had fought in the Revolution. In his prewar years he had been a carpenter, bank president, state legislator, mayor of his hometown of Rockland, and captain of the local militia. As colonel of the 4th Maine Volunteers, he saw action at First Bull Run and had been promoted to brigadier by the time he excelled in the Peninsular Campaign. Illness prevented him from fighting at Second

*Union major general
Hiram G. Berry.*
LIBRARY OF CONGRESS

Bull Run and in the Antietam Campaign, but he was in combat at Fredericksburg. Promoted major general on November 29, 1862, he commanded Joe Hooker's old division (the 2nd) in the III Corps of Maj. Gen. Dan Sickles.[72]

After Stonewall Jackson's flank attack on May 2, the Federals were still regrouping the next morning amid confused fighting, and Berry's division was rushed forward to try to blunt the Rebel onslaught.

Berry preferred to deliver orders in person and about 7 A.M. rode to the south side of the Orange Plank Road to issue instructions to one of his brigades. He did so and was returning to his headquarters when he was shot by an unidentified sharpshooter from Brig. Gen. Dorsey Pender's Confederate brigade.

"In crossing this road he passed under a perfect shower of bullets, one of which struck him in the left chest and passed through his lungs," the *New York Herald* reported. Berry slumped on his horse and tumbled onto the center of the road. He was assisted by members of his staff, whom he told quietly, "I am dying, carry me to the rear."[73]

Berry was taken to Hooker's headquarters at the Chancellor house, but didn't even live half an hour, dying in the arms of Capt. Le Grand Benedict of his staff. Hooker is said to have wept for his friend, exclaiming "O my God, Berry, why wasn't I taken and you left?" A Maine soldier recalled that Hooker "kissed his dead friend over and over again and seemed utterly overwhelmed and broken." Berry "died, peacefully, heroically," recalled Brig. Gen. Joseph B. Carr, his successor to division command. "I cannot describe the vacancy his absence creates, not only in the hearts of his command but in the army with which he has served in so distinguished a manner," Carr continued. "He had become endeared to all under him, around him, and to many above, through his honest kindness, amiability, and steady friendship. Gentleness and courage undaunted marked him as commander and leader. Endowed with sound judgment, actuated by a burning patriotism, impelled by a fiery ardor, his military career has appeared a success."[74]

In an aside, Berry's death gave his senior officer, Brig. Gen. Joseph W. Revere, temporary command of the brigade. Revere, a grandson of the legendary patriot Paul Revere, retreated with a portion of the brigade rather than attacking. The movement ultimately resulted in Revere's court-martial and dismissal from the service.

"This morning our army suffered an almost irreparable loss in the death of . . . Berry," Pvt. John W. Haley of the 17th Maine wrote in his journal that night. "When I say that General Berry was loved by this brigade, I use no idle phrase," he related, adding that seeing the stricken general being assisted to the rear was "a sad sight to us who fairly idolized him. He was our general from our own state, and we were justly proud."[75]

The story of the death of Brig. Gen. Edmund Kirby is tragically unique.

Kirby, twenty-three, was a New Yorker and a grandson of Gen. Jacob Brown, commander-in-chief of the U.S. Army from 1815 until his death in 1828. He also was a cousin of Confederate general Edmund Kirby Smith. Kirby graduated West Point in May 1861 and was immediately assigned to the 1st U.S. Artillery, being promoted to first lieutenant days later. He commanded a battery section and later the battery itself in all the major battles in the East leading up to Chancellorsville.[76]

On May 3, the young lieutenant was involved in the chaotic battle as the Union army was driven back. Maj. Gen. Darius Couch, commander of the U.S. II Corps, sent to the rear to bring up artillery to make a stand near the Chancellor house, but the roads were so clogged with troops and wagons that the guns couldn't move forward. General Meade of the V Corps, however, sent Couch the 5th Maine Battery, which wheeled into position behind the house along the road to the United States Ford.

The artillery began to bang away, but Confederate cannons answered with well-aimed fire, killing or wounding all of the battery's officers and many of the gunners. Couch called on "the gallant Kirby" to command the guns, his own battery stalled somewhere in the traffic jam.[77]

Kirby's thigh was shattered by a case shot fragment shortly afterward. Some of his men prepared to carry him to the rear, but Kirby shouted, "No! Take off that gun first." Kirby was taken to a military hospital in Washington where he lingered, "condemned to death by a wound which in World War II would have been considered routine," historian Ezra Warner noted. President Lincoln commissioned him as a brigadier general of volunteers "in recognition of his brilliant abilities, undaunted courage, and faithful service."[78]

But Kirby died on the day of his appointment, May 28, 1863, making him one of the youngest and briefest generals. In a page one note about his passing, the *New York Times* stated that he was promoted due to his "brilliant bravery" at Chancellorsville.[79]

Kirby was interred in his hometown of Brownville, New York.

┅┅ ≡♦≡ ┅┅

A day after Berry's death and Kirby's wounding, the Union III Corps would sustain the loss of another division commander. Maj. Gen. Amiel W. Whipple, forty-six, was a native of Greenwich, Massachusetts, who had been a teacher before being appointed to West Point. He graduated from the Military Academy in 1841, ranking fifth in a class that would include twenty-two Civil War generals, blue and gray. As an officer of topographical engineers, he helped survey the United States' boundaries with Canada and Mexico as well as serving in Arizona Territory and on the Great Lakes. Whipple had been in action at First Bull Run and served in the Washington defenses, being commissioned a brigadier general of volunteers in April 1862. Assigned to command the 3rd Division of Sickles's III Corps, Whipple saw minor service at Fredericksburg before being immersed in his first—and last—major battle at Chancellorsville.[80]

On May 4, Whipple was directing his troops as they erected field works near Sickles's headquarters amid the fire of Confederate sharpshooters. "They [the Rebels] had fired at and hit about every white or gray horse standing about," stated a May 10 *New York Times* account. "They perhaps thought it was the headquarters of Gen. Hooker, and that the white horses were his."[81]

One sniper perched in a tree was especially troublesome. "This sharpshooter had annoyed our officers very much, firing at those who seemed to him to be prominent, and whom he could readily single out," the *New York Herald* said.[82]

Sickles ordered Whipple to send some men (Berdan's Sharpshooters, according to newspaper accounts) forward to deal with the enemy riflemen. Sitting on his horse about one hundred feet to the rear of Sickles and his staff, Whipple was writing an order to dislodge the snipers when a bullet suddenly tore into the small of the general's back, barely missing his spine. Some accounts say he was hit in the stomach, the bullet exiting near his backbone. The May 8 *Herald* reported that as Whipple fell, a Union marksman spotted the sniper and fired. "The rebel sharpshooter fell from the tree a corpse."[83]

Taken to Washington, Whipple died on May 7, the same day he was appointed major general to rank from May 3. Sickles wrote in his battle report that "the brave and accomplished Brig. Gen. A. W. Whipple . . . had fallen, mortally wounded, while directing in person the construction of field-works in his front. . . . The gallantry of Whipple was gracefully acknowledged by his promotion before his wound proved to be mortal."[84]

Sickles continued: "The fall of Berry and Whipple deprived them of the opportunity of doing justice to the conspicuous merit and gallantry of their respective staffs. . . . The chivalrous Berry proved but too soon how well he had deserved the highest rank in our service." In a less than serious note, Maine private Haley wrote that Whipple's dirty uniform should have shielded him. "How any bullet ever pierced General Whipple's armor of dirt is a mystery of mysteries. I considered him perfectly safe from any missile weighing less than a ton, having a casing of dirt of unknown thickness supposed to be invulnerable."[85]

Berry's body was embalmed in Washington before it was buried at Achorn Cemetery in Rockland. Whipple was interred at South Cemetery in Portsmouth, New Hampshire, his wife's home.

CHAPTER 11

Mississippi Mourning and South Carolina

CONFEDERATE BRIGADIER GENERAL LLOYD TILGHMAN
Champion Hill, May 16, 1863

With a fought-out Confederate army streaming away in defeat at Champion Hill, Mississippi, on May 16, 1863, Brig. Gen. Lloyd Tilghman's Rebel brigade was ordered to hold as a rearguard at all costs. Tilghman did his duty—but at the cost of his life.

For more than two weeks before the fury at Champion Hill, the Rebels had been looking for any way to thwart the drive of the Federal army under Maj. Gen. Ulysses S. Grant, who was moving ever closer to the vital Confederate stronghold of Vicksburg on the Mississippi River. After the battle of Port Gibson south of Vicksburg on May 1, Grant had marched to the northeast, flicking aside a weaker Confederate force at Raymond eleven days later and forcing the Rebels to evacuate Jackson, the state capital, which Grant occupied on May 14.

From Jackson, the Yankees were in a prime position to strike Vicksburg, some fifty miles to the west, where they hoped to bag an isolated Confederate army under Lt. Gen. John C. Pemberton in addition to taking the city. Gen. Joseph Johnston had been sent to Mississippi but did not have enough Rebels to prevent Grant from taking Jackson. Johnston ordered Pemberton to drive east and attack the Yankees, but Grant got wind of the plan from a Union spy posing as a Rebel courier. Johnston was somewhere north of Jackson with a few thousand soldiers, but Grant knew that Pemberton posed the main threat. He realized that if he could destroy or

Confederate brigadier general
Lloyd Tilghman.
LIBRARY OF CONGRESS

seriously injure Pemberton's army he would have a much easier time taking Vicksburg.

Grant sent the XIII Corps of Maj. Gen. John A. McClernand and the XVII Corps of Maj. Gen. James B. McPherson—some 32,000 men—west on a collision course with Pemberton's 18,000 butternuts. The armies faced off on the morning of May 16, 1863, in the wooded ridges and gullies at Champion Hill, a rural plateau named for the Sidney Champion family who lived in the area.

Among Pemberton's officers was Lloyd Tilghman, a handsome forty-seven-year-old Marylander who led a brigade in Maj. Gen. William Loring's division. Tilghman was an 1836 West Point graduate who spent most of his prewar career as a railroad construction engineer, also serving in the Mexican War. Joining the Confederacy and promoted to brigadier in October 1861, he was in command at Fort Henry when it fell in February 1862. After his exchange that fall, he led a brigade at Corinth, and had been active in the Mississippi theater of operations ever since. One of Tilghman's officers later said of him that while he was "cool, collected and observant, he commanded the entire respect and confidence of every officer and soldier under him."[1]

Pemberton deployed his men at almost a right angle on Champion Hill and adjoining ridges, a battle line about three miles long overlooking Jackson Creek. Tilghman's men, along with the rest of Loring's command and Brig. John Bowen's division, composed the Confederate right flank, facing east and guarding the Raymond Road. The battle ignited with skirmishing about 7 A.M., and erupted in earnest before noon as two U.S. infantry divisions attacked Pemberton's left. Outnumbered and outflanked, the Rebels pulled back, and very quickly their entire position was in danger of destruction.

When Pemberton called desperately for reinforcements from his right, Bowen's division was rushed to the breaking point and made what historian Edwin Bearss describes as "one of the magnificent charges of the war."[2] Bowen's men halted the Federals and sent them reeling back off Champion Hill. But a fresh Union division and massed artillery cracked Bowen's impetus just short of capturing Grant's headquarters. In the back-and-forth fighting, the crest of Champion Hill changed hands three times before the overmatched Rebels gave way. By about 5 P.M. the Confederates were in retreat, an orderly withdrawal at first, but the federals soon routed the Confederates.

Tilghman was ordered to hold the Raymond Road until sundown while the rest of the army escaped to the west across Baker's Creek, over which engineers had erected a makeshift bridge.

Wearing a new uniform, Tilghman, on foot, joined the 1st Mississippi Light Artillery battery of Capt. James Cowan on a rise near the creek. Several artillery officers were mounted, making them conspicuous targets for Union sharpshooters, and Tilghman told them to dismount. He said to Cowan, "They are shooting pretty close to us, and I do not know whether they are shooting at your fine grey horse or my new uniform," according to E. T. Eggleston, a battery orderly sergeant. Tilghman's brigade also was being slammed by enemy artillery on the Coker house ridge where Tilghman had been posted before pulling back.[3]

About 5:30 P.M., Tilghman was standing behind Cowan's cannoneers, directing a change in the elevation of a gun when he was wounded by a shell fragment from a Union artillery round, the shard striking him in the chest and knifing through his body. He died moments later.

Eggleston gives a slightly different account, claiming that Tilghman sighted a 12-pound Napoleon and was standing on a little knoll, with binoculars raised, watching for the effect of his aim when he was fatally wounded by a solid shot.[4]

Some accounts state that the general was almost sliced in half by a fragment from a shell that exploded about fifty feet in front of him. The round then killed an officer's horse just to the rear.

Tilghman's young son, Lloyd Tilghman Jr., arrived at his father's side moments after the general was hit. "I shall never forget the touching scene

when with grief and lamentations he cast himself on his dying and unconscious father," Eggleston recalled. "Those of us who witnessed this distress-
ing scene shed tears of sympathy for the bereaved son and of sorrow for our
fallen hero, the chivalrous and beloved Tilghman."[5]

Pemberton wrote of Tilghman's rearguard action: "It was in the execution of this important trust, which could not have been confided to a fitter
man, that the lamented general bravely lost his life."[6]

When he was slain, Tilghman's Rebels were hotly engaged with the
Union brigade of Brig. Gen. Stephen G. Burbridge of the 10th Division in
McClernand's corps. The Federals claimed that a cannon shot from Bur-
bridge's artillery, either the Chicago Mercantile Battery or the 17th Ohio
Battery, killed Tilghman.

That night, Tilghman's son accompanied his father's body to Vicksburg. Behind them the Confederates counted their casualties at Champion
Hill at over 3,800 while Grant's losses were about 2,400. It had been a crucial Union victory because it kept Pemberton and Johnston from uniting
their forces against Grant and also forced Pemberton back to Vicksburg
where his army was essentially trapped. Tilghman's brigade would be
assigned to Brig. Gen. John Adams who himself would die at Franklin
about eighteen months later. Tilghman was buried in Vicksburg, but would
eventually be laid to rest in New York City's Woodlawn Cemetery.[7]

In defeat, the sullen Rebels still had heartened praise for Tilghman,
Loring stating:

> The bold stand of this [Tilghman's] brigade under the lamented
> hero saved a large portion of the army. It is befitting that I should
> speak of the death of the gallant and accomplished Tilghman.
> Quick and bold in the execution of his plans, he fell in the midst
> of a brigade that loved him well, after repulsing a powerful enemy
> in deadly fight, struck by cannon-shot. A brigade wept over the
> dying hero; alike beautiful as it was touching.[8]

Another of Loring's brigadiers, Abraham Buford, wrote of Tilghman:
"I would offer my tribute of respect to his gallant bearing, and his noble
devotion and untiring energy in behalf of our cause, alike on the field of
battle and in the private circle."[9]

Col. A. E. Reynolds of the 26th Mississippi, who assumed temporary
command of Tilghman's brigade, echoed their sentiments: "The tears shed
by his men . . . and the grief felt by his entire brigade, are the proudest
tribute that can be given the gallant dead."[10]

UNION BRIGADIER GENERAL EDWARD P. CHAPIN
Port Hudson, May 27, 1863

On the morning of May 27, 1863, Union assault troops readied for an attack on Port Hudson, a Confederate stronghold on the Mississippi River. Among the Federals was Col. Edward P. Chapin, a thirty-one-year-old New Yorker who would die this day, earning a posthumous promotion to brigadier general months later. Chapin commanded the 1st Brigade in Maj. Gen. Christopher Augur's 1st Division in Maj. Gen. Nathaniel Banks's XIX Corps.

Next to Vicksburg, Port Hudson was the most important Rebel bastion on the Mississippi and also guarded the mouth of the Red River. The town was defended by about 7,000 Confederates led by Maj. Gen. Franklin Gardner. These Rebels were hunkered in batteries on bluffs overlooking the Mississippi and in more than four miles of earthworks guarding Port Hudson's land approaches.

A native of Waterloo, New York, Chapin was the son of a Presbyterian minister and was an attorney in Buffalo when the war began. His experience with the local militia earned him a captaincy in the 44th New York. Promoted to major, he was seriously wounded at Yorktown, recovering to be commissioned colonel of the 116th New York in July 1862. His regiment, composed of his New York, Maine, and Massachusetts troops, had served in Baltimore's defenses and under Banks in Mississippi prior to Chapin being given command of his brigade, a few weeks before his death.[11]

On the morning of May 27, Banks launched a general assault, the fighting swirling amid stands of magnolias, thick underbrush, and fallen timber cut by the Rebels. Augur's men were on the left side of the Union line. Chapin was especially conspicuous in his dress coat and Panama hat.

"At the word Chapin's brigade moved forward with great gallantry, but was soon caught and cruelly punished in the impassable abatis," a Union officer wrote.[12]

Despite a murderous fire of grape and musketry, Chapin and some of his men reached a ditch below the enemy parapet. Here Chapin was shot in the head and killed instantly.

The attack failed and Banks began siege operations the next day. Another assault on June 14 also was repulsed. Still, when Vicksburg fell on July 4, it became a mere question of time before Port Hudson would follow. His men eating mules and rats, Gardner surrendered on July 9, the forty-eight-day siege the longest in American history.

Chapin, meanwhile had been buried in Waterloo's Maple Grove Cemetery. Four months after his death, he was posthumously promoted to brigadier general to rank from the date of his fall.[13]

CONFEDERATE BRIGADIER GENERALS
ISHAM W. GARROTT AND MARTIN E. GREEN
Vicksburg, June 1863

The Union siege of Vicksburg was in its third week by mid June 1863 when the first of two Confederate generals was killed in the trenches. The once beautiful city reigning over the Mississippi River had been transformed into hell's full acre by this campaign of attrition.

The sizzling Mississippi sun cooked Yankee and Rebel with no regard for causes while hundreds of Union artillery shells hurtled into the city, killing or maiming soldiers and civilians alike. Some 77,000 Federals, led by Ulysses S. Grant, formed a tight and deadly half moon around Vicksburg with U.S. gunboats prowling the river above and below the city and a strong force of Yankees just across the Mississippi in Louisiana.

In Vicksburg, John Pemberton had less than 30,000 Rebels to defend the city, many of whose residents had dug caves in hillsides to try to escape the bombardment. Food supplies quickly vanished, and even mule and horsemeat were beginning to run scarce. Snipers on both sides picked off any luckless soldier foolish enough to show himself over the rival earthworks.

Against this backdrop of total war, a Rebel officer was slain in the front lines, unaware of his promotion to general two weeks earlier. Col. Isham W. Garrott's commission to brigadier did not arrive in Vicksburg until after his June 17 death. Garrott was a North Carolinian who had been a peacetime attorney and legislator in Marion, Alabama He later helped recruit the 20th Alabama Infantry, and was named its colonel. The 20th was posted at Mobile in 1861–62 before being transferred to Mississippi as part of Brig. Gen. Edward Tracy's brigade.[14]

The forty-seven-year-old Garrott led his regiment at the battles of Port Gibson (where he temporarily took brigade command when Tracy was killed) and Champion Hill, but the Confederate forces had been unable to stymie Grant. They were steadily shoved back toward Vicksburg, the ultimate prize savored by these Federals.

When Grant began tightening the noose around the city in mid May, Garrott was a common sight in the earthworks, encouraging his men. On June 17 he was on the skirmish line and asked a soldier if he could borrow his musket to fire at the enemy. According to at least one account, Garrott raised the rifle to his shoulder and was aiming when a Federal bullet ripped into his chest. Without a word he crumpled and died.[15]

Brig. Gen. Stephen D. Lee had taken command of the brigade when Tracy was killed at Port Gibson on May 1. In a July 25 report he described

Garrott as "the pure patriot and gallant soldier" who fell "in the fearless discharge of his duties. Respected and loved by all who knew him, a more attentive and vigilant officer was not in our service." Garrott's division commander, Maj. Gen. Carter L. Stevenson, called the Carolinian "a true and gifted patriot." Garrott was buried in Vicksburg, supposedly near a friend's home, and was later reinterred at the Old City Cemetery.[16]

◆─ ▗◆▖ ─◆

Like Garrott, Rebel brigadier general Martin E. Green was frequently in the defensive lines, checking the progress and movements of the blue-coats across the way. Green sustained a slight wound on June 25, and was unable to make his rounds the next day when the Yankees along a portion of his front began digging an approach.

Green, forty-eight, led a brigade of Arkansas and Missouri infantry in John Bowen's division, and had boasted that the bullet had not yet been molded that would kill him. A native Virginian, he had settled in Missouri where he and his brothers established a sawmill in Lewis County. One of his brothers, James Stephen Green, would later become a U.S. senator. When the war started, Green organized a Missouri cavalry regiment and joined Sterling Price. Green fought at Lexington, Montana; Pea Ridge; Iuka; and Corinth, being commissioned a brigadier in July 1862. He had been very active in the Mississippi fighting leading up to Vicksburg's siege.[17]

About 9:30 A.M. on June 27, Green was peering out of the defenses at a Yankee sap, or narrow trench, about sixty yards from his line. Suddenly, he was shot in the head by a Union sharpshooter, dying moments later. "He was in the ditches, as was his custom," recalled Col. Thomas Dockery of the 19th Arkansas Infantry, "reconnoitering the positions of the enemy along his front. . . . Missouri has lost another of their bravest champions, the South one of its ablest defenders. . . . His soldiers regarded him with that reverence due a father, and many a tear was shed at his fall."[18]

Capt. John Bell of the 12th Arkansas Sharpshooters recalled that Green arrived at his fort that morning accompanied by two staff officers. "I warned him not to look through the portholes until we fired a few shots to keep the Yankees down," wrote Bell. "He failed to heed the warning, and at the second porthole through which he looked was shot and instantly killed. He was a gallant soldier and a gentleman."[19]

Bowen wrote a report a few hours later mourning Green's demise: "Devoted to our cause, without fear or reproach, his loss will be deeply felt by his entire command." Green's body was at first buried in the private lot of the George Marshall family in Vicksburg's city cemetery, but the present-day location of his remains is unclear. Six deserters from the 19th Arkansas came into the Federal lines the next day, bringing word of Green's death and the near-starvation conditions among the garrison and citizenry.[20]

The *Charleston Mercury* reported the "melancholy" news of Green's death on July 23, describing him as being "looked upon by his men, not as a General, but a father to his brigade. Many noble sons of Missouri have fallen during this war, but none of her martyrs . . . will be spoken of in more glowing terms, or more deserved praise."[21]

Green and Garrott were at least spared the final indignity of Vicksburg's fall. Food and morale at the barrel's bottom, Pemberton met with Grant on July 3 to discuss surrender terms, and on Independence Day 1863, some 29,500 Rebel defenders marched out of their works and stacked arms. Even as they did so, a thousand miles to the north Robert E. Lee was preparing his wrecked army for the retreat from Gettysburg after three days of monumental battle. The twin losses at Vicksburg and Gettysburg were defeats from which the Confederacy would never recover.

Pemberton's defeated Rebels would also mourn the death of thirty-two-year-old Gen. John Bowen who succumbed to illness on July 13. Bowen developed dysentery during the siege and died near Raymond after being paroled.

Pemberton described Green and Bowen as "two of the best soldiers in the Confederate service. . . . Always faithful, zealous, and brave, they fell as became them in the discharge of their duty. General Green died with a bullet in his brain upon the lines he had so long and so gallantly defended."[22]

UNION BRIGADIER GENERAL GEORGE C. STRONG
Fort Wagner, Morris Island, South Carolina, July 18, 1863

When Union troops splashed ashore under fire at Morris Island near Charleston, South Carolina, on July 10, 1863, Brig. Gen. George C. Strong was one of the first men out of the boats. Less than three weeks later, he would lie wounded and dying in New York City.

Strong, thirty, was born in Vermont, but due to his father's death had been raised by an uncle in Massachusetts. Earning an appointment to West Point, he graduated in 1857 as an ordnance officer and was posted at arsenals from New York to Alabama before the war. He had served on the staffs of Irvin McDowell and George McClellan and later helped organize Ben Butler's campaign resulting in the capture of New Orleans. Active in Louisiana between leaves due to illness, he was promoted brigadier in

Union brigadier general
George C. Strong.
LIBRARY OF CONGRESS

March 1863 (to rank from the previous November) and was sent to fight on the South Carolina coast.[23]

Strong commanded the 1st Brigade of Brig. Gen. Truman Seymour's 1st Division. His brigade of Connecticut, Maine, New Hampshire, New York, and Pennsylvania regiments also contained the 54th Massachusetts Colored Troops under Col. Robert Gould Shaw. Strong had been in the first wave when a Federal force gained a foothold on Morris Island during the amphibious assault on July 10. The island was important because it guarded the southern approaches to Charleston Harbor. Control of Morris would put the Yankees within siege-gun range of Charleston itself, but the Rebels were not quick to cede possession. While the Federals soon controlled two-thirds of this sandy spit, they still had to seize Battery Wagner, an earthen fort defended by about 1,800 Confederates.

Maj. Gen. Quincy Gillmore, commander of Union troops in the Charleston area, soon planned another attack for July 18 using Strong's brigade as the sword point. Marshy ground and a creek near the fort meant that the storming party would have to advance along a narrow stretch of beach and then approach Wagner along a strip of sand only a few hundred feet wide. Ships of the Union fleet off Charleston and land batteries pummeled the fort for several hours that afternoon in preparation for the infantry assault, which was set for dusk. Finally the bluecoats advanced, the troops of Strong's 54th Massachusetts leading the way and quickly coming under a terrible fire.

Minutes before the assault, Strong, accompanied by staff and orderlies, rode to the head of the attack column. The general, "mounted upon a spirited gray horse, in full uniform, with a yellow handkerchief bound around his neck," addressed his men, Capt. Luis Emilio of the 54th recalled. Emilio related Strong's brief encouragement:

> Boys, I am a Massachusetts man, and I know you will fight for the honor of the State. I am sorry you must go into the fight tired and hungry, but the men in the fort are tired too. There are but three hundred behind those walls, and they have been fighting all day. Don't fire a musket on the way up, but go in and bayonet them at their guns.

Strong then called for the regimental color bearer, saying, "If this man should fall, who will lift the flag and carry it on?" Standing close by, Shaw pulled a cigar from his mouth and said quietly, "I will," a response that drew wild cheers from his soldiers.[24]

The Yankees surged ahead, now enduring musketry from Wagner's defenders, who had emerged from their bombproof shelters after the shelling, but the 54th managed to plant its colors on the parapet despite heavy hand-to-hand fighting.

Strong was wounded in the thigh by a musket ball and was helped to the rear. He was being carried to an ambulance when Gillmore met him and inquired if he was badly hurt. "No General, I think not; only a severe flesh wound in the hip," Strong replied. The Federals managed to occupy a portion of the fort for about two hours before being compelled to withdraw. "The repulse was complete, and our loss severe, especially in officers," Gillmore stated.[25]

Captain Emilio added, "General Strong accompanied his column, and, as always, exhibited the utmost bravery." Strong, one of about 1,500 Union casualties in the attack, initially was treated in a field hospital on Morris Island. One observer wrote of the general lying on a stretcher there, "grieving all the while for the poor fellows who lay uncared for on the battlefield."[26]

Strong was taken that night to a Federal hospital in Beaufort, South Carolina, where he received "excellent attendance," Gillmore reported. "But he was seized with a yearning desire to go home, and, without my knowledge, took the first steamer for the North."[27]

After granting at least two interviews with New York war correspondents in which he praised the work of the 54th Massachusetts, Strong did indeed board the steam transport *Arago*, which left Port Royal, South Carolina, on July 23, bound for New York City. The three-day voyage was not without adventure, however. On the second day out, the *Arago* happened upon another vessel, whose crew immediately began tossing bales of cotton overboard.

Suspicious, the *Arago*'s captain overtook the other ship, sent aboard an armed party and found that the ship was the blockade runner *Emma* trying to reach Bermuda with a cargo of cotton and turpentine. With the *Emma* in tow, the *Arago* reached New York on July 26, with a weakening Strong being taken to the home of his father-in-law, W. A. Budd, to recuperate. His condition steadily declining, he died at the Budd house about 3 A.M. on July 30.

"Gen. Strong was a man of intense earnestness of character, of fine intelligence and generous instincts," stated a page one *New York Times* article on July 31 announcing his death. "He was devoted to and accomplished in his profession, and in his death . . . is lost a brave and valued officer."[28]

Gillmore blamed Strong's impetuousness in leaving South Carolina, his wound, and the sea journey for contributing to the general's end: "Being the senior officer on board, the excitement of the trip, aggravated by the chase and capture of a blockade-runner, brought on lockjaw, of which he died shortly after reaching New York."[29]

The day after Strong's death, Congress passed his appointment to major general of volunteers, to rank from the date of his fall at Fort Wagner. He was buried in Brooklyn's Greenwood Cemetery.[30]

CHAPTER 12

Gettysburg

CONFEDERATE MAJOR GENERAL WILLIAM DORSEY
PENDER; BRIGADIER GENERALS WILLIAM BARKSDALE,
RICHARD B. GARNETT, LEWIS A. ARMISTEAD,
PAUL J. SEMMES, AND JAMES J. PETTIGREW

UNION MAJOR GENERAL JOHN F. REYNOLDS;
BRIGADIER GENERALS ELON J. FARNSWORTH,
STRONG VINCENT, STEPHEN H. WEED, AND
SAMUEL K. ZOOK
Gettysburg Campaign, July 1863
Gettysburg.

Like other obscure places where armies collide and the fates of nations
are decided, this Pennsylvania village became the bloody canvas for America's destiny in July 1863.

In mid June, Robert E. Lee's gray hosts speared north, invading Pennsylvania in a campaign that would cost the South six generals and likely the
war. Five Union commanders paid with their lives to make it so.

Lee had launched this offensive to win a decisive battle on Union soil,
as well as to drive the enemy out of Virginia, a similar strategy to the strike
into Maryland less than a year earlier. Lee knew that his 75,000-man Army
of Northern Virginia would be outnumbered on the enemy's turf, but long
odds had rarely stopped him before. Scattered over the Pennsylvania countryside, his forces began concentrating near Gettysburg after he learned on

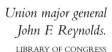

*Union major general
John F. Reynolds.*
LIBRARY OF CONGRESS

June 29 that the U.S. Army of the Potomac was moving to intercept him. These Federals, some 95,000 in all, had been whipped at Chancellorsville, but had a new and tough commander in Maj. Gen. George G. Meade, who had replaced Joe Hooker.

Lead elements of the armies clashed along McPherson's Ridge just west of Gettysburg on July 1, and both sides rushed troops toward the quiet crossroads town of about 2,400.

About 8 A.M. on July 1, Union cavalry under Brig. Gen. John Buford clashed with the Rebels' advance elements west of Gettysburg. Federal major general John F. Reynolds was there as well, riding ahead of his corps, and he dispatched orders for his lead division of the I Corps to hurry forward. He also sent a message to Meade, stating, "The enemy is advancing in strong force, and I fear he will get to the heights beyond the town before I can. I will fight him inch by inch, and if driven into the town I will barricade the streets, and hold him back as long as possible." Meade read the note and said to some of his aides, "Good! That is just like Reynolds, he will hold out till the bitter end."[1]

Watching the masses of butternut infantry in the distance, Reynolds, forty-two, had little time to think of his sweetheart and the lovers' ring he wore on a chain around his neck. He would be among the first—and certainly the highest ranking—of the thousands of bluecoats to die here, falling only about fifty miles from his birthplace in Lancaster, Pennsylvania. An 1841 West Point graduate, he served several years of garrison duty on the Atlantic coast before being sent to Texas. He was twice brevetted for gallantry in the Mexican War and after further frontier service had been appointed commandant at the Military Academy less than a year before the Civil War began. Assigned as an officer of the 14th U.S. Infantry in May 1861, Reynolds was promoted to brigadier general of volunteers in August. He led a brigade during the Peninsular Campaign and was captured in June 1862, but was exchanged in early August. Reynolds commanded a division at Second Bull Run, and in the Maryland Campaign led the called-up Pennsylvania militia to oppose the state's expected invasion. Given command of the Union I Corps and promoted major general in November 1862, he saw action at Fredericksburg. After Chancellorsville, Reynolds is said to have been offered command of the Army of the Potomac, replacing Joseph Hooker, but declined, because he felt Washington would not allow him enough freedom to command. Meade, who had been a junior officer to Reynolds, did accept the army's reins. Reynolds was assigned command of the army's left wing composed of the I Corps, now under Maj. Gen. Abner Doubleday, Maj. Gen. Dan Sickles's III Corps, and Maj. Gen. O. O. Howard's XI Corps.[2]

At Gettysburg, the first of Reynolds's units began arriving on the scene about 10 A.M., the general cursing and gesturing to push them into positions on either side of the Cashtown road, along which Rebels of A. P. Hill's corps were moving. Near the northeast corner of a group of trees on the John Herbst farm, Reynolds was bringing up the 2nd Wisconsin, the lead regiment of the Iron Brigade. The Wisconsin men swept by him to engage Southerners of Brig. Gen. James Archer's brigade who were pressing near. "For God's sake! Forward, my brave boys—forward!" Reynolds shouted to his men.[3]

Union major Joseph Rosengarten recalled that Reynolds was "a glorious picture of the best type of military leader, superbly mounted and horse and man sharing in the excitement of the shock of battle." He added that, "Reynolds was, of course, a shining mark to the enemy's sharpshooters."[4]

Reynolds was on his horse behind the 2nd and was turned, looking to see if the rest of the brigade was coming up, when he was shot about 11:15 A.M. The bullet struck him behind the right ear and he fell to the ground face down. Members of his staff scrambled to the general and turned him on his back, but he died moments later. Sgt. Charles Veil, Reynolds's eighteen-year-old orderly, helped drag the general's body out of the line of fire and then went to find an ambulance to carry it to the rear.

Most accounts state that Reynolds was the target of a Rebel rifleman firing from a barn at the edge of some nearby woods, but Rosengarten claimed that the sniper was "hidden in the branches of a tree almost overhead" which does not appear to be the case.[5]

Alfred Waud sketch of the death of John Reynolds. LIBRARY OF CONGRESS

One contemporary historian noted that the death wound, "probably high in the spinal cord or in the medulla oblongata," might have been prevented on a battlefield of the future: "A World War II type of helmet would probably have saved his life."[6]

The *New York Herald* reported that when Reynolds was hit, he fell against Capt. William H. Wilcox of his staff, who was riding beside him. The general exclaimed, "Good God, Wilcox, I am killed!" At almost the same time, Wilcox's horse was shot from under him, the captain sustaining severe bruises when he plunged to earth.[7]

Doubleday was on the field by now and soon learned of Reynolds's fall. "I took my position behind the left wing," he related. "I had hardly done so when I learned, with deep sorrow, that our brave and lamented . . . Reynolds had just been shot, and was no more." Doubleday added that it was a "melancholy event." Howard, despite Doubleday's claim that "The whole burden of the battle was thus suddenly thrown upon me," assumed command of Reynolds's wing.[8]

Soldiers initially carried the general's corpse on a blanket hung from two muskets to the Lutheran Theological Seminary. Later it was transported to a house on the Emmitsburg Road, then to Meade's headquarters by ambulance. Word of Reynolds's death passed rapidly through the ranks, but his men had no time for mourning as they were thrown into the battle line. Archer's Confederates, meanwhile, had been captured almost en masse and some of these Rebs were being hustled to the Federal rear as Reynolds's body was carried by them in the ambulance. Rosengarten wrote that the Southerners' "respectful conduct was in itself the highest tribute they could pay to him who had thus fallen." Thomas Westmoreland, a Rebel in the 6th Alabama, claimed that he was captured near the spot where Reynolds fell, the Federals telling him, "You killed our general," which Westmoreland denied.[9]

At the time, a puzzling aspect of Reynolds's death was revealed when one of his aides, Maj. William Riddle, was examining the body. Around the general's neck on a silver chain was a gold ring shaped like two clasped hands, with the engraving "Dear Kate" and a Roman Catholic medal. The inscription and the fact that Reynolds's West Point ring was missing from his finger led Riddle to believe that the bachelor general was romantically involved.[10]

Meade learned that Reynolds was either dead or badly wounded about 1 P.M. and immediately sent orders to Maj. Gen. W. S. Hancock to take overall command on the battlefield. The shock so overwhelmed Meade that he could barely speak.

As the battle heightened, Union troops rushing toward the action were sobered by the sight of the ambulance bearing Reynolds's body and accompanied by several aides, making its way to the rear. Many of the soldiers pulled off their caps in respect and one Yank recalled the look of the escort in the little procession: "Their faces showed plainly enough what load their vehicle carried." The soldier added that Reynolds's fall "affected us much, for he was one of the *soldier* generals of the army."[11]

Howard described Reynolds as "a noble commander [who was] long a personal friend." His loss was a "grievous cost to the army and the country," wrote Union artillery Brig. Gen. Henry Hunt. "It was not, however, until by his promptitude and gallantry he had determined the decisive field of the war, and had opened brilliantly a battle which required three days of hard fighting to close with a victory."[12]

Col. Henry Morrow of the 24th Michigan in Reynolds's command was wounded and captured on that first day. He had the chance to talk to several Confederates about Reynolds's death before he was released when the Rebels retreated from Gettysburg. "The death of Major-General Reynolds was well known to the enemy, and the highest opinions of his skill and bravery were freely expressed," Morrow wrote.[13]

Some Confederates credited gunners of Capt. Edward Marye's Fredericksburg Artillery, a battery in Maj. W. J. Pegram's battalion attached to

Henry Heth's division, with the shot that killed Reynolds. "A few shots from Pegram's battalion [Marye's Battery] scattered the cavalry vedettes," Heth reported. "One of the first shells fired by Pegram mortally wounded Major-General Reynolds, then in command of the force at Gettysburg." Rebel captain E. B. Brunson, commander of the army's Reserve Artillery Battalion, wrote in his report that Marye's guns were run forward, unlimbered in the road and began blasting at woods to the left of the pike where a "reconnoitering party of the enemy" was posted. "It was at this time and point that Major-General Reynolds, of the Yankee army, is reported to have been killed," Brunson wrote. Marye's men fired about ten rounds before limbering up and moving forward.[14]

In a postwar account, C. R. Fleet, who belonged to Marye's unit, recalled that the battery "fired into a group of officers, some of whom fell and one of whom was carried off on a litter. We supposed afterwards that this was General Reynolds, a gallant Federal officer, who did receive his death wound from an artillery shell." Rebels from Archer's 1st Tennessee also claimed to have killed Reynolds.[15]

The Rebels were closer to Gettysburg and more numerous, and they gradually pushed the Yankees back, paying with heavy losses. In the afternoon, the Confederate corps of Lt. Gen. Richard Ewell attacked the U.S. XII Corps north of town, A. P. Hill increasing the pressure with renewed assaults on McPherson's Ridge, near the scene of Reynolds's death. With much of Meade's army still to reach the field, the Federals fell back through the village and established defensive positions on high ground south of Gettysburg.

If the stage was set for the defining battle of the war, Reynolds, who should have been one of the primary players, was beyond caring. His body was taken by ambulance to Uniontown where it was embalmed, and then transported by train, via Baltimore and Philadelphia, to Lancaster for burial on July 4. A *New York Herald* correspondent viewed the remains in Baltimore and wrote: "The left side of the face and neck are much disfigured by his fall after being shot."[16]

It was in Philadelphia, at the home of Reynolds's married sister, Jennie Reynolds Gildersleeve, that the mystery of the "Dear Kate" ring was solved. Attractive twenty-four-year-old Catherine Mary Hewitt called at the Gildersleeve home and asked to see the general's remains. She revealed that she and Reynolds had met in 1860 when he was posted temporarily in San Francisco and she was a governess for a local family there. Their friendship had blossomed into a romance, but Reynolds had wanted to keep it a secret until the war was over. They had decided that if he survived the conflict they would marry and honeymoon in Europe. Should he die, she had his permission to enter a convent.[17]

He was to have met her family in Philadelphia in the second week of July. Instead, Kate Hewitt found herself entering a convent in Emmitsburg, Maryland, on July 12, about ten miles from the site of her sweetheart's death. The Reynolds family stayed in touch with her for several years, but she left the order in 1868 and they never heard from her again.

* * * ⚎ * *

Most of the remaining armies had arrived by the morning of July 2, the Northerners occupying a hook-shaped line facing east and northeast. Meade's position extended from Culp's Hill on the right to Cemetery Hill and Cemetery Ridge about two miles further to two hills called Big Round Top and Little Round Top. The Southerners were posted along the Hanover Road, looking up at Culp's Hill from Gettysburg and south along Seminary Ridge running almost parallel to the Emmitsburg Pike and Cemetery Ridge.

Between noon and 2 P.M. on July 2, Maj. Gen. Daniel Sickles moved the 11,000 men of his U.S. III Corps off Cemetery Ridge and on to high ground along the Emmitsburg Road. The last of Sickles's men were in position by 4 P.M., forming their salient well in advance of the rest of Meade's lines. On Lee's orders, but after hours of delays, Lt. Gen. James Longstreet attacked the Union left flank late in the afternoon with the divisions of Maj. Gens. John B. Hood and Lafayette McLaws. At about the same time, the Rebel division of Maj. Gen. Richard Anderson of Hill's Corps hit the Union center. There was rabid fighting as Hood's men seized Big Round Top and tried to take Little Round Top, blood puddling on stone amid the rocky slopes. McLaws, meanwhile, was trying to drive out Sickles's bluecoats who were entrenched in a grove of fruit trees that forever after would notoriously be known as the Peach Orchard because of the war savagery there. The boulder-strewn Devil's Den and the Wheatfield also entered the history books this day, their terrain smeared in red.

An unwitting contributor of his life in the Wheatfield butchery was one of McLaws's brigadiers, Paul J. Semmes, a forty-eight-year-old Georgian and a prewar banker and planter. Promoted brigadier general in March 1862, he had been in action on the Virginia peninsula, the Seven Days battles, the Maryland Campaign, Fredericksburg, and Chancellorsville.[18]

Other than these accomplishments, Semmes's fame rose from the fact that he was a first cousin of Raphael Semmes, commander of the renowned raider CSS *Alabama*. Semmes's Georgia Brigade had lost three-quarters of its men at Antietam. In the Wheatfield combat, Semmes was wounded in the thigh, during a counterattack by a U.S. II Corps brigade led by Col. John R. Brooke. The brigadier had carried a tourniquet on his person since early in the war and had not needed it. Gettysburg was different. "The fire of the enemy becoming more fearful than any he had ever witnessed in the many battles through which he had passed unscathed, he took the tourniquet from his bosom, and was holding it in his hand, when he was struck," the *Charleston Mercury* reported.[19]

The minié having penetrated his femoral artery, Semmes's soldiers carried him off the battlefield on a makeshift litter fashioned from a captured U.S. flag, the general likely saving his own life in the minutes after his wounding. "He applied the tourniquet with his own hands, and stopped the hemorrhage until a surgeon could take up the artery, otherwise he must have died in a few minutes," the Mercury said. Of Semmes at Gettysburg, Lee would write that he fought "with the courage that always distinguished him."[20]

The Federals also would lose a brigadier in this sector. Brig. Gen. Samuel K. Zook led the 3rd Brigade of Brig. Gen. John C. Caldwell's 1st Division in the II Corps. Zook, forty-two, was a Pennsylvanian who had spent much of his youth roaming the fields of Valley Forge, where Washington's army had wintered in the American Revolution. Before the war he was active in militia companies, and worked in the Philadelphia office of a telegraph company. A job promotion sent him to New York City where his militia service continued as lieutenant colonel of the 6th New York Militia. After Fort Sumter, he recruited the 57th New York and was commissioned its colonel in October 1861. He fought in the Peninsular Campaign, and at Fredericksburg suffered more than 500 casualties in his brigade, being wounded himself. Promoted brigadier to rank from November 1862, Zook was in combat at Chancellorsville before fate sent him to Gettysburg. A firm disciplinarian, his men also knew him well for his bellowed profanities, despite his Mennonite upbringing.[21]

Late in the afternoon, Zook's men marched south from Cemetery Ridge with the rest of Caldwell's division toward the Wheatfield fighting where II and V Corps troops also entered the fray. With his men on the move, Zook was stopped by one of Sickles's aides who asked the brigadier to come to Sickles's support. Zook rode to Sickles, saw his plight and returned to his command, leading them toward the III Corps' positions.

Longstreet's men, meanwhile, caved in a portion of Brig. Gen. James Barnes's V Corps division and Zook and his brigade soon found their way blocked by Barnes' disorganized troops. Other shifting units also disrupted Zook's advance amid the combat cacophony. On his horse and at the head of his men, Zook was a conspicuous target, but he was more concerned with the immediate obstacle of Barnes's men. "If you can't get out of the way," he shouted, "lie down, and I will march over you." Barnes ordered his men down and, Zook's soldiers marched over them to the battle line.[22]

The general rode into the action across the Wheatfield Road and up the wooded slope of Stony Hill, a rock-strewn little rise that Rebels of Brig. Gen. Joseph Kershaw's brigade were attempting to occupy.

Zook was soon shot in the abdomen—a soldier of Kershaw's 3rd or 7th South Carolina likely pulled the trigger—and he became one of the first casualties of his command. "Alas! Poor Zook soon fell, mortally wounded, and half his brigade perished with him," stated one account.[23]

Capt. Jonathan McCullough of the 140th Pennsylvania saw the general swaying in the saddle and, touching Lt. James Purman with the flat of his sword to get his attention, shouted, "There goes poor Zook." Zook's advance lost its steam when he fell, and the general was carried from the field, steadied in the saddle by an aide, Lt. Charles H. Broom, and a mounted orderly. Another staff officer, Lt. Josiah Favill quickly joined them when he saw Zook was wounded. The general clasped his hand, and said, "It's all up with me, Favill."[24]

Zook was soon placed in an ambulance and a surgeon pronounced that his wound was mortal. He was taken to a house on the Baltimore Pike that was serving as a field hospital and spent the night there amid a throng of other wounded.

The late afternoon was sunny and hot, and McLaws's Confederates who were not yet engaged were antsy for action. Brig. Gen. William Barksdale waited impatiently for the attack order, his long, cotton-white hair whipping about him as he rode among the soldiers of his Mississippi brigade. A Tennessee native, Barksdale, forty-three, had been a U.S. congressman from Mississippi, an attorney, and newspaper editor before secession. A Mexican War veteran, he led a brigade at First Bull Run, and was promoted brigadier in August 1862. He had already established a distinguished combat record in the Army of Northern Virginia before Gettysburg.[25]

Despite fire from a Union battery, the Mississippians occupied themselves by tearing down a rail fence in their front, filling canteens, and gathering cherries. Some helped roll Rebel guns into position to answer the enemy artillery.

Confederate brigadier general
William Barksdale.
LIBRARY OF CONGRESS

Barksdale was more than anxious to make the assault. When Capt. G. B. Lamar Jr., McLaws's aide-de-camp, brought him the order to advance about 6 P.M., Lamar recalled that Barksdale's "face was radiant with joy. He was in front of his brigade, hat off, and his long, white hair reminded me of the 'white plume of Navarre.'"[26] The 1,500 Mississippians moved out of the woods with Barksdale riding in front.

An Alabamian in another brigade noted that "Barksdale threw forward his Mississippians in an unbroken line in the most magnificent charge I witnessed during the war, and led by the gallant Barksdale, who seemed to be fifty yards in front of his brave boys."[27]

The attack swept over the Emmitsburg Road on the northern edges of the Peach Orchard and the Wheatfield, crushing Brig. Gen. Charles Graham's brigade of Sickles's corps. The Rebels had advanced about three quarters of a mile when they rammed into a stout Union defensive line of infantry and artillery dug in on a ridge behind Plum Run. Barksdale's men were somewhat disorganized by the long assault over rough terrain and stalled when they encountered these Federals.

Col. George C. Burling, who commanded a brigade in the III Corps in this sector, saw Barksdale leading his men and assigned a company of riflemen to shoot the enemy officer. Union brigadier general Joseph B. Carr also is said to have issued orders to bring down the Rebel officer on the white horse, whom they believed to be Barksdale.[28]

By this time Barksdale already had been wounded in the left leg by a musket bullet. A cannonball grazed his left foot, but despite his blood loss he did not leave the field. Now he was a marked man with Yank infantry-men drawing a bead on him from only a few yards away. What would prove to be the fatal minié struck Barksdale in the left side of the chest, and he tumbled from the saddle near the breastworks. "We killed or cap-tured everything in front of us until we were near their works," rem-embered J. W. Duke of the 17th Mississippi. "There Gen. Barksdale was shot."[29]

Longstreet had earlier sent one of his staff officers, William Young-blood, to tell Barksdale to press ahead with the stymied assault. When he received the order, Barksdale "put spurs to his horse, dashed a little way along his line, [and] gave an order to charge at double-quick," Youngblood recalled. "I distinctly heard a shot strike him and saw him fall from his horse. No troops were ever commanded by a braver man then General Barksdale."[30]

Before he fell unconscious, Barksdale gasped to Col. Benjamin G. Humphreys of the 21st Mississippi to take charge and pull the brigade back to their lines. Under heavy fire, the Rebels were unable to bring him away, his last words to his retreating men being quoted as "I am killed. Tell my wife and children I died fighting at my post."[31]

Lying near the general as the retreat passed over them was Pvt. J. C. Lloyd of the 13th Mississippi who had been wounded in the arm. Based on his account, Lloyd heard a weak voice and saw Barksdale. He crawled to him and held his canteen to the general's mouth, but it was empty, pierced by a musket ball. Lloyd tried to make his way to the rear to bring up litter bearers, but the Rebels retreated before he could return.[32]

Barksdale was captured by the Federals and carried unconscious on a litter to a field hospital on the Jacob Hummelbaugh farm. At least one report stated that the bluecoats waved their flag over his body when they reclaimed the contested ground.[33]

Barksdale had been shot within twenty yards of the line of the 7th Michigan Volunteers, who recovered two fallen Rebel battle flags near the stricken general. Some accounts state that Col. William T. Nichols of the 14th Vermont learned from a prisoner that Barksdale had been wounded in front of his position. Nichols then sent out a detail, which found the gen-eral and carried him to the hospital.[34]

Union surgeons treated Barksdale, but there appeared to be no chance that he could survive. Sickles's corps was smashed, but the Federals held along Cemetery Ridge, and the battle died out in this sector about dusk.

—◦— ⫘◦⫘ —◦—

Hood's Confederates were coming up the valley between the Round Tops when the V Corps command of Col. Strong Vincent entered Gettysburg legend. "If any one brigade saved George G. Meade's army at Gettysburg, it was Vincent's," wrote historian Ezra Warner. Vincent, twenty-six, commanded the 3rd Brigade, 1st Division, V Corps. He was a Pennsylvanian and Harvard graduate who had been a prewar lawyer in Erie. After serving in the state militia in the conflict's opening months, he was commissioned lieutenant colonel of the 83rd Pennsylvania. He had fought on the Peninsula, but his service had been limited due to a bout with malaria. Named colonel of his regiment in June 1862, Vincent and his men were in the thick of Fredericksburg, suffering some two hundred casualties. Vincent had risen to brigade command after Chancellorsville.[35]

With the rest of Barnes's division, Vincent's men had arrived at Gettysburg that morning and were hustled toward the Union left flank in the afternoon. As Barnes engaged in the Wheatfield, Vincent was held in reserve. About 4 P.M., Vincent flagged down a messenger from Maj. Gen. George Sykes, the V Corps commander, who had orders for Barnes to occupy Little Round Top. Maj. Gen. G. K. Warren, the army's chief engineer, had seen the threat of Hood's movement and was desperately trying to get troops in position to defend the hill.

On his own initiative, Vincent ordered his brigade up the slope. Enduring artillery fire, he posted the 20th Maine on his left, in what amounted to the left end of the entire army. The 83rd Pennsylvania and the 44th New York were in the center while the 16th Michigan composed his right flank, about 1,000 total men under Vincent's command.

No sooner had they deployed when the Rebels—Texans and Alabamians led by Brig. Gens. Jerome Robertson and Evander Law—stormed up out of a ravine, yelling and firing as they surged over the rocks and among the trees toward Vincent's line. The Yankees fought off several charges, but at one point the 16th Michigan gave way. Suddenly, Vincent's position and the army's flank were exposed. The ever-vigilant Warren, however, immediately ordered Brig. Gen. Stephen H. Weed to plug the gap with his V Corps brigade.

Weed, thirty-one, had been a brigadier less than a month. He was a New Yorker, West Point class of 1854, and an artillerist whose prewar Army duties had been out West, in Florida, Kansas, and with the Utah

Expedition. Weed led a battery in the Peninsular Campaign and was in battle at Second Bull Run and during the Antietam Campaign. He commanded the V Corps artillery at Fredericksburg and on June 6, 1863, had been promoted from captain to brigadier general of volunteers. His rise was accompanied by assignment to command a brigade in Brig. Gen. R. B. Ayres's division. Weed's men, with the 140th New York in the lead, charged with unloaded muskets and unfixed bayonets, causing the surprised Rebels to hesitate and pull back.[36]

Vincent was shot in the fighting and confusion of trying to remold this section of his line, the bullet hitting him in the left groin and lodging in his right leg, shattering his thigh bone. He was "rallying this part of his command [and] fell mortally wounded," General Barnes reported. When Vincent fell, Col. James C. Rice of the 44th New York took brigade command.[37]

Weed, meanwhile, had managed to manhandle a six-gun battery of the 5th U.S. Artillery over the rocks to the summit. His colleagues would later recall Weed's words before he went into action: "I lay down my life willingly. . . . I only hope its close will be the dawn of successive victories to our arms and a speedy end to this terrible war."[38]

Weed did not stand much longer than Vincent. He was directing the battery's fire when he was shot in the right arm, the bullet passing into his chest. "A few moments after General Weed . . . had placed his command in position on this ridge, he was mortally wounded on the summit, near the battery," reported Col. Kenner Garrard of the 146th New York Infantry.[39]

The fatal round likely came from a Rebel sharpshooter posted among the rocks of Devil's Den. One of the first to rush to Weed's assistance was Lt. Benjamin F. Rittenhouse who commanded a section of guns in the battery. He bent over Weed, discovering that the general was paralyzed from the shoulders down, Weed telling him, "I am cut in two, I want to see Hazlett."[40]

Rittenhouse immediately sent for the battery commander, Lt. Charles Hazlett, who came quickly, dismounted and knelt next to Weed. Rittenhouse heard Weed tell Hazlett something about paying off some small debts and then saw the general pull Hazlett closer to him, apparently for a confidential message. Seconds later, Hazlett crumpled forward, shot through the head.

Weed was carried to an aid station behind the hill and later to a field hospital on the Jacob Weikert farm. One of his aides, Lt. William H. Crennell of the 140th New York, tried to comfort him. "General, I hope that you are not so very badly hurt," Crennell said. Weed answered, "I'm as dead a man as Julius Caesar." Weed soon slipped into delirium and died about 9 P.M., Lt. Col. David T. Jenkins of the 146th New York reportedly hearing the general gasp, "My sister," with his last breath.[41]

The *New York Herald* said that Weed "lived some time after receiving his wound, and was conscious until within a few moments before breathing his last. A great and sublime soul as well as a true soldier." A *Herald* reporter also claimed that the dying general gave him a letter to deliver for him. The letter was to Weed's fiancée in Harrisburg, Pennsylvania, and had been written by Weed shortly before his fall. Some Federals would later remember seeing the general's body, along with those of Hazlett and a New York colonel, covered in sheets and lying on the porch of the Weikert house.[42]

The bluecoat defenders on Little Round Top hung on until sundown mercifully ended the bloodshed in this sector. "Night closed the fight," reported General Sykes, the V Corps commander. "The key of the battlefield was in our possession intact. Vincent, Weed, and Hazlett, chiefs lamented throughout the corps and army, sealed with their lives the spot intrusted to their keeping, and on which so much depended." General Ayres added, "In the death of Brig. Gen. Stephen H. Weed . . . the service lost a distinguished and gallant soldier."[43]

North of the Round Tops near sunset, elements of A. P. Hill's corps went into action and Richard Ewell, commanding another corps, opened an assault on Culp's Hill and Cemetery Hill, both in late support of Longstreet. It was during Hill's attack near the center of Lee's line that one of the best young generals in the Confederacy fell with a leg wound that would eventually kill him. Maj. Gen. William Dorsey Pender was a twenty-nine-year-old North Carolinian, West Point class of 1854, who had served primarily on the Pacific coast prior to hostilities. Promoted brigadier for his performance at Seven Pines, Pender was wounded three times during combat from Seven Pines to Chancellorsville. Promoted major general in late May 1863, he led Hill's old Light Division at Gettysburg.[44]

Pender was a hard hitter, known for his extreme coolness under fire, his boundless religious faith, and his devotion to his wife, Mary, to whom he wrote almost daily. His troops had driven the Federals off Seminary Ridge on Gettysburg's first day. Now, late on the afternoon of July 2, Pender was riding toward the right of his division, preparing for the attack on Cemetery Hill. He paid no mind to the explosions of Union artillery rounds nearby, but went down suddenly when a two-inch-square shell fragment hit his left thigh.

*Confederate major general
Dorsey Pender.*
LIBRARY OF CONGRESS

With the aid of his staff, Pender rallied his troops, but his attack was disrupted by his fall. Hill, who considered Pender his best division commander as well as a good friend, learned of the Tarheel's injury early in the evening and was saddened. Pender tried to mount his horse the next day but was unsuccessful. Unknown to him at the time, he would never take the saddle again. "The wound manifestly was serious," wrote Douglas Southall Freeman, "but Pender had been hit so often that he could not believe this injury mortal."[45]

Fighting continued into the darkness primarily at Culp's Hill, where Ewell made minimal gains, before the firing died away around midnight, the armies steeling for another mammoth struggle with the sun's rise.

THE PETTIGREW-PICKETT-TRIMBLE CHARGE

The stench of corpses from the previous two days of combat already fouled the summer air as the sun rose on what would be the most dramatic day of the Civil War—Friday, July 3, 1863.

Ewell had taken high ground at Culp's Hill the night before, but had lost it in the late morning, falling back to his previous positions. After failing to cave in the enemy flanks, Lee was intent on piercing the center of the Union line on Cemetery Ridge, and about 12,000 Rebels under Longstreet's overall command would be his longbow.

Maj. Gen. George Pickett's relatively fresh division of Longstreet's corps would form the nucleus of the attack. Pickett's division consisted of the brigades of Brig. Gens. Lewis A. Armistead, Richard B. Garnett, and James L. Kemper, and did not reach Gettysburg until early that morning. Pickett had two other brigades that had been left behind, on duty in the Richmond defenses. In addition to Pickett, Henry Heth's division—commanded by Brig. Gen. James J. Pettigrew since Heth's wounding on the first day— and a portion of Pender's division, now led by Maj. Gen. Isaac Trimble, would join in the assault.

The strike would be against the Union sector primarily occupied by Maj. Gen. Winfield S. Hancock's II Corps. The Confederates would move from their staging areas on Seminary Ridge, across gently sloping fields of wheat and clover to the Emmitsburg Road, then up the opposite slope to the enemy lines. Most of the Rebels would have to cross about three-quarters of a mile of open ground of to reach the Yankee positions. Armistead and Hancock had been the closest of friends before secession.

In this war, Armistead had been battle-tested in western Virginia, North Carolina, and during the Peninsular Campaign. He had commanded a brigade under Pickett since his promotion to brigadier in April 1862. Armistead was a forty-six-year-old North Carolinian who had been expelled from West Point in 1836 for smashing a mess hall plate over the head of fellow cadet Jubal Early. He was twice brevetted for gallantry in the Mexican War and was a brevet major stationed in California when he chose to join the Confederacy. At that time, Armistead's closest friend and fellow officer was Hancock, who had thrown a farewell party for Armistead and other Southerners, including Albert Sidney Johnston, who were leaving the Army to wear Rebel gray. At the little outpost of Los Angeles, California, they had reminisced and sung songs the night before the inevitable sad departure. Armistead had given Hancock's wife, Almira, a prayer book with the inscription, "Trust in God and fear nothing." At the end of the evening, a tearful Armistead had grasped Hancock's hand, looking him steadily in the eye and saying, "Hancock, good-by; you can never know what this has cost me, and I hope God will strike me dead if I am ever induced to leave my native soil, should worse come to worse."[46]

Armistead and Hancock had not seen each other since that night little more than two years earlier. Now at Gettysburg, Armistead looked across the field to where Hancock's bluecoats were bracing for the Rebel attack. He and Hancock were about to meet again, the song of reunion being the lethal zip of grape, canister, and musket lead.

Pickett deployed his brigades with Kemper and Garnett in front and Armistead following in support. Armistead protested heatedly, demanding that he should be placed in the first line as well, but his objections were in vain.

Hancock held the Union center with two veteran divisions, commanded by Brig. Gens. John Gibbon and Alexander Hays of his corps and two brigades from Doubleday's I Corps division—about 5,750 men total. Five batteries of II Corps artillery were also posted here, and Union guns from other sectors were within range. The most prominent features along this portion of Cemetery Ridge were a long, low stone wall, behind which the blue infantrymen were shielded, and a clump of trees, which would serve as a target for the assault.

Pickett and his three brigadiers had met at first light that morning for a "heart-to heart powwow," Pickett later wrote to his fiancée, Sally Corbell. As the officers spoke quietly, each offered regards to the future Mrs. Pickett and Armistead slipped a small ring from his little finger. Handing it to Pickett, he said, "'Give this little token, George, please, to her of the sunset eyes, with my love, and tell her the 'old man' says since he could not be the lucky dog he's mighty glad that you are.' Dear old Lewis—dear old 'Lo' as [General John] Magruder always called him, being short for Lothario." The generals clasped hands and wished each other good luck before departing for their commands.[47]

In preparation for the infantry assault, Confederate artillery began pounding the blue line about 1 P.M., and was soon answered by Federal cannons, the deafening bombardment making the earth tremble as it was ripped by explosions. Waiting for the order to advance, the gray troops lay down in ranks in the woods and fields, taking casualties from the enemy fire. Armistead remained on his feet, however, pacing in front of his brigade and inspecting the field. Armistead and Garnett were longtime friends and at one point stood together studying the imposing enemy positions, Garnett remarking, "This is a desperate thing to attempt."[48]

Garnett, forty-six, of Virginia, had already suffered the personal loss of his reputation and a relative in the war. His cousin, Brig. Gen. Robert Garnett, had been killed in 1861, the first general on either side to die in combat. The Garnetts had graduated from West Point together in 1841, Richard seeing army service in Florida and on the frontier.[49]

As a Rebel brigadier since November 1861, he led the Stonewall Brigade in the 1862 Shenandoah Campaign, enduring the brimstone of old Stonewall himself for his withdrawal after his men ran low on ammunition at Kernstown. Jackson arrested Garnett for a court martial, but there was never a trial. Garnett had fought in the Maryland Campaign, but this assault at Gettysburg would finally give him the chance to redeem his pride which he felt had been unjustly tarnished by Jackson.

"He was a perfect type of the gentleman and soldier," a Virginia infantryman recalled of Garnett. "His manner was charming, with almost the gentleness of a woman. As a soldier he was able, skillful and exacting; in battle a warrior and among the bravest . . . his dark eyes flashing and as black as coals. He wore a black beard and hair rather long."[50]

Garnett, however, had been ill and despite the July temperatures, was cloaked in a captured blue overcoat to stay warm. Adding to his misery, he had been kicked in the leg by a horse and could barely walk. Ignoring orders to go in on foot, he and a few others would be the only mounted Rebels in the assault. At his side, Garnett wore an elaborately engraved sword from his days in the U.S. Army, with the inscription "R. B. Garnett, U.S.A."

When the artillery storm ebbed about 3 P.M., Armistead was among the dozens of officers ordering soldiers to their feet, his voice booming down the brigade front "like a bugle blast in the air," a veteran remembered. "Men, remember what you are fighting for!" he shouted. "Your homes, your firesides, and your sweethearts! Follow me!"[51]

As the Confederates formed their lines, Armistead turned to the flag bearer of the 53rd Virginia, L. C. Blackburn, and asked, "Sergeant, I want you and your men to plant your colors on those works. Do you think you can do it?" Blackburn replied firmly, "Yes sir, if God is willing." Armistead then drew a small flask from his pocket and gave him a drink.[52]

With the deliberation of a parade ground review, the Rebels started forward in three ranks, the gray and brownish waves stretching in terrible splendor across the field. Armistead placed his battered black hat on his sword tip and led his brigade's onslaught.

Garnett rode with his advancing line calmly keeping the men well closed and dressed. One of his soldiers, Pvt. James W. Clay of the 18th Virginia, described the general as wearing "a black felt hat with a silver cord . . . a uniform coat, almost new, with a general's star and wreath on the collar, and top boots, with trousers inside, and spurs."[53]

Longstreet was conversing with his artillery chief, Lt. Col. E. P. Alexander, when "Pickett's division swept out of the wood and showed the full length of its gray ranks and shining bayonets, as grand a sight as ever a man looked on," Alexander remembered. "Joining it on the left, Pettigrew stretched farther than I could see. General Dick Garnett, just out of the sick ambulance, and buttoned up in an old blue overcoat, riding at the head of his brigade passed us and saluted Longstreet."[54]

Garnett also conversed briefly with Alexander, who described him as "a warm personal friend" whom he had not seen for several months. "We had served on the plains together before the war," Alexander noted. "I rode with him a short distance, and then we wished each other luck and a good-bye, which was our last." Longstreet recalled that Armistead and

Garnett "were veterans of nearly a quarter of a century's service. Their minds seemed absorbed in the men behind, and in the bloody work before them."[55]

Under cannon fire, Armistead trod about twenty steps in front of his troops. He had reached the vicinity of the Codori farm when General Kemper found him and asked that he move his brigade up in closer support. Armistead complied, marching his men faster. Their lines went over the rail fence along the Emmitsburg Road and were torn by Union infantry volleys as well as canister, the air hissing with flying metal.

Bloody gaps appeared in the gray ranks, but Armistead whipped his sword, his hat having slipped down the blade to the hilt by now, and continued on through the deadly blizzard. "Conspicuous to all, 50 yards in advance of his brigade, waving his hat upon his sword, [Armistead] led his men upon the enemy with a steady bearing which inspired all breasts with enthusiasm and courage, and won the admiration of every beholder," related Col. William Aylett of the 53rd Virginia.[56]

In Garnett's ranks men were dropping at every step now, including James Clay, who was wounded in the forehead by a shell fragment about 100 yards from the clump of trees in the Union position. Stumbling against some rocks, Clay fell as his comrades continued on. "The last I saw of General Garnett he was astride his big black charger in the forefront of the charge and near the stone wall," Clay recalled. "General Garnett was gallantly waving his hat and cheering the men on to renewed efforts against the enemy" and with his sword still on his side.[57]

Garnett rode along his ranks, keeping his men in order and telling them, "Don't double-quick. Save your wind and ammunition for the final charge." About this time, a line of Federals behind the wall rose and delivered a volley, hitting a number of Rebels, including Garnett. Some of his solders saw him bleeding and slumped in the saddle. Moments later general and mount fell together, the horse thrashing to its feet and galloping down the hill.[58]

With the issue much in doubt, some Federals surrendered, coming down the slope where two of them encountered Clay and Capt. Archer Campbell of the 18th Virginia, who was also wounded. Two of the Yankees offered to help these Rebels to the rear and they accepted. They also had dismal news for the Confederates. "These men told us that [Garnett] had been killed, having been shot through the body at the waist by a grape shot," Clay related. Clay and Campbell apparently were expecting the worst for Garnett, having seen his horse minutes earlier. "Just before these men reached us General Garnett's . . . horse came galloping toward us with a huge gash in his right shoulder, evidently struck by a piece of shell. The horse in its mad flight" hurdled the Virginians, Clay wrote.[59]

"There was scarcely an officer or man in the command whose attention was not attracted by the cool and handsome bearing of General Garnett," recalled Major Charles Peyton of the 19th Virginia. "He was shot from his horse while near the center of the brigade, within about 25 paces of the stone wall."[60]

Kemper was down with a desperate wound, his brigade all but blown to bits now, the survivors joining what was left of Armistead's and Garnett's commands in swarming up to the wall. Forty yards away, Armistead yelled "Charge!" and they made the final dash through double canister and point-blank musketry. With Armistead leading, the butternuts climbed over the rocks near the copse of trees and hurled back a portion of the 71st Pennsylvania in Brig. Gen. Alexander S. Webb's Philadelphia brigade. As he clambered over the wall, Armistead shouted, "Boys, we must use the cold steel. Who will follow?"[61]

About 150 or so Rebels followed him across the wall in front of two guns of Battery A, 4th U.S. Artillery, commanded by Lt. Alonzo Cushing. These cannons were seized by the onrushing Confederates, and Armistead charged toward a second line of guns about thirty yards away amid a mayhem of clubbed muskets, bayonets, and bare knuckle-fighting. The Rebels desperately tried to maintain their foothold inside the wall against elements of Webb's 69th and 72nd Pennsylvania, as well as what was left of the 71st, but Union reinforcements were also pitching into the chaos.

Armistead had almost reached the second row of artillery pieces when another Union volley staggered the attackers, including Armistead. He was hit in the left arm and left leg, but struggled forward to place his hand on an enemy cannon before he collapsed. As he fell, he gave the Masonic sign for distress, apparently hoping that some other member of the fraternity would come to his aid. Minutes later it was over, the charge crushed and the Rebel survivors streaming back across the smoky, body-littered fields toward Lee's lines.

"General Armistead passed over the fence with probably over 100 of his command and with several battle-flags," Webb reported. "Defeated, routed, the enemy fled in disorder. General Armistead was left, mortally wounded, within my lines, and 42 of the enemy who crossed the fence lay dead."[62] Pettigrew and Trimble had met with no better success, penetrating the wall further to the north after covering more ground than Pickett's men, but their divisions had to retire with ghastly losses as well. Both of these generals were wounded, Trimble captured. The attack had cost Lee more than half of his main attack force being killed or wounded, with scores of others taken prisoner.

Among the Confederates captured on Cemetery Ridge was Armistead, of whom Colonel Aylett wrote, "Far in advance of all, he led the attack till he scaled the works of the enemy and fell wounded in their hands, but not until he had driven them from their positions and seen his colors planted over their fortifications." Now, however, Armistead was being carried to the Union rear by Yankee stretcher bearers.[63]

Capt. Henry Bingham, a physician on Hancock's staff, saw the men with the Rebel officer and stopped them to ask his identity. After being told erroneously that the officer was Longstreet, Bingham ordered the soldiers to leave the officer in his care and sent them to rejoin their unit. Kneeling, Bingham had a brief conversation with Armistead, the general identifying himself and telling the captain that he and Hancock were old friends. He also asked Bingham, a fellow Mason (as was Hancock), to deliver a message. "Tell Gen. Hancock for me that I have done him and you all an injury which I shall regret or repent (I forget the exact word) the longest day I live," Bingham recalled Armistead saying.[64]

Armistead then gave Bingham his spurs, pocketbook, watch, chain, and seal which the captain later turned over to Hancock. Armistead had no way of knowing that Hancock had been wounded in the thigh about the same time that he had fallen. (Hancock would later return Armistead's personal effects to the general's sister, Cornelia.)

Bingham then sent Armistead to the U.S. XI Corps field hospital located on the George Spangler farm. Another wounded and captured Rebel officer recalled that as Armistead lay on a cot under shade trees at the hospital, he told busy corpsmen, "Please don't step so close to me."[65] Armistead was later moved into the Spangler kitchen where he was treated by Dr. Daniel G. Brinton, the chief surgeon.

Brinton gave this account:

On the afternoon of 3rd July about 4 o'clock the General was brought to my hospital and myself & Dr. Harvey late of Rochester N.Y. examined & dressed his wounds. They were two in number, neither of them of a serious character, apparently. The one was in the fleshy part of the arm, the other a little below the knee in the leg of the opposite side. . . . Both were by rifle balls, and no bone, or leading artery or nerve was injured by either. In conversation with the General he told me he had suffered much from over-exertion, want of sleep, and mental anxiety within the last few days. His prospects of recovery seemed good, and I was astonished to learn of his death. It resulted not from his wounds directly, but from secondary fever & prostration.[66]

Armistead remained defiant to the last. As Federal surgeons cleaned his arm wound, he reached into his pants and retrieved some kernels of raw corn. Showing the Yankees what passed for Rebel rations, he told them, "Men who can subsist on raw corn can never be whipped."[67]

Unaware of the fate of Armistead or Garnett, Lee gave Jefferson Davis a brief overview of the battle in a July 4 report and told of his command casualties: "General Barksdale is killed. Generals Garnett and Armistead are missing. . . . Generals Pender and Trimble are wounded in the leg . . . General Kemper, it is feared, is mortally wounded. Our losses embrace many other valuable officers and men."[68]

Without seeing his old friend Hancock, Armistead finally succumbed about 9 A.M. on July 5 and was buried with other Confederates on the Spangler farm grounds. His body was later exhumed and taken to Old Saint Paul's Cemetery in Baltimore.

Garnett's body was never recovered, and is believed to have been buried with other Rebel dead on the battlefield. Some accounts say that his sidearms and uniform insignia were taken by Union soldiers, thus preventing him from being identified. Years after the war, former Confederate brigadier general George H. Steuart discovered Garnett's sword in a Baltimore second-hand shop. Steuart bought it, and the sword was returned to Garnett's niece in 1905.

Pickett was in the habit of writing love letters to his Sally, but his words of July 6, 1863, were of a general haunted by the deaths of hundreds and the greatest failure of his life:

Ah, if I had only had my other two brigades a different story would have been flashed to the world. It was too late to retreat, and to go on was death or capture. Poor old Dick Garnett did not dismount, as did the others of us, and he was killed instantly, falling from his horse. . . . Dear old Lewis Armistead, God bless him, was mortally wounded at the head of his command after planting the flag of Virginia within the enemy's lines . . . I wonder, my dear, in the light of the Great Eternity we shall any of us feel this was the best and shall have learned to say, "Thy will be done." No castles to-day, sweet-heart. No, the bricks of happiness and the mortar of love must lie untouched in this lowering gloom. Pray, dear, for the sorrowing ones. —Your Soldier[69]

Even as the bloody gray tide receded from Cemetery Ridge, the day would still claim another general, this one a young Federal brigadier who had been promoted less than a week earlier. Looking to exploit the advantage of the enemy's repulse, Union cavalry Brig. Gen. Judson Kilpatrick decided to attack Longstreet's position to the south, believing the Rebels might be disorganized or demoralized even though these Confederates had not taken part in the assault. He ordered Brig. Gen. Elon J. Farnsworth to attack the right flank of Longstreet's position with his cavalry. It was a forlorn and hopeless effort that led to Farnsworth's controversial death.

Farnsworth, twenty-five, commanded the 1st Brigade in Kilpatrick's 3rd Division of the Cavalry Corps. His uncle, John Farnsworth, was a U.S. congressman who had been a brigadier in the Union army. Born in Michigan, Farnsworth's family had moved to Illinois when he was a teenager. He attended the University of Michigan, served as a civilian foragemaster on Albert Sidney Johnston's Mormon Expedition. In 1861 he enlisted in his uncle's regiment, the 8th Illinois Cavalry. Promoted to captain late that year, he served on Gen. Alfred Pleasonton's staff.[70]

In a rare promotion, Farnsworth was jumped from captain to brigadier to rank from June 29, even as the rival armies were only days away from the collision at Gettysburg. Being in the field, Farnsworth had no way of obtaining a new uniform, but Pleasonton loaned the new brigadier half of his wardrobe, including a coat with a single star that Farnsworth wore into action. Pleasonton would later write that "nature made him a general." He would have only five days to enjoy his new rank.[71]

Farnsworth's troopers—the 5th New York, 18th Pennsylvania, 1st Vermont, and 1st West Virginia regiments—skirmished with Confederate cavalry at Hanover and Hunterstown on July 1 and 2 respectively. On the morning of July 3, the brigade was posted near the center of the army and was ordered to the extreme left to guard against attack there, facing Longstreet. Farnsworth's men had been sniping with the Rebels for several hours that afternoon and knew they were up against veteran infantry posted behind stone walls and concealed in woods. Additionally, the charge would be over uneven ground peppered with boulders and broken by fences. Brig. Gen. Wesley Merritt's brigade tried a dismounted assault, but it was repulsed before Farnsworth made his attempt about 5 P.M. Scanning the enemy positions and seeing the bloody results of the cavalry's earlier thrusts, Farnsworth conferred with his officers, who agreed the attempt likely would be a costly mistake. He then voiced his opposition of the attack to Kilpatrick, the conversation quickly growing heated.

Capt. H. C. Parsons of the 1st Vermont recalled this last meeting between the cavalry generals:

> I was near Kilpatrick when he impetuously gave the order to Farnsworth to make the last charge. Farnsworth spoke with emotion: "General, do you mean it? Shall I throw my handful of men over rough ground, through timber, against a brigade of infantry? The 1st Vermont has already been fought half to pieces; these are too good men to kill." Kilpatrick said: "Do you refuse to obey my orders? If you are afraid to lead this charge, I will lead it." Farnsworth rose in his stirrups—he looked magnificent in his passion and cried, "Take that back!" Kilpatrick returned his defiance, but, soon repenting, said, "I did not mean it; forget it." For a moment there was silence, when Farnsworth spoke calmly, "General, if you order the charge, I will lead it, but you must take the responsibility." I did not hear the low conversation that followed, but as Farnsworth turned away he said, "I will obey your order." Kilpatrick said earnestly, "I take the responsibility."[72]

Parsons described Farnsworth as "tall, slight, stern, and pale, but rising with conscious strength and consecration . . . Farnsworth was courage incarnate, but full of tender regard for his men, and his protest was manly and soldierly." Shortly afterward, the brigade, about three hundred men strong, drew sabers and charged over the rocky fields, Farnsworth in the lead and accompanied by Maj. William Wells of his 3rd Battalion.[73]

The Rebels in their front belonged to Brig. Gen. Evander Law's brigade of John Hood's division in Longstreet's Corps. They were hunkered behind stone walls and in thickets and unleashed a heavy fire of musketry at the galloping blue horsemen, emptying a number of saddles. Still, Farnsworth's troopers smashed over the first line of gray infantry, penetrating some four hundred yards to the rear and threatening a North Carolina battery. The problem for the bluecoats was that the Confederates closed the breach behind them, leaving Farnsworth and his men surrounded.

In the violent mayhem within the Rebel positions, the Union riders became separated, their ranks dwindling as more of them were shot. Parsons related that Farnsworth's horse went down, whether from gunfire or from a stumble, but another trooper dismounted and gave the general his own mount, escaping on foot.[74]

The 15th Alabama of Col. William C. Oates in Law's brigade was hustled to the defense of the battery, Oates sending out skirmishers who soon clashed with the enemy cavalry. Law's 4th Alabama also was faced about to repulse the enemy thrust.

Oates recalled that "The [Union] officer commanding, with pistol in hand, ordered my skirmishers to surrender, to which they replied with a volley. The cavalry commander and his horse and one of his men fell to the ground, and the others dashed away."[75]

Law wrote that "Farnsworth, with his little handful of gallant followers, rode upon the skirmish-line of the 15th Alabama regiment, and, pistol in hand, called upon Lt. [John D.] Adrian, who commanded the line, to surrender. The skirmishers in return fired upon him, killing his horse and wounding Farnsworth in several places."[76]

Based on Oates's account, the Rebel lieutenant leading the skirmishers (apparently Adrian) ran forward, his repeating rifle at the ready, and called for the Federal to surrender, even as the enemy still clutched his revolver and tried to rise. "'I will not do it,'" the bluecoat officer answered, "and placing the pistol to his own head, shot his brains out," Oates stated. The colonel took no further notice of the dead officer, who lay a few yards away, until "one of the skirmishers brought me his shoulder straps, from which I discovered he was a general," Oates said. He went to the body and in looking through the officer's uniform found two letters which, he said, were addressed to "General E. J. Farnsworth." Oates said, "I was soon ordered to another part of the field, and left the body where it fell." Some of the 15th's officers claimed there were no more than ten men with Farnsworth when he was shot, his horse galloping through their lines.[77]

"A volley was fired which killed Gen. Farnsworth's horse and brought him down," recalled Maj. W. M. Robbins of the 4th Alabama. "Mortally wounded, and as a squad of Alabamians approached him he pulled a pistol and fired it into his own bosom, killing himself instantly."[78]

With their leader among about sixty-five casualties, the survivors of Farnsworth's brigade cut their way out of the Rebel beehive, managing to herd along a number of Confederate prisoners, but left the general's body behind. "This charge was made over severe obstacles, but succeeded in breaking the enemy's lines," related Lt. Col. A. W. Preston of Farnsworth's 1st Vermont. "Many of our dead, together with the body of General Farnsworth, were found in the rear of the position held by the enemy's second line." Col. Nathaniel Richmond of the 1st West Virginia was given brigade command the morning after Farnsworth's death. "General Farnsworth was ordered to charge the enemy's right, which he at once did, making one of the desperate, and at the same time most successful, charges it has ever been my lot to witness, and during which that gallant officer . . . was killed while in the thickest of the fight," Richmond wrote in his battle report. "In the loss of Brigadier-General Farnsworth this brigade suffered an almost irreparable loss, as a more gallant officer or perfect gentleman cannot, in my opinion, be found."[79]

Several Confederates contended that Farnsworth's troopers were drunk at the time of their charge. "Gen. Farnsworth (believed by us to be Kilpatrick himself) fell in the left front of our regiment, and one of the First Texans ran forward and got his epaulettes and spurs," recalled George Todd, an officer in the Texas regiment. "He also reported that he shot himself on account of the agony he was in. Their charging lines overlapped and outflanked our line . . . and several hundred of them dashed to our rear. They were checked by some teamsters and litter bearers, when they galloped back to our lines with sabers extended, in token of surrender. They were nearly all intoxicated and reeling in their saddles." Another Rebel veteran claimed that Farnsworth's horse was shot by a lieutenant in the 44th Alabama and that the animal fell on one of the general's legs. The lieutenant ordered Farnsworth to surrender, but the cavalryman refused, shooting himself in the temple. The Alabamian claimed to have retrieved Farnsworth's commission from one of his pockets.[80]

Brig. Gen. Henry Benning of Hood's Division gave this version of Farnsworth's end: "Some of the men engaged . . . told me that the prisoners said it was General Farnsworth's brigade, and that they were all drunk. The same men told me that in going over the field for spoils they approached a fallen horse with its rider by his side, but not dead. They ordered him to surrender. He replied wait a little, or something to that effect, and put his hand to his pistol, drew it and blew his brains out. This was General Farnsworth."[81]

The Federals disputed any claim that Farnsworth committed suicide, some stating that the Confederates likely confused the general with Capt. Oliver T. Cushman of the 1st Vermont. Cushman survived his Gettysburg wounds, but was killed at Cold Harbor in 1864. "A strange story which appears in all the Confederate reports shows how a mistake may make history," Parsons wrote. He contended that the Union officer wearing a linen coat and havelock and believed by the Rebels to be Farnsworth was actually Cushman. Parsons claimed that Farnsworth's body was left on the field when the Southerners retreated from Gettysburg, and that when

Union surgeons examined the general, they found "five mortal wounds in his body but no wound in his head."[82]

Parsons wrote that Cushman, not Farnsworth, rode in the charge on the 4th Alabama, but was at the brigadier's side in the combat with the 15th Alabama, falling "terribly wounded in the face" and fighting with his revolver until he fainted. "He was a notably handsome officer, and it was clear that he was mistaken throughout the fight for General Farnsworth," Parsons stated. Cushman "lay insensible and apparently dead until the next day, but finally revived."[83]

Whether Farnsworth died from Rebel bullets or his own hand, Kilpatrick lavished praise on his dead brigadier:

> Among the list [of casualties] will be found the name Farnsworth; short but most glorious was his career—a general on June 29, on the 30th he baptized his star in blood, and on July 3, for the honor of his young brigade and the glory of his corps, he gave his life. At the head of his men, at the very muzzles of the enemy's guns, he fell, with many mortal wounds. We can say of him, in the language of another, "Good soldier, faithful friend, great heart, hail and farewell."[84]

Kilpatrick's decision to order the attack was questioned, while Farnsworth's courage was not. "The charge in which Farnsworth lost his life was ordered by Kilpatrick and was unquestionably against the former's judgment," wrote Maj. James H. Kidd of the 6th Michigan Cavalry who had known Farnsworth since before the war. "But he was too brave a man and too conscientious to do anything else but obey orders to the letter. . . . He did not hesitate for one moment. Drawing his saber and placing himself at the head of his command, he led his men to the inevitable slaughter and boldly went to his own death. It was a pity to sacrifice such an officer and such men as followed him. . . . The charge was one of the most gallant ever made, though barren of results."[85]

General Pleasonton, Meade's cavalry commander, noted that the "noble and gallant Farnsworth fell, heroically leading a charge of his brigade against the rebel infantry. Gifted in a high degree with a quick perception and a correct judgment, and remarkable for his daring and coolness, his comprehensive grasp of the situation on the field of battle and the rapidity of his actions had already distinguished General Farnsworth among his comrades in arms. In his death was closed a career that must have won the highest honors of his profession."[86]

Parsons stated that Farnsworth "fell in the enemy's lines with his saber raised . . . and without fame." He added that the Alabamian colonel Oates kept a star cut from Farnsworth's coat, intending to return it to his family. Unfortunately it was lost or accidentally destroyed sometime after the war.[87]

General Barksdale of Mississippi, meanwhile, had died in a Union field hospital early that morning. "Among the circumstances worthy of mention . . . was the death of the rebel General Barksdale," Abner Doubleday, later reported. "He was brought into my lines by my acting assistant inspector-general, Lieutenant-Colonel [C.E.] Livingston. His dying speech and last messages for his family, together with the valuables about his person, were intrusted by him to . . . Livingston." Meade sent an 8 A.M. report to Maj. Gen. Henry W. Halleck, the army's general-in-chief: "Prisoners report Longstreet's and A. P. Hill's forces much injured yesterday and many general officers killed. General Barksdale's . . . dead body is within our lines."[88]

Barksdale ultimately would be laid to rest at Greenwood Cemetery in Jackson, Mississippi "We loved Gen. Barksdale," wrote W. G. Johnson of the 18th Mississippi, "because we knew he was proud of us, and would do any thing in his power for our welfare. No truer patriot ever fell on the field of battle."[89]

The Union general Zook outlasted Barksdale only a few hours. On July 3 he was transferred to another house occupied by several women who gave him chicken soup and whiskey. He inquired about the battle's progress during the day and his aide, Lieutenant Favill, told him of the Union victory with the repulse of the great charge. "Then I am satisfied and ready to die," Zook replied. About 5 P.M. he did just that. Zook was buried in Montgomery Cemetery, Norristown, Pennsylvania.[90]

General Caldwell wrote of his casualties, including Zook, in one of his battle reports: "While driving the enemy triumphantly before them, two of my brigade commanders, Brigadier-General Zook and Col. [Edward E.] Cross of the 5th New Hampshire Volunteers, fell, mortally wounded. They were both old and tried soldiers, and the country can ill spare their service. They both fell in . . . battle while driving back the invader, and lived long enough to know that their blood had not been shed in vain, but that the enemy had been driven back with terrible repulse. A grateful country will remember their virtues and hold them up to the admiration of posterity."[91]

Staggered by the loss of some 25,000 men, Lee stood his ground until the night of July 4 when his army withdrew from Gettysburg. In a blinding rainstorm, Lee's bloodied divisions limped south toward the Potomac, slowed by the flood and muddy roads. The retreat was especially agonizing for the approximately 10,000 wounded men being borne in about 4,000 wagons, the ghastly caravan sometimes stretching for thirty miles, a "vast procession of misery," wrote cavalry Brig. Gen. John Imboden who was in charge of the train.[92]

One of the lead ambulances bore Dorsey Pender and Brig. Gen. Alfred Scales of North Carolina, also severely wounded. Both generals, Imboden stated, were "resolved to bear the tortures of the journey rather than become prisoners." On the second day out and with the wagons waiting to roll, Imboden found time to visit the generals' ambulance. "I shared a little bread and meat with them at noon, and they waited patiently for hours for the head of the column to move. The trip cost poor Pender his life."[93]

Pender was transported to Staunton, Virginia, but his wound had become infected during the trek and hemorrhaged on the first night after his arrival there. Pender himself used a hairbrush and a towel as an impromptu tourniquet to stop the bleeding. His leg was amputated in an emergency surgery on July 18, but Pender did not recuperate from the operation, dying within hours. In his last moments Pender proclaimed his trust in God and lack of fear in dying, his only regret being that he would leave behind his pregnant wife, Mary, and two sons. "The three brigades lost heavily," Pender's commander, A. P. Hill, later related in a battle report. "On this day, also, the Confederacy lost the invaluable services of Maj. Gen. W. D. Pender, wounded by a shell, and since dead. No man fell during this bloody battle of Gettysburg more regretted than he, nor around whose youthful brow were clustered brighter rays of glory."[94]

"Seldom has the service suffered more in the loss of one man than it did when this valuable officer fell," related Rebel major Joseph Engelhardt. "Gallant, skillful, energetic, this young commander had won a reputation surpassed only by the success and ability of his services." Another Confederate officer described Pender as "young and handsome, brave and skillful. . . . He was known, admired, and trusted by his superior officers, beyond any of his age in the service." A heartbroken Mary Pender gave birth to their third son, Stephen Lee Pender, that fall. By then, her husband was at rest at Calvary Church Cemetery in Tarboro, North Carolina.[95]

⊷ ⊱✠⊰ ⊶

General Semmes, meanwhile, had died also. The Georgian had been taken to Martinsburg, (West) Virginia, carried across the Potomac in an ambulance before the retreat of the main army. There, "among friends who administered to every want and did all that human skill could to save his life, he passed away from the sphere of earthly duties" on July 10. As his life waned, Semmes is said to have spoken to a Southern war correspondent, saying, as his eyes filled with tears, "I consider it a privilege to die for my country." After temporary burial in Martinsburg, Semmes's body was later interred at Linnwood Cemetery in Columbus, Georgia, "as true a knight as ever drew a blade."[96]

The dying also was far from over among the Union commanders included in the approximately 23,000 Yankee casualties at Gettysburg. Taken to a field hospital after his wounding, Colonel Vincent's condition steadily worsened. At one point he asked to be sent home, but his surgeon informed him that he was too critically injured to be moved. While fighting one of the signature battles in American history, Meade found time on July 3 to send Halleck a request for the Pennsylvanian's promotion: "I would respectfully request that Col. Strong Vincent, 83rd Pennsylvania Regiment, be made a brigadier-general of volunteers for gallant conduct on the field yesterday. He is mortally wounded, and it would gratify his friends, as well as myself. It was my intention to have recommended him with others, should he live."[97]

Despite around-the-clock care and visits from many friends, Vincent died in a field hospital near Gettysburg on July 7. An impassioned Colonel Rice issued general orders five days later informing the brigade of the sad tidings:

> The colonel commanding hereby announces . . . the death of Brigadier General Strong Vincent. He died . . . from the effects of a wound received on the 2nd instant, and within sight of that field which his bravery had so greatly assisted to win. A day hallowed with all the glory of success is thus sombered by the sorrow of our loss. Wreaths of victory give way to chaplets of mourning, hearts exultant to feelings of grief. A soldier, a scholar, a friend, has fallen. For his country, struggling for its life, he willingly gave his own. Grateful for his services, the State which proudly claims him as her own will give him an honored grave and a costly monument, but he ever will remain buried in our hearts, and our love for his memory will outlast the stone which shall bear the inscription of his bravery, his virtues, and his patriotism. While we deplore his death, and remember with sorrow our loss, let us emulate the example of his fidelity and patriotism, feeling that he lives but in vain who lives not for his God and his country.[98]

General Sykes described Weed and Vincent as "officers of rare promise" who "gave their lives to the country. The former had been conspicuous during the war, won and adorned his promotion, and surrendered it and his life on the spot he was called to defend." General Barnes eulogized Vincent in a battle report: "He was a gallant officer, beloved and respected by his command and by all who knew him. His death is a serious loss to the army and the country. . . . He lingered a few days after the engagement. His promotion as a brigadier-general was sent to him at once as an appreciation of his services by the Government, but it reached him too late for his own recognition. He expired soon after its receipt."[99]

"Weed and Hazlett were killed, and Vincent was mortally wounded - all young men of great promise," related the artillery chief, General Hunt. Weed was initially buried on the battlefield (some accounts, including Lieutenant Crennell's, stating the location was near an apple tree on the Louis Bushman farm) but was later laid to rest on Staten Island, New York, in the Moravian Cemetery at New Dorp. "A more ardent soldier was not in the service, and a purer patriot has not lived," the *New York Herald* said of him. "He sacrificed his life through love for his profession and devotion to his country."[100]

Vincent was buried at Erie Cemetery while Farnsworth was laid to rest near his family's home in Rockton, Illinois. "Farnsworth will not be forgotten as long as a grateful people remember the name and the glory of Gettysburg," Colonel Kidd wrote. Parsons added this end to Farnsworth's obituary: "So fell this typical volunteer soldier of America—a man without military training or ambition; yet born with a genius for war which carried him to high command and to the threshold of a great career."[101]

⋆—⧉⧉—⋆

Like George McClellan after Antietam less than a year earlier, Meade counted his own terrific losses and did not mount a wholesale pursuit of Lee. He did, however, send cavalry to harass the Confederates, and his infantry was on the move, but in half spirited fashion. Reaching the Potomac at Falling Waters near Martinsburg, the Rebels found that the rains had swollen the river and that they would have to wait to cross.

Among those in the Confederate exodus was the scholarly General Pettigrew, his right hand bandaged from his wound sustained during the great charge. The North Carolinian had turned thirty-five on July 4 and was upbeat and cheerful in ensuring the march from Gettysburg progressed with his characteristic discipline. Pettigrew had been an assistant professor at the U.S. Naval Observatory as well as an attorney, South Carolina legislator, and militia colonel before the conflict. Commissioned a Confederate brigadier in February 1862, he had been seriously wounded and captured at the battle of Seven Pines. Exchanged, he served at Petersburg and in North Carolina before the Gettysburg Campaign.[102]

Pettigrew's North Carolina Brigade in Heth's Division of Hill's Corps had been the first to encounter the Federals at Gettysburg. These men had approached the town on June 30, looking for a supply of shoes reportedly there. Finding the enemy instead, Heth had sent his entire division forward, opening the battle on July 1. With Heth heavily engaged that afternoon, Pettigrew's Carolinians had attacked across Willoughby Run shoving the Yankees, including the famed Iron Brigade, off McPherson's Ridge after horrific fighting. Pettigrew's Brigade was maimed in the process, the 26th North Carolina losing almost 600 out of over 800 engaged in a half-hour of combat.

As the battle unfolded on July 2, the surviving Tarheels recuperated while Pettigrew was busy with the new experience of division command, Heth being wounded in the head the previous day. Pettigrew rustled up every cook and orderly he could find to fill his depleted ranks, even going to the field hospitals to turn out those with minor wounds who could wield a musket.

In the July 3 charge, Pettigrew led the four brigades of Heth's division. Unlike Pickett's division, which had not been engaged, the bandages of Pettigrew's men were conspicuous from their firefight on the first day. Pettigrew commanded almost as many troops as Pickett and covered more ground in the assault, prompting his Carolinians to later refer to the attack as "Pettigrew's charge." A portion of the division broke, but Pettigrew had led the remainder, including his Tarheels, to close range of the flaming Federal line along the stone wall. Pettigrew's horse was shot, and his right hand was mangled by a grape shot as he reached the wall, his division, unable to endure more, falling back. Pettigrew was one of the last survivors to return to the Confederate lines. His brigade had the highest casualty rate of any in the army at Gettysburg, the ninety percent decimation of the 26th North Carolina estimated by some as being the greatest loss by a single regiment on either side in any battle of the war.[103]

FALLING WATERS

Heth had been able to return to division command on July 7 and was in charge of the Confederate rearguard as Lee waited to cross the Potomac. The high water receded enough by the night of July 13 so that most of the army crossed on a makeshift pontoon bridge at Falling Waters, leaving the divisions of Heth and Pender—now commanded by James Lane after Trimble's wounding—on the hostile shore.

Meade, meanwhile, ordered a pursuit on the morning of July 14, the cavalry divisions of John Buford and Judson Kilpatrick leading the way. "Kilpatrick started off in hot haste . . . determined to strike the last blow on northern soil," wrote the cavalryman J. H. Kidd of the 6th Michigan Cavalry. The 6th was in the lead with troops B and F serving as the advance and commanded by Maj. Peter A. Weber. Kilpatrick spurred his men on the gallop for some five miles from Williamsport toward Falling Waters, the muddy roads hampering the advance and stringing out the column. About two miles from the bridge site, Weber's men found Heth dug in on a rise and guarding the river road.[104]

Exhausted by the campaign, many of Pettigrew's men, as well as Heth's other brigades, were resting or asleep about 10 A.M. The night had been rainy and the morning was misty and gloomy. Some of the more alert Rebels caught sight of horsemen in heavy woods about three to four hundred yards away, but there was no concern; this was merely Confederate cavalry on the move, they believed. In reality, these were Weber's troopers.

Weber's superior, Brig. Gen. George Custer, ordered him to dismount his men and send out skirmishers to determine the Rebels' strength. Kilpatrick however, instructed Weber to remount and charge the hill even though no other troopers had arrived to support the assault. Back in the saddle at the head of his less than one hundred horsemen, Weber led them with a shout, up the slope and into the surprised Confederates' camps. "The enemy's cavalry dashed in upon us, causing some confusion, as the men were just aroused from sleep," a North Carolina major recalled. "Soon as they saw what was the matter, they seized their guns."[105]

"We supposed that Stuart's Cavalry was in our front and that this body was a part of his force," related Sgt. June Kimble of the 14th Tennessee. "We had no pickets out, there was no fear or concern as to these troops. . . . Suddenly a body of horsemen came into the road . . . in a sweeping trot. About halfway up, they unfurled their pennants, drew sabers, and sprang into a rushing gallop." One of Pettigrew's aides, Capt. L. G. Young, added, "It was difficult to believe sane men would attack as this small body of cavalry did."[106]

Amid the sudden clatter of carbines, muskets, and revolvers, the Federals reached a field where Heth, Pettigrew, and other officers were conversing. Heth, his head swathed in a bandage, was on horseback while Pettigrew stood in the road. There was a flurry of shooting and hacking as the bluecoats wheeled among dazed Confederates scrambling to draw a bead on them. Pettigrew stepped to the rear of a Rebel infantry line, shouting, "Stand your ground, boys." His right hand basically useless and his left arm still weak from the Seven Pines wound, Pettigrew tried to mount his horse, but was thrown to the ground. One account states that he actually got into the saddle, but that the gunfire spooked his horse, causing it to rear and fall, toppling him as well.[107]

Regaining his feet, the general drew a small pistol from his coat with his left hand and moved toward a bluecoat corporal who had shot several Rebels. The Yankee fired his revolver, hitting Pettigrew in the left side of the abdomen just above the hip. As the general crumpled, a Rebel fatally brained the Federal with a rock. "The sharp crack of pistols rang out from the head of the enemy's plunging column, and the brave, noble Pettigrew fell with a mortal wound," Kimble recalled. Heth wrote of Pettigrew's misfortune: "It is probable when in the act of rising from the ground that he was struck by a pistol-ball in the left side, which, unfortunately for himself and his country, proved mortal."[108]

The Confederates quickly rallied from their initial surprise and "made short work of their daring assailants" Kidd wrote. Weber was killed, his command "more than decimated." Kilpatrick would later describe the attack, which lasted less than five minutes as "the most gallant ever made."[109]

More Union cavalry soon came up, and the action intensified as Pettigrew was carried to a barn nearer the river where physicians examined him. They quickly agreed that the wound was likely fatal unless Pettigrew was completely immobilized, and offered to leave him there so that Union surgeons could treat him. Pettigrew was adamant, however, that he would rather die than be captured again. Based on information from Kilpatrick, Meade erroneously reported Pettigrew's death in an evening dispatch to General Halleck that night: "General Pettigrew of the Confederate army was killed this morning in the attack on the enemy's rear guard. His body is in our hands."[110]

The next day a relay of stretcher bearers set out with Pettigrew, crossing the Potomac on the twenty-two mile trek to Bunker Hill, (now West) Virginia. With the masses of wounded from Gettysburg, there apparently was no ambulance available for the general. Pettigrew is said to have joked with the soldiers carrying him, and General Lee rode part of the way, expressing his regret about the Carolinian's wound. Pettigrew reportedly told Lee that he was perfectly willing to die for his country. Seeing the distressed look of his men at one point during his transport, Pettigrew called to them, "Boys, don't be disheartened; maybe I will fool the doctors yet."[111]

The journey took two days, but Pettigrew and his attendants finally reached Bunker Hill where the general was taken to Edgewood Manor, the fine, red-brick home of John Boyd that Stonewall Jackson had used as headquarters the previous fall. There he regained senses and strength enough on July 16 to divide his horses among his staff officers before lapsing into unconsciousness. An Episcopalian minister visited him later, offering him the sacraments, but Pettigrew sadly refused them, saying that he felt unworthy because he believed he was guilty of the sin of presumption.[112]

Pettigrew died at the Boyd home about 6:30 A.M. on July 17. His body would eventually be returned to his family home at "Bonarva" in Tyrrell County, North Carolina, for burial. "It was our sad misfortune . . . in this affair to lose General Pettigrew," wrote Lt. Col. S. G. Shepard of the 7th Tennessee. "No encomium that I might add could do justice to his memory. Both officers and men of the entire brigade feel that by his death the Confederacy has lost a model soldier and one of her most noble and gifted sons." "How we all loved him!" a Rebel soldier on A. P. Hill's staff mourned Pettigrew. "A Noble, gallant soldier and gentleman."[113]

Lee wrote of his losses in a July 31 report to Adjutant General Cooper:

> It is not yet in my power to give a correct statement of our casualties. Among them I regret to mention the following general officers: Major-Generals Hood, Pender, and Trimble severely, and Major General Heth slightly wounded. General Pender has since died. This lamented officer had borne a distinguished part in every engagement of this army, and was wounded on several occasions while leading his command with conspicuous gallantry and ability. The confidence and admiration inspired by his courage and capacity as an officer were only equaled by the esteem and respect entertained by all with whom he was associated for the noble qualities of his modest and unassuming character. Brigadier-Generals Barksdale and [R. B.] Garnett were killed, and Brigadier-General Semmes mortally wounded, while leading their troops with the courage that always distinguished them. These brave officers and patriotic gentlemen fell in the faithful discharge of duty, leaving the army to mourn their loss and emulate their noble examples.[114]

Lee mentioned his seven wounded brigadiers, including Armistead, before describing Pettigrew's death: "General Pettigrew, though wounded at Gettysburg, continued in command until he was mortally wounded near Falling Waters."[115]

Even though the war took many bloody twists and turns in the coming months, Lee appeared to still be affected by his loss of leadership at Gettysburg, especially Pender, when he penned a report to Cooper in January 1864: "The loss of Major-General Pender is severely felt by the army and the country. He served with this army from the beginning of the war, and took a distinguished part in all its engagements. Wounded on several occasions, he never left his command in action until he received the injury that resulted in his death. His promise and usefulness as an officer were equaled only by the purity and excellence of his private life. Brigadier-Generals Armistead, Barksdale, Garnett, and Semmes died as they had lived, discharging the highest duty of patriots with devotion that never faltered and courage that shrank from no danger."[116]

An account from Virginia brigadier gabriel Wharton also lends some insight into the value Lee placed on Pender. Wharton related that during a conversation Lee had with A. P. Hill and himself, the army commander said: "I ought not to have fought the battle at Gettysburg; it was a mistake. But the stakes were so great I was compelled to play; for had we succeeded, Harrisburg, Baltimore and Washington were in our hands; and we would have succeeded had Pender lived."[117]

CHAPTER 13

Chickamauga, Knoxville, and Bristoe Station

CONFEDERATE BRIGADIER GENERALS PRESTON SMITH, BENJAMIN H. HELM, AND JAMES DESHLER

UNION BRIGADIER GENERAL WILLIAM H. LYTLE
Chickamauga, September 18–20, 1863

The collision of great armies savaged the pristine north Georgia mountain country at Chickamauga in September 1863, resulting in a short-lived Southern victory and three Confederate generals who fought their last battles. On the Union side, a poet-general who was a celebrity known by many Yankees and Rebels was also among the dead.

In late summer, the U.S. Army of the Cumberland commanded by Maj. Gen. W. S. Rosecrans threatened Rebel-held Chattanooga, Tennessee, an important rail center that was also considered the gateway to the lower South. Rosecrans divided his troops and pressured Confederate general Braxton Bragg into abandoning the city on September 8. Bragg's Army of Tennessee retreated into Georgia, regrouping near the town of La Fayette.

Receiving reinforcements Bragg then decided to go on the offensive, trying to attack Rosecrans's scattered forces before they could concentrate. Bragg was unable to accomplish this, and by September 18, the rival armies had converged on Chickamauga Creek in northern Georgia, the fighting becoming heavier as more and more troops reached the field. Rosecrans's army, about 62,000 strong, was strung out facing east along the La Fayette and Brotherton roads and confronted by Bragg's 65,000. The battle flared

190

throughout the day on September 19 with neither side gaining a distinct advantage in the thick woods or across the small farm fields.

About 6 P.M., Confederate brigadier general Preston Smith was informed that a night attack was to be launched. Smith, thirty-nine, was a Tennessean who was a Memphis lawyer in peacetime. As colonel of the 154th Tennessee Infantry, he had been seriously wounded at Shiloh. He had returned to action in time to command a brigade in Maj. Gen. Patrick Cleburne's division during the 1862 Kentucky offensive, and temporarily led the division when Cleburne was wounded. Promoted to brigadier in October 1862, he was leading a Tennessee brigade in Maj. Gen. Benjamin Cheatham's division of Lt. Gen. Leonidas Polk's corps at Chickamauga.[1]

Smith's troops were to support Brig. Gen. James Deshler's brigade in the night assault. Both commands moved forward, but in the gathering darkness, Deshler's men became somewhat disordered, and the brigades were thrown into some confusion. Smith and Capt. Thomas H. King, a volunteer aide, rode ahead to determine what was causing the foul-up. They blundered into a Federal unit, but Smith apparently did not immediately realize his mistake, asking the men who was their commander. The Yankees saw that he was a Confederate officer and replied with a volley. Smith was hit several times and mortally wounded while King was killed.

"Our command had halted in line in the forest after the last advance," remembered Capt. W. W. Carnes, who temporarily commanded a battery under Smith. "General Smith, with his staff, riding a short distance in front, discovered a small body of detached troops. . . . When called on to surrender they fired a straggling volley, which killed General Smith. . . . Having safely passed through the dangers of the thickest fight he met his death, when least expected, after the battle had ceased."[2]

One of the enemy bullets struck Smith's gold watch, near his heart, but still deflected into his body. "The watch was shivered, but it only diverted the messenger of death to another vital point," related Confederate general John Gordon. A portion of the watch case "whirled for a great distance through the air" before falling at the feet of a Texas soldier who later returned it to Smith's family.[3]

Taken to the rear, Smith died less than an hour later. "At the head of his noble brigade . . . he fell in the performance of what he himself with his expiring breath said was his duty," Cheatham wrote of Smith. "Active energetic and brave, with a rare fitness for command, full of honorable ambition in harmony with the most elevated patriotism, the State of Tennessee will mourn his fall and do honor to his memory."[4]

The Confederates had endured a nightmarish day of battle, and as they hunkered in their positions that night, a chorus of moaning wounded filling the cold darkness, word passed down the line among Cheatham's veterans about Smith's fall. "Soon it is whispered that our Gen. Preston Smith is dead," a Rebel remembered.[5]

Amid this haunting landscape, Rosecrans's men strengthened their lines with log breastworks during the night. They would need them in the morning. Bragg planned a dawn attack on September 20, having divided his army into two wings led by Polk and Lt. Gen. James Longstreet, just arrived with a portion of his corps from Virginia. The assault was poorly coordinated, however, and delayed for several hours. When Polk's wing finally got underway between 9:30 and 10 A.M., a brigadier with close ties to Abraham Lincoln led his Rebel troops forward.

Brig. Gen. Benjamin H. Helm's family offered a unique perspective of a house divided by this war: his wife of some seven years was Emilie Todd Helm, a half sister of Mrs. Abraham Lincoln; Helm himself was a confidante of the president. Helm's command, the Kentucky Orphan Brigade, was in Polk's strike force as part of Maj. Gen. John Breckinridge's division in Lt. Gen. D. H. Hill's corps. A father of three, Helm was a thirty-two-year-old Kentuckian who was West Point class of 1851, a state legislator and an attorney before secession. Helm and Lincoln had been close before the war, and Lincoln apparently tried to persuade him to side with the Union, offering him an army paymaster's position. Helm refused it, and went with the Confederacy. After recruiting the 1st Kentucky Cavalry, he was promoted brigadier general as of March 1862. Helm served in Mississippi and Louisiana before assuming command of the Orphans after Gen. Roger Hanson was killed at Stones River in January 1863.[6]

Helm had been sitting against a tree talking to another officer that morning when he received word to advance. "The General got up and mounted his horse, laughing and talking as though he was going on parade," related infantryman John Jackman.[7]

With a shrill yell, Helm's 1,400 Kentuckians and Alabamians rolled forward against Union major general George Thomas's XIV Corps, dug in behind log breastworks near the La Fayette Road. Breckinridge was assaulting the far left of the Federal line, resulting in two of his brigades and a portion of Helm's command overlapping the Union flank and rear. Helm himself, however, was on the left of his line, riding forward with the Second Kentucky in a frontal assault on the enemy defenses, held in this sector by the U.S. division of Brig. Gen. Absalom Baird. Because Polk had not yet ordered Cleburne's division, on Breckinridge's left, to attack, Helm's men were punished by musketry and artillery from the front as well as their left flank. Some accounts state Helm led as many as three separate assaults against the Federals, each one being repulsed.[8]

At some point Helm was riding near the center of his troops, urging them to press ahead when he was shot in the right side, collapsing from his horse. Members of his staff, including Capt. Wallace Herr and Lt. John B. Pirtle, carried him nearly a mile to the rear under heavy fire. With almost 500 casualties and their general down, Helm's brigade fell back as Breckinridge's assault wilted.[9]

Now it was time for Cleburne, of D. H. Hill's corps, to take the offensive, as Polk sent in his divisions independently rather than attacking en masse. One of Cleburne's brigadiers was James Deshler, a thirty-year-old Alabamian whose command was composed of Arkansas and Texas troops. The son of Pennsylvanians who had moved south, he graduated West Point in 1854, ranking ahead of other future Confederates such as Jeb Stuart, Dorsey Pender, and Stephen Dill Lee, and served at army posts across the country. In Confederate service he fought in western Virginia, and was wounded in a skirmish at Alleghany Summit in late 1861. Deshler recovered to see action in the Seven Days battles before being transferred to the Confederate Trans-Mississippi Department. He was captured at Arkansas Post in January 1863, but exchanged and promoted to brigadier in July, being assigned to Cleburne.[10]

Deshler was not involved in the initial attack, but Cleburne soon called on him. "General, your brigade has not been engaged today," Cleburne is reported to have said to Deshler, who replied, "It is not my fault."[11]

Deshler's Brigade was sent forward to a low ridge to fill a hole in the Confederate line. His men lay down in a pine forest and blazed away, engaging a part of the Union line occupied by Maj. Gen. John Palmer's division of the U.S. XXI Corps. Behind logs and bolstered by artillery, the Yankees suffered few casualties while pouring a hot fire into the Rebels.

With their ammunition dwindling near midday, Col. R. Q. Mills of the 6th Texas sent word to Deshler that the men needed to be resupplied. The general immediately headed toward the firing line to personally see how dire the situation was. He was checking the cartridge boxes of his men when a three-inch artillery round blasted him, "his heart literally torn from his bosom."[12]

"In effecting the last disposition of his command, General Deshler fell, a shell passing fairly through his chest," Cleburne reported. "It was the first battle in which this gentleman had the honor of commanding as a general officer. He was a brave and efficient one. He brought always to the discharge of his duty a warm zeal and a high conscientiousness. The army and the country will long remember him." Deshler died among the casualties of his command, a fact that Mills later noted: "He poured out his own blood upon the spot watered by the best blood of the brigade."[13]

Even as Deshler was dying, Longstreet's Confederates to the south were flooding through a gap in the Union line that would alter the face of the battle. Reinforcements sent to Thomas from this sector had created this opening and the Rebels exploited it, breaking up the Federal units on either side, and surging into the Yankee rear. Most of Rosecrans's army was swept from the field, but Thomas managed to patch together a defensive line along Snodgrass Hill, preventing the rout from becoming wholesale.

Longstreet's breakthrough resulted in the death of Union brigadier general William H. Lytle who was famous as the writer of *Antony and Cleopatra*, a popular 1858 epic poem about the love and death of the Roman general and the Egyptian queen.

Lytle, thirty-six, commanded the 1st Brigade of Maj. Gen. Phil Sheridan's 3rd Division in the XX Corps of Maj. Gen. Alexander M. McCook. A native of Cincinnati, Lytle's father, Robert, had been a Congressman and surveyor general of the United States. Lytle was a lawyer before fighting in the Mexican War. He continued as an attorney after that conflict and also delved into politics, serving in the Ohio legislature and making an unsuccessful run for lieutenant governor. Lytle came into his own as a poet during this time, also being appointed a major general of state militia. Amid secession, he was commissioned colonel of the 10th Ohio Infantry in May 1861, and sustained a severe leg wound at Carnifex Ferry, Virginia, in September. He recovered to serve in Alabama and Kentucky.[14]

In leading a brigade at Perryville, Lytle had been wounded and left for dead on the battlefield. Captured by the Rebels and regaining his health, he was promoted brigadier general of volunteers in late November 1862, although not officially declared exchanged until the following February.[15]

At Chickamauga, Lytle's brigade was not involved in the combat on September 19, but arrived on the battlefield about 2 A.M. on September 20, taking position on a hill near Rosecrans's headquarters on the Union extreme right flank. Led by Bushrod Johnson's Tennessee brigade, Longstreet's thrust snapped the Union line, the Federals' right flank disappearing amid a massed mob of retreating bluecoats, many running in panic.

Astride his horse, Lytle watched the gray wave coming at him and pulled on his dark kid gloves, remarking, "If I must die, I will die as a gentleman." Lytle decided to try to mount a counterattack that would allow time for the shattered Union units to regroup and reform. "All right men, we can die but once," he shouted to the 88th Illinois. "This is the time and place. Let us charge." To the 24th Wisconsin he cried, "Boys, if we can whip them today we will eat our Christmas dinner at home."[16]

His men charged with a yell, but moments later a Rebel bullet plunged into Lytle's back. "Pirtle, I am hit," he gasped to his aide-de-camp, Lt. Alfred Pirtle, who was at his side. "If I have to leave the field, you stay here and see that all goes right." He then ordered Pirtle to the rear to bring up a regiment, but the aide was soon back with the general, bidding him goodbye. Lytle managed to remain in the saddle and was in the rear of the Illinois and Wisconsin regiments as they vainly tried to stymie the enemy onslaught.[17]

Suddenly, the brigadier was hit simultaneously by three bullets, one wounding him in the face, knocking out several teeth, and exiting his neck. Capt. Howard Green of the 88th was nearby and leaped from his horse to catch Lytle as he fell. Other Federals, including Col. William McCreery of the 21st Michigan, ran to the general and tried to carry him to safety, but McCreery was mortally wounded and two orderlies killed in the attempt. With Rebels sweeping up and around the hill, Lytle entrusted his sword to another orderly and waved for those around to leave him, uttering his last words, "brave, brave, brave boys."[18]

Among the onrushing Confederates was Col. William C. Oates of the 15th Alabama, who was struggling after being wounded in the hip. The 15th belonged to Brig. Gen. E. M. Law's brigade, but this day was temporarily assigned to Brig. Gen. Zachariah Deas's brigade of Alabamians. Oates saw a riderless horse and grabbed its reins, but quickly found the animal had been shot in the leg and was useless. Nearby, Pirtle saw the same horse, recognizing it as Lytle's, and realized that the general was likely dead or captured.

Atop the hill, Oates found Lytle's body and dragged it a short distance to some shade. With the Federals routed, Maj. Douglas West, also of Deas's brigade, was gathering up Yankee prisoners when he was approached by a young Union officer who had been wounded in the heel. The Yankee was Lt. Col. Theodore West of the 24th Wisconsin (despite the name coincidence, the soldiers soon determined they were not related) and he asked Major West to "save his general."[19]

They soon found Lytle lying face up in some leaves near some Union breastworks. Major West immediately recognized him: "He was bleeding from three wounds. . . . He was dressed in full regulation uniform, but was minus his sword, his scabbard and belt being still on his person. My first exclamation, on looking down at his graceful and manly form, so perfectly dressed and accoutered, was, 'I am dying, Egypt, dying!'"[20]

Other Confederates soon gathered around Lytle. One of them was William M. Owen of the New Orleans Washington Artillery, whose father was friends with Lytle's father. Owen noted that Lytle "was dressed in fatigue uniform. His shoulder straps—one star—indicated the rank of brigadier general. He wore high riding boots, a regulation overcoat, dark kid gloves." Rebel brigadier general William Preston, another longtime friend of Lytle's father, also came to the scene and expressed regret over the general's fall. Preston, who commanded Longstreet's reserve division, had Lytle's body taken to the division surgeon, E. W. Thomasson, who also had known Lytle before the war. Thomasson cleaned the remains, covered Lytle's face with silk netting and cut a lock of hair to send to the general's sister in Cincinnati.[21]

Major West offered a different version of these events, claiming that he had Lytle carried to the rear under guard to prevent anyone from robbing the body. However the general's remains were taken to the Confederate rear, Colonel West of Wisconsin told the major, "General Lytle's family will never forget you for this act of kindness."

The Federal insisted that they exchange swords, the Alabamian also taking custody of Lytle's personal effects, including his belt and scabbard, a pistol, pocketbook, and papers, including orders.[22]

⊷ ⊨✦⊨ ⊶

In a Rebel field hospital, medical staff cut off General Helm's uniform and tried to save him. He was soon removed to a house near Reed's Bridge where the more seriously wounded were being treated. At one point, Helm asked a doctor, "Is there hope?" The physician told him truthfully, "My dear General, there is no hope!" Helm lay for several hours, listening to the sound of battle into the night. When told later that the day had been a Confederate triumph, he whispered, "victory!" the last word anyone heard from him. Breckinridge came to see him that evening, but Helm was unconcious. In silence he suffered until near midnight when he succumbed.[23]

Lincoln was deeply saddened to hear of Helm's death, remembering the prewar times they had sat together and discussed law or swapped tales of life in rural Kentucky. "I never saw Mr. Lincoln more moved than when he heard of the death of his young brother-in-law," related Supreme Court Justice David Davis. "I called to see him about 4 o'clock on the 22nd of September; I found him in the greatest grief. 'Davis,' he said, 'I feel as David of old when he was told of the death of Absalom.' I saw how grief stricken he was so I closed the door and left him."[24]

There was no hint of grief in his message to his wife about their Rebel relative. Mary Todd Lincoln was on a shopping trip to New York and staying at the Fifth Avenue Hotel when she received a September 24 wire from her husband about Chickamauga. "We now have a tolerably accurate summing up of the late battle between Rosecrans and Bragg," the president said. "The result is that we are worsted, if at all, only in the fact that we, after the main fighting was over, yielded the ground, thus leaving considerable of our artillery and wounded to fall into the enemy's hands, for which we got nothing in return." Lincoln wrote of casualties on both sides, "including your brother-in-law, Helm."[25]

When Thomas finally pulled back with nightfall on September 20 after a legendary defense, the Rebels were left in possession of the tortured battlefield, and with it losses of about 18,500 compared to Rosecrans's casualties of just over 16,000. Bragg wrote to Adjutant General Cooper the following night:

> The victory is complete, and our cavalry is pursuing. With the blessing of God our troops have accomplished great results against largely superior numbers. We have to mourn the loss of many gallant men and officers. Brigadier-Generals Preston Smith, Helm, and Deshler are killed.[26]

Three days later, Bragg wrote that the slain generals "died upon the field in the heroic discharge of duty. They were true patriots and gallant soldiers, and worthy of the high reputation they enjoyed."[27]

About two weeks after the battle, Helm's officers met to draft resolutions expressing their sorrow over the general's death, and to extend their condolences to Emilie Helm. In an October letter to the new widow, Breckinridge wrote of Helm's bond with his Orphans: "Your husband commanded them like a thorough soldier. He loved them, they loved him, and he died at their head, a patriot and hero."[28]

Deshler's body was returned to his hometown of Tuscumbia, Alabama, for burial. Helm and Smith were at first laid to rest in Atlanta. Some twenty years after the war, Helm's remains were reinterred in his family's cemetery at Elizabethtown, Kentucky. Smith was eventually relocated to Elmwood Cemetery in Memphis.

⸺ ⚔ ⸺

With the battle smoke of Chickamauga still thick, Major West and Confederate brig. gen. Patton Anderson went through Lytle's things that night. Earlier in the war, Lytle had allowed Anderson's mother to pass through his lines and Anderson now wanted to repay the favor, asking to be allowed to return Lytle's personal effects to his family. West turned over everything to Anderson except a small wicker flask, which he kept as a souvenir.[29]

The Southerners found a sonnet written to Lytle by Illinois sergeant Richard Realf, an admirer of the general's literary work. Also in the coat was a poem titled "Company K," which, like *Antony and Cleopatra*, became a major part of Lytle's legacy, even though it likely was penned by Realf. There were also rumors that the dying Lytle had composed another stanza of *Antony and Cleopatra* on the battlefield. Lytle was buried that night alongside two Rebel officers killed that day.[30]

Anderson and Major West read many of Lytle's personal papers, including correspondence between Lytle and his sister Jodie. "We sat by the uncertain light of the campfire . . . and read quite a number of letters," West recalled, adding that they included articles of poetry clipped from the Cincinnati papers. "All of this was very interesting reading to us, but it was painful . . . to think that we had assisted in putting out so brilliant a light," West related.[31]

Lytle's death would result in some mild controversy among the Confederates, as to which brigade could claim credit for his fall. General Deas reported that "my men killed early in the fight and bore off the body of Brigadier-General Lytle, U.S. Army." Other Rebels contended that Lytle was slain by soldiers of Gen. Patton Anderson's brigade, possibly the 10th Mississippi.[32]

During the post-battle confusion, as Rosecrans reorganized his battered army in and around Chattanooga, there was hope that Lytle had been wounded and captured rather than killed. "Heaven grant that as at Perryville he may survive to the country," one Yankee wrote. The news was not long in coming that Lytle was dead.[33]

"While rallying the men to the formation of this line our noble and beloved commander fell (two or three times wounded previously)," wrote Col. Silas Miller of the 36th Illinois who assumed brigade command. "During this action he had persistently refused to leave the field, but gallantly doing more than his duty to the men he loved, and who worshiped him, he sacrificed himself without reluctance."[34]

"Among the killed early in the engagement . . . was Brigadier General W. H. Lytle, who was three times wounded, but refused to leave the field," reported Sheridan. "In him the country has lost an able general and the service a gallant soldier." Sheridan added that Lytle "behaved with great skill and bravery."[35]

"The devoted Lytle and the truest and bravest had fallen in vain resistance around him," another Union officer recalled. "His splendid fighting qualities and his fine soldiers had not had half a chance."[36]

Lytle's family sent a metal coffin to Rosecrans's army in Chattanooga, and on October 9 Rosecrans sent a message to Bragg requesting the return of the general's remains. Under a truce flag, Lytle's body and some personal effects were returned by the Confederates to the Union lines on October 12. The Confederate William Owen wrote:

> As the ambulance containing the remains passed on its way to the enemy's lines the road was lined with officers and men, who testified their respect for the dead General by removing their hats and looking on silently . . . As he was known to the gentlemen of the Southern army to be a gallant and chivalrous soldier, as well as the author of the beautiful poem, "Antony and Cleopatra," all were sincerely grieved at his taking off.[37]

Much of Cincinnati was draped in black for Lytle's October 21 funeral. Mobs of people came to see the general's body lying in state in the courthouse rotunda, his casket adorned with a battle-torn banner of the 10th Ohio. Amid tolling bells and flags flying at half staff, hundreds crowded the streets as the funeral procession made its way toward Spring Grove Cemetery. A military band and five regiments of troops preceded the hearse, which was drawn by six white horses with plumed black headdresses. Lytle's riderless horse followed behind.[38]

Colonel Miller wrote: "No words or eulogies of men can add any luster to his deeds of heroic daring or render more honored and revered among men the name and memory of William H. Lytle."[39]

UNION BRIGADIER GENERAL WILLIAM P. SANDERS
Knoxville Campaign, November 18, 1863

After Chickamauga, Bragg's army coiled around Union-held Chattanooga. In the first days of November, a force under Longstreet was detached to make a thrust at Knoxville and try to deal with the Federals in that sector commanded by Maj. Gen. Ambrose Burnside. Among the Yankee defenders of Knoxville was Brig. Gen. William P. Sanders, who had three brothers in Confederate service.

Sanders, thirty, was born in Kentucky, but his family had moved to Mississippi when he was seven. An 1856 West Point graduate, he had served on the frontier as an officer of dragoons and on the Utah Expedition. When the war erupted, he had seen duty with the 6th Cavalry in Washington's defenses, but missed significant time and action due to illness. Returning to service in February 1863, he was appointed colonel of the 5th Kentucky (U.S.) Cavalry and participated in operations against the notorious Rebel raider John Hunt Morgan. Promoted brigadier a month before his death, Sanders was given command of the 1st Division in the Army of the Ohio's cavalry corps. His brothers were troopers in Mississippi cavalry regiments.[40]

Throughout much of the day on November 17, Sanders led one of his brigades in a delaying action against Longstreet's advance on the Kingston road, buying time for Union engineers to strengthen Knoxville's defenses. These Yankees finally made a stand on a hilltop about a mile from the town. Sanders's other brigade, commanded by Col. C. D. Pennebaker, was engaged in similar fighting about a mile to the north, but Confederate efforts were aimed mainly at the brigade led by Sanders. The combat died out after sundown and in a conference with Burnside that night, Sanders expressed confidence that he could hang on until midday on November 18 when engineers estimated their work would be completed.

Fighting dismounted and outnumbered, Sanders's brigade was posted behind wood rail breastworks on the hilltop and stubbornly resisted Confederate efforts to dislodge them early the next morning. "The contest was very unequal, and occasionally a few of our men would leave their position . . . with the apparent intention of retreating," wrote Capt. Orlando Poe, Burnside's chief of engineers and a West Point classmate of Sanders. Poe and others were watching Sanders's stand in the distance as they worked on the defenses. He continued: "At such critical times Sanders would walk up to the rail piles and stand there erect, with fully half his height exposed to a terrific fire at short range, until every retreating man as if ashamed of himself would return to his proper place."[41]

The Rebels finally rolled up two Napoleons to within about 250 yards of the enemy position and blazed away, making "the rails fly at every shot," a Confederate recalled. As some of Sanders's troopers scampered for better cover, the 2nd and 3rd South Carolina regiments of Joseph Kershaw's brigade charged the Union line. "Sanders and his officers rallied their men gallantly and brought most of them back to the line, and poured a heavy fire upon the Carolinians," recalled Confederate colonel E. P. Alexander, Longstreet's artillery chief. The fight was brief but sharp before the Rebels captured the breastworks.[42]

Sanders was shot down in the process, however, his wound proving to be mortal. He had clung to the hill until about 2:30 P.M. when he fell, "the screen which he had so stubbornly interposed between the enemy and our hard-working troops was quickly rolled aside," Poe recalled. Sanders was taken to the Lamar Hotel in Knoxville where he lay in the bridal suite as surgeons tried vainly to save his life. He died on November 19.[43]

Burnside, in one of his campaign reports, described how important Sanders's resistance had been to the engineers' efforts. "During all this time the gallant Sanders, with his dismounted cavalry, held the enemy in check," Burnside wrote. "Just as I sent out orders to withdraw within the lines I received information that he was mortally wounded. He was brought into the city, where he received all possible attention, but he died the next day. The service lost in the death of General Sanders one of the most noble spirits, and we, his comrades, a beloved and faithful friend."[44]

After the war, Alexander recalled how he and Sanders had been friends while at West Point and that they had last seen each other in San Francisco in 1861 as Alexander was preparing to head south to join Virginia's forces. "We parted with no anticipations of such a meeting" in battle such as Knoxville, Alexander related.[45]

"The hours in which to work that the gallant conduct of our cavalry secured us were worth . . . a thousand men each," reported Poe. "It is sad that they were bought at such a price as the life of that most gallant, chivalric soldier and noble gentleman, General Sanders."[46]

To honor his friend, Poe suggested to Burnside that the fort nearest to where Sanders fell should be named in his honor. Burnside promptly complied. Reflecting after the conflict, Poe's praise of Sanders was undimmed. He wrote: "Every spadeful of dirt turned while Sanders was fighting aided in making our position secure, and he had determined to sacrifice himself if necessary for the safety of the rest of the army."[47]

Ezra Warner concludes that Sanders was probably first buried in the yard of Knoxville's Episcopal Church. He was later reinterred in the National Cemetery in Chattanooga. Burnside wrote to Gen. U. S. Grant on November 21, informing him of the strength of the town's defenses and mentioning Sanders's demise: "The death of General Sanders is a serious loss, and keenly felt by us all."[48]

Burnside issued general field orders on November 24 regarding Sanders's fall:

The commanding general has the sad duty of announcing to this army the death of one of the bravest of their number, Brig. General W. P. Sanders. A life rendered illustrious by a long record of gallantry and devotion to his country has closed while in the heroic and unflinching performance of duty. Distinguished always for his self-possession and daring in the field, and in his private life eminent for his genial and unselfish nature and the sterling qualities of his character, he has left both as a man and a soldier an untarnished name. In memory of the honored dead, the fort in front of which he received his fatal wound will be known hereafter as Fort Sanders.[49]

On November 29, the Rebels launched a daybreak assault on Fort Sanders. It was repulsed and the Confederates soon withdrew. The Rebels never seriously threatened Knoxville again, thanks in part to Sanders's stand.

CONFEDERATE BRIGADIER GENERAL CARNOT POSEY
Bristoe Station, Virginia, October 14, 1863

Surveying the corpse-strewn battlefield of Bristoe Station, Virginia, in a rainstorm the day after the fighting, Robert E. Lee rode with Lt. Gen. A. P. Hill, whose rashness had resulted in the Confederate defeat. "Well, well general, bury these poor men, and let us say no more about it," he told Hill.[50]

Even as Lee spoke, one of Hill's brigadiers, Carnot Posey, was being treated for a leg wound that would result in him joining the ranks of the deceased about a month later. After Gettysburg, Lee's troops and U.S. major general George Meade's Army of the Potomac had moved back into Virginia in the vicinity of Culpeper. By early October, however, Lee decided to take the offensive again and put his divisions in motion against the Federals. Learning of Lee's advance, Meade retreated north along the line of the Orange & Alexandria Railroad with the Confederates in pursuit.

Leading Lee's army, Hill reached Bristoe Station on the morning of October 14, believing that he had cornered the U.S. III Corps while its troops were waiting to ford nearby Broad Run. With little hesitation and no reconnaissance, Hill ordered an assault, not realizing that Maj. Gen. Gouverneur K. Warren's Union II Corps was on the field, dug in behind a railroad embankment. When Hill attacked with two brigades of Henry Heth's division as his spear point, the Rebels were rocked by the infantry and artillery fire of the Federals massed in the railroad cut. They did not falter long however, before turning and charging Warren's position. The result was murderous as the Confederates were mowed down or driven back, even as Hill's other divisions, under Maj. Gens R. H. Anderson and Cadmus Wilcox, were still trying to reach the field.

Posey and his Mississippi brigade were among the first of Anderson's men to arrive and join the attack. Posey was a forty-five-year-old Mississippian who had been the U.S. district attorney for the southern region of his state when the war started. He also served in the Mexican War and had been a planter. Elected colonel of the 16th Mississippi Infantry, Posey was in combat at First Bull Run, Ball's Bluff and the Army of Northern Virginia's other campaigns prior to his promotion to brigadier in November 1862. He had fought at Gettysburg, but his performance had not been noteworthy.[51]

Shortly after riding into action at Bristoe Station, Posey was wounded in the left thigh by a shell fragment. The injury did not appear to be life threatening at first, although Hill reported that Posey "was seriously wounded by a shell in the early part of the action." Hill lost about 1,400 men in less than an hour of combat, the battle ending near sundown, and the Federals continued their retreat the next day. Posey "was wounded severely, but not dangerously, in the leg," the *Charleston Mercury* said on October 23.[52]

That same day, Posey was taken to Gordonsville, Virginia, and transferred to a hospital at the University of Virginia in Charlottesville within hours. Infection set in, however, and he died at the home of a friend, Dr. John S. Davis in Charlottesville on November 13.[53]

For days afterward, news and rumors of Posey's passing trickled out of Charlottesville, the *New York Herald* finally confirming the reports based on the Richmond papers. "It is again announced in the Washington dispatches that General Posey, of the rebel army, is dead," the *Herald* said on November 30. "Rumors of his demise have reached us several times, but we have the positive intelligence of his death today."[54]

"He gave to his country the supreme gift, devoted service crowned with a patriot's death," a Confederate historian wrote. Posey lies in the University Cemetery on the University of Virginia campus, where he was buried with military honors on November 15, 1863.[55]

CHAPTER 14

The Red River Campaign— 1864

CONFEDERATE BRIGADIER GENERALS THOMAS GREEN, JEAN JACQUES ALFRED ALEXANDER MOUTON, HORACE RANDAL, AND WILLIAM R. SCURRY

UNION BRIGADIER GENERAL SAMUEL A. RICE

The Red River Campaign was a Union military debacle, but four Rebel generals paid with their lives to ensure that it was. A Federal brigadier also would die of wounds.

In late winter 1864, the Federals devised elaborate plans for an offensive they hoped would quell enemy operations in northwestern Louisiana and eastern Texas. One of their main objectives was to capture Shreveport, Louisiana, headquarters of the Confederate Trans-Mississippi Department.

Union major general Nathaniel P. Banks would lead the main force of some 30,000 troops, which would move up the Red River accompanied by ironclads and gunboats of the U.S. Mississippi Squadron under Rear Adm. David Porter. Coinciding with Banks's thrust, a column of 10,000 men commanded by Maj. Gen. Frederick Steele would strike toward Shreveport from Little Rock, Arkansas. The campaign opened on March 11, and Banks and Porter concentrated their forces at Alexandria, Louisiana, which was taken with little resistance. Within days, the expedition moved upriver toward Shreveport, some of the troops marching and others traveling with the navy on armed transports.

The Rebels trying to thwart these Yankees were few and far between, but Lt. Gen. Kirby Smith, commander of the Trans-Mississippi, ordered

Maj. Gen. Richard Taylor to stop Banks. Taylor had less than 10,000 soldiers for his effort and fell back before the enemy advance, looking for an opportunity to strike. On April 3, Banks left Porter's fleet at Natchitoches, marching overland to attack Shreveport. The Federals moved along the narrow Old Stage Road leading through thick pine woods and rolling hills, stringing their column out for some twenty miles.

With the enemy confined by the road, Taylor saw his chance. He posted his army of about 8,800 at Sabine Crossroads about three miles southeast of the town of Mansfield.

The infantry division of Brig. Gen. Jean Jacques Alfred Alexander Mouton held the east side of the main road while Maj. Gen. John G. Walker's division was on the west side. Rebel cavalry of Brig. Gen. Thomas Green supported both flanks.

The Louisianian Mouton, thirty-five, was a West Pointer, class of 1850, whose father, Alexander, had been a Louisiana governor and U.S. senator. A railroad engineer before the war, Mouton suffered a nearly fatal wound in the face at Shiloh as colonel of the 18th Louisiana Infantry, but survived to be promoted brigadier in 1862. Athletically built and with a strong voice, he was a strict disciplinarian who also mingled freely with his men when off duty. One Louisianian described him as "that peerless Bayard of our fighting Creoles."[1]

The Mansfield fight opened in the early afternoon of April 8, when U.S. infantry and cavalry probed the Rebel positions. Mouton's Confederates pushed these Federals back to the crest of Honeycutt Hill along the Old Stage Road. Over the next two hours more Yankees came up, and Brig. Gen. Thomas E. G. Ransom of the U.S. XIII Corps took command of the 5,700 Federals now on the battlefield.

Taylor decided to assail the enemy line before sundown. He ordered Mouton to open the assault, and the Cajun led his brigades forward about 4 P.M. "The charge made by Mouton across the open was magnificent," Taylor wrote later. "With his little division . . . the field was crossed under a murderous fire of artillery and musketry, the wood was reached and our little line sprang with a yell on the foe."[2]

The Southerners suffered heavy casualties, but surged across the field and ravine and up a hill, capturing some guns and buckling the Union line. As the Federals broke, Mouton encountered a group of thirty-five or so Yankees who had thrown down their weapons, appearing to surrender. Mouton whirled about, raising his hand to keep his soldiers from firing on these men. "Perhaps, out of that group, one did not see the hand of mercy," Louisiana soldier John Dimitry later wrote of these bluecoats. "It may be that a sudden blindness struck five of the group. That moment, while the mad charge was still sweeping by in pursuit, five of the Federals, picking up their guns, aimed straight at the heroic figure, which had, by a signal, given them back their own unworthy lives."[3]

Hit by several bullets, Mouton tumbled dead out of the saddle, the sight of his fall enraging his men who converged on the bluecoats, soon littering the field with their bodies near where Mouton fell. "With the yells of battle was mingled yet another yell; wilder, fiercer, more curdling, a yell for vengeance!" wrote Dimitry. "Before their officers could check the savage impulse, thirty guiltless Federals had paid with their lives for the cowardly act of five. As they lay around Mouton, one might have fancied them a guard of honor drawn from the foe to show him reverence."[4]

The Yankees "had a white flag flying, and [Mouton] rode up to receive their surrender," when he was shot, related B. G. Goodrich in the 16th Texas Infantry. "They paid dearly for the dastardly act."[5]

Adding the weight of Walker's Infantry and Green's Cavalry, the Confederates smashed Ransom's line despite Mouton's loss. The Federals fell back in disorder, twice using reinforcements to make stands before sunset.

Instrumental in the pursuit was Col. Horace Randal, one of Walker's brigade commanders, who captured some 500 prisoners as well as the blue cavalry's wagon train. Randal fought so well at Mansfield that Kirby Smith assigned him to duty as a brigadier general to date from April 8. The thirty-one-year-old Tennessean would have little time to enjoy his promotion.[6]

Mouton's body was buried at Mansfield next to his old friend Col. Leopold Armant of the 18th Louisiana, who also was killed in the battle. Earlier, veteran soldiers had filed past both their bodies, many in tears as they paid their respects. After the war, Mouton's remains were transferred to St. John's Cathedral cemetery in Lafayette, Louisiana.

⚓

The shaken Federals retreated almost twenty miles from Mansfield to Pleasant Hill where Taylor attacked the next day. The April 9 battle achieved little, only adding more casualties to each side (1,300 Union, 1,600 Confederate), and Banks continued his retreat to the Red River, abandoning hope of capturing Shreveport. Hampered considerably by low water, Porter's squadron joined in the retreat down river, harassed by Rebel forces on the banks.

Thomas Green's cavalry was among Confederates that engaged several of Porter's gunboats and transports near Blair's Landing on April 12. Green, fifty, was a Virginian who had fought in the Texas war of independence and the Mexican War. With a law background, he was clerk of the Texas Supreme Court for twenty years before the war. As colonel of the 5th Texas Cavalry, Green fought in the New Mexico Campaign, in Texas and Louisiana before his promotion to brigadier in May 1863.[7]

At Blair's Landing, Green was killed by an enemy shell, possibly fired from the ironclad *Osage*, which had run aground, or from the gunboat *Lexington*. A Rebel prisoner gave U.S. brigadier general A. L. Lee information about Green's death, which Lee related in an April 14, report:

> General Green, with two brigades of cavalry, came to the river on this side and, dismounting his men, attacked the gun-boats. His men were exposed in an open field and suffered much from our shells. Green gave the order to retire, and as he was mounting his horse a shell burst and took off the top of his head. This man [the prisoner] was three miles from the spot, saw friends who had seen Green's body, which was to be carried back for burial.[8]

The Southerners claimed their fire from shore was so intense that the transports raised white flags several times, but were kept from surrendering by the Union gunboats, which didn't stop their shelling. Taylor wrote that the Federal vessels would not have escaped if Green had not fallen: "It is believed that the result would have been the capture of the whole fleet but for the unfortunate fall of the noble Green, killed by a discharge of grape from one of the gun-boats."[9]

"Gen. Tom Green was killed while fighting gunboats at Blair's Landing," wrote the Texas infantryman B. G. Goodrich. "It was a sad loss for us." Brig. Gen. Hamilton Bee assumed Green's command upon the latter's death.[10]

"For two miles the bank was strewn with the wounded and dead," Banks reported to Secretary of War Edwin Stanton. "Among other rebel officers killed was General Green, who was left dead upon the field. The troops of the transports saw him fall, and claim that his death was the work of their artillery, the gun-boats and transports all firing at the same time."[11]

Union brigadier general A. J. Smith related that the Rebels were inundated by grape and canister, and that Green was decapitated after he "had behaved with great gallantry throughout the fight." Other Federals claimed a round fired by one of four 30-pounders in an Indiana battery aboard the steamer *Rob Roy* also may have killed Green. He was "seen to fall from a discharge of canister," reported Capt. William S. Hinkle of the 1st Indiana Heavy Artillery aboard the vessel.[12]

Green's remains were returned to his camp on April 13 and, that night, lay in a torch-lit tent guarded by a squad of Texas cavalrymen. Banks mentioned the deaths of Mouton and Green in an April 14 dispatch to Maj. Gen. William T. Sherman, commander of the U.S. Military Division of the Mississippi, describing Green as "the ablest officer in their service."[13]

Green's body was taken to Austin where his entourage was met by an honor guard. He lay in state for several days in the state House of Representatives before being buried in his family's plot at Oakwood Cemetery.

After Pleasant Hill, Kirby Smith ordered most of Taylor's infantry to Arkansas to deal with Steele's Federals who had accomplished little in their advance. After losing minor battles at Poison Springs and Marks Mills, Steele began an April 26 retreat from Camden, Arkansas, toward Little Rock with Smith's force in pursuit. Cold, rainy weather, boggy roads and scant rations tortured both armies. The Federals headed toward the Saline River where they hoped to cross at Jenkins' Ferry on a pontoon bridge, destroying the span before the Rebels could follow.

Among Smith's men were the newly promoted General Randal and his brigade and Brig. Gen. William R. Scurry's command. Both were in Walker's division, known as "Walker's Greyhounds" due to the men's marching speed and stamina. Randal was the son of a Texas congressman (the family had moved to Texas when he was very young) and an 1854 graduate of West Point where he roomed with John Bell Hood. The boy-faced general was an accomplished horseman who had commanded cavalry and infantry in the war and was a brother-in-law of Confederate major general G. W. Smith. Jenkins' Ferry would be his first—and last—major battle as a general.[14]

Scurry was a forty-three-year-old Tennessean who had migrated to Texas as a teenager. He had a fine combat record in the Mexican War and had entered Confederate service as lieutenant colonel of the 4th Texas Cavalry. Scurry was a veteran of the New Mexico Campaign and was promoted brigadier in September 1862. He participated in the recapture of Galveston in January 1863 before the Red River Campaign brought him to the forefront again.[15]

The Federals reached the ferry on the afternoon of April 29 and began crossing, the high water slowing the operation. There was skirmishing during the day as the Confederates approached the field. By the next morning, all but about 4,000 of Steele's infantry and two cannons had crossed the river as the Southerners prepared to attack, some of their brigades still miles away on the march. The combat ignited before sunup and swirled over cornfields, muddy bottomland, and dripping woods, but two piecemeal

Rebel assaults failed to break Steele's battle line. Walker's Greyhounds began arriving late in the morning and Smith hustled the lead brigade of Brig. Gen. Thomas Waul into action. Scurry and Randal, meanwhile, hurried on a side road to hit the Union left flank. Walker deployed Randal in the center of the Rebel line with Scurry to his right, both brigades posted in heavy timber.

With all of his units finally on the field, Smith readied for a third assault—but it was not to be. Walker's Texans were preparing to charge when Randal and Scurry both fell with mortal wounds shortly after noon. Scurry refused to be carried to the rear and bled to death on the battlefield. With Waul also seriously wounded, the attack dissolved in confusion before it could be launched.[16]

Suffering about 700 casualties, Steele managed to get the rest of his little army over the river within two hours and torched the bridge behind him. Greatly assisting his exodus was Brig. Gen. Samuel A. Rice who fought in his rear guard.

Rice, thirty-six, was born in western New York before his family moved to Pennsylvania and then Ohio. As a youth he made several trips down the Mississippi and Ohio Rivers to New Orleans for his father's business. Rice graduated from Union College in Schenectady, New York, in 1849, and, after a year of law school there, established himself as an attorney in Oskaloosa, Iowa. He flourished as a lawyer, being elected state attorney general in 1856 and winning reelection two years later. Also active in the militia, he organized the 33rd Iowa and was commissioned its colonel, the regiment entering Federal service in October 1862. Rice's war service was in Arkansas and Missouri, and he fought well in the battle of Helena, Arkansas, resulting in his promotion to brigadier general of volunteers in August 1863. He also participated in the capture of Little Rock.[17]

His brigade of Midwesterners was a part of Brig. Gen. Friedrich Salomon's 3rd Division of the U.S. VII Corps. Rice's younger brother, Elliott W. Rice, would also become a Union brigadier and survive the war despite being wounded seven times.

In Steele's retreat, Rice had been wounded slightly in the head by a shell fragment on April 4 near Moscow, Arkansas, but did not relinquish command. "We have had two severe skirmishes," Steele reported on April 7. "General Rice was in the thickest of both fights." A piece of Rice's scalp was ripped away by a canister shot, Steele saying that "upon retiring from the field he presented a very sanguinary appearance, his wound having bled profusely."[18]

Rice would not be so lucky at Jenkins' Ferry. In the last stages of the battle, a bullet drove pieces of his spur into his right ankle, shattering the bone at the joint. Salomon was one of apparently many who didn't believe Rice's injury was life-threatening as he complimented his brigadier in his battle report. Rice "merits special mention, not only for conspicuous gallantry, cool and correct judgment in action, but also for his continual personal attention to his command," Salomon wrote. "During the entire expedition his services have been invaluable, and it is not without reluctance that I am obliged to part with him, even temporarily."[19]

Steele was even more praiseworthy in a May 4 report: "General Rice has been twice wounded during the recent campaign. At Jenkins' Ferry he received a wound which will cause the loss of his right foot. His self-possession, good judgment, energy, and faculty for managing men in the camp as well as in the field entitles him to distinguished honor. He was wounded in a charge upon the enemy's battery."[20]

Taken to Little Rock by May 8, Rice was ultimately sent to his home in Oskaloosa. There the wound would not heal and his condition worsened. A doctor removed several pieces of bone from the foot on June 15, but Rice died on July 6, Ezra Warner writing that "the primitive surgical procedures of the day virtually condemned him." Rice was buried in the town's Forest Cemetery.[21]

While they held the field and claimed victory, the Rebels had missed a prime chance to destroy the enemy while he was backed against a flooded river and had lost about 1,000 men, including their generals, for the effort.

Randal died on May 2 and was first buried near the battlefield. "The serious loss in officers and men, the fall of the gallant and daring Scurry and Randal, the only general officers from Texas, save myself, on the field, fully sustain the well-earned reputation of the troops from that State," Waul wrote.[22]

From his headquarters in Camden, Kirby Smith issued a May 3 message to his soldiers: "Once more in the hour of victory we are called upon to mourn the heroic dead. Generals W. R. Scurry and Horace Randal have fallen upon the field of honor. At Jenkins' Ferry they offered themselves up precious victims on the altar of liberty. Mouton and Green are gone; Scurry and Randal have followed on the same glorious path. Be it ours to emulate their virtues and valor, and to act as men not unworthy to associate with such heroes. The colors of their respective brigades will be draped in mourning for thirty days."[23]

Scurry was initially buried near the hamlet of Tulip, Arkansas, but later was interred in the Texas State Cemetery in Austin. Randal's remains later were moved to Greenwood Cemetery in Marshall, Texas. A Confederate soldier recognized the missed opportunity of Jenkins' Ferry when he later wrote:

> Hope for a season bade the world farewell,
> And freedom shrieked when Scurry and Randal fell.[24]

CHAPTER 15

The Wilderness

UNION MAJOR GENERAL JAMES S. WADSWORTH AND BRIGADIER GENERAL ALEXANDER HAYS

CONFEDERATE BRIGADIER GENERALS JOHN M. JONES, LEROY A. STAFFORD, AND MICAH JENKINS

The Wilderness, May 5–6, 1864

During the first days of May 1864, the jungly thickness of the Wilderness again became the chessboard for the foes' main armies in Virginia, a year after Chancellorsville was fought over much of the same killing ground.

Gen. George Meade's Army of the Potomac, some 110,000 strong, was on the march again, and the grim woods were about to claim three more Confederate generals and two Federal commanders—one of them a wealthy New Yorker—among thousands of men whose blood would soak the earth here.

Under Gen. Ulysses S. Grant's direction, Federal armies were advancing on four fronts simultaneously in an effort to overload the Confederacy's military capabilities. Meade's army, accompanied by Grant, was to attack and hopefully defeat Robert E. Lee's Army of Northern Virginia. Other Union forces were aimed at Virginia's Shenandoah Valley and Petersburg while the army of Maj. Gen. William T. Sherman ground toward Atlanta. Additionally, about 10,000 Federal cavalrymen led by Phil Sheridan were set to strike toward Richmond. Grant was squeezing five enemy pressure points at once, and Meade crossed the Rapidan River, entering the

Wilderness on May 4. Lee had only about 62,000 troops to meet this threat, but he knew that if he caught and attacked while the Yanks were trying to find their way out of the thick woodlands, Meade's numbers might be negated.

Lee's three corps were still separated in winter quarters, and he immediately ordered all of them to converge on the enemy toiling through the Wilderness. Lt. Gen. Richard Ewell's corps moved east along the Orange Turnpike while about three miles to the south, Lt. Gen. A. P. Hill's corps marched almost parallel to Ewell on the Orange Plank Road. Lt. Gen. James Longstreet's corps was about a day's march behind the rest of Lee's men.

Leading Ewell's advance was the Virginia brigade of Brig. Gen. John M. Jones, a forty-three-year-old Virginian and West Point class of 1841 who had spent several years as an instructor of infantry tactics at the Military Academy. In the war's first two years he served on the staffs of Gens. John Magruder, Richard Ewell, and Jubal Early, frequently being commended for gallantry. Promoted to brigadier in May 1863, he was badly wounded at Gettysburg and again in fighting at Payne's Farm the following November. His command was in Maj. Gen. Edward Johnson's division.[1]

Jones was destined to open the Wilderness fighting, but he would not live to see much of the battle. Shortly before noon on May 5, his men collided with elements of U.S. major general Gouverneur K. Warren's V Corps along the turnpike. Ewell sent in two brigades to support Jones, but a sudden attack on Jones's front and right flank sent the Virginians reeling. Jones and his aide-de-camp, Capt. Robert D. Early, were shot and killed "in a desperate effort to rally their brigade," Ewell reported.[2] Another account relates that as his men broke, Jones was on horseback and cooly watching the approaching enemy when he was slain.[3]

By this time the fighting had spread south where Hill met Union cavalry. The U.S. VI Corps of Maj. Gen. John Sedgwick was also engaged against Ewell and Hill. With only two-thirds of his army, Lee had wanted to avoid a large-scale battle until Longstreet reached the field, but more and more units poured into the increasingly fierce combat. The enemies rarely saw each other in the tangled forests that made coordinated attacks impossible, soldiers stumbling through thorny underbrush where smoke from thousands of muskets hung in the trees, obscuring the sun. The gunfire sparked brush fires that consumed a number of soldiers too badly wounded to escape. The battle in Ewell's sector ebbed and flowed through the early afternoon with both sides making thrusts and digging in along temporary trench lines in the deep woods.

Brig. Gen. Leroy A. Stafford's Louisiana brigade of Johnson's Division was in position near the turnpike. The forty-two-year-old Stafford had been a planter and parish sheriff before the war, and had a wife and nine children at home. He was a Mexican War veteran who went to fight the Yankees as lieutenant colonel of the 9th Louisiana Infantry. Stafford fought in Jackson's Valley Campaign, the Seven Days battles, at Cedar Mountain, Second Bull Run, and the Maryland Campaign, as well as Fredericksburg, Chancellorsville, and Gettysburg. Commissioned a brigadier in October 1863, Stafford was given command of the 2nd Louisiana "Tigers" Brigade of the Stonewall Division, which he led at Mine Run.[4]

In their swiftly dug Wilderness defenses, the Tigers suddenly heard a volcano of musketry roaring through the thickets off one of their flanks. Sedgwick's corps was launching an assault on Ewell. Unknown to Stafford due to the rugged terrain, there was a gap between his brigade and James Walker's Stonewall Brigade to his left, and the attacking Yankees poured into it, most notably the New Jersey brigade of Col. Henry W. Brown. Stafford desperately tried to swing some of his men around to face these Federals, but with no success. He also sent an aide to try to find the brigade on his right and link with it, but blue infantry crashing through the underbrush there captured the officer. Assailed on both flanks, Stafford ordered a withdrawal, calmly sitting on his horse as the Louisianians pulled back.

As the last soldiers passed him, Stafford turned to follow when he was shot, a musket ball piercing his right shoulder and damaging his spine. He toppled from his mount and several of his men carried him to the rear where he was laid in the shade of a tree near the turnpike. Hurrying to the front, the Louisianians of Brig. Gen. Harry Hays's brigade saw the stricken general by the roadside. A number of them had been in the Stafford Guards, which Stafford had organized at the war's outset, later to become a company in the 9th Louisiana. Now these Tigers paused in their rush to offer a quick word of encouragement or sympathy to the wounded leader. Stafford told them "he was ready to die if need be," and urged them to fight to the last man. Leaving his side, many of the men were confident that he would recover from his injuries.[5]

In the fighting to the south that afternoon, Hill's Rebels also began to encounter Maj. Gen. Winfield S. Hancock's II Corps, which was just arriving on the battlefield. The combat was back and forth when Union brigadier general Alexander Hays, one of Grant's longtime friends, was added to the casualty list. Hays, forty-four, was a native of Franklin, Pennsylvania, who graduated near the bottom of the West Point class of 1844. While his grades were average, he did become close to Grant, who was in the preceding class, and their friendship endured into the war years. Hays

*Union brigadier general
Alexander Hays.*
LIBRARY OF CONGRESS

saw combat in the Mexican War, but left the Army in 1848 to go into the iron business. He also prospected for gold in California and was a bridge construction engineer. When the Civil War came, he rejoined the Army and was appointed colonel of the 63rd Pennsylvania Volunteers. Hays led his regiment through the Peninsular Campaign and was seriously wounded at Second Bull Run. He was promoted brigadier general of volunteers in September 1862, and fought well at Gettysburg, commanding a II Corps division. In early 1864, however, the Union III Corps was merged into the II Corps and, due to seniority among generals, Hays was relegated to command of a brigade in Maj. Gen. David Birney's division of Hancock's corps.[6]

Hays was killed about 2 P.M., shot through the head while leading his brigade near the intersection of the Brock Road and the Orange Plank Road. Described by a Union officer as "one of the most gallant officers in the service," Hays had ridden forward to rally his broken line when he was hit. Soldiers placed his body in an ambulance and it was carried to the rear. Lt. Col. Horace Porter of Grant's staff was at the front and later returned to relay the "sad intelligence" of Hays' death. He recalled, "General Grant was by no means a demonstrative man, but upon learning the sad intelligence I brought, he was visibly affected. He was seated on the ground with his back to a tree, still whittling pine sticks. He sat for a time without uttering a word, and then, speaking in a low voice, and pausing between the sentences, said: 'Hays and I were cadets together for three years. We served for a time in the same regiment in the Mexican war. He was a noble man and a gallant officer. I am not surprised that he met his death at the head of his

*Union brigadier general
James S. Wadsworth.*
LIBRARY OF CONGRESS

troops; it was just like him. He was a man who would never follow, but would always lead in battle.'"[7]

That night, one of Hays's staff officers rode to General Meade's headquarters and asked permission to transport the body to Washington. The request was granted, and Hays's corpse was carried to the rear in an ammunition train.

Sundown brought an end to the hellish fighting with thousands of casualties on both sides. "By the blessing of God we maintained our position against every effort until night, when the contest closed," Lee wrote to Confederate secretary of war James Seddon that night. "We have to mourn the loss of many brave officers and men. The gallant Brig. Gen. J. M. Jones was killed, and Brig. Gen. L. A. Stafford, I fear, mortally wounded while leading his command with conspicuous valor."[8]

Grant and Meade greeted dawn on May 6 with assaults against the Rebels along the Orange Turnpike and the Orange Plank Road. Ewell's men were well dug in, however, and blunted the Union thrust on the turnpike. But Hancock's attack on Hill's lines met with much more success, and suddenly Lee's right flank was in danger of collapse. At this critical juncture, Longstreet's divisions arrived in the nick of time, having been on the march since midnight. The vicious counterattack stunned Hancock. Longstreet followed up this success with a flank assault on the Federals' left with four brigades about 11 A.M. This surprise blow, led by Lt. Col. Moxley Sorrel of Longstreet's staff, and a simultaneous assault on his front sent Hancock's men pulling back to entrenchments along the Brock Road. Among the Union troops in this melee was the division of Brig. Gen. James S. Wadsworth in Maj. Gen. G. K. Warren's V Corps.

Wadsworth, fifty-six, was from one of the most affluent families in New York State, born in the village of Geneseo where his father presided over the Wadsworths' vast land holdings. As a young man, Wadsworth had spent two years at Harvard and became a lawyer, but soon immersed himself in politics. He was one of the organizers of the Free Soil Party and in 1861 participated in the Washington peace conference, an unofficial meeting where Northern and Southern leaders tried to find a way to prevent bloodshed. When the war came, Wadsworth volunteered his services and, despite his lack of military training, was appointed a brigadier general in August 1861. He served as military governor of the District of Columbia and mounted an unsuccessful bid for the governorship of New York that year. Assigned command of a I Corps division after Fredericksburg, he was in heavy fighting at Gettysburg. Amid a reorganization of several Union corps, Wadsworth had been assigned to lead a division in Warren's corps a few weeks before his last battle at the Wilderness.[9]

On this fateful morning, Wadsworth continued in command despite being ill. His Federals fought their way across the II Corps front and to the south side of the plank road, driving back the Confederates. The advantage was short-lived when Longstreet's men blunted the Union attack and hurled it back. "The accumulating force of the enemy staggered his [Wadsworth's] advance, and the line became confused in the dense woods," Warren later reported.[10]

In the confused combat, Wadsworth was trying to rally not only his own men but those of some II Corps troops as well, including Brig. Gen. Alexander Webb's brigade. Webb recalled that Wadsworth ordered the 20th Massachusetts to attack, but was told by officers that the regiment, posted behind log defenses, had changed its front and was holding its line there. "Wadsworth answered that the men were afraid, leaped his horse over the logs and led them in the charge himself," Webb wrote. "He was mortally wounded, and my line was broken."[11]

Wadsworth fell from his horse when a minié to the forehead lodged in his brain. "In the very van of the fight General Wadsworth was killed by a bullet through the head," Warren wrote. At least one other account states that the fatal shot, fired by a Rebel sniper posted in a tree, struck the general on the top of his head and emerged from the back of his neck.[12]

The Federals were unable to bring him from the field and he was captured by Rebels of Brig. Gen. William Mahone's brigade. "As our troops reached the plank-road . . . a volley was given to the enemy who were trying to rally on the opposite side," a Rebel colonel remembered. "By this volley General Wadsworth and his horse (while trying to rally his men), were both killed, and his soldiers could make no stand against us." Another officer in Mahone's brigade noted, "we soon had the entire force of the enemy . . . routed, leaving in our hands a large number of dead and wounded, among the latter General Wadsworth, whom I remember seeing lying on the ground as we passed along." In the battle frenzy, a Rebel officer noticed Wadsworth and ordered two of his men to erect a makeshift awning over him using muskets and a blanket.[13]

Even his Rebel captors knew of Wadsworth and his millionaire status. On a litter, the Confederates carried him to an officers' field hospital where other Confederates came for a look at the white-haired general. One of the Southerners later wrote of the socialite who had "more wealth than the treasury of the Confederate government" dying among his enemies and so far from his loved ones.[14]

Wadsworth "was placed alone in an officer's tent, which had been put in position for his especial benefit" and was treated by Dr. James W. Claiborne, Mahone's surgeon, who also was tending to a number of other Union wounded. A captured and injured Federal physician also examined Wadsworth, finding that the unconscious general's eyes did not react when his eyelids were lifted. Wadsworth's pulse was regular and his breathing was slightly labored, but his face betrayed no signs of pain.[15]

After his success in the late morning and early afternoon, Longstreet quickly prepared to try to finish Hancock with another attack, making hasty plans to renew the assault with Brig. Gen. Joseph Kershaw's division and the fresh South Carolina brigade of Brig. Gen. Micah Jenkins of Maj. Gen. Charles Field's division.

Jenkins also had been sick and traveled in an ambulance, mounting a horse to lead his brigade in the battle. Jenkins, twenty-eight, was a member of a prominent South Carolina family who had graduated from the state military academy at the head of his class in 1854. He fought at First Bull Run as colonel of the 5th South Carolina Infantry and organized the Palmetto Sharpshooters regiment, which he led in the Seven Days battles. Promoted brigadier in July 1862, he was severely wounded at Second Bull Run, but recovered to see action at Chickamauga where he led John Hood's division, and participated in the Knoxville Campaign.[16]

While successful, Sorrel's flank attack had further disorganized the positions of the armies. There was a lull in the battle about 1 P.M., and Longstreet rode up to Field to congratulate him for the conduct of his division so far that day. Longstreet was now ready to renew the offensive. At the head of Jenkins's Brigade, Longstreet, Jenkins, and Kershaw proceeded down the plank road, Kershaw's men crunching forward through the underbrush. Jenkins's men were wearing new uniforms of deep gray that appeared to be blue or even black in the woods.

Jenkins was exuberant, calling for his men to raise a cheer for Longstreet, which they did, momentarily drowning out the sound of distant gunfire. "I am happy," the Carolinian told Longstreet. "I have felt despair for the cause for some months, but I am relieved now, and feel assured that we will put the enemy back across the Rapidan before night." Jenkins had earlier thrown his arm around Sorrel and exclaimed, "We will smash them now."[17]

The generals were now in the vicinity of where Stonewall Jackson had fallen little more than a year earlier, and the banshees of Confederate misfortune still lurked in these tortured woods.

Kershaw and Jenkins were riding together, conferring about their assault when two or three shots came from the north side of the road. They were followed immediately by a volley from the other side where Mahone's Virginians, who had been involved in Sorrel's flank assault, mistook the advancing troops for Federals and opened fire. Longstreet was critically wounded, coughing blood from a round that caught him near the throat and plunged into his right shoulder.

As soldiers tended to him, life ebbed away for Jenkins and two others. The brigadier had been shot in the forehead, the bullet penetrating his brain and paralyzing one side of his body. In the dusty road lay the bodies of Capt. A. E. Doby of Kershaw's staff and orderly Marcus Baum, both instantly killed by the volley. When the musketry flared, Jenkins's lead ranks had wheeled toward the gunfire, preparing to return it, but Kershaw, seeing what had happened, galloped among them shouting, "They are friends!"[18]

Mahone's 41st or 61st Virginia apparently fired the mistaken shots, but in the shock of the moment no one was pointing fingers. Field recalled that the generals "had gotten about thirty yards in my front when I heard a scattering fire from the bushes on the right of the road, and saw General Longstreet's party in great confusion."[19]

Longstreet was lifted from his horse and propped against a tree at the roadside. He would live; Jenkins would not. He was rushed to a field hospital, but surgeons quickly saw there was little to be done for him. Semi-conscious and delirious, Jenkins could not recognize those around his bed, but called for his men to press forward. The brigadier "would cheer his men and implore them to sweep the enemy into the river, until he became too weak to talk," recalled one observer. He died about five hours later, leaving his wife, Carrie, to raise their four small children alone.[20]

That night an obviously battle-jaded captain in the 61st Virginia scribbled a few thoughts in his diary: "The Union General Wardsworth [*sic*] was killed in front of our line. Lieutenant-General Longstreet was wounded, and General Jenkins, of South Carolina, was killed, both in front of our line by our troops. So much for bad generalship." Grant, meanwhile, learned of Longstreet's wounding and Jenkins's death from prisoners, and noted these Confederate losses in several dispatches.[21]

Amid the battle, word reached the Federal brass about Wadsworth's fall, one of the general's aides, a lieutenant, bringing the tidings shortly after noon. "He [the lieutenant] reports that the general is killed; that he was with him when he was struck in the head about half an hour ago," Union major E. R. Platt wrote in a dispatch to Maj. Gen. Andrew Humphreys, Meade's chief of staff, at 12:45 P.M. "The body was left on the ground."[22]

Lee noted Wadsworth's wounding and capture in a dispatch that night to Secretary of War Seddon. Grant wrote to Gen. Henry Halleck on the morning of May 7, making note of Hays and Wadsworth. "Among the killed we have to deplore the loss of Generals Wadsworth and Hays," he wrote, although Wadsworth still clung to life in Rebel hands. In one of his many reports about the Wilderness, Meade wrote of "the gallant Wadsworth falling mortally wounded while exerting himself to rally the retiring columns."[23]

That night, a Rebel surgeon examined Wadsworth and removed a piece of the skull while probing the wound. It was noted that the general was unable to swallow, teaspoonfuls of water placed between his lips dribbling out of his mouth.[24]

—+— ≋✚≋ —+—

"I grieve to announce that Lieutenant-General Longstreet was severely wounded and General Jenkins killed," Lee wrote to Secretary Seddon on the night of May 6. "[Brigadier] General [John] Pegram was badly wounded yesterday. General Stafford, it is hoped, will recover." Stafford would not rally, however. From the battlefield, the paralyzed general had been taken to the Institute Hospital in Richmond, where he died about 10 A.M. on May 8. "In his death the country is called to mourn the loss of a good man and a gallant and skillful officer," the *Richmond Whig* said a day later.[25]

President and Mrs. Davis attended Stafford's funeral, and were among the mourners who gathered at Hollywood Cemetery where he was buried next to Maj. Roberdeau Wheat, another popular Louisiana officer, who had been killed at Gaines' Mill. A year after the war's end, Stafford's remains were returned to his ancestral home near Cheneyville, Louisiana. "General Edward Johnson once said of General Stafford that he was the bravest man he ever saw," Dick Ewell wrote of his brigadier. "Such a compliment from one himself brave almost to a fault and habitually sparing of praise needs no remark."[26]

After a funeral in Richmond, Jenkins's body was returned to South Carolina. He was first buried in Summerville, but was moved to Charleston's Magnolia Cemetery in 1881, where he and Carrie would lie side by side.

The similarities between the deaths of Jenkins and Stonewall Jackson shocked the South. "We fear, too, that he fell by the hands of our own men, another victim of the carelessness which deprived us on the same ground, and by the same misfortune, of the illustrious Stonewall," the *Charleston Mercury* said. Jenkins "led his impetuous battalions in a score of stormy fights, and fell with sword in hand, at the close of a well-stricken field, the light of the setting sun crimsoning his victorious bayonets, and the shouts of triumph ringing in his ears."[27]

John Jones's body, meanwhile, was taken to Charlottesville, his hometown, where he was buried in Maplewood Cemetery. "I considered his loss an irreparable one to his brigade," Ewell reported of the Virginian's fall.[28]

With the hard fighting and confused reports flowing from the battlefield, Hays's death was not confirmed publicly for several days, but the sad intelligence gradually seeped out. "There seems to be no doubt of the death of General Hays," the *New York Herald* noted on May 9. "He held the position which bore the brunt of A. P. Hill's attack, and fell at the head of his command just at the moment that the support that he had ordered forward reached him." "We learn that in the action in the Wilderness he sustained his reputation of being one of the most splendid officers in the veteran Army of the Potomac," the *New York Times* said of Hays on May 10. The general was "a gallant and intrepid soldier and dearly loved by his men," the *Herald* added on May 14. "They had often said they would follow him to the death, and many of them did."[29]

Wadsworth died at the Rebel field hospital on May 8 without regaining consciousness. The Federals, meanwhile, were receiving scattered information about his fate, although most of it indicated his demise. Charles A.

Dana, the U.S. Assistant Secretary of War, was with Meade's army and sending regular updates to Secretary of War Edwin Stanton. Even as Wadsworth breathed his last, Dana's May 8 message included the latest the Federals then knew of him and Hays: "Our last report from General Wadsworth is that yesterday morning he lay senseless in a rebel hospital, shot though the brain, and sure to die. . . . General Hays is killed."[30]

Union cavalry that afternoon had also picked up more information about Wadsworth, although it was outdated. "A captured rebel courier informs me that General Wadsworth is not yet dead, though insensible from a wound in the head, and expected to die eventually," cavalry Brig. James Wilson reported. "I will send more details when I ascertain them." The news gradually trickled back to the Federal lines regarding Wadsworth's fate. Dana wrote to Stanton on May 11: "We learn from prisoners that Wadsworth is dead."[31]

In his correspondence to Meade the next day, Stanton mentioned Wadsworth: "I beg to suggest that on the first occasion that may offer for a flag of truce, every effort be made to recover the remains of the gallant General Wadsworth, which are understood to be still in the hands of the enemy, and those of any other officers who may be in a like situation."[32]

The *Times* published a lengthy editorial on Wadsworth's loss in the May 11 edition: "Gen. Wadsworth's death excites feelings of intense regret everywhere. There has been no instance in this war of a more high-toned surrender of comfort, fortune and life itself to principle, than that offered in his career." Despite his wealth and social standing, Wadsworth joined the army when the war came because "he believed the cause of the Union to be the highest and noblest in which the sword was ever drawn, and because he could not sit at ease . . . while leaving others to fight the battle of human liberty and republican government. . . . The State . . . and the country have, by his fall, lost one of their finest and truest sons. But for himself, both the manner and the occasion of his death were all that could be desired. The oldest and the bravest soldier that ever lived could not have craved a more glorious close of his career than came, unsought but scarcely unwelcome, to crown the brief but splendid service of this noble son of the Empire State."[33]

Despite its verbal dirges, the *Times* was more optimistic about Wadsworth's survival two days later: "It is not yet certain that Gen. Wadsworth was killed . . . the belief exists among some of his friends here that he may yet be heard of living." By the next day, however, Union authorities had confirmed that Wadsworth was dead. "The question of the death of Gen. Wadsworth is at length settled," the *Times* said on May 14. "A Rebel captain was taken to-day who helped to bury him, and who took his official papers from his person." In the same edition, another article mentioned that Rebel major general Edward Johnson, captured at Spotsylvania, "though he did not know the fact personally, had very little doubt of his [Wadsworth's] death."[34]

A May 15 *New York Herald* piece stated that based on information from a captured Rebel lieutenant, Wadsworth had lived three days in Confederate hands and had been "very kindly treated," which appears to be the case. Even so, the report contributed to the confusion about Wadsworth's end and continued: "He was conscious up to the hour of his death, and his only regret was, not that he had fallen mortally wounded, but that he should die among the enemies of his country, for which he had given his life a cheerful sacrifice." The article also stated that the Rebels had buried Wadsworth near the crossroads of Parker's Store and in a ravine near the plank road.[35]

At the front that day, Meade sent a dispatch to the "Officer Commanding Confederate Forces, In Vicinity of Parker's Store" to try to retrieve Wadsworth's body:

> Sir: I would esteem it a personal favor for which I shall be grateful if you will permit the bearer, A. K. St. Clair, assistant surgeon, First Michigan Cavalry, to pass within your lines sufficiently far to obtain the remains of the late Brigadier General J. S. Wadsworth, for the purpose of transferring them to his affected widow and relatives.

Lee sent a May 16 reply to Meade agreeing to release Wadsworth's remains, but by the time Meade received the note, arrangements had already been made for St. Clair to return with the body. Learning that St. Clair had returned with Wadsworth, Meade wrote a dispatch to Lee, offering "my sincere thanks for your kind consideration."[36]

Wadsworth's remains were accompanied back to the Union lines by Dr. W. J. McDermott, a surgeon with the 66th New York who had been captured in the fighting. McDermott was impressed with the care the Confederates exhibited for the general's body and the neat, black coffin in which it was placed.

"It is but just to say that Gen. Lee gave free consent to have the body exhumed and brought home," said the *Times*, "but some of his officers did all in their power to thwart the party seeking the body, by objecting to slight informalities in the arrangement for the flag of truce." In a grisly aside, the paper noted that the remains were too decomposed to embalm.[37]

General Hancock lamented the loss of Hays and Wadsworth:

Brigadier-General Alexander Hays, that dauntless soldier, whose
intrepid and chivalric bearing on so many battle-fields had won for
him the highest renown, was killed at the head of his brigade . . .
Brigadier-General Wadsworth whose brilliant example and fearless
courage always had such an inspiring effect upon his soldiers, fell
while leading them against the enemy.[38]

All in all, however, the deaths of three Confederate and two Union
generals were quickly forgotten in the two-day holocaust of the Wilderness, which cost Grant about 18,000 casualties compared to Lee's 10,800.
But the butcher's bill for this campaign was far from being totaled. Grant
ordered the army to move on the evening of May 7, tramping to the
southeast to try to get behind Lee's right flank. Lee countermarched as the
lethal minuet ground toward the crossroads of Spotsylvania Court House.

Hays was posthumously brevetted major general from the date of his
death, and was buried in Pittsburgh's Allegheny Cemetery. Wadsworth's
remains arrived in Washington by steamer on May 18 on its return to New
York State. Laid to rest at Temple Hill Cemetery in Geneseo, Wadsworth
also was honored with a posthumous promotion to major general to rank
from the date of his wounding.[39]

A few years after the war Grant traveled to Pittsburgh during his presi-
dential campaign. He asked to be taken to Allegheny Cemetery and cried
at the resting place of Hays, his old friend.

CHAPTER 16

John Sedgwick and Other Virginia Dead, May–June, 1864

UNION MAJOR GENERAL JOHN SEDGWICK AND BRIGADIER GENERALS JAMES C. RICE AND THOMAS G. STEVENSON

CONFEDERATE BRIGADIER GENERALS JUNIUS DANIEL AND ABNER M. PERRIN
Spotsylvania, May 9–12, 1864

Despite the awful carnage of the Wilderness, the armies seemed locked in a death grip as they toiled across the Virginia countryside, the hamlet of Spotsylvania Court House being next to earn a battle name in the history books. Sniping or wholesale assaults were almost nonstop as Lee and Grant moved out of the ghoulish Wilderness, both eyeing the road junction at Spotsylvania. The Confederates got there first and began digging earthworks while the rest of the rival forces filtered into lines in the vicinity.

By the time a Rebel sharpshooter killed Union major general John Sedgwick of the U.S. VI Corps along the Spotsylvania lines on May 9, the war here had become a meat grinder of men on both sides: four more generals—two each in blue and gray—joined Sedgwick among the slain.

Sedgwick, fifty, is described by historian Ezra Warner as "one of the most beloved soldiers in the Army of the Potomac," and was born in Cornwall Hollow, a village in Connecticut's Berkshire Mountains. An 1837 graduate of West Point, his classmates included Joseph Hooker and future Confederate generals Braxton Bragg, Jubal Early, and John Pemberton. He

*Union major general
John Sedgwick.*
LIBRARY OF CONGRESS

fought in the Seminole wars and participated in the relocation of the
Cherokees from Georgia to Oklahoma, also seeing combat in the Mexican
War. He also served as major of the 1st U.S. Cavalry under Robert E. Lee
and William J. Hardee.[1]

After secession, Sedgwick was commissioned brigadier general of volunteers to rank from August 31, 1861. He led a II Corps division in the
Peninsular Campaign before being wounded on June 30, 1862. A few
weeks later he was promoted to major general. Sedgwick recovered from
his injuries in time to fight at Antietam, where he was wounded three
times and carried unconscious from the field. Given command of the VI
Corps in early 1863, Sedgwick played a key role in the Chancellorsville
Campaign, but saw little action at Gettysburg, his corps held in reserve.
Sedgwick was the victor at Rappahannock Bridge in November, 1863,
however, leading the V and VI Corps.[2]

In the Wilderness and Spotsylvania fighting up to the dawn of May 9,
he had offered his usual steadiness and reliable generalship. Rising before
daybreak, Sedgwick was in good spirits on his last morning alive, joking, as
was his nature, with members of his staff. He issued orders to his division
commanders for them to remain in position, distribute rations and ammunition, and send in their estimated casualty and strength totals.

Meade, meanwhile, sent a 6:45 A.M. dispatch to Maj. Gen. Gouverneur K. Warren, the V Corps commander, showing his trust and
reliance on Sedgwick. Meade stated that in the event of any combined

action involving the V and VI Corps, Sedgwick would take command of both in Meade's absence. (The VI Corps had moved into position to support Warren's corps the previous day.) About an hour later while in the Union breastworks, Sedgwick encountered one of Warren's staff officers, saying to him, "just tell General Warren to go on and command his own corps as usual. I have perfect confidence that he will do what is right, and knows what to do with his corps as well as I do."[3]

Sedgwick also had a brief, early-morning talk with Grant, the generals conferring on horseback behind the VI Corps positions. Sedgwick "seemed particularly cheerful and hopeful . . . and looked the picture of buoyant life and vigorous health," related Lt. Col. Horace Porter, one of Grant's aides. "When his chief uttered some words of compliment upon his recent services, and spoke of the hardships he had encountered, Sedgwick spoke lightly of the difficulties experienced, and expressed every confidence in the ability of his troops."[4]

After Grant's party passed further to the Union left, Sedgwick sat on a hardtack box, issued orders and watched some of his soldiers digging rifle pits near a two-gun battery that occupied an angle in the Union front line where several officers had been dropped by Rebel fire.

At one point, Lt. Col. Martin T. McMahon, Sedgwick's chief of staff, had gestured toward the guns and in a "half-jesting manner" told his commander, "General, do you see that section of artillery? Well, you are not to go near it today." McMahon continued his account: "He [Sedgwick] answered good-naturedly, 'McMahon, I would like to know who commands this corps, you or I?' I said, playfully, 'Sometimes I am in doubt myself,' but added, 'Seriously, General, I beg of you not to go to that angle; every officer who has shown himself there has been hit, both yesterday and today.' He answered quietly, 'Well, I don't know that there is any reason for my going there.'"[5]

About 9:45 A.M., an hour or so after this conversation, Sedgwick noticed that the line of infantrymen occupying the newly-dug rifle pits was overlapping the battery. He told McMahon to have the infantry move away from the cannons and both officers walked to the angle, forgetting their earlier talk, according to McMahon. The order was issued and the soldiers began to shift positions, attracting a smattering of fire from the Confederates.

McMahon described what happened next:

As the bullets whistled by, some of the men dodged. The general said laughingly, "What! What! Men dodging this way for single bullets! What will you do when they open fire along the whole line? I am ashamed of you. They couldn't hit an elephant at this distance." A few seconds after, a man . . . separated from his regiment passed directly in front of the general, and at the same moment a sharp-shooter's bullet passed with a long shrill whistle very close, and the soldier . . . dodged to the ground. The general touched him gently with his foot, and said, "Why, my man, I am ashamed of you, dodging that way," and repeated the remark, "They couldn't hit an elephant at this distance." The man rose and saluted and said good naturedly, "General, I dodged a shell once, and if I hadn't, it would have taken my head off. I believe in dodging." The general laughed and replied, "All right, my man; go to your place." For a third time the same shrill whistle, closing with a dull, heavy stroke, interrupted our talk; when, as I was about to resume, the general's face turned slowly to me, the blood spurting from his left cheek under the eye in a steady stream. He fell in my direction; I was so close to him that my effort to support him failed, and I fell with him.[6]

McMahon's cry as he collapsed with Sedgwick drew the attention of several officers, including Col. Charles Tompkins, commander of the VI Corps artillery, who shouted for his brigade surgeon, a Dr. Ohlenschlager. All rushed to Sedgwick's aid.

"A smile remained upon his lips but he did not speak," McMahon wrote of the general. "The doctor poured water from a canteen over the general's face. The blood still poured upward in a little fountain. The men in the long line of rifle-pits, retaining their places from force of discipline, were all kneeling with heads raised and faces turned toward the scene; for the news had already passed along the line." Brig. Gen. Horatio Wright was ordered by Meade to take command of the VI Corps about 10 A.M.[7]

"The only fighting during the day was between the pickets and sharp-shooters, in which, however, we sustained a heavy loss in the death of . . . Sedgwick," reported Surgeon Thomas McParlin, the Army of the Potomac's medical director. "His death was almost instantaneous, the ball entering just below the left eye and traversing the base of the brain."[8]

Followed by grieving members of his staff, Sedgwick's body was carried by ambulance to Meade's headquarters. "A bower was built for it of evergreens, where, upon a rustic bier, it lay until nightfall, mourned over by officers and soldiers," McMahon wrote.[9]

Grant, meanwhile, had sent Colonel Porter back to find Sedgwick and clarify some matter when Porter heard musket fire and saw an officer being taken to the rear. "Such a sight was so common that ordinarily it would have attracted no attention, but my apprehensions were aroused by seeing several of . . . Sedgwick's staff beside the body," Porter remembered. "As they came nearer, I gave an inquiring look. Colonel [E. B.] Beaumont, of the staff . . . looked at me with an expression of profound sorrow, and slowly shook his head. His actions told the whole sad story. His heroic chief was dead."[10]

Porter informed the general-in-chief of Sedgwick's fall shortly afterward and recalled Grant's reaction: "For a few moments he could scarcely realize it, and twice asked, 'Is he really dead?' The shock was severe, and he could ill conceal the depth of his grief. He said: 'His loss to this army is greater than the loss of a whole division of troops.'"[11]

"The army remained comparatively quiet during the day; it was, however, called upon to mourn the death of one of its greatest leaders, the gallant and noble hearted Sedgwick," reported Maj. Nathaniel Michler, the Army of the Potomac's acting chief engineer.[12]

Later in the day on May 9, Meade issued orders for Sedgwick's body to be sent home to Connecticut, accompanied by several staff officers.

The May 12 *New York Times* stated that Sedgwick was "superintending the mounting of some heavy guns, in an angle the men had just prepared. There was no skirmishing at the time, but an occasional sharpshooter sent a bullet in that direction, which caused the men to be on the alert to dodge them." The general, "who was standing near them, was smiling at their nervousness, when a bullet struck him in the forehead, the blood oozed from his nostrils, and he fell back dead into the arms of his Assistant Adjutant-General."[13]

A day earlier, the *Times* had eulogized Sedgwick, as well as General Wadsworth, on its editorial page:

> The death of this gallant soldier will cause a deep feeling of sorrow throughout the country, only to lose his life at the hands of a murderous sharpshooter, instead of falling, as he would have chosen to fall, in the heat of battle, inspiring his men by a brilliant example. To no one will his death come with deeper sorrow than to his command, who loved him, and the avenging arm of the noble Sixth Corps will strike surer and swifter blows upon the tottering rebellion as they remember the fall of their brave leader.[14]

"Sedgwick was essentially a soldier," related Porter. "He had never married; the camp was his home, and the members of his staff were his family. He was always spoken of familiarly as 'Uncle John,' and the news of his death fell upon his comrades with a sense of grief akin to the sorrow of a personal bereavement."[15]

Word of Sedgwick's end still was spreading through the army the next day when two other Federal generals were mortally wounded in the Spotsylvania woods.

Brig. Gen. Thomas G. Stevenson, twenty-eight, commanded the 1st Division in Maj. Gen. Ambrose Burnside's IX Corps. He was a Bostonian whose lifelong interest in the military had led him through the ranks of the state militia to a major's appointment. When the war came he had recruited the 24th Massachusetts, many of the men coming from his militia battalion, and had been named its colonel. The regiment had tasted action in Burnside's expedition to coastal North Carolina, and subsequent campaigning there led to his promotion to brigadier general in April 1863. Stevenson was active in the combat around Charleston, South Carolina, in summer 1863, and after illness debilitated him that winter, had been assigned to lead a division in Burnside's corps the following spring.[16]

On the morning of May 10, Stevenson's command was among IX Corps units involved in a reconnaissance toward Spotsylvania. Near the Ny River, he was killed by a Confederate sniper.

Burnside received word of Stevenson's death in a 9 A.M. dispatch from Brig. Gen. O. B. Willcox, another of his division commanders: "General: It is with deep sorrow I have to report that the gallant commander . . . General Stevenson, is killed. He was, at his headquarters in front, hit by some chance shot. Colonel [David] Leasure [of the 100th Pennsylvania] takes his command. Will send his body to you." Burnside replied to Willcox in a 9:45 A.M. message: "I am pained beyond measure to hear of the death of General Stevenson. We will send for his body at once."[17]

Burnside elaborated on Stevenson's loss in one of his action reports. "During the forenoon we met with a severe misfortune in the loss of the gallant General Stevenson, who was killed by one of the enemy's sharpshooters," he wrote. "This officer commenced his services in the war with me in the expedition to North Carolina, and on all occasions proved himself a brave and efficient soldier."[18]

Stevenson was "among the more prominent losses on the Union side in the battle," the Times said on May 13. Despite his relatively young age, he "had lived long enough to win a fine reputation as a soldier, and do much good service for the country in whose defence [sic] he laid down his life."[19]

Stevenson's body was returned to Boston for burial and lay in state at City Hall. Flags at the city's public and many private buildings flew at half staff on May 16, the day of his funeral. The service was held at the home of

Stevenson's father, "without public display," the general later being buried at Mount Auburn Cemetery in Cambridge.[20]

⸺ ⸺ ⸻ ⸻

Before sunset on May 10, Brig. Gen. James C. Rice would join Stevenson on the casualty list, the fifth Union general to be mortally wounded in six days of Wilderness fighting.

Rice, thirty-four, was a native of rural Massachusetts and an 1854 Yale University graduate, and had been a teacher and an attorney in New York City before the war. After hostilities opened, he had been an officer in the 44th New York, rising to colonel of the regiment and leading it in the Peninsular Campaign of 1862. He fought at Second Bull Run and Chancellorsville, but the highlight of his combat record came at Gettysburg, where his defense of Little Round Top on July 2 helped save the day for the Union. Promoted brigadier general in August 1863, he commanded a brigade of New York and Pennsylvania troops in the late Wadsworth's V Corps division at the Wilderness and Spotsylvania. Riding into the Wilderness, Rice had forged a reputation as "one of most trusted and respected" brigadiers in the army.[21]

After more than a day occupying breastworks about six hundred yards from the Rebel lines, Rice's men were ordered to attack about 2 P.M. on May 10 as part of a strike involving elements of the II and V Corps. Rice led his brigade in the assault but he was quickly repulsed, a musket ball to the thigh severely wounding him in the process. At least one account states that Rice was standing on a breastwork, urging on his men, when he was hit. The bullet shattered his femur and punctured an artery and Rice went into shock from blood loss before a tourniquet could be administered.[22]

A physician amputated the leg and asked Rice "which way he desired to be turned that he might rest more easy," recalled Col. J. W. Hoffman of the 56th Pennsylvania. "He [Rice] replied, 'Turn me with my face to the enemy.' These were his last words, and indicated the true character of the man, the soldier, and the patriot." Rice also asked if he was dying and was told that he was. Three hours after his wounding, he was dead. General Meade wrote that Rice was "ever distinguished for personal gallantry," in mentioning the brigadier's death in a campaign report.[23]

Rice "bore the brunt of many terrible conflicts," his uniform torn a number of times by enemy bullets, but had never been previously wounded. "In him the country has lost not only a true and brave soldier, but a devoted citizen—a man who understood the full meaning of liberty—who was a democrat in the best sense of the word," the *Times* said on May 13.[24]

Rice's funeral was held on May 15 at the Madison Avenue church in New York City where he had been married some eighteen months earlier. His coffin was draped with a U.S. flag, his gloves, hat and sword laid atop it. Union officers and members of the New York bar served as pallbearers. Rice was later interred at Rural Cemetery, Albany, New York. "The country mourns the loss of this gallant soldier, in common with our City and his own family," the *Times* stated on May 14.[25]

Sedgwick's remains, meanwhile, lay in state at New York's City Hall on May 12 on their way to his home in Cornwall Hollow. Hundreds stood in line to view the uniform-clad body, Sedgwick appearing "just as he fell when struck by that fatal bullet." The coffin was adorned with the national flag and bouquets and wreaths of flowers. "The martial face of the departed hero, bronzed by exposure to the fierce blaze of battle, wore in death a calm and serene aspect, marred only by the wound in the left cheek—nay, not marred, for that sad token of his stern and high fidelity unto death to the cause of his country and of liberty, was a nobler decoration than was ever the star or cross bestowed by royalty for success in war," the *Times* said.[26]

After the remains reached Connecticut, the funeral was held at Sedgwick's home on May 15, attracting an estimated 3,000 mourners, including military and political dignitaries. "All seemed deeply impressed with the solemnity of the occasion," the *Times* said, adding that the theme of the Reverend Charles Wetherly's service was "How the Mighty Have Fallen in Battle."[27]

In 1868 a monument to Sedgwick, composed of melted down guns captured by his beloved VI Corps, was erected at West Point.

No Rebel was officially credited with killing Sedgwick, but in 1908, forty-four years after the general's fall, friends of an old soldier named Thomas Burgess claimed he had pulled the trigger. Burgess, of the 15th South Carolina, was among pickets posted out in front of Jenkins's Brigade of Anderson's Division, Longstreet's Corps, stated an account in *Confederate Veteran*. The pickets had strict orders not to fire and possibly give away the position of their brigade, which was posted in the edge of some woods. The Confederates knew the Federals were advancing in heavy force. Suddenly, the Carolinians saw several enemy officers ride out into an open field in their front, apparently reconnoitering. All of the pickets resisted the urge to fire—except Burgess. One of the horsemen tumbled from his saddle and was soon carried back into the Union lines. The Rebels later learned it was Sedgwick.[28]

If he indeed did shoot the general, which is highly doubtful, since Sedgwick, by Union accounts, was on foot at the time, Burgess apparently never gloried in the act. In fact, he always avoided the issue. "When the matter was mentioned in his presence, he always changed the topic . . . or retired," related a comrade, V. M. Fleming. "Somehow he was sensitive on the subject, and could never divorce the thought from his mind that the occurrence was something akin to murder." On his deathbed in 1908, the eighty-four-year-old Rebel's mind returned to the horrors of Spotsylvania, and in his delirium, according to Fleming, spoke about "the tragic death of Sedgwick."[29]

Lee's men had burrowed into earth and log defenses that included a half-moon of trenches jutting from the Confederate line, soldiers soon dubbing it the "Mule Shoe Salient" due to it shape. Grant soon took aim at this bulge in the enemy defenses. An assault on the west side of the salient on May 10 resulted in a Union breakthrough, but the Federals could not hold their ground and were driven back. Grant decided to make another attack on this strongpoint with Hancock's II Corps.

On the foggy and damp morning of May 12, Hancock's 20,000 men rushed forward, striking the apex of the mule shoe about 4:35 A.M. Gen. Edward Johnson's defending Confederate division was smothered quickly, many of the Rebels unable to fire their muskets due to wet gunpowder. The Federals scooped up about 3,000 prisoners, including Johnson, most of the famed Stonewall Brigade and twenty guns, before spearing about half a mile further into the heart of the Rebel position. Lee's army was suddenly in danger of being cut in half.

In the defenses on both sides of the salient, dazed Confederates desperately tried to stem the Federal flow or fell back in disorder. The division of Maj. Gen. Robert E. Rodes was posted to Johnson's left and attempted a stand, the North Carolinians of Brig. Gen. Junius Daniel's brigade among them. Daniel was a thirty-five-year-old North Carolinian, West Point class of 1851, and U.S. Army veteran who had run his father's plantation in Louisiana prior to the conflict. As colonel of the 14th North Carolina Infantry, he had fought in the Seven Days battles and earned promotion to brigadier in September 1862. At Gettysburg, his brigade sustained the heaviest of any in the Second Corps in the first day of fighting.[30]

Now Daniel urged his men forward to drive out Hancock's Federals, saluting the 14th's Tarheels as they swept into battle. Minutes later he was shot in the stomach and, mortally wounded, was carried from the field.

A. P. Hill, meanwhile, had been ordered to dam the breach and sent in three brigades, including Brig. Gen. Abner M. Perrin's Alabamians in Dick Anderson's division. A South Carolinian, Perrin, thirty-seven, was a lawyer and Mexican War veteran who had fought in all of the Army of Northern

Virginia's major campaigns. Promoted to brigadier as of September 1863, he had continued his stellar combat performance at the Wilderness before the armies converged on Spotsylvania Court House. "I shall come out of this fight a live major general or a dead brigadier," Perrin is said to have remarked at Spotsylvania.[31]

In Hill's counter-punch, Perrin's brigade was the first to arrive, Hancock's men pouring an awful fire into his ranks. The combat now centered on an unfinished trench line at the open end of the salient. Into this tumult of musketry Perrin rode, whipping his sword and trying to inspire his troops. Suddenly rocked by seven bullets, he was hurled dead from the saddle as his horse leaped over the incomplete breastwork.

Confederate reinforcements gradually drove the Yankees back to the exterior of the salient. Here the Federals refused to yield any more and the battle degenerated into some of the most brutal fighting of the war. Separated only by the log and earth breastworks, blue and gray shot and stabbed at each other through chinks in the defenses, or handed up muskets to riflemen who climbed to the top of the trenches to fire down into the enemy on the other side. The massed men fought in calf-deep mud and a pouring rain drenched living and dead while helpless wounded and corpses sank into the ghastly quagmire. The battle horrors of what men on both sides later referred to as the "Bloody Angle" screamed into the night before the outnumbered Rebels withdrew to the inner line at the salient's base.

"The brave General Perrin was killed and Generals [James] Walker and Daniel severely wounded," Lee said in closing a report of the battle to Secretary of War Seddon that night.[32]

Daniel lingered into the next day. In his last hours, his physicians conferred as to whether his wife, Ellen, might be able to reach him before he breathed his last. When it was deemed that she could not, Daniel sent his "last message of love to her—love from the tomb." He then entrusted his pocketwatch to Maj. Edward Badger to be given to Ellen and requested that she provide for his servant, William. He also wanted his horse, John, to receive the best of care. Daniel's last inquiry was about his brigade and how they had fared in the battle.[33]

In a postwar account, D. H. Hill Jr. described the Carolinian as "a thorough soldier, calm, resolute and unpretending" whom Lee had recommended be promoted to major general.[34]

"General Daniel's services at Gettysburg, as well as on the bloody field where he fell, were of the most distinguished character," wrote Dick Ewell, Daniel's corps commander. "General Daniel was killed while leading his men with characteristic impetuosity," Gen. John Gordon wrote after the war.[35]

One of Daniel's sharpshooters, Pvt. Louis Leon of the 1st North Carolina, had been captured in the May 5 fighting and was settling in as a prisoner of war at Point Lookout, Maryland, when he learned of Daniel's death. "Our General Daniel was killed, which is certainly a great loss for us," he wrote in his diary, "for he was a good and brave man."[36]

North Carolina colonel Bryan Grimes ascended to command Daniel's brigade, but his attitude was somber in a May 14 letter to his wife, a few hours after the general's fall. "He was an excellent officer, and although I probably gained a Brigade by his death, I would have preferred to remain in statu[s] quo rather than his services should be lost to the country," Grimes wrote. "North Carolina has suffered seriously." Grimes was promoted to brigadier five days later.[37]

Col. John C. C. Sanders took command of Perrin's brigade, and his conspicuous service during the remainder of the battle earned him a generalship. But Sanders himself would die in battle near Petersburg little more than three months later.

Perrin was buried in the City Cemetery in Fredericksburg, Virginia, while Daniel's body was returned to his hometown of Halifax, North Carolina, for interment in the Old Colonial Churchyard Cemetery.

CONFEDERATE BRIGADIER GENERAL
ALBERT G. JENKINS
Cloyd's Mountain, May 9, 1864

From the western Virginia hills, Albert G. Jenkins had journeyed to Washington as a congressman in 1856. As a Confederate brigadier some eight years later, he would die in these mountains, fighting the Union he once served.

With a dark bushy beard flowing well past his chest, Jenkins, thirty-three, was an eye-catching officer in the ranks of the Rebel cavalry and had developed a reputation as a wily and daring raider in independent command. A lawyer with a Harvard degree, he had spent about five years in the U.S. Congress before resigning his seat in 1861. Elected a Confederate congressman, Jenkins was promoted to brigadier in August 1862. The highlight of his military career had been when he led his horsemen in a 500-mile raid into western Virginia and Ohio, but he had been severely wounded at Gettysburg.[38]

Still recovering from this head injury, Jenkins received orders on May 5, 1864, to take command of the sparse and scattered Rebel units in southwestern Virginia. Within hours of receiving this assignment, word came that a Union force was on the move in the Roanoke area with the Virginia

*Confederate brigadier general
Albert G. Jenkins.*
LIBRARY OF CONGRESS

& Tennessee Railroad as its possible target. These Federals, some 6,500 in all, were led by Brig. Gen. George Crook and indeed were aiming at the railroad, which was the Confederacy's last rail link to eastern Tennessee. Jenkins hastily scraped together a force of about 2,400 men, including some home guards and an artillery battery, to meet this threat. When it appeared Crook was marching to strike the railroad bridge over the New River near Dublin, Virginia, Jenkins marched to stymie the enemy advance. The Confederates dug in on two wooded ridges along the Dublin Road east of Cloyd's Mountain.

Just after sunrise on May 9, Crook's army approached Jenkins's positions, which extended about a half mile. Believing that a frontal attack might be too costly, Crook instead decided to send his men on a sweeping blow at the Rebels' right flank. After an artillery duel, the Union infantry attacked, West Virginia and Ohio troops driving in and meeting a sleet of cannon and musketry. "The enemy . . . kept up a grave-yard whistle with their artillery," Crook remembered.[39]

Soldiers engaged in hand-to-hand combat around the Rebel earthworks and gunfire ignited the woods, incinerating many of the wounded. Crook, however, had more men than Jenkins and poured in reinforcements, including the Ohio brigade of Col. Rutherford B. Hayes, the future U.S. president. The numbers began to tell and the Yankees overran Jenkins's artillery.

It was at this point, as the battle tide turned for the Federals, that Jenkins's left arm was shattered near the shoulder by a gunshot. He was on horseback and waving his sword to rally his men when he was hit, and was helped from the saddle by members of his staff. Jenkins immediately dispatched a messenger to his second-in-command, Brig. Gen. John McCausland, to take charge of the Rebel force. McCausland led a brief rearguard action before ordering a retreat, but Jenkins was captured. The hour-long firefight cost the Confederates over 500 men while Union losses were almost 700, although Crook estimated Southern casualties at well over 1,000.[40]

Even as Jenkins was being treated the Federals pushed on to Dublin where they cut the railroad. With other Rebel wounded, Jenkins was taken to the John Guthrie home near Dublin where he received medical care. "General A. G. Jenkins and Lieutenant-Colonel [Thomas] Smith fell into our hands, seriously wounded . . . gave their paroles to report at Charleston as soon as their wounds will admit, if not properly exchanged before that time," Crook reported.[41]

On May 13, a Union surgeon, with Confederate physicians in attendance, amputated Jenkins's mangled arm at the shoulder, Guthrie's son and a black youth wrapping the limb in a sheet and burying it in a nearby orchard.

Cared for by his wife and Guthrie's daughters, Jenkins appeared to be recovering. Pneumonia set in, however, and on May 21 Jenkins was destined to lose one last battle—this one for his life. He developed a secondary hemorrhage and bled to death in a few minutes. After two interments, Jenkins was buried in Spring Hill Cemetery, Huntington, West Virginia, where he rests today.[42]

CONFEDERATE BRIGADIER GENERALS JAMES B. TERRILL AND GEORGE P. DOLES
Bethesda Church, May 30–June 2, 1864

Confederate brigadier general James B. Terrill was not the first general in his family to be killed in this war; however, his deceased brother had worn Union blue.

Indeed, when Terrill fell at Bethesda Church, Virginia, on the afternoon of May 30, 1864, he did not know that he would be a general himself. As colonel of the 13th Virginia Infantry, Terrill, twenty-six, had been nominated to the Confederate Senate for promotion to brigadier. His appointment came on June 1, and gave him the rank as of May 31, the Rebel Congress not realizing that he had fallen in battle.[43]

His brother, U.S. brigadier general William R. Terrill, had been killed at the battle of Perryville in 1862.

James Terrill was a Virginian who graduated from Virginia Military Institute in 1858. A lawyer, he was elected major of the 13th Virginia before seeing action at First Bull Run and in Stonewall Jackson's Valley Campaign of 1862. Terrill fought in almost every major engagement of the Army of Northern Virginia through Gettysburg, being promoted colonel of the 13th Virginia in May 1863. As part of John Pegram's brigade in 1864, his regiment engaged in the Wilderness and Spotsylvania battles.

Terrill was killed during a clash with Warren's V Corps, the Federals learning of his death from a Virginia colonel who was wounded and captured by Warren's men. "Poor Terrill, gallant, brave soldier," lamented one of his company commanders, Capt. S. D. Buck. "His commission as brigadier general was at Lee's headquarters, but he did not know of the high esteem in which he was held. Peace to the ashes of that brave spirit."[44]

As related in the earlier narrative about Gen. William Terrill, a popular story at the time was that the father of the Terrill brothers buried his sons in the same grave. In actuality, Federal soldiers recovered the Rebel Terrill's body on the battlefield, and buried it near the spot where he died. His Yankee brother was interred at West Point.

Warren briefly mentioned Terrill's death and burial in a May 31 dispatch to U.S. major general Andrew A. Humphreys. Terrill's widow, Charlotte, meanwhile, was left to raise their two children on her own, including a daughter who was only months old. In memory of the brothers, the Terrill family erected a headstone in Bath County, Virginia, with the haunting engraving, "God Alone Knows Which Was Right."[45]

On June 2, another Rebel general met his end in battle near Bethesda Church. Georgia brigadier general George P. Doles was overseeing his soldiers as they dug in when a Union sharpshooter killed him, the bullet plunging into the left side of his chest.[46]

Doles, thirty-four, was considered by some to be among the best brigadiers in the army. He was a prewar businessman and saw his first major action as colonel of the 4th Georgia Infantry. Doles fought well in the Maryland Campaign, earning promotion to brigadier in November 1862, and had added to his service record at Fredericksburg, Chancellorsville, Gettysburg, and the Wilderness.[47]

In the fighting at Bethesda Church, Lt. Gen. Jubal Early's corps had attacked Warren's corps, shoving it back to the Shady Grove Road. A *Rich-*

mond Dispatch correspondent mentioned Doles's demise in a June 4 article about the combat: "General Early commanding Ewell's corps attacked the enemy's right . . . and drove him with great slaughter out of his works, suffering but slight loss himself. Among his killed was the brave General Doles of Georgia."[48]

Confederate historian Joseph Derry offered this postwar epitaph for Doles: "This gallant soldier offered up the life which had from the very first sound of arms been devoted to his country. His loss was sadly felt by the gallant men whom he led, and by whom he was fondly loved, and in his native city, where he was known as a modest gentleman and earnest Christian, his death was deeply deplored."[49] Doles's remains were sent south for burial at Memory Hill Cemetery in Milledgeville, Georgia, his hometown.

CHAPTER 17

Jeb Stuart's Final Glory

CONFEDERATE MAJOR GENERAL JEB STUART AND BRIGADIER GENERAL JAMES B. GORDON

Sheridan's Raid, May 1864

Pvt. John A. Huff of the 5th Michigan Cavalry was considered a dead aim and had won a prize for being the best shot in his former regiment, the famed Berdan's Sharpshooters. Yet as he and his fellow troopers prepared for battle at Yellow Tavern, Virginia, on May 11, 1864, Huff was fated to kill one of the Confederacy's most revered generals at so close a range that his marksmanship mattered little.

Yellow Tavern itself was no more than a rundown inn located near a crossroads about two miles north of Richmond's outer defenses. Confederate major general J. E. B. "Jeb" Stuart, commander of Robert E. Lee's cavalry corps, waited here to do battle. Some 10,000 Union horsemen under Maj. Gen. Phil Sheridan had broken loose from the Wilderness fighting two days earlier and were on a hell-bent raid toward Richmond, tearing up railroad tracks and destroying Rebel stores. Stuart had, by an exhaustive ride, concentrated two of his cavalry brigades—those of Brig. Gens. Lunsford L. Lomax and Williams C. Wickham—to stop Sheridan short of the capital. He would be outnumbered about three to one.

Like a musketeer who had ridden out of the pages of an adventure novel, the debonair, thirty-one-year-old Stuart was the personification of the Southern cavalier. An 1854 West Point graduate, he had served on the frontier before the war and had been the driving force in molding the

Army of Northern Virginia's cavalry corps into a formidable weapon. Stuart had fought splendidly in all of the army's major campaigns other than Gettysburg, where he failed to provide Lee necessary information on the enemy's movements and positions (twice he and his cavalry had ridden completely around Union armies on raids). With his plumed hats, grand uniforms, and massive beard, Stuart was bigger than life, easily the most flamboyant of Lee's generals but with the military savvy and skills to back it up.

A native of Patrick County, Virginia, Stuart had served primarily in the U.S. 1st Cavalry in Kansas and had been wounded in an Indian fight at Solomon's River in 1857. When Virginia seceded, he resigned his lieutenancy to become a colonel in the 1st Virginia Cavalry. Stuart excelled at First Bull Run and was promoted to brigadier in September 1861. The following June he was advanced to major general and given command of the Army of Northern Virginia's cavalry, a post he held until his death. Stuart also had the distinction of being a son-in-law to Union brigadier general Philip St. George Cooke.[1]

The fighting at Yellow Tavern exploded before noon and crackled for about three hours with significant casualties on both sides, the Rebels forced to give ground. There was a lull in the combat for about two hours as more of Sheridan's units reached the field to face the Confederates, who by now were formed in a somewhat straight battle line along both sides of the Telegraph Road.

Union brigadier George Custer restarted the fireworks about 4 P.M. He spied Lomax's Rebels in some woods on a slight hill and noted the three artillery pieces the Southerners had in this position. Custer ordered the 1st Michigan Cavalry of Lt. Col. Peter Stagg to charge the battery from Stuart's left flank. To keep the Rebels busy in front, Custer would send in the 5th and 6th Michigan, both dismounted. Their carbines snapping, Stagg's horsemen caved in Lomax's flank, capturing two of the guns. Seeing this threat, Stuart rode to the scene to rally Lomax's rattled brigade. As he did so, he was caught up in the charge of the dismounted 1st Michigan driving past him.

These Federals were met momentarily by a countercharge from a portion of the 1st Virginia Cavalry, blunting their assault. Capt. George W. Dorsey of the 1st Virginia's Company K, was fighting on the Telegraph Road when Stuart rode up about 4:30 P.M., shouting to Dorsey's men, "Bully for old K! Give it to them boys!" From astride his horse Stuart fired his LeMat revolver at some nearby Federals. The Yankees in the thwarted charge retreated, running back toward the point where Stuart had managed to regroup a few of his troopers.[2]

Confederate major general
Jeb Stuart. LIBRARY OF CONGRESS

One of the bluecoats was Huff, a forty-eight-year-old trooper in Company E of the 5th Michigan. Nearing a mounted Southern officer, resplendant with a plumed hat and fine uniform, Huff leveled his revolver and fired once from about thirty feet away before loping back toward his own lines. His shot, however, would be one of the most important of the war, the .44-caliber round hitting Stuart in the right side of the stomach. Stuart "reeled on his horse and said: 'I am shot,' and then, 'Dorsey, save your men,' the captain recalled. I told him we would take him with us."[3]

Clutching his side, Stuart was able to stay in the saddle and Dorsey tried to lead the animal to the rear, but it spooked. He and other soldiers eased the now hatless general to the ground and propped him against a tree. A trooper asked if he was badly hurt, to which Stuart replied, "I am afraid I am but don't worry, boys. Fitz [Robert E. Lee's nephew Maj. Gen. Fitzhugh Lee of the cavalry] will do as well for you as I have done."[4]

Facing the very real threat of Stuart being captured, the soldiers placed him on another horse and led him to a safer place where he was put in an ambulance. As he was being carried to the rear, his head cradled by Pvt. Charles Wheatley of the 1st Virginia, Stuart was incensed by the sight of some of his troopers retreating. "Go back! Go back! and do your duty, as I have done mine and our country will be safe," he called to them. "Go back! Go back! I had rather die than be whipped."[5]

Some of the Virginians were preparing to charge when a tearful Fitz Lee galloped in front of their ranks and told them that Stuart was wounded, probably mortally, and that the cavalry was to retreat. "I never saw such a distressed looking body of men in my life as they looked to be, many of them shedding tears when they heard our gallant General had been shot," recalled Sgt. William Poindexter of the 1st Virginia. "He [Fitz Lee] knew too well what a shock such sad news would be to the Old First. He knew what the men thought of Stuart, and what their beloved General thought of him."[6]

In awful pain, Stuart was taken by ambulance to the home of his brother-in-law, Dr. Charles Brewer, on Grace Street in Richmond, arriving after an excruciating six-hour journey. The bullet had sliced through his abdomen and into his liver, and doctors saw that his condition was hopeless. Stuart survived the night and lingered into Thursday, May 12, President Jefferson Davis recalling that "the intense anxiety for his safety made us all shrink from realizing his imminent danger."[7]

Brewer, Dr. John B. Fontaine, Stuart's surgeon, and two other physicians, along with several clergymen and friends, kept watch over Stuart as he weakened, lapsing in and out of delirium throughout the day. In his irrational state, his rants contained snippets of orders and combat commands.

Maj. Henry B. McClellan, Stuart's chief of staff, spent an hour at Stuart's bedside as cannons rumbled in the distance. Hearing the guns, Stuart asked what they meant and McClellan told him of Confederate movements to slow the Federal advance. McClellan related: "He [Stuart] turned his eyes upward, and exclaimed earnestly, 'God grant that they may be successful.' Then turning his head aside, he said with a sigh—'But I must be prepared for another world.'"[8]

As McClellan was leaving the room about noon, Davis came in, one of a number of dignitaries to visit Stuart. Davis grasped the general's hand and asked how he felt. Stuart answered, "Easy, but willing to die, if God and my country think I have fulfilled my destiny and done my duty."[9]

Davis later recalled his final meeting with Stuart:

When I saw him in his very last hours, he was so calm, and physically so strong, that I could not believe that he was dying, until the surgeon, after I had left his bedside, told me he was bleeding inwardly, and that the end was near.[10]

Meanwhile, Stuart's wife, Flora, and children, Jimmy and baby Virginia, were desperately trying to reach the general's bedside that afternoon. The Stuarts were staying at the home of Col. Edmund Fontaine near Beaver Dam Station and Confederate authorities had some difficulty in contacting them due to cut telegraph lines. Flora had been helping treat wounded soldiers at the depot that morning when Fontaine finally received word about noon that Stuart was badly wounded and that his family should come at once. In an hour the Stuarts were put aboard a special train bound for Richmond.

The bouts of delirium intensified in the afternoon as Stuart's mind galloped from battlefields to thoughts of his family. "As the evening wore on, the paroxyms of pain increased, and mortification set in rapidly," the *Richmond Examiner* stated. "Though suffering the greatest agony at times, the General was calm," even holding ice to his own wound to alleviate his suffering. Toward twilight, Stuart asked Brewer if he might survive, at least through the night. When Brewer told him that neither was likely, Stuart nodded, saying, "I am resigned if it be God's will; but I would like to see my wife. But God's will be done." Several times he roused and asked if Flora had come to him.[11]

About 7:30 P.M., Brewer and the other physicians concluded that Stuart had little time to live and Brewer told him so, asking if he had any last messages. Whether he did so in these his final minutes or in his last hours, varies by account, but Stuart did take care of his personal affairs. He gave McClellan and another aide, Col. Charles Venable, each one of his horses, and bequeathed a pair of spurs to a lady in Shepherdstown, Virginia. He also arranged for the return of a small battle flag sent to him by a belle from Columbia, South Carolina. To Robert E. Lee's wife he bestowed his golden spurs, in honor of his esteem for her husband. His sword was to go to his son.

The Episcopal Reverend Joshua Peterkin had gathered everyone in the house at Stuart's bedside just after 7 P.M. Peterkin prayed and then the sorrowful group sang Stuart's favorite hymn "Rock of Ages." Stuart weakly tried to join in and after the song and a prayer told Brewer, "I am going fast now; I am resigned; God's will be done." He lapsed into unconsciousness and died at 7:38 P.M.[12]

Flora Stuart and the children did not reach the Brewer house until about 11:30 P.M., the solemnity and quiet they encountered bearing mute reality for Flora that she was now a widow. The train had carried the family to Ashland where they transferred to an ambulance to proceed across country. Over bad roads and through a thunderstorm's driving rain, they had arrived at the Chickahominy River to find a bridge destroyed. Their driver finally found a ford and they continued on, almost being fired on while approaching the Confederate lines before reaching Richmond.

Flora Stuart wore mourning black for the final forty-nine years of her life.

━━ ━◆━ ━━

Lee was embroiled in the fighting at Spotsylvania on the night of May 12 when word of Stuart's fall reached him. W. G. McCabe, an artillery staff officer, was sitting on his horse nearby when Lee was given the dreadful telegram and read its contents. "Gentlemen," he said (evidently greatly moved), "we have very bad news," McCabe recalled of Lee's reaction. "General Stuart has been mortally wounded." He paused for a few moments, and then exclaimed impressively: "He never brought me a piece of false information." Lee remarked later that night, "I can scarcely think about him without weeping."[13]

"No incident of mortality, since the fall of the great Jackson, has occasioned more painful regret than this," the *Examiner* said on May 14. "Major-General J.E.B. Stuart, the model of Virginia cavaliers and dashing chieftain, whose name was a terror to the enemy, and familiar as a household word in two continents, is dead—struck down by a bullet from the foe."[14]

Yellow Tavern was the first decisive victory of the Union cavalry over its Confederate counterpart; never again would the Rebel horse exercise the superiority it had enjoyed earlier. Sheridan considered Stuart's defeat critical to the war effort: "Since the beginning of the war this general had distinguished himself by his management of the Confederate mounted force," he wrote in his memoirs. "Under him the cavalry of Lee's army had been nurtured, and had acquired such prestige that it thought itself wellnigh invincible; indeed, in the early years of the war it had proved to be so."[15]

Stuart left "behind him a record in which those who wore the blue and . . . gray take equal pride," one of Custer's troopers wrote after the war. "He was a typical American cavalryman."[16]

Henry Kyd Douglas gave a brief but apt comparison of the rival cavalry chiefs:

> It is no reflection on Phil Sheridan's reputation to say that he did not do anything which Jeb Stuart could not have done as well. Whether Sheridan could have done as well as Stuart with what Stuart had, may well be doubted. General Stuart's loss was simply irreparable.[17]

Not since Stonewall Jackson's death would the Confederacy weep so deeply for a fallen leader. "Stuart had few equals as a commander of cavalry on either side or in any war, and his fall was a serious blow to that branch of Lee's army," wrote Gen. John Gordon.[18]

John Huff did not long survive Stuart. Less than three weeks after Yellow Tavern, he was mortally wounded in the May 28 battle of Haw's Shop.

The day after his death, Stuart's funeral was held at Saint James Episcopal Church with Reverend Peterkin presiding. Seven generals and a commodore served as pallbearers. The cortege arrived at the crowded church about 5 P.M., "without music or military escort, the Public Guard being absent on duty," the *Examiner* said. In the congregation were Jefferson Davis, General Bragg, and a host of other military and civilian officials. After the ceremony, the mourners stood with heads covered as Stuart's metallic coffin was borne to a hearse adorned with black plumes and drawn by four white horses, the church organ's dirge echoing through the sanctuary. Trailed by carriages occupied by Stuart's family and members of his staff, the hearse trundled to Hollywood Cemetery where the casket was placed in a vault, the Episcopal Reverend Charles Minnigerode conducting the graveside service. Flora Cooke Stuart would join her husband there upon her death in 1923. "Thus has passed away, amid the exciting scenes of this revolution, one of the bravest and most dashing cavaliers that the 'Old Dominion' has ever given birth to," the *Examiner* said. "Long will her sons recount the story of his achievements and mourn his untimely departure."[19]

May 12 also brought a death wound to one of Stuart's commanders, Brig. Gen. James B. Gordon, who fell at Meadow Bridge as the Confederates tried to trap Sheridan.

Gordon was a forty-one-year-old North Carolinian and a distant relative of Gen. John Gordon. Before the war he had been a merchant, farmer and state legislator. As major of the 1st North Carolina Cavalry, he had been assigned to Stuart's corps in 1862, receiving his brigadier's commission in September 1863.[20]

Gordon's Brigade was detached and had not been with Stuart at Yellow Tavern, but these troopers harassed the rear of Sheridan's column as the Federals pressed toward Richmond's outskirts early on the morning of May 12. Sheridan decided against trying to take the city, but he and his corps soon found themselves about to be boxed in by the enemy. Blocking Sheridan's now eastward advance was Fitzhugh Lee's cavalry division, dug in on the opposite bank of the Chickahominy River at Meadow Bridge. To the south were the Richmond defenses, while behind Sheridan was Gordon's cavalry. The Rebels had torn out much of the footboards from the bridge and also had damaged a nearby railroad span to impede the Yankees.

In a rainstorm, Gordon attacked Sheridan near Brook Church, encountering Brig. Gen. David M. Gregg's Union division, which was supported by artillery. Outnumbered, Gordon could not dent Gregg's line. He sent for reinforcements, and a gleaming battery of new guns galloped into position, manned by raw cannoneers from the Richmond lines. But at the first sting of canister from Sheridan's artillery, these rookies scampered for cover, to the derisive laughter of Gordon's veterans. Gordon, however, was not amused, alternately railing and pleading for them to stand, but in vain. Disgusted, he rode back into the combat.

By mid-morning, Gordon had received more artillery and some infantry support, and continued to attack Gregg with little to show for the effort. At some point, Gordon was riding along his battle line, encouraging his Tarheels as enemy carbine bullets cut the air around him. Another officer urged him to dismount, but Gordon refused saying, "No, we must set the men an example of gallantry today."[21]

Shortly afterward a bullet hit him in the front of the left arm, tearing out of his elbow. The general turned to an aide, telling him calmly, "I am wounded, bring a surgeon here to me, I cannot leave my post to go to him." When the soldier returned with a physician, they found Gordon lying in the road and carried him to safety. The general was soon in an ambulance bound for Richmond, relinquishing command to Col. Clinton Andrews of the 2nd North Carolina Cavalry. Sheridan, meanwhile, was able to establish a foothold on the Chickahominy's north bank, despite Lee's resistance. With George Custer's Michigan troops leading the way, the Federals repaired Meadow Bridge and poured across late in the afternoon, routing Lee. Sheridan had fought his way out of the snare and, two days later, he and his cavalry were safely back within Union lines.

Gordon was taken to the Officers' Hospital in Richmond where doctors tried to sustain him without amputating the shattered limb. The result was that Gordon worsened, finally dying on May 18. "The immediate cause of death was mortification, the wound not being considered by the surgeons a dangerous one," the *Richmond Examiner* said in announcing Gordon's loss in its May 20 edition. "Had amputation been resorted to at first, the result would doubtless have been different; but the surgeons attempted to save the limb, and the result is his valuable life is lost to the cause and the country."[22]

Sheridan was less descriptive in noting Gordon's death in a May 22 report: "The rebel General Gordon, wounded in the engagement at Meadow Bridge, has since died of his wounds." Custer wrote that the battle was "a hard contest, from which we suffered severely . . . the enemy lost heavily in officers, among others General Gordon, mortally wounded."[23]

Gordon was "among the bravest and best," one of his Tarheels later related. "Active, alert, and vigilant, he was never taken by surprise, and was always quick to take advantage of any mistake of his adversary and to meet any emergency. . . . His death was a heavy blow to the cavalry arm . . . and was felt as a personal loss by . . . his brigade, all of whom were warmly attached to him." With Gordon's death, "The esprit de corps was gone," another cavalryman recalled, "and the croaking of the raven became louder."[24]

Accompanied by a home guard unit and a band, Gordon's body was escorted to the Danville railroad depot for conveyance to North Carolina, where he was buried in St. Paul's Episcopal Church Cemetery in his hometown of Wilkesboro.

"Our great loss at Brook Church was the gallant and glorious James B. Gordon," remembered a trooper in the 5th North Carolina, "He was the Murat of the Army of Northern Virginia."[25]

CONFEDERATE BRIGADIER GENERAL
WILLIAM E. "GRUMBLE" JONES
Piedmont, June 5, 1864

Brig. Gen. William E. "Grumble" Jones was infamous among Rebel cavalrymen for his Saturday night saber grindings, which most of the Confederates believed to be a useless practice since they rarely drew their swords in battle.

At Piedmont, Virginia, on June 5, 1864, Jones hoped to dull his blade on Yankee flesh to stop a marauding Union army burning its way down the Shenandoah Valley. Facing Jones was a force of 12,000 Northerners under Maj. Gen. David Hunter, who had assumed command of the Federal army in the valley on May 21 after its defeat at New Market six days earlier. Rather than let his men lick their wounds, Hunter put them on the offensive on May 26, marching on Staunton where he hoped to join the cavalry of Brig. Gens. George Crook and William Averell.

On June 2 at Mount Crawford, the bluecoats tangled with Brig. Gen. John Imboden's cavalry, which was quickly brushed aside. Imboden wired a desperate call for help to stop Hunter's march. His plea resulted in Jones's infantry brigade being sent by railroad from Bristol, Virginia, to reinforce him. The Rebels also gathered local militia, quartermaster soldiers and basically anyone else who could pull a trigger to swell their ranks to about 5,600.

Deemed a "gruff soldier and woman-hater" by one Confederate officer, Jones, forty, was a Virginian and 1848 West Point graduate who saw frontier service with the army before his state's secession. After organizing a mounted rifle company he fought under Jeb Stuart at First Bull Run, and remained with Stuart's cavalry, excelling in particular at Brandy Station. Promoted brigadier as of September 1862, Jones participated in the Gettysburg Campaign before friction with Stuart resulted in his transfer to command in the obscure post of southwestern Virginia and eastern Tennessee. Organizing an infantry brigade there, Jones was in action in the Knoxville Campaign and at Cloyd's Mountain.[26]

Trying to block Hunter, the Confederates concentrated about half a mile north of the village of Piedmont on June 5. Along with Jones's infantry and the reserve troops were the cavalry of Imboden and Brig. Gen. John C. Vaughn. Since Jones had seniority, he would have overall command in the expected battle.

The gray infantry and reserves dug in to form the left flank while the cavalry was posted on the right. Inexplicably, their positions left a gap in their center along the East Road, which ran into the village. As the Rebels deployed in the rain, Imboden confronted Jones, asking why he had not stationed the Southerners on the higher ground of nearby Mowry's Hill.

Imboden gave this postwar account of their heated exchange:

> I exclaimed, "My God, General! You are not going to fight here, and lose all the advantage of position we shall have at Mowry's hill?" . . . Jones replied: "Yes! I am going to fight right here, if Hunter advances. . . . If he don't, I will go over there and attack . . ." I answered: "We have no advantage of ground here, and he outnumbers us nearly three to one, and will beat us." This seemed to anger him, for he replied with great warmth and an oath: "I don't want any advantage of ground, for I can whip Hunter anywhere."[27]

The argument escalated with Imboden continuing his protest and Grumble's ire rising as he snapped, "Sir! I believe I am in command here today." Imboden responded, "You are sir, and I now ask your orders and will carry them out as best I can; but, if I live, I will see that the responsibility for this day's work is fixed where I think it belongs."[28]

The quarrel ended when an artillery officer galloped up to Imboden asking where his guns should be posted. Hearing the bark of these cannons, Grumble calmed down, according to Imboden, who added that Jones "was brave to a fault, and I believe enjoyed the roar of the battlefield." The two generals then rode together, checking the lines and Jones told some of his staff officers, "Gentlemen, I don't want any of you killed, and don't want to be killed myself today."[29]

Hunter's troops had driven south down the valley that morning, warding off gray cavalry before coming upon the enemy at Piedmont. With the skies clearing about noon, Hunter and his infantry commander, Brig. Gen. Jeremiah Sullivan, decided to attack Jones's foot soldiers. Jones himself was leading his infantry, leaving the cavalry to Imboden. Earlier, he had issued final orders to Imboden to hold the Confederate right flank. The generals then parted to attend to the battle. "That was the last time I ever saw General William E. Jones," Imboden remembered. "In an hour afterwards he was dead."[30]

Two Union brigades under Cols. Joseph Thoburn and Augustus Moor attacked the butternut infantrymen, who were hunkered behind makeshift defenses of fence rails and logs. Rebel musketry and artillery repulsed at least two Federal assaults, but the Yankees soon discovered the gap in the Southern center. Thoburn's men assailed this point while Hunter's cavalry occupied Imboden's troopers. The 54th Pennsylvania unleashed a volley on their bellies and then charged, overrunning the enemy works in some woods, the fighting now man on man. "A most desperate struggle took place, bayonets and clubbed guns were used on both sides, and many hand-to-hand encounters took place," recalled the 54th's Col. Jacob M. Campbell.[31]

The Pennsylvanians and the 34th Massachusetts soon gained the upper hand, dislodging Confederates along a fence line where Grumble Jones had vainly urged them to hold their ground. Jones had been riding to various danger points when he was shot in the head and instantly killed amid the melee of Thoburn's assault. His death plus the flood of Yankees was too much for the Rebel infantry to bear, and their ranks melted in retreat, compelling their cavalry to do so as well.

"It was here that Brigadier-General Jones commanded in person, and was killed while encouraging and rallying his troops," Campbell remembered. The Confederates "upon the fall of their chief commander . . . gave way in utter confusion."[32]

In the chaos of the Southern withdrawal, Jones's body was recovered by the Federals. Hunter noted Jones's death in his battle report and stated that documents taken from the general's body revealed the Rebel troop strength in the battle.[33]

Piedmont was indeed a severe Confederate setback. The army was wrecked, with Jones among some 1,600 casualties, and the southern end of the Shenandoah Valley now lay almost defenseless against Hunter's raiders. Jones's remains were later turned over to friends who had him buried at Old Glade Spring Presbyterian Church not far from his home in Washington County, Virginia.[34]

Hunter occupied Staunton on June 6, his men destroying railroad bridges, factories, and other facilities before Crook and Averell joined him there two days later. With his army now numbering more than 17,000, and with Jones dead, Hunter continued his relentless drive through the Shenandoah.

CHAPTER 18

Mcpherson, Bishop Polk, and the Atlanta Campaign

CONFEDERATE LIEUTENANT GENERAL LEONIDAS POLK; MAJOR GENERAL W. H. T. WALKER; AND BRIGADIER GENERALS CLEMENT H. STEVENS AND SAMUEL BENTON

UNION MAJOR GENERAL JAMES B. MCPHERSON AND BRIGADIER GENERALS CHARLES G. HARKER AND DANIEL MCCOOK JR.

Atlanta Campaign, 1864

On the morning of June 14, 1864, Lt. Gen. Leonidas Polk, the "militant bishop of the Confederacy," went to the mountaintop, never to return in this world. Polk would be the first and highest ranking general to die in the Atlanta Campaign. "Pine Mountain, a lone sentinel of nature, was made sacredly historic by the blood of the great preacher, General Bishop Polk," a Rebel soldier wrote.[1]

Since the first week in May, Gen. Joseph E. Johnston's Confederate Army of Tennessee had been forced steadily backward through the Georgia mountains as elements of three Union armies commanded by Maj. Gen. William T. Sherman struck south from Chattanooga toward Atlanta. Sherman had about 100,000 men on which to draw, against Johnston's approximately 65,000, including Polk's Corps from the Rebel Army of Mississippi, which reinforced Johnston in mid May. As the Federals marched south, the enemies collided at Dalton and Resaca with Sherman repeatedly flanking

*Confederate lieutenant general
Leonidas Polk.*
LIBRARY OF CONGRESS

the Confederates out of mountaintop strongholds. Amid Johnston's retreat
there was fierce combat at Dallas, New Hope Church, and Pickett's Mill.
By early June 1864, the Rebels had fallen back to a defensive line anchored
by Lost Mountain, Pine Mountain, and Brush Mountain a few miles north
of Atlanta.

On the Tuesday morning of June 14, Polk was among several Confederate generals and their staffs who rode to Pine Mountain near Marietta on
a reconnaissance. The group included Johnston, Lt. Gen. William J.
Hardee, another of Johnston's corps commanders, and Brig. Gen. William
H. "Red" Jackson of the cavalry. Union troops were dangerously close to
surrounding the Rebels on Pine Mountain, who belonged to Maj. Gen.
William Bate's division, and the generals were discussing the feasibility of
holding the position.

Polk, fifty-eight, was a North Carolinian who finished West Point in
1827, but he had a higher calling than the U.S. Army. He left the service just
after graduation and entered the Episcopalian ministry, later becoming Missionary Bishop of the Southwest. At the Military Academy, Polk had developed a close friendship with Jefferson Davis, and this served him well when
the war began. Despite his lack of military experience, Polk was appointed
major general in June 1861 and lieutenant general as of October 1862. His
major duties early on were supervision of Confederate defenses along much
of the Mississippi River and organizing the Army of Mississippi. Polk commanded a corps at Shiloh, Perryville, Stones River, and Chickamauga.[2]

When Johnston joined Polk shortly after 8 A.M., the generals rode to the summit, encountering the Kentucky Orphan Brigade, which was among the Rebels posted on or around Pine Mountain. One of the Kentuckians, Sgt. Lot Young, recalled seeing Polk and the other generals ascending the slope, writing that he "could not but admire the graceful and dignified bearing of the grand old man as he saluted in true military style as he passed."[3]

J. M. Crawford, a Georgia sharpshooter, related that as Polk rode past him, the general said, "Young man, you are exposing yourself unnecessarily, and had better get to cover." Crawford replied, "General, you are worth more than I am, and you are exposing yourself."[4]

The weather had been rainy, but the morning had dawned bright and clear and the officers had a panoramic view of the surrounding country as well as both battle lines. Distant fields were white with the covers of Union wagons while soldiers on both sides sweated with axes and shovels amid the rattle of heavy skirmish fire and the occasional boom of cannons. "All combined to make the scene one of unusual beauty and grandeur," recalled Capt. William M. Polk, a staff officer for his father.[5]

As the Confederate officers were studying the enemy positions from an exposed area, Rebel infantrymen in earthworks nearby repeatedly warned them that the Yankees had found the artillery range for their location. The Union batteries, located 600 to 700 yards away, were under orders to conserve ammunition, but Sherman himself rode among the gunners and saw the clustered Rebels on the slope above. He pointed out the enemy to Maj. Gen. O. O. Howard of the U.S. IV Corps and ordered him to fire on them, the 5th Indiana Battery of Capt. Peter Simonson obeying in minutes.

G. H. Blakeslee of the 129th Illinois Infantry later wrote that his unit was lying in close support of Simonson's battery and were some 600 to 800 yards from the Rebel line. He recalled:

> We had for some moments been watching a group of men, supposed to be officers evidently viewing our lines, when Gen. Sherman came along, and, noticing this group, ordered the battery to fire three shots and make them keep under cover. This was done, and after the second shot they kept out of sight. We shortly learned that Gen. Polk was killed.[6]

The first round plunged into the ground a short distance in front of the Southerners sending most of them scurrying for cover, but Polk did not appear to be in a hurry as he and Johnston moved around the crown of the hill. These generals parted soon afterward with Polk retracing his steps from their earlier position. "Upon reaching a commanding point he paused for a moment, either to make a final examination of the scene before him, or, as is more probable, to spend a short interval in silent communion with his God," wrote the Bishop Stephen Elliott, one of Polk's colleagues.[7]

It was here that another round from Simonson's Parrotts found its mark, striking Polk in the left arm, tearing through his body and out the other arm before hitting a nearby chestnut tree. "As he stood thus occupied, his arms folded upon his breast, and his face wearing the composed and reverent look of a humble and trusting worshipper, a second shot was heard, and the cry arose that General Polk had fallen," Elliott wrote. Several of Polk's staff officers, including his son and son-in-law, Maj. William D. Gale, rushed to him, but there was nothing to be done for him. "His body, badly torn, was lying on the ground at full length, with the face upturned, and retaining its last expression of prayerful faith, and the arms, though broken, still crossed upon the breast," Elliott related.[8]

Johnston is said to have stood over Polk's twisted corpse and wept, Polk having baptized him earlier in the campaign. "The death of this eminent Christian and soldier who had been so distinguished in every battle in which the army of Tennessee had been engaged produced deep sorrow in our troops," Johnston recalled.[9]

William Polk wrote that the general "walked to the crest of the hill, and, entirely exposed, turned himself around, as if to take a farewell view. Folding his arms across his breast, he stood intently gazing on the scene below. While he thus stood a cannon shot crashed through his breast, and opening a wide door, let free that indomitable spirit."[10]

Rumors persisted for years that Sherman himself fired the gun that killed the bishop-general—and that he actually knew he was aiming at Polk. Sherman denied this:

> The fact is, at that distance we could not even tell that the group were officers at all; I was on horseback, a couple of hundred yards off, before my orders to fire were executed, [and] had no idea that our shot had taken effect.[11]

Sherman also claimed that Johnston gave him a postwar account of Polk's end. Johnston and others had scattered when they saw the Union battery preparing to fire, "but General Polk, who was dignified and corpulent, walked back slowly, not wishing to appear too hurried or cautious in the presence of the men, and was struck across the breast by an unexploded shell, which killed him instantly," Sherman wrote of his conversation with Johnston.[12]

The Kentuckian Lot Young gave this version of the general's death: "I saw the smoke from and heard the thunder of Simonson's guns as they sent the fatal shot that tore his body and ended his earthly career. Sad and awful moment for the Confederacy!"[13]

Soldiers hastily carried Polk's body to a rear area. In his left coat pocket was found his Book of Common Prayer. In the right were four copies of a thin pamphlet titled *Balm for the Weary and Wounded*. On a front page of three of these, Polk had written the names of Johnston, Hardee, and Lt. Gen. John B. Hood and the inscription, "with the compliments of Lieutenant-General Leonidas Polk, June 12, 1864." Polk had penned his name in the fourth copy. The five booklets were soaked in the general's blood.[14]

Johnston broke the sad tidings of Polk's death to his soldiers in a general field order issued a few hours after he left Pine Mountain:

> Comrades! You are called to mourn your first captain, your oldest companion-in-arms. Lieutenant-General Polk fell to-day at the outpost of this army—the army he raised and commanded—in all of whose trials he has shared—to all of whose victories he contributed. In this distinguished leader we have lost the most courteous of gentlemen, the most gallant of soldiers. The Christian, patriot, soldier, has neither lived nor died in vain. His example is before you—his mantle rests with you.[15]

"[T]he fatal missile of death deprived us of a hero," related Col. J. N. Wyatt of the 12th Tennessee. "In him the troops of Tennessee lost their best friend and the whole country one of its ablest commanders." Tennessee infantryman Sam Watkins added, "Every private soldier loved him. Second to Stonewall Jackson, his loss was the greatest the South ever sustained. . . . I felt that I had lost a friend whom I had ever loved and respected, and that the South had lost one of her best and greatest generals."[16]

The Union army learned of Polk's death later on Tuesday by reading the signal flags of the Confederates, having broken their code. Federal signalmen intercepted a message from Hood that Polk was dead, his body having been taken to Marietta. Other communication called for an ambulance to be sent for Polk's remains. Sherman was more concerned about eliminating the threat of Rebel cavalryman Nathan Bedford Forrest in a June 15 dispatch to U.S. Secretary of War Edwin Stanton, but mentioned Polk's death as well: "Forrest is the very devil . . . There will never be any peace in Tennessee till Forrest is dead. We killed Bishop Polk yesterday, and have made good progress today."[17]

In a report to Maj. Gen. Henry Halleck an hour later, Sherman elaborated on Polk's death: "An intercepted dispatch reports the death, by cannon-shot, of Bishop Polk, and it is confirmed by the prisoners." The Confederates abandoned Pine Mountain before daybreak on June 15, the Rebels showing their angry grief in a sign nailed to a tree and meant for the Yankees: "You sons of bitches killed poor old General Polk." Simonson who was the artillery chief for Maj. Gen. David Stanley's 1st Division in the U.S. IV Corps, did not have long to savor his achievement. A sharpshooter's bullet killed him on June 16 as he repositioned his guns at Pine Mountain.[18]

From Marietta, Polk's body was carried to Atlanta where he lay in state at St. Luke's Church for several hours before a service was conducted by Rev. Charles Quintard, the church rector and chaplain on Polk's staff. His remains were then conveyed to a railroad car for the trip to Augusta, Georgia, where Polk's family had requested he be buried. The train arrived in Augusta early the next day, and the body was taken to St. Paul's Church. Polk's funeral was held on June 29 at Augusta's City Hall and was attended by Gen. James Longstreet, recuperating from his Wilderness wound. "Our brother fills the grave of a Christian warrior!" Bishop Elliott said in eulogizing Polk during the service. "Although a minister of the Prince of peace and a Bishop in the Church of God, he has poured out his life-blood for us upon the field of battle." His remains and those of his wife were later reinterred at Christ Church Cathedral in New Orleans.[19]

"Our army, our country, and mankind at large sustained an irreparable loss . . . in the death of that noble Christian and soldier," Jefferson Davis wrote of Polk after the war. "Since the calamitous fall of General Albert Sidney Johnston and of General T. J. Jackson at Chancellorsville, the country sustained no heavier blow than in the death of General Polk."[20]

The bishop was not the only Southern general in the Polk family to spill his blood in the wild country around Atlanta. Thirteen days after his uncle's death, Brig. Gen. Lucius E. Polk was so severely wounded at Kennesaw Mountain that his military career was finished.

KENNESAW MOUNTAIN, JUNE 27, 1864

Johnston withdrew to Kennesaw Mountain on the night of June 18–19 to what would be the center of the new Confederate line guarding Atlanta. Sherman followed and, confident that Johnston had stretched his army too thin, decided to make a frontal attack on Kennesaw. One of Sherman's few significant mistakes, this offensive would deprive him of two brave young officers, including one whose father and brother, the latter a Union brigadier, would also die in the war, as part of one of the conflict's most famous families.

The assault would be made by two columns, one of which would be led by the IV Corps division of Brig. Gen. John Newton, Army of the Cumberland. Among Newton's commanders was Brig. Gen. Charles G. Harker, a twenty-eight-year-old New Jersey native and seasoned battle veteran. Harker was an 1858 West Point graduate who had seen action on the western frontier and who had been commissioned colonel of the 65th Ohio Infantry in the war's first months. He had been in combat at Shiloh, Perryville, Stones River, and Chickamauga, where he had greatly assisted Gen. George Thomas in the legendary defense of Snodgrass Hill. His exploits at Chickamauga earned him a brigadier's promotion in April 1864.[21]

On four previous occasions, Harker had horses shot from under him in battle, but had not been seriously injured. He decided to lead his troops on horseback at Kennesaw even though he still was recovering from a minor leg wound sustained at Resaca on May 14.

Also preparing for the attack was Col. Daniel McCook Jr., who was leading a XIV Corps brigade in Brig. Gen. Jefferson C. Davis's division. McCook was one of the "Fighting McCooks," fifteen men from an Ohio family who would fight for the Union in the Civil War, four as generals. McCook's brother, Brig. Gen. Robert McCook, had been killed in 1862 while his father, Maj. Daniel McCook, had been mortally wounded in July 1863 at Buffington Island, Ohio, battling John Hunt Morgan's Rebel cavalry. Another brother, Alexander D. McCook, and a cousin, Edward M. McCook, also were Union generals. Daniel Jr., twenty-nine, was born in Ohio, attended college in Alabama and studied law before moving to Leavenworth, Kansas, where he became a law partner of Sherman and Thomas Ewing, both future Federal generals. The three were soon in uniform when the war came, and McCook fought at Wilson's Creek as a captain of the 1st Kansas Infantry. In July 1862, he was commissioned colonel of the 52nd Ohio and assigned a brigade command under Sherman. McCook was in combat at Perryville, Chickamauga, Chattanooga, and Knoxville. His brigade was attached to Davis's division in the Atlanta Campaign.[22]

The attack was set for the morning of June 27 and was preceded by an artillery bombardment of Johnston's defenses. The assault against the Rebel left centered on a hilltop salient defended by two brigades of Maj. Gen. Benjamin F. Cheatham's command (the rise is now known as Cheatham's Hill). After this day the position would be immortalized as the Dead Angle.

Gazing up at the enemy works, McCook realized the odds of success were slim. After his men were aligned for the assault, he moved along their ranks, calmly reciting lines from Thomas Babington Macaulay's epic poem *Horatius*.

The Federal infantry plunged forward about 9 A.M. with Yankee skirmishers brushing back the Rebel pickets, the main Union line following immediately. Under intense fire, Harker's brigade advanced through thick brush, struggling through abatis to reach the foot of the enemy works. Unable to proceed, the brigade fell back a short distance.

Harker then started his men forward again and was shot from his horse about fifteen feet from the Confederate line. Hit in the arm and chest and mortally wounded, he died that night.

"Harker, moving with them cheered on his men; when they were forced to stop, he rallied them again and made a second vigorous effort, in which he fell," related the Union general Howard.[23]

"We were forced to witness the fatal fall of our beloved commander . . . who fell mortally wounded in the very midst of our ranks," recalled Maj. Frederick Atwater of the 42nd Illinois Infantry. Union colonel Luther P. Bradley, who led the brigade after Harker's fall, wrote: "No more gallant soldier has fallen in the war. Conspicuous for gentleness and generosity as well as courage, he won the confidence and respect of all who knew him, and was everywhere recognized as a true gentleman and soldier."[24]

McCook, meanwhile, also had pushed up the slope amid the sleet of bullets. "On and up the brave men rushed, with their gallant leader at their head, until some of them reached the base of the enemy's parapet," reported Lt. Col. James W. Langley of the 125th Illinois. Some of the Yankees were "knocked down with stones and clubs hurled by the enemy," Langley recalled. The desperate defenders here were the 1st Tennessee Volunteers who held on with "the hot blood of our dead and wounded spurting on us, the blinding smoke and stifling atmosphere filling our eyes and mouths," one Rebel recalled. McCook had reached the Confederate line when he suddenly crumpled to the ground. "Here the gallant Colonel McCook fell mortally wounded, while present and cheering his men on," Langley wrote. The Illinois colonel who replaced McCook was killed within minutes, and McCook's men joined the rest of the blue wave receding from Kennesaw Mountain.[25]

The assaults were repulsed and by noon the battle was over. Sherman had sustained about 3,000 casualties while Rebel losses were about 1,000. General Thomas described the failed offensive in a 6 P.M. dispatch to Sherman that also mentioned Harker and McCook. Both "were wounded on the enemy's breast-works, and all say had they not been wounded we would have driven the enemy from his works," Thomas stated. Replying with instructions, Sherman told Thomas, "I regret beyond measure the loss of two such young and dashing officers as Harker and Dan. McCook."[26]

McCook was taken to the home of his brother George in Steubenville, Ohio. He was promoted to brigadier general of volunteers on July 16, but died the next day, five days short of his thirtieth birthday.

Sherman realized how critical Harker and McCook had been to his attack, later writing to General Halleck: "Had Harker and McCook not been struck down so early, the assault would have succeeded, and then the battle would have all in our favor on account of our superiority of numbers, position, and initiative." In an earlier report to Halleck, Sherman had described how each column's attack had failed, "costing us many valuable lives, among them those of Generals Harker and McCook." George Thomas described them as "skillful, brave, and accomplished officers."[27]

A few weeks later, Sherman wrote to one of Harker's relatives regarding that family's loss:

> The position we attacked was a difficult one, but very important, and had General Harker lived I believe we would have carried the parapet, broken the enemy's center, and driven him pell-mell into the Chattahoochee [River]. General Harker, though quite young for his rank, was regarded as one of our best young generals, of rising fame, and his loss was deeply felt by me. He was universally esteemed, none more so; but death, you know, chooses a shining mark. . . . The nature of the country, its forests, its narrow defiles and mountain passes, all expose the leaders to the danger of ambush and unexpected shots; but General Harker fell in an assault, always one of the most dangerous moves of our dangerous life. I beg to record the high opinion I had of General Harker, and the hopes I had of a long and bright future to him, but it is ordered otherwise and we must submit.[28]

Sherman realized his direct attack on the Kennesaw fortress was a sanguine mistake, and he returned to his flanking maneuvers to uproot Johnston. By the first week of July, Union losses in the campaign were some 17,000, but from the hills the Federals could finally see Atlanta.

Frustrated by Johnston's retreats and inability to stop the enemy, Jefferson Davis replaced him on July 17, handing the Rebel army's reins to Gen. John B. Hood. Hood had the reputation of being an impetuously aggressive warrior, and Sherman braced for some type of offensive action from him, even though the Federals still had more men. Hood did not dawdle; on July 20, he attacked at Peachtree Creek with Hardee's Corps as his juggernaut.

In this Confederate assault force were the Georgians of Brig. Gen. Clement H. "Rock" Stevens. The son of a U.S. Navy officer, Stevens, forty-two, was born in Connecticut, but the family had relocated to Florida and then to South Carolina when he was very young. He had spent several years at sea serving with two commodores to whom he was related, but had been a Charleston, South Carolina, banker for many years when war came.[29]

Stevens had been seriously wounded at First Bull Run while serving on the staff of his brother-in-law, Gen. Barnard Bee, who was killed. He fought at Secessionville, South Carolina, as colonel of the 24th South Carolina Infantry, and in the Vicksburg Campaign before being severely wounded again at Chickamauga. Promoted to brigadier in January 1864, he was assigned to a brigade in Maj. Gen. W. H. T. Walker's division of Hardee's Corps.

In the assault at Peachtree Creek he was grievously wounded in the head, and two officers who carried him to the rear also were hit by enemy fire. The Rebel onslaught was repulsed with heavy losses on both sides. Hood sent a brief dispatch to Secretary of War James Seddon that night, mentioning that Stevens was seriously injured. Across the trenches the Yankees soon got wind that another Rebel general had fallen—they just weren't sure who it was. General Thomas shed light on the mystery in a July 21 message to Sherman: "Prisoners say that our shells yesterday fell into Atlanta, producing great consternation. They also say that General Stevens . . . was killed, not [C. L.] Stevenson."[30]

The information was premature, but only for a matter of days. Stevens was transported to Macon on July 22 where he was treated at Ocmulgee Hospital. Doctors there quickly saw that his skull had been shattered behind the jaw. Using chloroform anesthesia, they extracted the bullet and bone splinters, but Stevens died on July 25.[31]

His body was initially taken to Charleston for burial at Magnolia Cemetery but was later moved to the St. Paul's Episcopal Church cemetery in Pendleton, South Carolina, where he was laid to rest near Bee.

On July 22, Hood launched another titanic strike, this time on the Union left against Maj. Gen. James B. McPherson's Army of the Tennessee east of Atlanta. Walker, the fiery Georgian, and his division led Hardee's corps in this offensive. Walker, forty-seven, had the flint-eyed gaze and demeanor of an Old Testament prophet. Col. Arthur Fremantle, a British observer, described him as "a fierce and very warlike fire-eater" when they met in May 1863. Graduating West Point in 1837, Walker had fought in the Seminole Wars and the Mexican War, being desperately wounded in both conflicts. Because his body had absorbed so many bullets in Florida and Mexico, his men nicknamed the slightly built officer "Shotpouch." He had been appointed a Confederate brigadier in May 1861 and served in Florida, Virginia, and Georgia, resigning from the service at one point supposedly due to his health, but more likely because of his impatience with promotion. Appointed major general in May 1863, he participated in the Vicksburg Campaign and fought at Chickamauga.[32]

Even though his wife, Mary, was a New Yorker whom he had met before the war, Walker was vicious in his anti-Northern venom, telling his two children to "grow up hating the Yankee nation more & more every day."[33]

With Walker's division leading, Hardee made a night march through Atlanta and then north through thorny thickets and swamps to get into position for the attack on McPherson. The Confederates hoped to launch a surprise assault that would push the Federals away from Atlanta, at least temporarily. The rough country, however, greatly hampered the Rebels' progress, fraying nerves already on end by expected battle.

At one point early in the morning, Walker asked Hardee if some of his men might be allowed to go around a thick tangle of briars, but Hardee was in no mood for even the slightest deviation of plans after hours on the march and much lost time. "No sir! This movement has been delayed too long already," he barked at Walker. "Go and obey my orders!" Glaring at Hardee, Shotpouch stifled his rage, saluted stiffly, and returned to his command, but moments later spat to one of his officers, Joseph B. Cumming, "Major, did you hear that? I shall make him remember this insult. If I survive this battle, he shall answer to me for it!" Hardee soon sent an officer to apologize to Walker for his "hasty and discourteous language," but Walker would have none of it, thundering, "He must answer for this."[34]

Shortly afterward, the Rebel column abruptly came to a stop, a millpond half-mile-long blocking their advance. Walker and some of his officers tried to ride around the west end of the pond, but their horses sank to their bellies in mud. The already seething Walker exploded in anger, drawing his revolver and threatening to shoot the civilian guide responsible for leading them. Cumming and other aides were able to calm him, but the Confederates still faced a lengthy detour around the pond.

*Union major general
James B. McPherson.*
LIBRARY OF CONGRESS

Thus, Walker was probably still simmering near noon when he reached high ground to the north and decided to study the terrain ahead. He had ridden ahead of his troops and reined in to inspect some distant woods with his field glasses. As he did so, he was killed by a single shot, his binoculars still in his hands when his soldiers reached him. Walker's limp body was hustled to the rear as his division headed into combat. Lt. William R. Ross of the 66th Georgia claimed that as the general was being carried away he covered Walker's face with the general's own handkerchief. Walker was taken to a house near the pond and later in the afternoon was conveyed by mule-drawn wagon into Atlanta.[35]

A Federal version of Walker's death is that he was trying to rally some of his troops who were falling back from a rail fence when he was shot in the chest, apparently by a picket of the Union XVI Corps. "A general officer [supposed to be General Walker] rode out from the woods, and swinging his hat made a great effort to urge forward his troops," reported Union brigadier John W. Fuller, a division commander in the XVI Corps. "The next moment his horse went back riderless, and so sharp was the fire of our men that the enemy disappeared almost immediately, and nobody seemed to heed the cry of their officers to 'bring off the general.'"[36]

About the same time and a short distance from where Walker fell, General McPherson was killed. At age thirty-five, he would have the tragic distinction of being the only Union army commander killed in the war.

McPherson was born on a farm near Hamer's Corners (present-day Clyde), Ohio. As a teenager, he worked in a general store to help his mother support the family and eventually won an appointment to the Military Academy. He graduated in 1853, first in a class that included John Hood and Philip Sheridan. It would be Hood's decision to launch an offensive at Atlanta that would result in his classmate McPherson's death eleven years later. Fresh from the Military Academy, McPherson served in the Corps of Engineers in New York and on the Pacific coast, and supervised construction of defenses on Alcatraz Island in San Francisco Bay. When the Civil War opened, McPherson's star ascended more rapidly than any other officer in the Union armies. A first lieutenant in August 1861, he rose to become a major general of volunteers by October 1862. During those fourteen months, he was an aide-de-camp to Henry Halleck, chief engineer to U. S. Grant in the campaigns against Forts Henry and Donelson, was under fire at Shiloh and superintended railroads in western Tennessee. Promoted brigadier in August 1862, he rose to major general after the battle of Corinth.[37]

McPherson commanded the XVII Corps in the Vicksburg Campaign, earning appointment as a brigadier in the Regular Army in August 1863. He assumed command of the Army of the Tennessee in March 1864 and led it throughout the Georgia Campaign to the gates of Atlanta. McPherson had planned to take leave in the winter of 1864 to marry Emily Hoffman of Baltimore, to whom he was engaged. But Sherman had denied it because so much was happening, the war's pace too frantic to allow such a romantic personal luxury.

McPherson had conferred with Sherman at the Howard house that morning and had left him about 12:30 P.M., riding toward the action as the Rebels poured into a gap between his XVI and XVII Corps. About thirty minutes later, Lt. Col. William T. Clark, McPherson's adjutant-general, rode to Sherman and reported that McPherson was either dead or a prisoner. "The suddenness of this terrible calamity would have overwhelmed me with grief, but the living demanded my whole thoughts," Sherman reported.[38]

Clark told Sherman that after leaving the Howard house, McPherson had ridden to Maj. Gen. Grenville Dodge's column (Dodge commanded the XVI Corps) and had sent off most of his staff and orderlies on various errands. McPherson had then "passed into a narrow path or road" leading to the left rear of Brig. Gen. Giles Smith's division on the extreme left of Maj. Gen. Francis Blair's XVII Corps line. Clark also stated that "a few minutes after he had entered the woods a sharp volley was heard in that direction, and his [McPherson's] horse had come out riderless, having two wounds." Sherman quickly dispatched a staff officer to Maj. Gen. John

Logan, commander of the XV Corps, ordering him to assume command of the Army of the Tennessee.[39]

Specific details of McPherson's death remain in dispute, even to the number of soldiers with him when he was shot. Orderly A. J. Thompson claimed to be with McPherson when they were surprised by Confederates in the woods. At least three officers of the U.S. Signal Corps gave versions of McPherson's death that do not mention Thompson. Two of them, Capt. O. H. Howard and Lt. William H. Sherfy, claimed in official reports to have been with the general when he fell.

Thompson, who stated he was riding slightly behind the general, gave this account:

> All at once the rebels rose on our left and cried, "Halt! Halt!" General McPherson turned quickly from them to the right and I followed. Just as we turned they fired a volley. . . . I dodged down and hung on to the side of my horse and several balls came so close that they fairly blistered the back of my neck. They shot over me and killed the General.[40]

Thompson said that he saw McPherson fall and that the general's horse, followed by his mount, galloped between two saplings. The orderly hit his head on one of the trees and was knocked from the saddle, momentarily senseless.

He described the scene when he regained consciousness seconds later: "When I came to, McPherson was lying on his right side with his right hand pressed against his breast, and every breath he drew, the blood flowed in streams between his fingers. I went up to him and said to him, 'General, are you hurt?' He raised his left hand and brought it down upon his left leg and said, 'Oh, Orderly, I am,' and immediately turned over on his face, straightened himself out, trembling like a leaf." Thompson said he knelt to turn the general over, but was grabbed by the pistol belt by a Confederate "who jerked it until he broke the buckle, at the same time calling me rough names." The Rebel threatened to shoot Thompson if he did not head toward the Confederate rear, and the orderly complied.[41]

The accounts of the signal officers, written within days of the battle, appear to be more reliable, but while they do not mention the orderly, offer no evidence that Thompson's version is inaccurate.

Sherfy reported that he had been riding along the line that morning and, after the fighting flared, had seen Rebel infantry moving toward the gap between the XVI and XVII Corps. Shortly afterward, he encountered

McPherson who was about to ride toward the XVII Corps. "I rode up and warned him of the danger [of nearby Confederates]," Sherfy wrote. "He disregarded it though, and went on, and as he was accompanied by but one orderly, I went with him, being followed by several other members of the Signal Corps. Sherfy continued: "We had gone but a short distance when the enemy appeared on our left within a few yards of the road, and ordering us to halt, fired a volley at us. We all wheeled off the road to retreat, but at that instant the general was struck, and a moment afterward my horse dashed me against a tree with such force as to hurl me to the ground almost insensible. . . . I narrowly escaped, losing horse, hat, and signal glass."[42]

Captain Howard stated that he, Lt. W. W. Allen of the Signal Corps and Sherfy accompanied McPherson "through the broken line and into an ambush, where the general was killed, and we had a very narrow escape." Howard mentioned Sherfy's injury and added that Allen was "badly bruised by coming in contact with a tree."[43]

Samuel Edge, a first lieutenant who belonged to the same Signal Corps detachment as the others, wrote in a report that McPherson was riding with Captain Howard, Allen, and "other officers and men" when they "were fired upon by the enemy, resulting in the death of the general" and Allen's broken ankle from the tree. With Southerners closing in, the signalmen evidently made their way to safety before Thompson had his final encounter with McPherson.[44]

McPherson had apparently encountered Rebels of the 5th Confederate Tennessee Regiment attached to Lucius Polk's brigade of Maj. Gen. Patrick Cleburne's division, the 5th's Cpl. Robert F. Coleman being credited with shooting McPherson. In postwar accounts, Capt. Richard Beard, who led Coleman's company, related that the Tennesseans were in a battle line that crashed through the woods and underbrush before emerging on a narrow dirt lane. Moments later the Rebels saw an officer later identified as McPherson come "thundering at the head of . . . his staff."[45]

Beard continued his account:

> He [McPherson] was certainly surprised to find himself suddenly face to face with our line. My own company and possibly others had reached the road when he discovered that he was within a few feet of where we stood. . . . McPherson checked his horse for a second just opposite where I stood. I could have touched him with the point of my sword. Not a word was spoken. I threw up my sword to him as a signal to surrender. He checked his horse slightly, raised his hat as if he were saluting a lady, wheeled his

horse's head . . . and dashed off to the rear in a full gallop. Corporal Coleman, who was standing near me, fired on him. . . . It was his bullet that brought Gen. McPherson down. He was shot as he was passing under the thick branches of a tree, and as he was bending over his horse's neck, either to avoid . . . the limbs or, more probably, to escape the death dealing bullets that he knew were sure to follow him. A number of shots were also fired at his retreating staff.

Beard said he ran to the general who lay "just as he had fallen, upon his knees and face. There was not a quiver of his body to be seen. Not a sign of life perceptible. The fatal bullet had done its work well."[46]

As he reached McPherson, Beard claimed that Rebel captain W. A. Brown of his regiment picked up McPherson's hat, removed the gilt headband and replaced his own worn-out cap with the captured trophy.

Based on Beard's account, a slightly injured Union soldier, apparently Orderly Thompson, lay near McPherson who appeared only slightly injured, He asked the Federal the identity of the fallen officer and the soldier replied, with tears in his eyes, "Sir, it is Gen. McPherson. You have killed the best man in our army." In the battle storm, these Rebels quickly moved on and amid the fluctuating positions of the rival lines, Beard, Brown and a number of others from their regiment were captured.[47]

General Blair meanwhile, claimed that he likely heard the musketry that slew McPherson. "I was but a short distance from him at the time, and saw him enter the woods and heard the volley which probably killed him and the yells of the rebels which perhaps followed his fall," he wrote. He added that he immediately sent word to Logan that McPherson had either been killed or captured and that Logan, as senior general, might consider taking command of the Army of the Tennessee.[48]

Pvt. George J. Reynolds of the 15th Iowa in the XVII Corps had been wounded in the arm and was trying to evade capture when he happened upon McPherson shortly after the Confederate battle line passed. He raised the general's head, placed it on a blanket and tried to give McPherson water from a canteen, but the latter was unresponsive. Reynolds asked McPherson if he had any message, but the general did not reply. The private managed to make his way back to the Union lines and told some officers about McPherson's death. He led two of them back to where the general's body lay and, despite his wound, helped them place McPherson in an ambulance while under fire. Reynolds would win the Medal of Honor for his actions.

The 64th Illinois of Fuller's XVI Corps division was credited with driving back the Confederates and effecting the retrieval of the general's remains. The day cost the 64th several officers and more than fifty men as casualties, but they also captured a Rebel flag and forty prisoners, some of whom were found to be in possession of McPherson's field glass and personal papers.[49]

McPherson's body was returned to the Howard house even as enemy artillery shells battered the residence and grounds. Despite being in the midst of battle, Sherman is said to have wept openly when he saw McPherson's body lying on a bier improvised from a door. The fighting lasted until late in the afternoon, but the Rebels eventually had to withdraw with heavy losses. News of the general's death stunned his soldiers, many of whom charged into combat shouting "Remember McPherson!"[50]

Within the Union lines, the captured Rebel captain Beard found himself being questioned by a Federal officer of McPherson's staff, not only about the circumstances of McPherson's death, but about the general's personal possessions taken from the corpse. "He told me what he [McPherson] had on his person when killed, money, watch, etc., and that his body had been recovered. . . . I assured him that, so far as I knew, nothing on his person was touched while I was near it."[51]

Stunned Federals, meanwhile, examined the general's wounds. Dr. John Moore, medical director of the Army of the Tennessee, recorded that McPherson "was killed by a ball through the chest. . . . Thus prematurely fell an officer pre-eminent for his genius and attainments as a soldier, and as a man peculiarly beloved by all who had the good fortune to know him." Another physician, H. S. Hewitt, said the bullet hit McPherson in the back and came out at the left breast after passing near his heart.[52]

Sherman had the general's remains escorted to Marietta by members of McPherson's staff on the first leg of the journey home. "He was a noble youth of striking capacity, and with a heart abounding in kindness that drew to him the affections of all men," Sherman wrote in a report. "His sudden death devolved the command of the Army of the Tennessee on the no less brave and gallant General Logan, who nobly sustained his reputation and that of his veteran army and avenged the death of his comrade and commander."[53]

By heartbreaking accident, a dispatch about McPherson's death was read by Emily Hoffman, who until then was unaware of his loss. The message had been sent to her mother who, unable to see well without her glasses, passed it to her daughter to read. The general's bride-to-be scanned the terrible words and fainted. Most of Emily's family was strongly pro-Southern and did not approve of her engagement to McPherson. Emily was mortified to hear one of these relatives say, "I have the most wonderful news—McPherson is dead." Devastated by the news, Emily retired to her bedroom where she would spend the next year, curtains drawn, speaking to no one, meals brought to her door three times a day.[54]

General Grant was visibly upset when he learned of McPherson's fall. His eyes welling with tears and his voice breaking, he remarked, "The country has lost one of its best soldiers and I have lost my best friend."[55]

General Blair of the XVII Corps also was among those to praise McPherson: "The . . . Corps maintained the fair renown it had won under its first commander, Major-General McPherson, the youthful and illustrious leader of the Army of the Tennessee, who, in this battle, laid down his unsullied life for the cause to which he had consecrated it. Yet his genius survived in the discipline, valor, and constancy with which he had inspired his veterans."[56]

General Fuller lamented the Union dead, especially McPherson, whose lives helped buy the victory: "Many a grave was shutting from sight forever those who had stood manfully in the ranks for years; hundreds more were borne maimed and bleeding to the hospital, and . . . McPherson, who had secured our unbounded confidence and regard, had fallen just when his usefulness seemed at its zenith and when his assistance seemed most required."[57]

"A Sad Loss To Our Arms," read the page one headline regarding McPherson's death in the July 25 issue of the *New York Times*. "In this brilliant young officer the country loses one of its ablest Generals," the *Times* stated. Logan, in one of his battle reports, wrote that McPherson "was an earnest patriot, a brave and accomplished officer, in all his intercourse with others a true gentleman, and held in the highest degree the confidence and esteem of the officers and men of his command. He met the death of a patriot soldier, universally lamented by those he commanded and by the nation whose Government and flag he gave his life to defend."[58]

General Howard described McPherson as "so young, so noble, so promising, already commanding a department! . . . His death occasioned a profound sense of loss, a feeling that his place can never be completely filled."[59]

McPherson's loss rocked Grant and Sherman like the death of no other Union general in the war. Sherman wrote to Miss Hoffman himself, grieving with her over their mutual loss:

I yield to no one on earth but yourself the right to exceed me in lamentations for our dead hero. I see him now, so handsome, so smiling, on his fine black horse, booted and spurred, with his easy seat, the impersonation of the gallant knight.

Sherman's thoughts turned to the firebrands on both sides who contributed so greatly toward starting the war as he continued:

The loss of a thousand men such as Davis and Yancey and Toombs and Floyd and Beechers and Greeleys and Lovejoys, would not atone for that of McPherson. . . . Though the cannon booms now, and the angry rattle of musketry tells me that I also will likely pay the same penalty, yet while life lasts I will delight in the memory of that bright particular star which has gone before to prepare the way for us more hardened sinners who must struggle to the end.[60]

Sherman further displayed his eloquence and sadness regarding McPherson's end in this excerpt from a report to the War Department:

History tells us of but few who so blended the grace and gentleness of the friend with the dignity, courage, faith, and manliness of the soldier. His public enemies, even the men who directed the fatal shot, ne'er spoke or wrote of him without expressions of marked respect; those whom he commanded loved him even to idolatry, and I, his associate and commander, fail in words adequate to express my opinion of his great worth. I feel assured that every patriot in America on hearing this sad news will feel a sense of personal loss and the country generally will realize that we have lost not only an able military leader but a man who, had he survived, was qualified to heal the national strife which has been raised by ambitious and designing men.[61]

Grant's emotions must have been further stirred on August 3 when he received a letter from McPherson's eighty-seven-year-old grandmother, Lydia Slocum, who wrote:

I hope you will pardon me for troubling you with the perusal of these few lines from [my] trembling hand . . . When it was announced at his funeral, from the public prints, that when Gen-

eral Grant heard of his death he went into his tent and wept like a
child, my heart went out in thanks to you for the interest you
manifested in him while he was with you. I have watched his
progress from infancy up. In childhood he was obedient and kind;
in manhood interesting, noble, and persevering, looking to the
wants of others. . . . When it was announced to us by telegraph
that our loved one had fallen, our hearts were almost rent asunder;
but when we heard the commander-in-chief could weep with us
too, we felt, sir, that you have been as a father to him; and this
whole nation is mourning his early death. . . . [H]is remains were
conducted by a kind guard to the very parlor where he spent a
cheerful evening in 1861, with his widowed mother, two brothers,
only sister, and his aged grandma, who is now trying to write. In
the morning he took his leave . . . little dreaming he should fall by
a ball from the enemy. His funeral services were attended in his
mother's orchard, where his youthful feet had often pressed the
soil to gather fruit, and his remains are resting in the silent grave,
scarce half a mile from the place of his birth. . . . I pray that the
God of battles may be with you, and go forth with your armies till
the rebellion shall cease, the Union be restored, and the old flag
wave over our entire land.[62]

Grant replied to her a week later:

A nation grieves at the loss of one so dear to our nation's
cause. . . . It is a selfish grief, because the nation had more to
expect from him than from almost anyone living. I join in this selfish grief, and add the grief of personal love for the departed. He
formed for some time one of my military family. I knew him well,
and to know him was but to love him. It may be some consolation
to you, his aged grandmother, to know that every officer and every
soldier who served under your grandson felt the highest reverence
for his patriotism, his zeal, his great, almost unequaled ability, his
amiability, and all the manly virtues that can adorn a commander.
Your bereavement is great, but can not exceed mine.[63]

The news of McPherson's fall also saddened Hood. "No soldier fell in
the enemy's ranks, whose loss caused me equal regret," he recalled. In his
memoirs, Hood wrote of the "sincere sorrow" he felt at McPherson's death
and described their relationship:

Although in the same class, I was several years his junior, and, unlike him, was more wedded to boyish sports than to books. Often, when we were cadets, have I left [the] barracks at night to participate in some merry-making, and early the following morning have had recourse to him to help me over the difficult portion of my studies for the day. . . . Neither the lapse of years, nor the difference of sentiment . . . in the late war, had lessened my friendship.[64]

In special field orders issued on September 8, Sherman thanked his soldiers and paid tribute to his slain generals:

In our campaign, many, yea, very many, of our noble and gallant comrades have preceded us to our common destination—the grave. But they have left the memory of deeds on which a nation can build a proud history. McPherson, Harker, McCook, and others dear to us all, are now the binding links in our minds that should attach more closely together the living, who have to complete the task which still lays before us in the dim future.[65]

Harker was laid to rest in the New Episcopal Cemetery in his hometown of Swedesboro, New Jersey, while McCook was interred at Cincinnati's Spring Grove Cemetery.

On July 29, McPherson was buried near his father on a hill in his family's orchard. In 1881, dignitaries including Sherman and former President Rutherford B. Hayes gathered for the dedication of a grave monument through the efforts of the Society of the Army of the Tennessee. The war's end would also see Kansas veterans of McPherson's command return home to establish a town and county both named McPherson in his honor. A statue of the general on horseback was unveiled there on July 4, 1917, amid much fanfare in which many of the old soldiers took part.

⊷ ≼✦≽ ⊶

As he had with Stevens, Hood noted Walker's death in a report to Secretary Seddon on the night of July 22, and Jefferson Davis later referred to the Georgian as "that preux chevalier and accomplished soldier" who was foremost among Southern losses that day. "Here, I regret to say, the brave and gallant Maj. Gen. W. H. T. Walker was killed," Hood reported. Reflecting after the war, he called Walker the "noble and gallant hero" who was "generally beloved by his officers and men."[66]

Walker's body was sent by train to his hometown of Augusta, but because of the proximity of Union troops and the sorry state of the Confederacy's railroads, the roundabout journey wove through Macon, Millen, and Waynesboro. The general's sword and scabbard were lost or stolen during the trip but were later recovered. The remains arrived in Augusta on the morning of Sunday, July 24, about the time that word of his death reached the city. His funeral was held that afternoon.

Among the many condolences received by Mary Walker was a letter from the wife of Gen. Joseph Johnston. "You have been so incessantly on my mind for the last week and I have wept so many bitter tears with you and for you, since the loss of our glorious, brave hero," wrote Lydia Johnston. "Your dear, noble husband was our dear friend, his country's glorious defender, and we all weep for him, and as I dearly loved him . . . I ask to weep with you."[67]

Walker's division was dismantled on the day of his funeral, and his three brigades were transferred to other divisions in Hood's army. The general was buried in his family's plot on the grounds of the old Augusta Arsenal (now on the campus of Augusta College) and today lies next to his wife.

In the aftermath of the July 22 fighting, another Confederate officer lay dying, unaware that his promotion to brigadier was en route to Atlanta. Col. Samuel Benton of Tennessee, forty-three, was a nephew of the famous U.S. senator Thomas Hart Benton. In the prewar period he had settled in Holly Springs, Mississippi, where he was a lawyer and state legislator. He had seen action in Mississippi and central Tennessee in 1862–63, and in the Atlanta Campaign had been assigned to lead a Mississippi brigade in Gen. Stephen D. Lee's corps.

Benton was in action on July 22 when he was hit over the heart by a shell fragment. He also sustained a foot wound which later necessitated amputation. "In the desperate charge of that day he was mortally wounded, and the career of this able and gallant officer came to an end before he had an opportunity to enjoy the honors of his new position," Mississippi colonel Charles Hooker wrote after the war.[68]

Benton died on July 28, in a hospital in Griffin, Georgia, before receiving his brigadier's commission to rank from July 26. He was buried temporarily in Griffin before his remains were transferred to Hillcrest Cemetery in Holly Springs after the war.[69]

Hood had been stymied in his first two offensives, but he would still fought at Ezra Church and Jonesboro before Sherman's army forced him to evacuate Atlanta on the night of September 1. Within weeks Sherman would continue his trek across Georgia, embarking on a fiery march to the sea.

CONFEDERATE BRIGADIER GENERAL JOHN H. KELLY
Wheeler's Raid, Franklin, Tennessee, September 2, 1864

On August 10, 1864, some 4,000 Rebel cavalrymen under Maj. Gen. Joseph Wheeler trotted out of Covington, Georgia, intent on disrupting the communications and supply lines of the Union armies besieging Atlanta.

In the ranks of his division was Brig. Gen. John H. Kelly who, at age twenty-three, had been the youngest general in the Confederacy when he was promoted in November 1863. The Alabamian had been in his third year at West Point when the South seceded. He had resigned from the Academy in late December 1860, and headed home to join the Rebels. After serving on General Hardee's staff, then-Major Kelly led an Arkansas battalion at Shiloh where his gallantry earned him a promotion to colonel. He fought at Perryville, Stones River, and Chickamauga before his appointment to brigadier brought with it assignment to lead a cavalry division under Wheeler. "A young man of slight figure, fair complexion, light hair and moustache, a superb horseman, from the training school at West Point, nothing in man could be more inspiring than his presence on the field, with the enemy in front," one of Kelly's troopers recalled of him. "He dashed down his lines like a ray of light."[70]

With Sherman clamping his vise on Atlanta by late summer, Hood decided to send Wheeler on a strike at the enemy's lifelines in northern Tennessee and Georgia. The cavalry would destroy as much railroad as possible, hopefully weakening the Yankees and forcing Sherman to retreat from Atlanta. It was a forlorn hope, but Hood was rapidly running out of options if his vastly outnumbered army was to hold the city.

Wheeler's horsemen raided Marietta, Dalton, Cassville, and Calhoun, ripping up a few miles of track, and continued north into Tennessee. On September 2, the raiders were destroying a portion of the Nashville & Decatur Railroad about two miles from Franklin when they clashed with Union cavalry under Maj. Gen. Lovell H. Rousseau. The soldiers on both sides in this minor engagement had no way of knowing that at the same hour, Sherman's army was marching through the streets of Atlanta, Hood having evacuated the night before. Rousseau had infantry, but they had been marched to a frazzle in chasing Wheeler and did not reach Franklin in time to fight.

The combat was brief but costly to the Confederates before Wheeler's troopers abandoned the field. While leading his men, Kelly was shot in the chest by a sharpshooter and collapsed from his horse. The Rebels placed him on a blanket and cut off his bloody uniform coat to examine the wound. Kelly was then taken to a nearby house, but shortly thereafter moved to the home of the William Harrison family on the Columbia Pike a few miles south of town. Doctors soon found that the bullet entered just below the right shoulder and ranged downward, penetrating the right lung, one of Kelly's officers reported. Too seriously hurt to be moved again, he had to be left behind and was captured. The Confederates retreated across the Harpeth River toward Columbia, Tennessee, while the "Rebel General Kelly is mortally wounded, and in our hands," a Union brigadier wrote on September 3. "We have driven the enemy off . . . after a fight with his whole force," Rousseau said in a brief report written a few hours after the engagement. "Our loss is considerable, though not heavy." He made no mention of Kelly.[71]

In a postwar letter to Kelly's brother, Col. William S. McLemore of the 4th Tennessee Cavalry in Kelly's Division, described the general's end. "Of course we were forced to leave him, but I am glad to be able to say that he was tenderly cared for as long as he lived," McLemore wrote. "He had the best medical attendance and nursing." Kelly died on or about September 4, and his body was temporarily buried in the Harrisons' garden in a metallic coffin paid for by many of Franklin's residents. Kelly was dressed in new clothes other than his tunic, McLemore explaining that "we thought it best he should be buried in the uniform coat he wore when he fell."[72]

Writing to a superior officer that day, Lt. Col. J. B. Park of the 4th Michigan Cavalry, who was the post commander at Franklin said, "General Kelly's friends have asked me to furnish a small escort to bury him. Shall I do it?" Wheeler's troopers, meanwhile, continued to cause general alarm and some damage before crossing the Tennessee River to the relative safety of Alabama on September 10. The raid was over and did not negatively affect Sherman's siege operations, as he did not have to swat at the pesky Rebel cavalry in the final weeks of the campaign. Wheeler, however, expressed his grief over Kelly's loss, writing: "To my brave division commander . . . who gave up his life at Franklin . . . while gallantly fighting at the head of his division, I ask his country to award its gratitude. No honors bestowed to his memory could more than repay his devotion."[73]

"Allow me to mourn with you for his loss," McLemore wrote to Kelly's brother. "I honored him as an officer and loved him as a brother. No braver soldier ever faced a foe—no truer gentleman ever walked the earth." In March 1866, Kelly's remains were disinterred and returned to Mobile, Alabama, for reburial in a family plot at Old Magnolia Cemetery. Before the casket was taken to the gravesite, a funeral service was held at St. Francis Street Methodist Church. A reporter offering this description: "It was a solemn scene, and the bitter memories of the past seemed to rise up, unbidden, and tinge with melancholy the hearts of the large audience who listened to the history of the dead soldier whom they had come to bury. He slumbers with the great army of the brave dead. . . . Let us be as true to our country as he was to his."[74]

CHAPTER 19

Shrouds in the Shenandoah

CONFEDERATE MAJOR GENERAL ROBERT E. RODES AND BRIGADIER GENERAL ARCHIBALD C. GODWIN

UNION BRIGADIER GENERAL DAVID A. RUSSELL
Opequon Creek (Third Winchester), September 19, 1864

Winchester, in the northern reaches of the Shenandoah Valley, changed hands almost one hundred times during the war, local historians claim. At the battle of Opequon Creek, also known as Third Winchester, on September 19, 1864, the town was captured for the last time by the Union army. Three generals—two Confederate and one Yankee—were among those who died in the violent exchange.

The Federals of Maj. Gen. Philip Sheridan's Army of the Shenandoah who descended on Winchester that morning were intent on destroying Lt. Gen. Jubal Early's scattered Rebel Army of the Valley before it could reassemble. In raiding the Baltimore & Ohio Railroad near Martinsburg, (now West) Virginia, Early had dispersed his four infantry divisions. Maj. Gen. John Gordon's command was at Bunker Hill about thirteen miles north of Winchester, while at Stephenson's Depot, about five miles north of town, the divisions of Maj. Gens. Robert E. Rodes and John Breckinridge were posted. Maj. Gen. Stephen Ramseur's division guarded Winchester itself, these Rebels posted on slightly elevated ground along the Berryville Pike about a mile east of town.

Sheridan wanted to seize Winchester and assail Early before the Confederates could concentrate. In the predawn hours of September 19, his army advanced on Winchester along the Berryville Pike, the U.S. VI and XIX Corps crossing Opequon Creek. After bluecoat cavalry made their initial contact with the Confederate outposts, Early sensed Sheridan's plans and quickly ordered Gordon and Rodes to reinforce Ramseur. Sheridan also lost momentum when the XIX Corps was slowed in reaching its attack positions due to the VI Corps wagon trains on the pike. By about 10 A.M., Rodes and Gordon had arrived to support Ramseur, who had been involved in a fighting withdrawal throughout the early morning. Yet even though he had been allowed to gather most of his army, Early was still substantially outnumbered; he had only about 12,500 troops to face Sheridan's approximately 40,000. The Rebels were gradually pushed back toward Winchester with Ramseur bearing the brunt of the action.

About 12:30 P.M. the Confederates saw an opportunity: a gap several hundred yards wide had opened between the attacking VI and XIX Corps. Gordon and Rodes took aim at this vulnerable point, deploying their men for a counterstrike.

Rodes, thirty-five, had been promoted major general after leading Stonewall Jackson's flank attack at Chancellorsville. An 1848 graduate of Virginia Military Institute, he had been an assistant professor there before the war and also had worked as a railroad engineer. His combat resume ran from First Bull Run to Seven Pines, where he was seriously wounded, to Antietam, Gettysburg, the Wilderness, and Spotsylvania. Handsome and over six feet tall, Rodes was known for his battle ferocity.

Rodes's men started forward with his old brigade, the Alabamians of Brig. Gen. Cullen Battle, as the spearhead. "Rodes was a few paces behind us," recalled infantryman J. L. Schaub, adding that the general was having trouble controlling his "fine black horse" as cannon fire from the VI Corps artillery of Col. Charles H. Tompkins pummeled the Confederates. "Charge them, boys! Charge them!" Rodes yelled, riding behind Battle's line in an open field.[1]

As his men began their attack, a shell exploded overhead, and a fragment hit Rodes behind the ear. As he crumpled from his horse, Rodes was caught by Lt. J. S. Battle, a staff officer for Brig. Gen. William R. Cox who was in the vicinity. Rodes's men were already in motion and did not see their leader fall. He would die a few hours later without regaining consciousness.[2]

In his postwar memoir, Gordon said that he and Rodes had just conferred about making the attack while sitting on their horses. Gordon wrote

Confederate major general Robert E. Rodes.
VIRGINIA MILITARY INSTITUTE ARCHIVES

of what happened next: "As the last words between us were spoken, Rodes fell, mortally wounded, near my horse's feet, and was borne bleeding and almost lifeless to the rear."[3]

Gordon did not have time to grieve for Rodes as he was carried from the field. He continued:

> There are times in battle—and they come often—when the strain and the quick shifting of events compel the commander to stifle sensibilities and silence the natural promptings of his heart as cherished friends fall around him. This was one of those occasions. General Rodes was not only a comrade whom I greatly admired, but a friend whom I loved. To ride away without even expressing to him my deep grief was sorely trying to my feelings; but I had to go. His fall had left both divisions to my immediate control for the moment, and under the most perplexing and desperate conditions.[4]

The 12th Alabama of Rodes's division was on the move when Alabama captain Robert E. Park saw Maj. Green Peyton of Rodes's staff arrive on their line. Park did not know the general was down, but something compelled him to approach Peyton. "I know not what carried me to his side as he sat upon his horse," Park remembered. "I had heard nothing, not even a rumor nor whispered suggestion, yet something impelled me to ask, in a low tone, 'Major, has General Rodes been killed?' In an equally low, subdued tone, the gallant officer answered, 'Yes, but keep it to yourself; do not let your men know it.' The dreaded news . . . distressed and grieved me beyond expression."[5]

Battle's Brigade barged into the enemy weak point, smashing two Union divisions, and suddenly the struggle hung in the balance, the Confederates on the brink of a miraculous victory against overwhelming odds. Brig. Gen. Bryan Grimes now led Rodes's Division and he brought up the rest of his brigades to bolster Battle. But Sheridan had many more infantry and sent in reinforcements that launched a counterattack and regained the momentum.

"Rodes' division made a very gallant charge, and he was killed conducting it," Early said in a battle report. Writing after the war, Early had more to say, stating that Rodes "had been killed in the very moment of triumph, while conducting the attack of his division with great gallantry and skill, and this was a heavy blow to me."[6]

"The chivalric and heroic Rodes, after much brilliant service, fell on this field," recalled Maj. Henry Kyd Douglas of Early's staff. "In the charge, General Rodes, one of the most promising officers and accomplished soldiers in Lee's army, was killed," added Confederate historian D. H. Hill Jr.[7]

⊷ ⊱✦⊰ ⊶

This phase of the action also brought the death of Union brigadier general David A. Russell, a forty-three-year-old native of Salem, New York, whose father, David Abel Russell, had been a U.S. Congressman. A graduate of West Point class of 1845, Russell was a Mexican War veteran who had seen service in the Pacific Northwest. Before the war, Sheridan had served under Russell, but the fortunes of the conflict had now reversed their roles.

In the Civil War's first months, Russell had returned east and been assigned to Washington's defenses. Appointed colonel of the 7th Massachusetts Infantry in January 1862, he fought in the Peninsular and Maryland campaigns. Russell was promoted brigadier general in November, his brigade in heavy combat during the Chancellorsville Campaign. Russell's career zenith had come at Rappahannock Station on November 7, 1863. Temporarily commanding a division, he had personally led a bayonet charge that overran a strong Confederate position, resulting in Rebel losses of more than 1,600 men, four guns, and eight battle flags. At Gen. George Meade's urging, Russell, recovering from a battle wound, personally escorted the captured banners to Washington.[8]

Russell was given a division command in Maj. Gen. Horatio Wright's VI Corps and fought at the Wilderness and against Early's raid toward Washington before further operations in the Shenandoah. "He was a son of New York, who had carved his way from a captaincy to the command of a

*Union brigadier general
David A. Russell.*
LIBRARY OF CONGRESS

division by his own trusty sword," the *New York Herald* said. At Winchester, Russell led the VI Corps' 1st Division and was placed in reserve initially. Seemingly destined to watch the fighting from this vantage point, Russell had asked his friend Sheridan, "Phil, why do you put me in the rear?" Sheridan had replied, "Because I know what I shall have there in a commanding officer if the line should break at or near that point."[9]

Russell's chance for action came early in the afternoon when he rushed his command forward to try to stem Early's attack into the Union gap. Through Wright, Sheridan ordered Russell's division forward, but Russell, seeing the crisis, already was on the move. Russell was supervising the deployment of some of his units along the Berryville Pike when a minié ball hit him in the left side of his chest. He did not inform any of his staff that he had been wounded and did not leave the field, "continuing to urge forward his troops," recalled Maj. Henry Dalton, Russell's assistant adjutant general.[10]

His division soon became heavily engaged with attacking elements of the late Rodes's division, now led by Grimes. Russell was encouraging two of his brigades, leading them to a crest, when he was killed by a shell fragment ripping through his heart. Learning of his loss, Wright ordered Brig. Gen. Emory Upton, one of Russell's brigade commanders, to lead the division for the rest of the battle.

By mid afternoon, Union infantry and cavalry had turned the Confederate left flank, and Early ordered a retreat south down the Valley Pike.

Some of the Rebels ran while other units maintained their cohesion and withdrew in fighting order. Rodes's and Gordon's divisions fell back through Winchester, followed by Ramseur's men with Brig. Gen. Archibald C. Godwin's North Carolina Brigade serving as the rearguard.

Godwin, a thirty-three-year-old native of Nansemond County, Virginia, had been a general little more than a month. He had no formal military training, but had been a successful miner and rancher in California prior to the conflict, narrowly losing the Democratic gubernatorial nomination there in 1860. He had served in the Confederacy's military prison system before recruiting the 57th North Carolina Infantry, which he led at Fredericksburg. Godwin also fought at Chancellorsville and Gettysburg before being captured at Rappahannock Bridge. After his exchange he was promoted to brigadier in early August 1864. He was a "tall, lithe, auburn-haired man, who was a born soldier," recalled Capt. Clarence Hatton, the brigade adjutant.[11]

Like the rest of Ramseur's exhausted men, Godwin's brigade had been engaged almost continually since well before daylight. Now these Carolinians were trying to save the rest of the army from annihilation. There was a brief lull in the fighting near sunset, and Godwin rode up to his line at a point on the Berryville Pike where he found Capt. John Beard who commanded Godwin's 57th North Carolina. "I am proud of the conduct of my old regiment today," Godwin reportedly remarked to Beard. "It saved the day." Beard then warned him that he should move off the road because the Union artillery had found the exact range there. Before the general could reply, a shell burst over them, and a fragment hit Godwin in the head. He pitched forward off his horse, dead, with Beard catching him. Godwin's rearguard action saved the Confederates from a defeat "worse for us than at Cedar Creek," Captain Hatton claimed, even though the enemy "had killed our much beloved General Archie Godwin."[12]

The Confederates had Godwin's body taken to the home of a friend in Winchester, identified as Mrs. Long, with whom he had supposedly attended a church service the night before. In the 57th North Carolina's regimental history, Godwin was described as a "gallant gentleman and brave soldier, universally loved by all his comrades throughout the entire service." Hatton added, "The Tarheels who followed him on many fields until he was killed . . . were worthy of him and he of them."[13]

＊━ ⚔ ━＊

During the chaotic Confederate exodus from Winchester, a captured Union cavalry officer watched as Robert Rodes's body was prepared to be taken away. The Federal saw "an ambulance, the driver nervously clutching the reins, while six men in great alarm were carrying to it the body of General Rodes." The Alabama captain Park had been shot in the leg after learning of Rodes's mortal wounding. He was taken to a hospital set up in Winchester's Union Hotel where he told others of Rodes's division about their general's fall. "Many of my wounded comrades wept aloud and bitterly on learning . . . the fate of their brave and beloved commander," Park recalled. "All seemed overcome with real, unaffected grief."[14]

Confederate captain Jed Hotchkiss was at New Market, well south of Winchester, the following day when he heard of the battle and Rodes's death. Hotchkiss had reached Rude's Hill a few hours later and met Rodes's body being transported by his grieving soldiers. "A severe loss, his men along the road lamenting it deeply," Hotchkiss wrote in his journal. Rodes was survived by his wife, Virginia, and two children.[15]

Several Federal reports written just after the battle claimed that Gordon had been killed or gravely wounded, which was untrue. Lee informed Confederate secretary of war James Seddon about the Winchester fight in a September 20 dispatch: "Our loss is reported severe. Major-General Rodes and Brigadier-General Godwin were killed nobly doing their duty."[16]

Among the more than 3,600 Rebel casualties, in addition to Rodes and Godwin were four generals wounded, while the Federal losses of about 5,000 included Russell and three generals injured.

Russell "lost his life while bravely leading his command into action at a critical period of the battle," Wright later reported, "an officer whose merits were not measured by his rank, whose zeal never outran his discretion, whose abilities were never unequal to the occasion, a man tenderly just to his friends and heartily generous to his foes. In the memory of this entire command there will ever live a sincerity of admiration and respect, a richness of glorious recollections to foster the widespread influence which his life created, worthy only of such a character and of deeds like his." Writing to Gen. U. S. Grant that night, Sheridan added, "Our losses are severe, among them General D. A. Russell . . . who was killed by a cannon-ball." In another report Sheridan referred to "the lamented Russell," stating, "He had been previously wounded, but refused to leave the field. His death brought sadness to every heart in the army."[17]

Russell's body was taken to Harpers Ferry, arriving on September 20. It was embalmed there and then forwarded to New York. "General Russell had the entire confidence of his officers and men; there was not a single exception," wrote Major Dalton. "He had won their respect and confidence by an unselfish life, devoted to no other interest but that of his country. His death will long be regretted by them. To his nearer friends General

Russell's life will always be remembered with affection, his death most deeply mourned."[18]

"While the country rejoices over one of the most brilliant achievements of the war in Sheridan's victory . . . it is called upon to mourn . . . the loss of one of its bravest, most gallant and faithful general officers," the *Herald* said of Russell, and describing his Rappahannock Station victory. "He was . . . almost idolized by his troops, from officer to man." Russell was buried at Evergreen Cemetery in his hometown of Salem.[19]

Before he joined the flight of Early's army, Captain Hatton paid a local undertaker to take care of Godwin's body, and the brigadier was buried in the town's Stonewall Cemetery. Rodes, meanwhile, was interred at the Presbyterian Cemetery in his hometown of Lynchburg, Virginia, after lying in state at the courthouse. "There was no better officer in the entire army than he," Captain Park said of Rodes, "very few as brave, skillful and thoroughly trained. His men regarded him as second only to General Lee." The Rebel infantryman J. L. Schaub agreed, stating Rodes's death "was a great loss to the army. . . . He was brave without rashness, and General Lee often complimented him. Could more be desired?"[20]

CONFEDERATE MAJOR GENERAL STEPHEN D. RAMSEUR

UNION BRIGADIER GENERALS DANIEL D. BIDWELL AND CHARLES R. LOWELL
Cedar Creek, October 19, 1864

Confederate major general Stephen D. Ramseur wore a white flower in honor of his new baby as his division opened its attack against the Federals at Cedar Creek early on the morning of October 19, 1864.

Three nights earlier, Ramseur had received the joyous news that his wife, Ellen, had given birth to their first baby. Married only a year, Ramseur sat down the next day and expressed his happiness in a letter to her, not knowing if he was the father of a son or a daughter:

> Camp near Strasburg-Va.
> My own Darling Wife-
> I rec'd late last night through the Signal Corps, the telegram [about the birth]. It has relieved me of the greatest anxiety of my life. I hope that my darling precious wife & our darling babe too are well. . . . I cannot express my feelings. . . . I don't know how I can bear the separation from you much longer. . . . I must see you & be with you & our little Darling & The telegram did not state

whether we have a son or a daughter! . . . Tell Sister Mary for
pity's sake if not for love's sake to write me a long letter about my
little wife & baby! May God bless my Darlings & me, & soon
reunite us in happiness & peace—a joyful family. Goodbye, sweet-
est. With love inexpressible Yr devoted Husband[21]

The twenty-seven-year-old Ramseur did not have long to savor father-
hood's exuberance before the brutal campaign for control of the Shenandoah flamed again. Sheridan's army of 32,000 was arrayed along Cedar
Creek north of Strasburg, confident after victories over Jubal Early at Winchester on September 19 and at Fisher's Hill three days later. But Early
regrouped and plotted a massive surprise attack against these Federals set for
dawn on October 19.

A North Carolinian, Ramseur was an 1860 West Point graduate and
had been wounded three times in combat. He had seen action from the
Seven Days battles to Antietam, Chancellorsville, and Spotsylvania, and was
the youngest West Pointer to attain the rank of major general in the Southern service. Ramseur was "an officer whose record was equaled by few in
the Confederate army," Gen. John Gordon related.[22]

Early's plan called for the divisions of Ramseur, Gordon, and Maj.
Gen. John Pegram, some 21,000 troops, to cross the north fork of the
Shenandoah River and strike Sheridan. As the Rebels swung into position
after midnight that morning, Gordon and Ramseur sat together on a bluff,
Gordon later recalling their exchange: "He [Ramseur] talked most tenderly
and beautifully of his wife and baby . . . whom he longed to see." Henry
Kyd Douglas of Early's staff also remembered seeing Ramseur shortly
before the battle:

> In the morning's onset he had cried out to me joyously as he
> rushed past on his bay, "Douglas, I want to win this battle, for I
> must see my wife and baby." . . . Aside from his ability and bravery
> he was one of the most attractive men in our army.[23]

When the fighting kindled about 5 A.M., the Rebels were at first successful in driving back the stunned Federals. Only a tenacious stand made
by a U.S. VI Corps division likely saved the Yankees from disorganized
defeat. Sheridan, meanwhile, was en route back to his army after attending
a conference in Washington. He had spent the night in Winchester, twenty
miles to the north, and awoke that morning to hear the distant boom of
cannons at Cedar Creek.

The spitfire general galloped toward the crash of the guns, rallying his retreating men, in what would become one of the more glamorized exploits of the war. Coupled with Early's hesitation to press his initial advantage, Sheridan's efforts regrouped the Federals and set the stage for a Union counterattack about 4 P.M. This blow, with massed cavalry and infantry, was too much for the Southerners to withstand. Now it was their turn to run, their retreat soon turning into a rout.

Ramseur was among the Confederates who vainly tried to stem Sheridan's onslaught and two horses were shot from under him. Maj. R. R. Hutchinson of Ramseur's staff was near the general about 5:30 P.M. when the latter was shot in the right side, the bullet penetrating both lungs. "He exposed himself to every shot, cheering and encouraging all," Hutchinson later wrote to Ellen Ramseur. "I ran over to him, got some men, and bore him to the rear."[24]

The Rebels put Ramseur on a horse to try to reach safety and then found an ambulance for him, and Hutchinson returned to action. Squadrons of blue cavalry pursued the fleeing Rebels into the night, capturing artillery and wagons, many of which the Confederates had seized from the Federals earlier in the day.

Amid this confusion Ramseur's ambulance was stopped just south of Strasburg by a Union trooper of the 1st Vermont who asked the driver who was inside. Ramseur had enough strength to call out: "Do not tell him."[25]

Union brigadier general George Custer, leading his cavalry in the chase, was nearby and recognized the voice. He and Ramseur had been at West Point together. Custer climbed into the vehicle and saw how severely Ramseur was wounded. He ordered the stricken general taken to Sheridan's headquarters at Belle Grove plantation on the battlefield.

The day would not be without sacrifice among Union commanders. Brig. Gen. Daniel D. Bidwell was not on the field to see Sheridan's Ride or the reverse of fortunes. He fell when all seemed lost for the Federals.

Bidwell, forty-five, commanded the 3rd Brigade in Brig. Gen. George Getty's 2nd Division of the VI Corps. His brigade was composed of New York, Maine, and Pennsylvania troops. Born at Black Rock, just outside Buffalo, New York, Bidwell had been a well-known and well-liked civic leader of the city for two decades. When war erupted, he resigned as a city judge to enlist as a private in the 65th New York Infantry. His prominence was not overlooked, however, and Bidwell was made colonel of the 49th New York in October 1861. Bidwell fought at Fredericksburg, Chancellorsville, Gettysburg, and in the Overland Campaign as well as at Petersburg. Promoted to brigadier general in August 1864, he led his command at Winchester and Fisher's Hill before Cedar Creek.[26]

At Cedar Creek, Bidwell's men repulsed two assaults and were holding a rise when they were attacked by Confederates including Bryan Grimes's North Carolina Brigade. The intensity of the onslaught forced back Bidwell's 61st Pennsylvania and 77th New York, causing a breach in the Union line. Amid the blue and gray infantry battling only yards apart and Rebel shellfire, Bidwell rode to the right of his position to try to fill this gap.

His bravery cost him his life. An artillery round exploded over him, iron fragments ripping into his chest and shoulder and toppling him from his horse. As men rushed to help the mortally wounded general, Capt. G. S. Orr of Bidwell's staff lost an arm to another shell moments later. Lt. Col. W. B. French of the 77th New York was able to patch the line back together and the Rebels were eventually repelled.

Bidwell died that night, saying, among his last words, "I have tried to do my duty."[27]

In three years of war, Union colonel Charles R. Lowell had twelve horses shot from under him without even minor injury to himself. Fate turned terribly at Cedar Creek, however, and Lowell was twice wounded, the latter injury killing him on the day he was promoted to brigadier general. Lowell, twenty-nine, commanded the cavalry Reserve Brigade in Brig. Gen. Wesley Merritt's 1st Division and was one of the most popular and acclaimed officers in the cavalry. His younger brother, James Jackson, had been mortally wounded at the battle of Glendale in June 1862. Lowell "was a young man, not much past his majority, and looked like a boy," recalled J. H. Kidd of the 6th Michigan Cavalry. "He had a frank, open face, a manly, soldierly bearing, and a courage that was never called in question."[28]

Born in Boston, Lowell was a nephew of the famed poet James Russell Lowell and graduated Harvard at the head of the class of 1854. After traveling abroad, he was managing an ironworks in Maryland when the war flared. Lowell was commissioned captain in the 3rd U.S. Cavalry in May 1861 and fought in the Peninsular Campaign. Assigned to Gen. George McClellan's staff, Lowell was under fire while delivering orders and helping rally troops at Antietam. His bravery resulted in him being selected to carry captured Confederate flags from the battle to Washington. In the fall, Lowell recruited and organized the 2nd Massachusetts Cavalry, being named colonel of the unit in May 1863. He served in Washington's outer defenses during winter of 1863–64 and assisted in thwarting Early's raid on the capital in July 1864. Lowell fought well in the Shenandoah, including Third Winchester, and Tom's Brook on October 9.[29]

A few days before his death, Lowell wrote a letter to his pregnant wife, Josephine Shaw Lowell. "I don't want to be shot til I've had a chance to come home," he penned. "I have no idea that I shall be hit, but I want so much not to now, that it sometimes frightens me."[30]

In the confusion of Cedar Creek, Lowell's brigade held its position on the Union left flank against three Confederate attacks during the morning. During the last assault, however, a spent bullet ricocheted off a stone wall and smacked into Lowell's chest (some accounts state he was wounded in the arm and side). Despite bleeding from the mouth, Lowell would not quit his post. "He was wounded painfully . . . soon after which I met him," Merritt reported, "he was suffering acutely . . . but to ask him to leave the field was to insult him almost; a more gallant soldier never buckled on a saber."[31]

Sheridan was on the field by now, and earlier had asked Lowell if he could hold his position, the colonel replying that he could. Now Lowell, possibly suffering from a collapsed lung, knew that Sheridan was gathering the army for a counterattack and wanted to lead his command despite his injuries. Some of his soldiers erected a small earthwork behind which Lowell rested and waited for the counterstroke.

When the Yankees commenced their counterattack, Lowell was lifted into the saddle to lead his troopers against the Rebel infantry. He drew his sword and weakly told an aide to sound the charge. Now, however, his luck finally ran out. Kidd wrote that Lowell "was killed by a bullet from the gun of a sharpshooter in Middletown," the colonel slipping off the back of his horse. Minutes after his fall, the Confederate line broke under the Union attack.[32]

The mortally wounded Lowell was taken to a house in Middletown where surgeons, including Dr. Oscar DeWolf of the 2nd Massachusetts Cavalry, found that the bullet had cut through his body and severed his spinal cord.

Meanwhile, the Confederate major Hutchinson had been captured by the Federals and also taken to Belle Grove where he was granted permission to remain with his wounded chief, General Ramseur. Dr. James Gillespie, a Rebel surgeon, was assisted by Union medical personnel in trying to save Ramseur, while other Academy classmates, including Wesley Merritt and Union colonel Alexander Pennington, gathered at his bedside. Ramseur was "made as comfortable as circumstances would permit," Hutchinson wrote, adding that despite the doctors' efforts, Ramseur "suffered a good deal from his wound."[33]

Given an anesthetic to relieve the intense pain, Ramseur lingered through the night, but died just before 10:30 A.M. the next day. Hutchinson described his last moments to Ellen Ramseur:

> The end was peaceful and quiet. He spoke continually of you, and sent very many messages to his family, but above all, to his wife. . . . He told me to "give his love and send some of his hair to his darling wife," and often wished he could "see his wife and little child before he died." He told me to tell you he had a "firm hope in Christ, and hoped to meet you hereafter." He died as became a Confederate soldier and a firm believer.[34]

Custer clipped the lock of his hair to send to Ellen and the new daughter that Ramseur would never see. "A Union officer—a friend—watched by his side in his last moments and conveyed to his southern home his last words of affection," Merritt remembered.[35]

Shortly after Ramseur's death, Hutchinson sat down to write his widow, which Ramseur had requested of him. He opened thusly:

> Dear Madam: I do not know how to write to you; how to express my deep sympathy in your grievous affliction; but the Christian soldier who has gone before us . . . has asked me to do it, and I must not shrink from the performance of this duty, however painful. I am writing by the side of him whose last thought was of you and his God, his country and his duty.[36]

Despite his own suffering, Colonel Lowell spent much of the night trying to soothe at least one of four or five other seriously wounded men who lay around him in the room. At DeWolf's urging, he also managed to write a few lines to Josephine. But his life was ebbing by the hour as dawn came and by 8 A.M., he was gone. A saddened Sheridan already had used his influence and connections to ensure that Lowell's commission as brigadier general of volunteers was signed on the day of the battle.

"Into that fearful charge rode many a noble spirit who met his death," Merritt reported. "One more prominent than the rest, if individual prominence among a band of heroes is possible, received his death wound—the fearless Lowell, at the head of as gallant a brigade as ever rode at a foe, fell in the thickest of the fray, meeting his death as he had always faced it—calmly, resolutely, heroically. His fall cast a gloom on the entire command. No one in the field appreciated his worth more than his division commander."[37]

Brig. Gen. Alfred Torbert, Sheridan's cavalry chief, reported, "Thus the service lost one of its most gallant and accomplished soldiers. He was the beau ideal of a cavalry officer, and his memory will never die in the command." Kidd wrote, "The gallant Lowell, who so bravely did his duty and who exhibited in every stage of the battle the highest quality of leadership . . . laid down his life for the cause he so valiantly served."[38]

On a rainy October 28, Lowell's funeral was held at the Harvard chapel in Cambridge, Massachusetts. His flag-draped coffin was borne by soldiers whose fresh blue uniforms contrasted greatly with Lowell's worn, soiled gauntlets and cap and battered sword and scabbard all laid atop the casket. He was buried in Cambridge's Mount Auburn Cemetery. A few weeks after the service, Josephine Lowell, a widow after one year of marriage, gave birth to a daughter, Carlotta, who never knew her father. Josephine would go on to become a well-known philanthropist in New York City. Merritt wrote of Lowell:

> His coolness and judgment on the field were unequaled. An educated and accomplished gentleman, his modest, amiable, yet independent, demeanor endeared him to all his superiors in rank; his inflexible justice, temperate, yet unflinching, conduct of discipline made him respected and loved by his subordinates. He was upright as a man, pure as a patriot, and pre-eminently free from the finesse of the politician. His last breath was warm with commendations of his comrades in arms and devotion to his country's cause. Young in years, he died too early for his country, leaving a brilliant record for future generations, ending a career which gave bright promise of yet greater usefulness and glory.[39]

The *New York Times* described Lowell as a "singularly modest" officer who also was "one of the most faithful, brave and competent [to] ever draw a sword. Quick, genial, accomplished and young, the country mourns a choice spirit gone."[40]

⚔

On Sunday, October 30, hundreds of people crowded Buffalo's streets to watch the passage of General Bidwell's funeral procession. Services were held at St. Paul's Church before the general was laid to rest at Forest Lawn Cemetery, his escort composed of "a large body of military and by the masonic fraternity."[41]

Brig. Gen. Lewis A. Grant had served with Bidwell for most of the war and expressed his grief over his loss: "As regimental commanders and also as brigade commanders we have often performed the duties of the camp and the march and fought side by side, and it is but just to say that on every occasion he bore himself with gentlemanly deportment and with marked coolness and intrepidity." Bidwell, "endeared to all by his many soldierly virtues, kindness of heart, and sterling patriotism, has at last fallen in the first line of battle," reported Col. Thomas Hyde, who succeeded Bidwell in brigade command.[42]

General Getty was full of praise for Bidwell in his battle report:

> Actuated by a true sense of duty and patriotism General Bidwell took up arms at the outbreak of the rebellion, and for more than three years followed the banner of the Republic, sharing with his troops the dangers and privations of active field service. As a regimental and brigade commander in the Army of the Potomac he took part in all the arduous campaigns and bloody battles of that army from Yorktown to Petersburg, and was always at the head of his command, at the post of duty and danger. Brave and devoted as an officer, earnest, upright, and single-minded as a man, he was beloved by his command and respected by everyone. In his death the country and service have suffered a great loss.[43]

Embalmed at Belle Grove, Ramseur's body was later taken through the lines to Lincolnton, North Carolina, his hometown, where he was buried at St. Luke's Church Cemetery. "He was a most gallant and energetic officer whom no disaster appalled," Early later wrote of Ramseur, "but his courage and energy seemed to gain new strength in the midst of confusion and disorder. He fell at his post fighting like a lion at bay."[44]

Years after the war, John Gordon recalled his last meeting with Ramseur on the hill overlooking Cedar Creek. Before daybreak, Ramseur had ridden away to lead his men in the assault, telling Gordon, "Well, general, I shall get my furlough to-day." Gordon related: "I did not know what he meant. I did not ask what he meant. It was not a time for questions. But speedily the message came, and his furlough was granted. It came not by mail or wire from the War Department at Richmond, but from the blue lines in his front, flying on the bullet's wing. The chivalric soldier, the noble-hearted gentleman, the loving husband, had been furloughed—forever furloughed from earth's battles and cares."[45]

In 1920 Ramseur's daughter, Mary, helped unveil a Cedar Creek battlefield monument, dedicated to the father she never knew.

CHAPTER 20

More Dirges in Virginia—1864

CONFEDERATE BRIGADIER GENERALS
JOHN R. CHAMBLISS JR. AND VICTOR J. B. GIRARDEY
Second Deep Bottom, Virginia, August 16, 1864

Before daybreak on August 16, 1864, a combined force of U.S. infantry and cavalry readied for a thrust at Rebels entrenched north of the James River below Richmond. The day's actions would claim two brigadier generals among the Confederate dead, including one who was in his first battle since being promoted from captain.

For two days prior, these Federals, commanded by Maj. Gen. W. S. Hancock, had been frustrated in puncturing the enemy lines despite a sizable manpower advantage. Lt. Gen. Ulysses S. Grant had ordered this feint toward Richmond in an attempt to lure Rebel troops away from the Petersburg defenses to meet the threat. If successful, Grant hoped that other Union forces could attack and capture weakened Petersburg.

Hancock had about 29,000 troops—including his II Corps from the Army of the Potomac, Maj. Gen. David Birney's X Corps of the Army of the James, and the Army of the Potomac cavalry division of Brig. Gen. David M. Gregg. By transport and pontoon bridge the Yankees had come ashore on the north bank of the James beginning early on the morning of August 14. To oppose Hancock, the Confederates had only Maj. Gen. Charles Field's division and Brig. Gen. Martin Gary's cavalry, less than 8,000 men total.

There was inconclusive fighting that day and the next as the Rebels shifted their units to successfully repel every Federal threat. Record heat boiling to 100 degrees cooked the soldiers, and many died on the roadsides. Matters turned in the Confederates' favor on August 15, however, with the arrival of Gen. Robert E. Lee and reinforcements from Petersburg. By evening, Field had about 17,000 men; he was still outnumbered, but the odds were better now.

Hancock ordered a two-pronged dawn attack for August 16. Birney was to attack Rebel positions in the area of Fussell's Mill. As a diversion for this lunge, Gregg's cavalry was to move up the Charles City Road with Brig. Gen. Nelson Miles's infantry brigade under Gregg's temporary command. The late arrival of Miles's infantry, however, caused Gregg to open his assault about forty-five minutes later than expected, jumbling Hancock's plans.

After finally embarking about 6 A.M., Gregg's force soon approached Deep Run, finding Confederates of the 9th Virginia Cavalry entrenched in rifle pits on the south side of the little creek. Miles's men fanned out in adjoining woods and opened fire on these Rebels. With this covering musketry, Col. John Gregg's cavalry charged into a ravine and across the creek. Colonel Gregg was shot in the wrist, but his troopers uprooted the Virginians, who retreated in disorder. Most of the Confederates fell back along the Charles City Road toward White's Tavern before they could be rallied for another fight a mile and a half from the creek. "We pursued at a gallop . . . when he made a stand," reported Union major W. G. Mitchell of Hancock's staff, who was riding with the cavalry.[1]

With the Confederates again starched for a fight, the Federals reined in and waited for their infantry to catch up. When Miles' troops arrived, the Yankees charged, again snapping the Rebel line. This time, however, they also killed an enemy general whom General Gregg had befriended when they were West Point cadets.

Brig. John R. Chambliss Jr. was a thirty-one-year-old Virginian who graduated from the Academy in 1853, and ranked well ahead of classmate and future Confederate general John Bell Hood. He had been a gentleman planter before the war, and was an officer of infantry and cavalry in the war's first year. Service in Virginia as colonel of the 13th Virginia Cavalry brought a promotion to brigadier as of December 1863 and command of a Virginia cavalry brigade in Maj. Gen. W. H. F. "Rooney" Lee's division. He and Gregg had been at West Point at the same time, Gregg graduating in 1855.[2]

Now as Gregg's troopers pounded down the road, Chambliss tried to rally his men and was shot through the body, sagging to the ground. General Gregg reined in beside his friend's corpse moments later, but not before some Yankee troopers had cut buttons and insignia from Chambliss's uniform. "We are getting along and driving the enemy," Gregg said in an 8 A.M. dispatch to Hancock. "I have the body of General Chambliss, killed a few minutes ago. I am having some loss, but not very considerable."[3]

The *New York Herald* gave this account of Chambliss's end:

> This rebel general endeavored to rally his troopers, but without avail; for when the head of our charging column was close upon the rear of the flying fugitives he was seen almost alone upon the field where his men had deserted him. . . . It was an exciting scene . . . our cavalry dashing forward . . . and their general, at the post of danger, attempting to inspire them with his own courage and high sense of military honor. But a bullet . . . pierced the breast of the youthful general.[4]

Major Mitchell updated Hancock in an 8:15 A.M. note that mentioned Chambliss's death: "Generals Gregg and Miles are advancing, with sharp skirmishing. . . . Have not met enemy infantry yet. We have killed Brigadier-General Chambliss, of the rebel service. His body is in our possession."[5]

In searching Chambliss's clothing, the Federals found a map they believed would be of military importance. They also discovered a pocket Testament in which Chambliss had written his name and the inscription, "If I am killed in this struggle, will some kind friend deliver this book to my dear wife? J. R. C., Jr., June 8, 1864." The Testament also contained several Bible verses scribbled by Chambliss.[6]

"General Gregg found a valuable map on General Chambliss' body, which I will send you when it comes," Hancock, wrote to Grant that day. "It is said to have the enemy's line marked on it." The map indeed detailed the Richmond fortifications and the surrounding countryside. Despite his involvement in the battle, Hancock was concerned that the Rebels might retake Chambliss's remains. He sent this dispatch to Gregg: "In order to prevent the enemy's recapturing General Chambliss' body as a trophy in any of the subsequent operations of the day . . . send it back in an ambulance."[7]

The Confederates first got wind of Chambliss's ill fortune when his horse scampered back to their lines, but there was no word whether the general had been killed, wounded, or captured. Within hours of his death, Union II Corps soldiers had placed Chambliss in a wooden coffin and buried him near the corner of an icehouse at the Potteries, a country hamlet near Hancock's headquarters. They also erected a crude headboard, which a *Herald* reporter interpreted as a gesture of civility:

> [T]his incident illustrates the fact that we bear no individual malice against our common kindred who have blindly made themselves our enemies in arms; but that we can afford to be as magnanimous towards even those who attempt to destroy the Union as we are confident in the justice and final triumph of our cause.[8]

About four hours after Chambliss died, a French-born Rebel general was killed a short distance away in trying to stave off Birney's attack. Brig. Gen. Victor J. B. Girardey was a twenty-seven-year-old native of Lauw whose family had emigrated to the U.S. when he was a child and settled in Augusta, Georgia. Orphaned by age sixteen, Girardey spent the next few years in New Orleans where he completed his education and was married. The war saw Girardey assigned to the staff of Brig. Gen. A. R. Wright as captain and assistant adjutant general—a post punctuated by many commendations—that he held until May 1864. Transferred to the staff of Gen. William Mahone in the same capacity, Girardey earned even more recognition for helping organize Mahone's counterattack at the battle of the Crater. Four days later, Girardey was promoted from captain to brigadier with temporary rank from July 30, the only time such a jump in rank was made in the Confederate military. "In organizing and timing the attack of Mahone's division . . . Girardey won the admiration of the entire army," wrote Douglas Southall Freeman. "Girardey had every promise of being a brilliant officer."[9]

Now, less than a month after his promotion, Girardey was killed near Fussell's Mill on the Darbytown Road. About 5,000 Union troops under Brig. Gen. Alfred H. Terry assailed the Confederate line on the east end of the Richmond defenses about noon. Girardey was temporarily leading Wright's Brigade, and was among the Rebel units trying to repel the assault, but Terry's troops, primarily the brigade of Col. Francis B. Pond, punched a hole in the Confederate line. Girardey had only about 800 men to defend his position, the Georgians arrayed in a single rank in earthworks atop a hill.

Pond's Illinois, Ohio, and Pennsylvania troops charged out of a ravine to attack a portion of Girardey's defenses. From a range of only thirty yards, the Rebels fired a volley that momentarily staggered the Yankees, "a withering fire, carrying with it almost every man in the front division of each regiment," Pond reported.[10]

The Federals came on with a yell over their own dead and wounded. The Confederate defenders here belonged to the 2nd and 10th Georgia

Battalions, but they were too few to hold the trenches, and Pond's Yankees stormed through the abatis and were among them before they could fire another volley. The fighting was hand-to-hand for several minutes, but many of Girardey's men lacked bayonets for such combat. The two Rebel units were soon overpowered, and some of Pond's troops streamed south along the enemy entrenchments. They smashed into the rear of the 64th Georgia Battalion, which also was outmatched and soon broken.

In desperation, Girardey grabbed the 64th's flag and tried to keep his line from dissolving, but a skirmisher of the 67th Ohio shot him in the forehead. Girardey slumped dead in a trench, a Georgia private retrieving the banner and carrying it to the rear. "The fire of my skirmishers caused the death of the rebel general Girardey," Col. Alvin Voris of the 67th Ohio wrote in his action report. With Girardey down, Col. William Gibson assumed brigade command and tried to reform the Georgians, as Pond's men rounded up scores of prisoners. "The enemy fought desperately inside their breast-works, but nothing could withstand the determined valor of our men, who swept over them like a tornado," Pond wrote.[11]

General Gregg received word of the X Corps' progress, including Girardey's demise, in a 2 P.M. dispatch from Hancock's headquarters: "General Birney has captured 200 or 300 prisoners and 3 battle-flags. One general officer, supposed to be Girardey, is dead within our lines." "The fighting north of the river today has resulted favorably for us," Grant said in a dispatch to Gen. Henry Halleck that night. "Two brigadier-generals [Chambliss and Girardey] were killed and their bodies left in our hands."[12]

A Rebel counterattack later in the day restored the Rebel line, and by sundown little or nothing had been gained by either side. The Southerners still were unsure of Chambliss's fate, but Rooney Lee feared the worst in sending this message under a truce flag on August 17:

> General Gregg or Officer Commanding Federal Cavalry: General: I am led to believe, from statements of prisoners captured yesterday, that Brigadier General J. R. Chambliss of my command may have been killed during the action. Should such prove to be the fact, I have the honor to request that you will inform me whether any arrangement may be effected by which I may obtain possession of his body.[13]

Gregg replied promptly, telling Lee of Chambliss's death and writing that the general's body would be returned to the Confederates later that day if possible. He also included a description of Chambliss's burial site so that if the remains could not be transferred the general's friends could find it later. In an August 19 dispatch to Maj. Gen. Wade Hampton, praising the work of his cavalry, Robert E. Lee mentioned Chambliss's void: "The loss sustained by the cavalry in the fall of General Chambliss will be felt throughout the army, in which, by his courage, energy, and skill, he had won for himself an honorable name."[14]

The Federals soon exhumed Chambliss and returned him to the Confederates near Fussell's Mill during an exchange of the dead. With the body was a letter of condolence written by General Gregg to Chambliss's widow in Emporia, Virginia, where Chambliss's remains were eventually buried.

Girardey was laid to rest at Magnolia Cemetery in Augusta, Georgia. "No more valiant soldier than Victor Girardey laid down his life for the Southern cause," a Confederate historian wrote.[15]

CONFEDERATE BRIGADIER GENERALS
JOHN C. C. SANDERS, JOHN GREGG, JOHN DUNOVANT, AND ARCHIBALD GRACIE JR.

UNION BRIGADIER GENERAL HIRAM BURNHAM
Richmond-Petersburg Campaign, August–December, 1864

At age twenty-four, John C. C. Sanders was one of the youngest generals in the Confederate armies. Assigned to Mahone's Division, he had distinguished himself in the Petersburg siege, in the combat at the Crater and in leading his own and a North Carolina brigade at Deep Bottom. The boyish Alabamian had been severely wounded at Frayser's Farm before promotion to colonel at age twenty-two after the Maryland Campaign. Sanders fought well at Fredericksburg, Gettysburg, and in the Overland Campaign but had shone brightest at Spotsylvania, taking over the brigade of the dying Abner Perrin and earning a brigadier's promotion.[16]

On August 21, 1864, Sanders's Brigade was involved in fierce fighting along the Weldon Railroad south of Petersburg. The railroad was one of Robert E. Lee's crucial supply lines, linking Richmond and Petersburg with the Confederacy's last major seaport of Wilmington, North Carolina. But on August 19, the Federals had seized a section of the tracks at Reams Station, forcing the Confederates to try to retake the line. Mahone's Division, including Sanders, attacked two days later.

Sanders was leading his Alabamians on foot when a minié ball sliced through both of his thighs, ripping his femoral arteries. Despite his injuries, Sanders did not collapse, instead telling his adjutant, "Take me back." Bleeding heavily, the general was carried a short distance to the rear before he asked to be laid down. He died minutes later and Mahone's assault was repelled. "Prisoners report the death yesterday of General Sanders, commanding brigade." Maj. Gen. George Meade wrote to Ulysses Grant on August 22, "but I place no reliance on the reports of prisoners in such matters, as they are generally only camp rumors."[17]

Grant wrote to Meade on the morning of August 24 about the attrition of enemy commanders in the recent fighting: "Richmond papers of yesterday show great despondency over the affair on the Weldon road, and report five generals killed, but only know positively of . . . Sanders . . . being actually dead. They seem to be unable to learn anything official of the affair, but have to depend entirely upon citizens going from Petersburg to Richmond for information."[18]

The Alabamians lamented the "sad loss" of Sanders, "our young and gallant brigadier, who gave his life to the cause," one of his men recalled. "I knew that none were braver than he," added a private in the 11th Alabama. "He was stern but kind, and always looked after the comfort and safety of his men, and as the war progressed he grew continually in their estimation."[19]

The *Charleston Mercury* described the battle casualties, stating that "none was more beloved, or will be more regretted, than the gallant" Sanders. The article added that he was "a thorough soldier . . . yet a gentleman and a patriot . . . devoted to his duties, modest in deportment, of no unselfish disposition."[20]

The Confederates reclaimed the railroad in more fighting at Reams Station on August 25. The Yankees had destroyed the tracks at several other points, but Lee still could use the line with wagon trains carrying supplies where the rails had been demolished.

Sanders, meanwhile, was buried in Richmond's Hollywood Cemetery. "He had proven his fitness for command," Gen. Joseph Wheeler wrote of him after the war. "A man of serene courage and unblemished moral character, he won general admiration."[21]

—— ✠ ——

A few weeks after Sanders's fall, the name of a Union commander from Maine was added to the lengthening casualty lists. Brig. Gen. Hiram Burnham commanded a brigade in the 1st Division of the U.S. XVIII Corps. Burnham, fifty, had been a county commissioner and coroner as well as a lumberman in what is now the Maine community of Cherryfield before hostilities. He became colonel of the 6th Maine, which he had helped to recruit, in July 1861, and was in combat in the Peninsular Campaign, Antietam, Chancellorsville, and in the Overland Campaign. Promoted brigadier general of volunteers to rank from April 26, 1864, he led his brigade in the Petersburg fighting.[22]

On September 29, Burnham's men were involved in a probing attack against Fort Harrison, a bastion in Richmond's outer defense ring below Chaffin's Bluff. The fort was a formidable work, but with Confederate manpower and weaponry stretched thin, was understrength, only about 200 Rebels equipped with poor artillery defending the place.

The Federals quickly overran the fort, but Burnham did not live to savor the victory.

"Brigadier General Burnham was killed as he was about entering the fort," wrote John Brady, a correspondent for the *New York Herald*. "He lived a few moments after he was struck, but every attempt to save his life proved futile. General Burnham had but just returned from a leave of absence."[23]

"The column had scarcely entered the works when the brave . . . Burnham was mortally wounded by a musket-ball in the bowels," reported Brig. Gen. George J. Stannard, Burnham's division commander. "He survived but a few moments."[24] Lee believed Harrison was such a key to his defenses that he personally organized an attack to recapture it the next day. The assault failed, however, and the victorious Yankees renamed the stronghold Fort Burnham to honor the slain general.

The October 2 *New York Times* featured two full front-page columns about the career and death of famed Confederate general John Hunt Morgan, killed by Union raiders in Tennessee, while Burnham's demise garnered only two separated paragraphs and a brief obituary. Burnham "fell at the head of his brigade while leading a charge," stated one mention. The other said that his body had been sent by ship to Fortress Monroe, arriving on September 30 on the mourned general's return to Maine.[25]

The obituary, however, was much more generous. "It is simple truth to say that a braver and more conscientious soldier never lived," it stated. "Not bred a professional military man, yet entering into military service with all the enthusiasm of a national soldier, combined with that high sense of duty which he felt as a patriotic citizen . . . [Burnham was] foremost in every place of danger. Under the lead of such a man it was no wonder that his old regiment, the Sixth Maine, loved him, and followed his brilliant example through many fiery streams of death." Burnham's soldiers were "worthy of such a leader, and their leader was thrice worthy of all the honors he ever received. He was a man who never failed to do his duty." The obit went on to praise Burnham's bravery in the "great charges" at Fredericksburg and Rappahannock Ford. "He fell in another charge, but it is worthy to note that the position charged was taken. Such men we cannot afford to lose." Burnham, meanwhile, was buried at Pine Grove Cemetery in Cherryfield.[26]

In a written address to his soldiers on October 11, Maj. Gen. Benjamin F. Butler praised the Army of the James for its victories, also mentioning the cost:

> All these triumphs have not been achieved without many loved and honored dead. Why should we mourn their departure? Their names have passed into history emblazoned on the proud roll of their country's patriot heroes. Yet we drop a fresh tear for the gallant General H. Burnham—a devoted soldier leading his brigade to the crest of Battery Harrison, where he fell amid the cheers of the victorious charge.[27]

Confederate brigadier general John Gregg had been left for dead at Chickamauga, his "corpse" robbed by Yankee soldiers. Gregg had lived to fight again, but his charmed life ended on a fall morning punctuated by battle in the Virginia countryside.

Born in Alabama, Gregg, thirty-six, was a transplanted Texan who had been a lawyer and district judge in Fairfield, Texas, before being elected to the Confederate Congress. He resigned his seat to recruit and lead the 7th Texas Infantry, but was captured at Fort Donelson. Exchanged and promoted to brigadier in August 1862, he fought in Mississippi and was seriously wounded at Chickamauga. When he was shot, Gregg fell from his horse and was about to be captured by Federals, some of whom, apparently believing him dead, took his spurs, sword and other valuables from his person. Gregg's Texans rushed forward and drove off the enemy, bringing the general and his horse to safety. Gregg recovered to command the Texas brigade at the Wilderness and in the Overland Campaign.[28]

Gregg was killed in action on the Charles City Road below Richmond on the morning of October 7, 1864, while temporarily commanding Maj. Gen. Charles Field's division in an assault on the Federal lines. Gregg and Brig. Gen. John Bratton led their men on foot, "my gallant fellows" as Field called them. Under a murderous fire—a number of the Yankees were armed with the new repeating Spencer rifles—the Rebels managed to penetrate the abatis in front of the Yankee positions. But Gregg was fatally shot near the throat, and Bratton fell with a shoulder wound, the attack failing as the Texans and South Carolinians were driven off with heavy losses.

"These gentlemen were both brave and able officers," Field wrote of Gregg and Braxton, "and the fall of General Gregg was felt as a great calamity by the whole army, and was a misfortune from which his brigade never recovered."[29]

"We had a hard fight on the Charles City Road," W. L. Timberlake of the 2nd Virginia Battalion recalled of the battle, adding that he saw "the brave General Gregg of the Texas brigade lying cold and dead with a bullet through his neck." Gregg's body was taken into Richmond and lay in state at the Capitol, showing the "high esteem in which General Gregg was held by the government and his soldiers" said Col. A. C. Jones of the 3rd Arkansas. Gregg was temporarily buried at Hollywood Cemetery, his brigade, according to Jones, receiving permission from General Lee to leave the lines and escort his body there.[30]

Word of her husband's death reached Gregg's widow, Mary, in Decatur, Alabama, days later. Naturally grief-stricken, she decided to bring her husband home. Accompanied by Sgt. E. L. Sykes, a Rebel soldier and friend of the family, she set out for Virginia in January 1865. The trip took a month, but Mary Gregg found and claimed her husband's body. The rigorous journey, however, had taken a toll on her and she suffered a breakdown, having to recuperate for several weeks before starting home. After another month of travel through the war-spent South, she and Sykes finally reached Aberdeen, Mississippi, where her family owned land. Mary Gregg had her husband buried in the town's Odd Fellows Cemetery where she would eventually join him.

The death of Rebel brigadier John Dunovant of South Carolina would earn the Medal of Honor for the Union soldier who killed him. Dunovant, thirty-nine, fought in the Mexican War and had been a captain in the U.S. 10th Infantry when he resigned his commission at the war's onset. As colonel of the 1st South Carolina Regulars, Dunovant was cashiered for drunkenness in June 1862 and dismissed from the army with President Jefferson Davis's full approval.[31]

Dunovant, however, was not long removed from duty. South Carolina governor Francis Pickens soon appointed him colonel of the 5th South Carolina Cavalry, which was ordered to Virginia in March 1864. Assigned to Brig. Gen. M. C. Butler's cavalry, Dunovant must have proved himself to Davis over the next few months, for in August the president suggested to Robert E. Lee that he be temporarily promoted to brigadier general. Dunovant was given command of a South Carolina brigade in Maj. Gen. Wade Hampton's cavalry corps.

On a chilly and wet October 1, 1864, Dunovant led his brigade with the rest of Butler's Division in action near the McDowell farm on the James River below Petersburg. His left arm still in a sling due to an unhealed hand wound sustained in late May, Dunovant rode his favorite chestnut while directing his dismounted troopers as they engaged Union cavalry of Gen. David Gregg's division along the Vaughan Road. In this sector the Rebels were battling Brig. Gen. Henry Davies's brigade of Gregg's command.

Butler's cavalry, shielded by a makeshift work of logs and fence rails, had been fighting for most of the day as the Federals made repeated attacks against them. By about 3 P.M., however, the Southerners took the offensive with Butler ordering Dunovant and Brig. Gen. P. M. B. Young to advance. The gray troopers ran forward, enduring sharp fire from Gregg's men posted behind breastworks on the far side of a narrow swamp. Butler ordered the Southerners to take cover at the base of a hill while he decided how best to proceed. A small log causeway led from near the center of the Rebels' position across the swamp and appeared to be the only way to get through the tangle. Dunovant rode up to Butler and said that he believed one more thrust would take the enemy line and Butler, trusting his opinion, ordered the brigades forward.

"Dunovant gave the command, 'Attention, men,' in a loud voice," Butler recalled after the war. "They had been subjected to such a terrible fire a short time before that they were a little tardy in heeding the order. He called out a second time . . . and every man jumped to his feet and moved forward, firing across the swamp." The Rebels "came on at a double-quick, shouting and yelling like so many fiends," a Union officer reported.[32]

Ahead of their troopers, Butler and Dunovant rode to the causeway and were greeted by a Yankee volley. Dunovant was hit and tumbled forward off his horse and onto the bridge, his spooked mount galloping into the Union position. Butler, who was uninjured, later recalled that Dunovant's "gallant life went out almost in the twinkling of an eye."[33]

Charles Montague, a courier in the 6th South Carolina Cavalry, recalled seeing Dunovant "fall from his horse . . . and reigning [*sic*] my horse back for fear of treading on him, two men picked him up instantly, and as they did so, General Butler leaned almost over on his horse's neck and called out, 'Who is shot?'" When Montague answered, Butler told the men, "Carry him back, and don't let the men know it." The Confederate assault was repulsed shortly afterward, the Carolinians carrying their dead general to the rear.[34]

Sgt. James T. Clancy of Company C, 1st New Jersey Cavalry, in Davies's brigade was commended for shooting Dunovant, who was within

ten yards of the Federal line. "No doubt his death assisted in a great measure to demoralize the enemy," the 1st New Jersey's major Myron Beaumont said of Dunovant in his battle report. Clancy's aim earned him the
Medal of Honor, which was awarded on July 3, 1865, the citation stating
that Dunovant's death confused the attacking Confederates, and aided in
their repulse.[35]

Dunovant's loss was multiplied by the death of Dr. J. B. Fontaine, medical
director of the cavalry corps. Fontaine was summoned to aid Dunovant and
was making his way to the front when he was mortally wounded by Union
artillery fire. "Each of these officers, in his own sphere, was an admirable
one," Hampton wrote, "both were zealous in the performance of their duties
and both were a loss to the service and to the country." Little more than four
months earlier, Fontaine had worked feverishly but vainly to save Jeb Stuart's
life. Now he too was gone. Learning of the deaths of Dunovant and Fontaine,
Lee told Hampton, "I grieve with you at the loss of General Dunovant and
Dr. Fontaine, two officers whom it will be difficult to replace."[36]

When he first examined Dunovant's body, Butler said it appeared the
general had been shot in the forehead. A closer look showed that Dunovant
was wounded in the chest, the head injury apparently suffered when he fell
from his horse. Dunovant was buried in his family plot near Chester, South
Carolina. "He died as I know he would have liked to die," Butler said of
him, "with his face to the enemy and every throb of his manly, brave heart
pulsating for the glory and welfare of his country."[37]

On December 2, a New York–born Confederate general was killed in
the Petersburg trenches, never to see a baby daughter born the day
before—on his thirty-second birthday.

Brig. Gen. Archibald Gracie Jr. led a brigade of Alabama troops in
Bushrod Johnson's division that had been fighting in the Petersburg
defenses since late spring. Born to Southern parents in New York City,
Gracie was educated in Germany and graduated West Point in 1854.
Resigning from the Army two years later, he joined his father in business as
a merchant in Mobile, Alabama. Gracie was active in organizing Alabama
infantry units when the war came, and was elected colonel of the 43rd
Alabama in 1862. Most of his family however, remained loyal to the Union
and lived in New York for the war's duration. Promoted brigadier in
November, Gracie served in eastern Tennessee, in the Kentucky Campaign
and at Chickamauga. Seriously wounded at Bean's Station, Gracie recovered to join General Beauregard in Virginia in May 1864.[38]

Not far from the position of Gracie's brigade at Petersburg was his grandfather's house, a fine brick home located near the foot of Sycamore Street. The first Archibald Gracie had settled here after emigrating from Scotland shortly after the Revolutionary War, and had become a successful merchant and prominent citizen. He later moved to New York City where his prosperity continued, and he soon became one of the city's wealthiest men.

The week before his death was among the most eventful of General Gracie's life. On his birthday his wife, Josephine, gave birth to a daughter in Richmond. He was also credited with possibly saving Robert E. Lee's life when the army commander was inspecting Gracie's defenses. Gracie's troops occupied one of the most dangerous stretches of the works, which some called "Gracie's Mortar Hell," located only a few hundred feet or so from the Union lines. Lee raised his head over the parapet to look at the enemy positions, ignoring entreaties from his staff that he should not expose himself so carelessly. Seeing this, Gracie climbed onto the parapet in front of the surprised Lee. "Why, Gracie, you will certainly be killed," Lee said to him, to which Gracie replied, "It is better, General, that I should be killed than you. When you get down, I will." Lee smiled and climbed down, followed by Gracie.[39]

On December 2, Gracie was using a telescope to inspect the Federal works. Soldiers in the trenches nearby asked him what he saw and Gracie replied that he spied a Union general accompanied by his staff riding behind the enemy front lines.

Gracie had been granted a leave of absence to visit his wife and new baby, intending to leave for Richmond the next day. He would never make it. As he exposed the top of his head over the earthwork, an exploding Parrott shell killed him and two soldiers of the 43rd Alabama, his old regiment, the men falling together in a heap. The blast broke Gracie's neck and also inflicted three shoulder wounds.[40]

"We all loved General Gracie, and I was not the only one who cried that day," an Alabamian wrote after the war. Union reports credited the artillery of Maj. Gen. John G. Parke's IX Corps with firing the round that claimed Gracie's life. Maj. Gen. George Meade routinely mentioned Gracie's death in a December 4 dispatch to Ulysses Grant:

> General Parke yesterday afternoon opened his batteries on some working parties of the enemy in front of Fort Sedgwick. From deserters who came in last night he is informed that the rebel general Gracie was killed by one of our shells.[41]

In a December 11 letter to his wife, Lee wrote that Gracie's death was "a great grief to me. I do not know how to replace him. . . . May his wife, whom he loved so tenderly, be comforted in the recollection of his many virtues, his piety, his worth, his love! I grieve with her and for her daily." Lee also wrote to Gracie's widow, describing his friendship with Gracie since West Point days when Lee was superintendent and Gracie a cadet and stating that Lee's "esteem and admiration for [Gracie] increased to the day of his death."[42]

(Gracie had two other claims to fame in addition to his Confederate service. His family's former home in Manhattan, Gracie Mansion, has been the official residence of New York City's mayors since 1942. His son, Archibald Gracie, IV, sailed on the ill-fated *Titanic* in 1912, and survived to write a first-hand account of the sea disaster.)

In the years just after the war, the younger Gracie encountered an Army officer in New York City who claimed that he had commanded the battery that fired the fatal shot. The officer opened their conversation with the startling comment, "I killed your father."

"My blood boiled, while my arms and legs seemed to rebel against keeping still," Gracie recalled. "I calmed myself, knowing that no offense was intended."[43]

After the war, General Gracie's remains were moved to New York's Woodlawn Cemetery where they rest with other members of his war-divided family. An unsent letter to his father, found in the general's tent after his death, would have provided fitting words for his gravestone: "If I be shot down to-morrow, may my last words be 'I was right.'"[44]

CHAPTER 21

John Hunt Morgan's Inglorious End

CONFEDERATE BRIGADIER GENERAL
JOHN HUNT MORGAN
Greeneville, Tennessee, September 4, 1864

Just after sunrise on September 4, 1864, Union troopers dodged through the quiet streets of Greeneville, Tennessee, intent on capturing notorious Confederate cavalry raider Brig. Gen. John Hunt Morgan. The general was sleeping in a house in the town, and the Federals were preparing to give him an unpleasant, and ultimately fatal, wakeup call.

What transpired would be the ugliest incident involving a Southern general's death during the war.

Morgan, thirty-nine, had been a biblical plague to the Union military in Kentucky and Tennessee while waging his far-flung raids into Indiana and Ohio where no other armed Confederate had been able to tread. He had the flamboyance of Jeb Stuart, the warrior temperament of Nathan Bedford Forrest, and the rare ability and opportunity among Confederate leaders to strike the enemy's homeland. To many in the pro-Union population of eastern Tennessee, however, he was no more than a glorified horse thief and highwayman.

Born in Alabama, Morgan was educated in Kentucky and fought in the Mexican War. He later settled in Lexington, Kentucky, his mother's home, and was a hemp manufacturer and general merchandiser. In 1857 he organized the Lexington Rifles, a militia unit that would be the nucleus of his command when he joined the Southern cause.

Morgan's family was a little Confederacy of its own, with six brothers in Rebel gray and two of his sisters married to Confederate generals—Dolly to A. P. Hill and Henrietta to Basil Duke. Yet none of them would equal the notoriety of John, who was promoted colonel of the 2nd Kentucky Cavalry in April 1862, and brigadier general the next December. His horsemen conducted raids in Tennessee and Kentucky, his strikes into Indiana and Ohio, earning a vote of thanks from the Confederate Congress.[1]

In 1863 Morgan led his most famous raid into Ohio where he and many of his officers were captured near New Lisbon. They were held at the Ohio State Penitentiary, but Morgan would escape and head south to join the war again. Back in the saddle, Morgan was assigned command of the Department of Southwestern Virginia in April 1864. In late August, Morgan led his command of about 2,000 troopers on a thrust into eastern Tennessee. Joe Wheeler's cavalry was also raiding into Tennessee during this time (resulting in General Kelly's death), but the operations were not coordinated.

Morgan's command was organized into three brigades led by Brig. Gen. John C. Vaughn and Cols. H. L. Giltner and Howard Smith, but all was not well in the Rebel ranks. On a recent foray into Kentucky, some of Morgan's men had robbed a bank and been accused of other possibly illegal activity, prompting his brigade commanders to request an official investigation. Because of this, Morgan had been suspended from command four days earlier and ordered to appear before a military court of inquiry. Yet when Morgan camped at Greeneville on the night of Saturday, September 3, he was ignoring the order and remained in charge.

Morgan made his headquarters in the elegant mansion of Catharine Williams, the widow of local physician Alexander Williams and a distant relative of Morgan's wife. The three-story Williams home was the grandest in town, with elaborate architecture, a formal garden, and a small vineyard; the house and grounds occupied an entire block.

Amid this finery, Morgan may have become too careless. One of his officers, Capt. George T. Atkins of the 4th Kentucky Cavalry, later described how Morgan spread his units too thin to thoroughly cover the town's approaches, and kept only his staff with him that night. "I have always regarded . . . Morgan's death as the result of his own lack of caution," Atkins recalled years later. "He said he would take quarters in the Williams House, pointing it out to us. . . . He thus practically isolated himself from his command and rendered accessible and easy the sudden dash that cost him his life."[2]

Because the weather was rainy that night, he allowed his headquarters guard to stay in the house rather than outside. Morgan also reversed an order to move out at sunrise the next day, resetting the time for 7 A.M. so the men would have more time to dry their weapons.

Meanwhile, a Union cavalry force led by Brig. Gen. Alvan C. Gillem was camped at Bull's Gap about sixteen miles from Greeneville. Gillem's men were resting and refitting after an exhaustive pursuit of Wheeler's raiders. Gillem received word on the night of September 3 that Morgan was concentrating his troopers to attack him. He also had intelligence that the Confederates had not yet assembled. Based on this, Gillem decided to attack first in hopes of destroying the separated enemy units. A teenager named Jimmy Leady (or Leddy) had also ridden into the Union camp and informed Gillem that Morgan himself was in Greeneville.

Gillem's men moved out during the night in two columns to surprise the Rebels, Gillem leading the main force while the other was composed of the 13th (U.S.) Tennessee Cavalry under Lt. Col. William H. Ingerton. Wind and blinding rain buffeted the troopers. "The night was one of the darkest and stormiest I ever witnessed, the rain poured down in torrents, and had it not been for the vivid and almost constant lightning it would have been impossible to have continued the march," Gillem reported.[3]

Before dawn Gillem's column indeed surprised and routed some of Morgan's men a few miles from Greeneville while Ingerton's bluecoats swept toward the town. When Ingerton's men arrived at Greeneville's out-skirts before sunrise, he learned from a black youngster who rode out to meet them that Morgan was at the Williams mansion, according to Col. J. W. Scully, Gillem's chief of staff.[4]

Ingerton ordered Capt. Christopher C. Wilcox to take two companies and surround the house in an effort to capture Morgan. As Wilcox's men were moving into position there was no alarm from the Confederates apparently still asleep inside the house and in the Williams stable. Rebel artillerists on nearby College Hill, however, were more vigilant and opened fire on Wilcox's Federals in the streets shortly after 5 A.M.

The cannons awakened Morgan and his staff, who were in rooms on the third floor, but by this time the Yankees had encircled the house. Some accounts state that Mrs. Williams had offered Morgan breakfast about thirty minutes earlier but that upon seeing the misty dank dawn through his win-dow, the general had decided to stay in bed. Suddenly aware of the danger outside, Morgan hustled to his feet and pulled on a pair of Union cavalry pants and a pair of slippers. In his white muslin nightshirt, he grabbed his belt and holsters, bolted into the hallway and down the spiral stairs. Before darting out the back door with a Colt revolver in each hand, Morgan bade farewell to Mrs. Williams, saying, "The Yankees will never take me a prisoner again."[5]

The general ran through the Williams's garden toward the stable, but Union soldiers were there and he and some of his officers found brief refuge under Saint James Episcopal Church just south of the house. While this was occurring the Yankees were exchanging sporadic gunfire with the few Confederates actually posted in the village.

Capt. James T. Rogers of Morgan's staff later reported that Morgan "handed me one of his pistols, and said that he wished me to assist him in making his escape. I told him it was almost useless, as we were entirely surrounded. He replied, saying that we must do it if possible."[6]

Now Morgan and the other officers heard crashes overhead as Union troopers smashed at the church door in their search. Morgan then led them in a dash across a pathway and into the Williams's vineyard where they hid among tangles of grapevines. The Federals were momentarily distracted by a small group of Morgan's troopers who charged into town in a vain effort to save their leader, these graybacks being quickly dispersed.

Morgan, however, had been seen by a Union sympathizer, Mrs. David Fry, as she stood at the rear door of the Lane House, a local inn and tavern. She and several other women yelled to the bluecoats, telling them of Morgan's location. On their chief's order, the Rebel officers separated and crawled away in different directions to try to make their escape. Captain Rogers recalled that he and Morgan were still hiding in a clump of bushes when they saw a soldier wearing a brown jacket ride up to the white wooden fence around the yard. Believing the rider to be a Confederate, they stepped out from the bushes. The trooper, however, was a Federal.

"The soldier demanded a surrender, much to our surprise," Rogers wrote. Wilcox and other Yankees rode up about then and Rogers said that he and another Rebel soldier named Johnson headed toward them while "hearing cries, 'kill him! kill him!' from every quarter" except from Wilcox. "I saw General M. throw up his hands exclaiming 'Oh my God!'" Rogers said. "I saw nothing more of him until he was brought to the street dead." Rogers added that he believed that he and Johnson were fired on after they surrendered, but that the Federals likely did not realize they had given up. "If General M. surrendered before he was shot I do not know it."[7]

Other Confederates, however, claimed that Morgan had dropped his other revolver and was unarmed when he was killed in cold blood. Union private Andrew Campbell of the 13th Tennessee's Company G was credited with firing the carbine shot that killed Morgan.

"I had not crawled over ten feet when I heard the General call out: 'Don't shoot; I surrender!'" recalled Maj. C. A. Withers, Morgan's adjutant general.[8]

Colonel Scully wrote that Morgan was shot in the back, the bullet "penetrating his heart, and death was instantaneous." Withers added, "The General fell forward on his face. As his distance was only twenty feet the shot must have caused instant death which was subsequently proved." Based on Withers's account, the man later identifed as Campbell "began shouting, 'I've killed the d——d horse thief.'"[9]

Morgan's assistant adjutant general, Capt. Henry Clay, who had been captured by the Federals, identified the general's body, sobbing to Wilcox, "You have killed the best man in the Southern Confederacy." Several blue-coats then hoisted the body onto Campbell's horse, draping it across the saddle. The private rode through the streets to the cheers of other soldiers as Morgan's night-shirted corpse bounced grotesquely in front of him.[10]

"I had the pleasure of seeing the lifeless carcass of their fallen chief . . . with his body thrown on the neck of his horse, his head and face covered with blood," wrote Col. John Brownlow of the U.S. 9th Tennessee Cavalry. "I pointed the men of the 9th to the corpse, assuring them it was the veritable John Morgan. They made the welkin ring with shouts of applause."[11]

Campbell then rode to the edge of town where Gillem had arrived and set up headquarters. He announced that the body was that of Morgan and shoved it off the horse and into a rain-filled ditch. A crowd of pro-Union civilians soon gathered by the roadside to celebrate and dance around the corpse in a macabre spectacle. The body soon was stripped down to its underwear, the clothing being torn into pieces for souvenirs.

Withers, meanwhile had been captured and was being taken to the Federal camp when he and his guards encountered the gruesome scene:

> On the outskirts of town we approached a crowd shouting and dancing around an object lying in a ditch by the roadside. They called to the Sergeant, "Bring that d——d rebel over here; we want to show him something." Making me dismount, I was led to that "object" and wiping the mud and blood out of his face with my shirt sleeves, I recognized, what I anticipated, the features of my General.[12]

Withers contended that he asked to see General Gillem and vigorously protested that Morgan's remains were being treated like that of a dog. Gillem was unsympathetic, replying, "Ay Sir, and it shall lie there and rot like a dog!"[13]

Withers and Captain Rogers later received permission to retrieve Morgan's body and were taken to the scene by a Union cavalry escort. These

Federals had to threaten force against the screeching mob before the corpse could be removed and placed in an ambulance. The body was returned to the Williams mansion where Yankee soldiers had already taken all of the general's clothing and other personal effects.

Scully gave a much different version of the treatment of Morgan's remains. He stated that he and Gillem were riding toward town when they met Campbell riding with Morgan's body. "We both denounced Campbell's conduct, had the remains placed on a caisson and carried back to Mrs. Williams' house where they were decently cared for," Scully claimed.[14]

With the assistance of a Williams family servant, Withers and Rogers washed the corpse and dressed it in their own clothes, although the general's coat and vest were returned by the Federals for his burial. To these Confederates, Morgan's death wound appeared to be in the left breast and his face was scraped and cut from the ride on Campbell's horse. A Greeneville undertaker embalmed the body later in the day.

All but one of Morgan's staff officers was captured and "all of General Morgan's papers fell into my hands," Gillem reported.[15] The general would receive one of Morgan's Colt revolvers as a war trophy, Col. John K. Miller, commander of the 13th Tennessee, taking the other pistol. (Miller had ridden with Gillem that morning while Ingerton led the regiment.) Brownlow took Morgan's pipe and razor for his trophies.

Other versions of Morgan's last stand sprang up as they always do with the death of a legend. Sarah Lane Thompson was the widow of a Federal soldier and an active Union sympathizer in the Greeneville area. When she learned of Morgan's presence in town, she slipped away and alerted Federal troops as to his whereabouts, one story goes. Mrs. Thompson, by her account, also pointed out where Morgan was hiding near a garden fence to a Yankee who killed the general. Union reports of the action do not mention her. Captain Wilcox wrote after the war that his cavalry learned Morgan was in the Williams house when they captured a Rebel messenger bearing a dispatch to the general there.

Mrs. Williams's daughter-in-law, Lucy, is also incorrectly credited, or blamed, for the general's betrayal. She was seen leaving the house, but this turned out to be an innocent mission to find some watermelon for Morgan. At the time, however, she was described in Southern newspapers as a "betrayer" and a "murderess."[16]

Scully wrote that the "negro boy" who told Ingerton of Morgan's whereabouts "was lost sight of in the tumult and never again appeared at headquarters."[17]

On the morning of September 5, a small party of Rebel troopers from the 4th Kentucky rode in to Greeneville under a flag of truce to retrieve

Morgan's body. The general had been laid out in the Williams parlor and the Confederates had to wait while a walnut coffin was constructed. Accusations, however, were already spreading in both armies that Morgan had been shot after surrendering. Lt. O. C. French of Gillem's staff moved to discredit this version of Morgan's end, saying that it would have been a "direct violation of the rules of war."[18]

He wrote to the captured Rebel captain Rogers on September 5: "You will confer a personal favor upon myself, and be doing an act of justice to this command, by stating what you know to be the facts connected with the killing of the general." On the same day, Rogers sent French his account of what happened.[19]

The Confederate brass was as much embarrassed as saddened by Morgan's loss. "The enemy, in consequence of a failure on the part of some offices to have one of the roads leading into the town properly guarded and picketed, charged into the town soon after daylight and at once surrounded the house where General Morgan's headquarters were established, and, I regret exceedingly to say, killed him," Rebel brigadier John Echols, department commander of Confederate forces in the region, wrote to Adjutant General Cooper on September 5. Echols also said that he would order an investigation "of the affair at Greeneville, in order to ascertain by whose neglect or misconduct the surprise occurred."[20]

From Greeneville, Morgan's body was taken by wagon to Jonesboro, Tennessee, where a funeral was held at Saint Thomas Episcopal Church on September 6. The remains were then taken by train to Abingdon, Virginia, where they were placed in a vault and later moved to Hollywood Cemetery in Richmond.

Accusations about Morgan's death and the mistreatment of his body by the Federals continued to fly years after the war, and Jefferson Davis himself was among the most vitriolic. He wrote:

Among the atrocious, cowardly acts of vindictive malice which marked the conduct of the enemy, none did or could surpass the brutality with which the dying and dead body of Morgan was treated. Hate, the offspring of fear, they might feel for the valorous soldier while he lived, but even the ignoble passion, vengeance, might have been expected to [end] when life was extinct.[21]

The Union colonel Scully tried to address these accusations in a 1903 letter to the *New Orleans Picayune*: "Wild stories about the 'barbarous' manner in which General Morgan was treated by General Gillem prevailed through the South for years, but Gillem and I refrained from contradicting them."[22]

Scully appeared to try to exonerate Gillem, but not his soldiers, lending some credence to Confederate claims of an atrocity. Scully also wrote that Captain Rogers "was my guest for over a week after his capture, and he afterwards spoke in the highest terms of the manner in which they were treated by General Gillem, and also of the treatment of Morgan's remains, with the exception, of course, of Campbell's conduct."[23]

Scully also disputed Campbell's claim of killing Morgan:

> It was not believed by General Gillem, Colonel Miller, myself or any of the field officers . . . that Campbell knew who shot General Morgan, for he was in the midst of a crowd of men, and outside of the fence, and all of them firing as fast as they could load. He probably was the first to discover the body as it lay within seventy-five feet of the fence and was partially hidden in a clump of gooseberry bushes. I examined the place at the time, and was then convinced that on that damp, foggy morning, before sunrise, a man's figure would appear only as a shadow, and that Morgan was killed by a volley.[24]

Scully maintained that Jimmy Leady, whose mother was a widow, was taken to Nashville by Gillem and placed in a school. Leady, however, tired of his new life and returned home.

In April 1868, Morgan reached his final resting place in his hometown of Lexington, Kentucky. In an elaborate double ceremony, the general was buried beside his brother, Confederate lieutenant Thomas Morgan, who had been killed earlier in the war and whose remains were returned to Lexington for the reinterment. About a hundred of General Morgan's men attended the funeral. These veterans "saw their dead comrades laid away in that calm, untroubled slumber which the loving voice of friend nor the battle cry of foe may never break."[25]

The furor over Morgan's death still laced Southern opinion almost half a century later when a monument to the general was unveiled in Lexington in 1911. Dr. G. Carlton Lee of Baltimore, one of the featured speakers said of Morgan, "He was done to death by ruffians who disgraced the flag of our fathers."[26]

CHAPTER 22

The Franklin Generals

CONFEDERATE MAJOR GENERAL PATRICK R. CLEBURNE
AND BRIGADIER GENERALS JOHN ADAMS,
JOHN C. CARTER, STATES RIGHTS GIST,
HIRAM B. GRANBURY, AND OTHO F. STRAHL
Franklin, November 30, 1864

When he spied a Union army dug in at Franklin, Tennessee, on November 30, 1864, Confederate general John Bell Hood was seething, and thousands of his soldiers, including many of his commanders, would pay for his angry impatience with their lives.

On no other battlefield would the blood of Southern generals flow as freely as at Franklin in a single hellish hour that eclipsed the ferocity of Pickett's Charge at Gettysburg. Five would be killed outright, another would die within days, and six others would be wounded or captured. "The death-angel was there to gather its last harvest," a Tennessee Rebel related. "It was the grand coronation of death."[1]

The Union forces entrenched before Hood on a low ridge had been in his pocket less than a day earlier at Spring Hill, Tennessee, but had escaped due to incompetence and miscommunication among Hood and his generals. U.S. major general John M. Schofield's army of 23,000 had slipped out of the bag on the night of November 29, and marched some twelve miles before digging in just south of Franklin, with their backs to the Harpeth River. At Spring Hill, Hood had maneuvered his Army of Tennessee into position behind the surprised Schofield (Hood and Schofield were West

*Confederate major general
Patrick R. Cleburne.*
LIBRARY OF CONGRESS

Point classmates, graduating in 1853) and had issued orders for what should have been the destruction or capture of the enemy. The orders were bungled however, and Schofield had been able to retreat unmolested toward Nashville. Hood faulted his commanders, primarily Maj. Gen. Benjamin F. Cheatham, for the breakdown, while they blamed him for Schofield's escape.

Thus it was an antagonistic group of Rebel brass that led their troops north along the Columbia Pike in pursuit of Schofield on November 30. Hood saw the Federals at Franklin as an opportunity to make up for the mistakes at Spring Hill, and as a chance to earn the first major victory of his drive into Tennessee. After losing Atlanta to the army of Maj. Gen. William T. Sherman, Hood's forces had retreated to northern Alabama. In late November, the Confederates had marched north into Tennessee on a forlorn hope with several objectives. Hood hoped to divert Sherman from his march across Georgia to the sea and possibly reclaim Nashville, which had become a formidable Union base of operations. If all went according to vague plans, the Rebels would continue north toward the Ohio River.

As his troops arrived at Franklin, Hood decided on an immediate, wholesale attack. Maj. Gen. Patrick R. Cleburne, who commanded a division in Cheatham's corps, advised against it, but to no avail. Cleburne rode off to join his infantry, telling them, "If we are to die, let us die like men."[2]

Described as the "Stonewall Jackson of the West," Cleburne was a thirty-six-year-old Irishman who was one of two foreign-born officers to earn the rank of major general in the Confederate military. Born near Cork, Cleburne served three years in the British army before purchasing his discharge, coming to the United States in 1849. An apothecary by trade, he lived in New Orleans and Cincinnati before locating to Helena, Arkansas, where he was a partner in a drugstore, and eventually became a successful lawyer and property owner. The war's outbreak saw Cleburne elected colonel of the 15th Arkansas Infantry, and he was promoted brigadier in March 1862, leading a brigade at Shiloh and at Perryville. Commissioned major general in December 1862, Cleburne performed well at Stones River, and was the only rock in the Rebels' calamitous defeat at Missionary Ridge, his command fighting an effective rearguard action that saved the army's trains.[3]

In early January 1864, Cleburne had caused a stir when he was the first to advocate arming slaves for Confederate military service. The suggestion met with much criticism and ridicule at the time, but Richmond instituted the idea in the war's closing months.

Cleburne, however, was better known for his battle prowess and coolness under fire. His loss at Franklin was a telling blow to the South, the Irishman having said often that he did not want to survive if the Confederacy fell. As Civil War historian Ezra Warner noted of Cleburne: "A savage fighter of the Bedford Forrest stamp, his death . . . was a calamity to the Confederate cause perhaps only exceeded by the demise of Stonewall Jackson."[4]

Among the stories circulated after the war was the account that Cleburne might have ridden to his death barefooted. In the army's march toward Franklin, Cleburne is said to have seen some of his soldiers trudging along the road without shoes, including one who was leaving bloody footprints. Cleburne reined in and told the Rebel to take off his boots, saying "You need them more than I do," based on the account. Some wondered whether Cleburne had a premonition that he would die in battle and no longer need his boots.[5]

The Rebel corps of Lt. Gen. Stephen D. Lee had not yet reached the field, but Hood deployed the remainder of his army for the massive assault. With Cheatham on the left and Lt. Gen. A. P. Stewart's corps on the right, some 20,000 soldiers would make this assault in what would be one of the war's grimmest and grandest martial spectacles. The industrious Federals had thrown up earthen breastworks some five feet high and ten feet thick which shielded them well. The Rebels meanwhile would attack this strong position across open ground of about two miles, Hood planning to throw in Bedford Forrest's cavalry and his reserves if and when the Yankee line cracked.

The imposing gray lines stepped off about 4 P.M. and Col. Ellison Capers of the 24th South Carolina in Cheatham's corps described the scene:

Just before the charge was ordered the brigade passed over an elevation, from which we beheld the magnificent spectacle the battle-field presented—bands were playing, general and staff officers and gallant couriers were riding in front of and between the lines, 100 battle-flags were waving in the smoke of battle, and bursting shells were wreathing the air with great circles of smoke, while 20,000 brave men were marching in perfect order against the foe.[6]

"It looked to me as though the whole South had come up there and were determined to walk right over us," an Indiana Yankee later recalled.[7]

In addition to Cleburne attackers were the five other generals who would not survive this battle—Brig. Gens. John Adams, John C. Carter, States Rights Gist, Hiram B. Granbury, and Otho F. Strahl.

Adams and his wife, Georgia, had been married just over ten years and had six children. The thirty-nine-year-old Tennessean was an 1846 graduate of West Point (where he roomed with George Pickett) and had served with the 1st U.S. Dragoons in the Mexican War. A frontier veteran, he joined the Confederacy and was promoted to brigadier general to rank from December 1862. He served in the Vicksburg and Atlanta campaigns before following Hood into Tennessee with his brigade of Mississippians in Maj. Gen. W. W. Loring's division of Stewart's Corps.

Carter, Gist, and Strahl led brigades in Maj. Gen. John C. Brown's division of Cheatham's Corps. A Georgian by birth, Carter was practicing law in Memphis when the war started. He fought with distinction at Shiloh, Perryville, Stones River, and Chickamauga, being appointed a brigadier in July 1864. He was nineteen days short of his twenty-ninth birthday when he took the field at Franklin.

Gist was a thirty-three-year-old South Carolinian who had a Harvard law degree and had been a general in his state militia before the conflict. He was an aide to Barnard Bee at First Bull Run and assumed command when Bee was killed. Named a Confederate brigadier in March 1862, he had seen action at Vicksburg, Chickamauga, Chattanooga, and Atlanta.

Strahl was a thirty-three-year-old Ohio native who moved to Tennessee after college to study and practice law. He was living and working in Dyersburg at the time of secession. He saw combat at Shiloh and Stones River before being appointed brigadier in July 1863, and had fought in all of the Army of Tennessee's major campaigns since then. As his troops prepared to attack at Franklin, Strahl "was quiet, and there was an expression of sadness on his face," a Rebel sergeant recalled.[8]

In Cleburne's Division was the thirty-three-year-old Granbury, a Mississippian who had relocated to Texas, and who was a prewar attorney and judge in Waco. He had been captured at Fort Donelson, but was exchanged and fought at Vicksburg, Chickamauga, and Chattanooga. Promoted to brigadier to rank from February 29, 1864, he led the Texas Brigade in the Atlanta battles before Hood made his Tennessee thrust. During the Atlanta fighting, Gen. William Hardee had described Granbury as "the stately Granberry [*sic*], as great of heart as of frame, a noble type of the Texan soldier."[9]

As soon as the long gray lines were within range, Schofield's infantry and artillery commenced a devastating fire. "They had no protection and were mowed down like grass before the scythe," a Yankee recalled, adding that the Southerns "fell by thousands."[10] A Rebel officer added, "The [Confederate] general officers riding behind their men or in line with them were shining marks for the deadly rifles aimed from a rest behind breastworks."[11]

"The death-angel shrieks and laughs and old Father Time is busy with his sickle, as he gathers in the last harvest of death, crying, More, more, more! while his rapacious maw is glutted with the slain," related Tennessee infantryman Sam Watkins.[12]

Cheatham's Corps charged along the Columbia Pike with Cleburne's veterans coming under fire first after bulling through a locust grove and overwhelming some weak Federal outerworks, Cleburne riding behind his infantry. "It was his custom . . . to follow his troops into the midst of the battle, and it has frequently been a cause of wonder to his friends that he came from so many dangers unscathed; but up to this time he seemed to have borne a charmed life," recalled Cleburne's aide-de-camp, Lt. L. H. Mangum.[13]

Some accounts state that Cleburne's horse was hit, but the general plunged ahead on foot through the maelstrom of lead. He did not reach the Federal defenses, falling just short of the works. "Cleburne was killed in a charge at double-quick," Confederate colonel John Harrell wrote. "His horse was first killed under him, and he pressed forward with his men on foot, when he was killed within a hundred feet of the parapet. He fell pierced through by a single rifle ball."[14]

Another of Cheatham's commanders, Brig. Gen. George Gordon, described Cleburne's end differently: "It seemed to me if I had thrown out my hand I could have caught it full of the missiles of death, and it is a mystery how any of us ever reached the works," he related. Cleburne "came charging down our lines . . . toward the enemy's works, his horse running at full speed, and if I had not personally checked my pace as I ran on foot, he would have plunged over and trampled me to the earth. On he dashed, but for an instant longer, when rider and horse both fell, pierced with many bullets, within a few paces of the enemy's works . . . The intrepid Cleburne had fallen."[15]

Mangum stated that he last saw Cleburne near the center of his division before the general galloped away to direct a portion of the assault. Cleburne's last command to Mangum was for the aide to join Granbury. In his postwar account, Mangum wrote that Cleburne's horse was killed and that another mount was riddled by bullets as the general attempted to climb into the saddle. Cleburne then charged forward on foot to within less than a hundred yards of the enemy line before he fell, "pierced by a single minnie [sic] ball which passed through his body and probably caused instant death. Hidden by smoke and enveloped by thunder he sank on the couch of his glory unattended and alone."[16]

A later examination of Cleburne's body showed that he died from a gunshot to the left side of the abdomen.[17] Some of Cheatham's Confederates managed to climb the defenses and plant their colors while others fought their way up and into the Federal works. These few Rebels were soon killed or captured. Near the pike, many of Strahl's men poured into a three-foot ditch at the base of the Federal defenses where they were raked by musketry. The mound was so steep that men scaled the side and were handed rifles from their comrades below to fire down into the enemy trench on the other side. Inevitably, the exposed Rebel was shot and tumbled back into the ditch, another quickly taking his place.

Strahl was here himself, thrusting muskets to the marksmen above as the heap of dead and wounded grew deeper in the ditch and on the embankment. Sgt. Sumner Cunningham of the 41st Tennessee made his way up the hill and began firing with muskets Strahl handed him, the former bracing himself with a foot on the bodies around him. As Confederate numbers dwindled, Cunningham called to the general, asking what they should do. Strahl replied, "Keep firing," based on Cunningham's account.[18]

Soon afterward, a Rebel near Cunningham was hit and slumped against him, groaning in his death throes. Strahl was shot at almost the same time. "He threw up his hands, falling on his face, and I thought him dead," Cunningham related of the general. The sergeant asked the wounded man lying against him about his injury, but Strahl, still alive and thinking the question was directed to him, replied that he was shot in the neck and wanted to turn his brigade over to his second in command, Lt. Col. F. E. P. Stafford.

Some of Strahl's men tried to carry him out of the death trap, but the general was wounded twice more in the attempt and died.[19]

Cunningham, who survived the war and established *Confederate Veteran* magazine, wrote that he later learned Strahl was being assisted to the rear by a soldier named T. F. Ledsinger when an enemy bullet struck the general in the back of the head.[20]

Gist's Brigade, meanwhile, brushed through the outer Union defenses before steeling for the charge against the main enemy works. "General Gist . . . rode down our front, and returning, ordered the charge," wrote Colonel Capers of the 24th South Carolina. "In passing . . . the regiment the general waved his hat to us, expressed his confidence in the 24th, and rode away in the smoke of the battle, never more to be seen by the men he had commanded on so many fields."[21]

Gist's horse, "Joe Johnston," was skittish under fire, and when it was shot in the neck shortly afterward began bucking, forcing Gist to dismount. He continued to lead his brigade on foot until he fell with a mortal chest wound.

Coming in behind Gist's Rebels was John Carter's brigade, Carter riding in front of his troops. He was within about 150 yards of the abatis guarding the Federal line when he was shot in the body, reeling in the saddle. His adjutant caught him as he fell, easing him to the ground, and Carter was soon carried to the rear.

Granbury's Texans had become intermingled with Gordon's infantry as they closed on the enemy defenses, Granbury leading his men on foot. "On all sides men sank out of sight, the ground was thick with the dead, the fallen seemed more numerous than living. Officers and soldiers, general and privates, fell side by side," wrote Lieutenant Mangum who had reached Granbury as he cheered on his charging infantry. "Forward men, forward!" Granbury shouted. "Never let it be said that Texans lag in the fight!" A moment later a bullet struck Granbury just under the right eye and passed through his head. "Throwing both hands to his face as in the impulse of the instant to find where the pain was, he sank forward on his knees," remembered Mangum, who claimed to have been some ten feet from Granbury when he was killed.[22]

The Confederates of John Adams's brigade, meanwhile, advanced against works manned by the U.S. 3rd Division of Brig. Gen. Jacob Cox (who was leading the Union XXIII Corps at Franklin). Despite the awesome fire, Adams rode in front of his battle line, and was seriously wounded by a bullet in his right arm near the shoulder. Members of his staff, including his cousin, Capt. Thomas Gibson, urged him to leave the field, but Adams refused, saying "No, I am going to see my men through."[23]

Driven back several times, with bloody gaps torn in their ranks, the Rebels fell back, regrouped and came on again. In one of these charges, Adams rode for the breastworks, apparently intending to leap his horse over them and grab an enemy flag there.

Horse and rider were riddled and fell on top of the embankment, with Adams pinned under the animal and gashed by nine bullet wounds.

At this point, Adams's fate is lost in the fog of war, as a number of soldiers contradicted his final moments. With their general down and under murderous enemy musketry, Adams's Brigade pulled back without him. As the Confederates withdrew, Federals climbed atop the mound, some lifting the horse while others pulled Adams free, many accounts state.

"He was perfectly conscious, and knew his fate," Edward A. Baker, an officer in the 65th Indiana Infantry, recalled years later in a letter to Adams's widow. "He asked for water, as all dying men do in battle. . . . One of my men gave him a canteen of water, while another brought an armload of cotton from an old gin near by and made him a pillow. The General gallantly thanked them, and, in answer to our expressions of sorrow at his sad fate, he said, 'It is the fate of a soldier to die for his country,' and expired."[24]

James Barr of the 65th Illinois related how his regiment's Col. W. Scott Stewart tried to save Adams as he charged the Union line. Stewart "called to our men not to fire on him, but it was too late," Barr remembered. "Adams rode his horse over the ditch to the top of the parapet, undertook to grasp the 'old flag' from the hands of our color-sergeant, when he fell, horse and all, shot by the color-guard."[25]

Col. John S. Casement who commanded the brigade which included the 65th Indiana and the 65th Illinois in Cox's division, reported that after the firing died down in the night skirmishers were sent out, finding the dying Adams among the Rebel dead and wounded in front of their line. After Adams's death, Casement had the general's pocket watch, chain and ring later sent through the lines under a truce flag to be returned to Mrs. Adams. Casement presented the general's pistol to one of his officers, while his soldiers gave Adams's saddle to Casement as a war trophy. The saddle hung forgotten in the attic of Casement's Ohio home for years, with his young sons apparently taking the wooden stirrups for use on their pony.[26]

"Your men went down like leaves in the fall of the year," Tillman H. Stevens of the 65th Indiana wrote to Confederate Veteran in 1903 in giving one of the more stirring accounts of Adams's last charge:

We looked to see him fall every minute, but luck seemed to be with him. We were struck with admiration. . . . He was too brave to be killed. The world had but few such men. His valiant soldiers were close behind him, though each second . . . reduced their numbers. . . . Gen. Adams reached our line, but was shot down with his faithful horse, both falling together on top of the slight entrenchment that we had on this line. Adams was mortally wounded and soon died, and his command was badly shattered. . . . [W]e saw scores of officers fall from their mounts, but of course we did not know who they were by name. We saw the Phil Sheridan of the Southern army, Gen. Cleburne, fall. We saw the pride of Texas, Gen. Granbury, fall . . . but the one great spirit who appealed the strongest to our admiration was Gen. John Adams. . . . He was riding forward through such a rain of bullets that no one had any reason to believe that he would escape them all, but he seemed to be in the hands of the Unseen, but at last the spell was broken and the spirit went out of one of the bravest men who ever led a line of battle.[27]

O. W. Case, another member of the 65th Illinois, gave yet another version of the Adams story. Case agreed with Casement that skirmishers from their brigade found Adams, but that the general was already dead. Based on Case's account, Adams's body was carried back to the Union positions and then taken by stretcher bearers to Casement's headquarters near the cotton gin where it was placed under guard. When the Federals retreated from Franklin, Adams's corpse was abandoned, leaving "some writers in the South" with the impression that the general was killed inside the Union works, Case stated. Lt. George Brown of the 65th Illinois retained Adams's watch, later returning it to Confederate officers when the armies were in their battle lines at Nashville, Case claimed.[28]

"Their officers showed the most heroic example and self-sacrifice, riding up to our lines in advance of the men, cheering them on," related Cox in his official report. "One general officer [Adams] was shot down upon the parapet itself, his horse falling across the breast-work. In all this part of the line our men stood steadily without flinching, and repulsed the enemy, inflicting terrible loss upon him and suffering little in return."[29]

In November 1891, Casement wrote to Georgia Adams after Baker informed him of her desire to reclaim the general's saddle. Casement also described her husband's end:

It was my fortune to stand in our line within a foot of where the General succeeded in getting his horse's forelegs over the line. The poor beast died there, and was in that position when we returned over the same field more than a month after the battle. . . . Gen. Adams fell from his horse . . . just over the line of

works, which were part breastworks and part ditch. As soon as the
charge was repulsed, I had him brought on our side of the works and
did what we could to make him comfortable. He was perfectly calm
and uncomplaining. He begged me to send him to the Confederate
line, assuring me that the men that would take him there would
return safely. I told him that we were going to fall back as soon as we
could do it safely, and that he would soon be in possession of his
friends. . . . I was too busy to again see the General until after his
gallant life had passed away. . . . The saddle will be expressed to you
to-morrow. Would that I had the power to return the gallant rider![30]

Tom Gore of the 15th Mississippi in Adams's Brigade, added another
twist to the general's death. According to his postwar account, Adams was
wounded about the time his horse was killed atop the Federal earthwork.
Gore related that the general was staggering to the rear when he was
"pierced with nine balls." After the battle, Gore was caring for the
wounded when he came across Adams's bootless body, based on his
account. The dead general was put into an ambulance also bearing Cleburne's corpse and, Gore stated, both were taken to the home of John
McGavock near the battlefield.[31]

Capt. Thomas Gibson, Adams's adjutant and cousin, backed the versions of Casement and Baker and offered an explanation for why some may
have claimed Adams and his horse fell outside the Federal works. Gibson
related that Adams' mount, "Old Charley," would sometimes squat to the
ground when under fire. Old Charley might have done this at Franklin,
leading to the assumption that "horse and rider had fallen."[32]

Another Rebel veteran, John McQuaide, claimed that he was among
soldiers who found Adams's body outside the base of the Federals' works.

One thing *is* certain in all of this: In the battle inferno of Franklin,
undiluted exaggeration and pure fact combined to ensure that we will
never know precisely how or where Cleburne, Adams, or the others died.
The accounts of Casement, Baker, and Gibson, however, do seem to be the
most believable.

"Our troops fought with great gallantry," Hood wrote to Confederate
secretary of war James Seddon on December 3 as the Rebel army dug in
near Nashville. "We have to lament the loss of many gallant officers and
brave men. Major-General Cleburne, Brigadier Gens. John Adams, Gist,
Strahl, and Granbury were killed."[33]

Hood would later report his total casualties at Franklin as 4,500, although the figure was closer to 6,500, with Union losses considerably less. Brown's Division was hardest hit by its loss of leadership. Three of its brigadiers were dead or dying—Gist, Carter, and Strahl—while the fourth, George Gordon, had been captured. Brown himself had been shot and four of Hood's other brigadiers—Arthur M. Manigault, Francis M. Cockrell, Thomas Scott, and William A. Quarles—were wounded.

Among the generals' bodies found in the piled slain on the battlefield was that of Granbury, "half sitting, half crouching, with his hands over his face he was found . . . rigid in the attitude in which the bullet with its blow and its swift coming death had left him," Mangum wrote.[34]

McQuaide, an artillerist in Stewart's Corps, claimed to have been the one to discover Cleburne's body. On horseback, he was riding forward to determine if the Yankees had evacuated Franklin and encountered heaps of dead as he neared the enemy works. Picking his way through them, he happened upon Cleburne. "There was not a sign of life anywhere, and the deathly silence was oppressive," McQuaide wrote. "I bent down, and as I looked into the marble features of our hero, our ideal soldier, my first thought was to have the body taken to a place of safety, so that it might be secured to the people for whom he died." McQuaide stated that he was about to carry Cleburne's body to the rear when he encountered Rev. Thomas R. Markham, chaplain of Gen. W. S. Featherston's brigade, who was accompanied by two corpsmen and their ambulance.[35]

Based on McQuaide's account, Markham and the medics were in the process of lifting General Adams's body into the wagon when he approached them. "I told Dr. Markham that Gen. Cleburne had been killed, and his body lay upon the field, pointing in the direction, and asked him to come with me and take charge of it," McQuaide wrote. "We went together and put it in the ambulance beside Adams, and I left him with his sacred trust."[36]

A popular, but untrue, tale of Franklin is that the bodies of the five slain Southern generals were laid out side-by-side on the back porch of Carnton, the John McGavock home located near the battlefield. At least three of the fallen commanders *were* taken there—Cleburne, Granbury, and Strahl—but the bodies of at least two of the other officers were aides (Col. R. B. Young, Granbury's chief of staff, and Lt. John H. Marsh, who served with Strahl). A day or so after the battle, these officers' remains were taken to Columbia, Tennessee, and buried in the "potters' field" section of Rose Hill Cemetery. Hearing of this, Confederate brigadier General Lucius E. Polk, who had served with them in the Army of Tennessee, was angered that these heroes of Franklin had been interred among the less fortunate. Aided by Confederate chaplain Charles Quintard, Polk had the five exhumed and reburied at St. John's Episcopal Church at Mount Pleasant, near his home in Ashwood, Tennessee.

During the advance of Hood's army four days before his death, Cleburne had stopped at this pretty little church and admired its tranquil setting, including the cemetery. "It is almost worth dying to rest in so sweet a spot," he remarked to one of his staff officers. Young and Marsh rest there still, but the generals were later exhumed again for burial elsewhere.[37]

Cleburne was reburied in his adopted hometown of Helena, Arkansas, in the Confederate Cemetery, while Strahl was disinterred in 1900 for reburial at Dyersburg, Tennessee.

In 1893, Granbury's remains were removed to Granbury, Texas, a town that had been named in his honor. "The General's uniform and army blanket in which he was buried were in a tolerably fair state of preservation" after almost 30 years, read one account at the time.[38]

It remains unclear if a fourth general—Adams—was taken to Carnton. Saddened soldiers of his brigade retrieved his body at some point and carried it by wagon to his home in Pulaski, where he was buried on December 1.

Gist never made it to the Carnton porch, despite common belief. After he was wounded, the Carolinian was treated at a field hospital set up near the Franklin home of a Judge White and died about 8:30 P.M. Gist's servant, Wiley Howard, found the general's body there after searching the battlefield for him. With the aid of the medical staff, Howard procured a cedar box to serve as a coffin. He then went to the Whites' home and asked Mrs. White for permission to bury Gist in the family cemetery. Mrs. White had the general brought into her parlor and requested a minister, who performed a funeral ceremony attended by officers and men of Gist's Brigade. Gist was afterward buried in the Whites' cemetery. When Hood's army was further mangled at Nashville, the Confederates limped back through Franklin. In doing so, Howard or members of Gist's Brigade, or both, disinterred the general's body and sent it home. Gist was finally laid to rest in the Trinity Episcopal churchyard in Columbia, South Carolina.

"Perhaps you have not heard of the enemy's loss of generals at the battle of Franklin," Maj. Gen. Lovell H. Rousseau, commander of the

U.S. District of Tennessee, wrote to a colleague on December 8. "I have it definitely from prisoners; it is this; Killed, Major-General Cleburne, Brigadier-General Gist, Brigadier-General Strahl, Brigadier-General Adams, Brigadier-General Carter, Brigadier-General Granbury, and three others wounded. It is reported by citizens here that [Maj. Gen. William B.] Bate was killed on yesterday, and I think the report very probably true."[39]

Carter, however, was still alive, although not for long. He was among Rebel wounded taken to Hood's headquarters at the William Harrison home, about three miles south of the battlefield, but there was little anyone could do for him. Under similar conditions in September, Rebel brigadier general John Kelly had been brought to the Harrison house where he gasped out his life.

Carter lingered into the first week of December and was visited by his friend Chaplain Quintard, who was often at the home comforting the wounded and praying with the Harrison family. On December 8, Quintard wrote in his diary of a conversation he had with Carter about religious matters. Carter was semiconscious and in great pain but was unconvinced that he was going to die of his wound.

"General, if you do die, what do you wish me to say to your wife?" Quintard asked him. Carter roused enough to reply in a whisper, "Tell her I have always loved her devotedly and regret [leaving] her more than I can express." He then asked for chloroform and some was administered to him.[40]

Quintard never had the chance to speak to Carter again, as the general died near midnight on December 10. His body was taken to Rose Hill Cemetery in Columbia where Quintard performed the burial service.

━━ ≍✦≍ ━━

Schofield's army withdrew from their Franklin defenses and crossed the Harpeth during the night of November 30, making its way to the safety of the Union lines at Nashville and leaving Hood in possession of a smoky field of corpses and wounded from both sides. After burying the dead, Hood's maimed divisions limped in pursuit, settling into positions just south of Nashville, bloodied, outnumbered, and exhausted. On December 15, Union major general George H. Thomas's army emerged from Nashville and hammered the Confederates. The Rebels were overwhelmed in a two-day, one-sided battle, most fleeing in rout.

The once-vaunted Army of Tennessee died at Nashville, but the bayonet had been driven home at Franklin. Hood himself was relieved of command at his own request less than a month later.

Diarist Mary Boykin Chesnut wrote of Franklin in her December 14 entry and criticized the South Carolina politicians who had opposed Gist's promotion to general:

> Hood and Thomas have had a fearful fight, with carnage and loss of generals excessive in proportion to numbers. That means they were leading and urging their men up to the enemy. I know how [Colonel Francis] Bartow and Barnard Bee were killed bringing up their men. One of Mr. Chesnut's [her husband James was a South Carolina lawmaker, Confederate congressman and brigadier general] sins thrown in his teeth by the Legislature of South Carolina was that he procured the promotion of . . . Gist by his influence in Richmond. What have these comfortable, stay-at-home patriots to say of General Gist now?[41]

The story of Cleburne's fiancée, Susan Tarleton of Mobile, Alabama, is a sad footnote to the battle tragedy. Days after Franklin, she was walking in her garden when she heard a newspaper boy on the street crying "Big Battle near Franklin, Tennessee! General Cleburne killed! Read all about it!" She fainted and soon entered mourning for her beloved. Two years after the war, Miss Tarleton married a former Confederate captain, but she died less than a year later. Many who knew her felt that Susan never recovered from the shocking way she learned of Cleburne's death.[42]

In October 1889, U.S. senator William Bate stood on the Franklin battlefield during a school dedication ceremony and spoke of Cleburne. Bate, a Confederate major general who fought at Franklin (Union general Rousseau erroneously reporting his death), was elected as Tennessee's governor after the war, and later to Congress.

"Just to the left there fell Major-General Cleburne, whose name in history is circled with a halo as bright as the sunburst on the green flag of his native Ireland," Bate told the crowd.[43]

In his *Rise and Fall of the Confederate Government* written after the war, Jefferson Davis paid tribute to Cleburne and described the magnitude of his loss:

> Around Cleburne thickly lay the gallant men who in his desperate assault followed him with the implicit confidence that in another army was given Stonewall Jackson; and in the one case, as in the other, a vacancy was created which could never be filled.[44]

And the Indianan Tillman Stevens, whose brigade likely shot John Adams, summed up the army that held its ground at Franklin and killed six enemy generals among thousands of other Rebels:

> We were just the common ordinary "Western soldiers". . . . Casement used to call us "squirrel shooters." We were mostly boys from the woods and small towns . . . and knew how to shoot when we were ten years old. We did not have to go to war.[45]

CHAPTER 23

The Engineer and the Newlywed—1865

CONFEDERATE MAJOR GENERAL
WILLIAM HENRY CHASE WHITING
Fort Fisher, North Carolina, January 15, 1865

Maj. Gen. W. H. C. Whiting had helped transform North Carolina's Fort Fisher from a few big mounds of dirt into one of the strongest forts on the planet by January 1865. He would be shot down within the walls of his greatest wartime creation and die a few miles from West Point where his academic record was unsurpassed for decades.

The colossal earthwork was the keystone of Rebel defenses guarding Wilmington, North Carolina, the last seaport open to the Confederacy in the first weeks of 1865. Located on the Atlantic Ocean at the mouth of the Cape Fear River, Fort Fisher had withstood a Union army/navy attack weeks earlier thanks to the exhaustive buildup of the fort by Whiting and the garrison commander, Col. William Lamb.

The son of Massachusetts parents, Whiting, forty, had been born on an Army post in Mississippi where his father was stationed. He never strayed from his Southern sympathies, especially after he married a North Carolina belle. He graduated West Point in 1845 with the highest grades ever earned at the Academy at that point, and had a fine Army career as a military engineer before joining the Confederacy. Promoted brigadier in July 1861, Whiting saw combat at Seven Pines, in the Shenandoah Valley, and in the Seven Days battles. His soldiers called him "Little Billy" due to his diminutive height.[1]

In November 1862, Whiting was sent to Wilmington to strengthen coastal defenses. The gem of his work would be Fort Fisher, at that time a modest battery on Confederate Point about eighteen miles below the city. Over the next two years the plans and engineering of Whiting and Lamb, along with the sweat and labor of a thousand slaves, transformed the sandy position into possibly the most formidable fortress in the world. The L-shaped bastion ran for about 700 yards across the throat of the peninsula, from the ocean to the river and more than a mile down the beach with sandbagged earth walls thirty to more than forty feet high and twenty-five feet thick. The fort mounted about 170 guns, including dozens of pieces of heavy artillery, and was also guarded by a minefield, ditches, and a palisade of sharpened pine logs. Its Mound Battery jutted some sixty feet high and could be seen for miles at sea. Yet while the fort itself was awesome, the perpetual problem of the Confederacy would plague it: there were not enough soldiers to man it properly.

Whiting was promoted major general in April 1863, and briefly reassigned to service in Virginia in summer 1864. It would be an inglorious return. He failed to get his troops into combat at Port Walthall Junction, and was accused of being under the influence of drugs or alcohol although there were no formal charges.[2] He returned to Wilmington and Fort Fisher in late May, and was in district command by fall 1864, reporting to General Braxton Bragg, who was in charge of the Department of North Carolina.

The next combat test for Whiting and Lamb came in December when a Union army and navy strike force under Maj. Gen. Benjamin Butler and Rear Adm. David Porter tried to take the fort during Christmas week. Their attack failed, but by the second week of January 1865, Porter's fleet was back, this time carrying troops commanded by Maj. Gen. Alfred Terry and set for another attempt. On January 13, Porter opened an around-the-clock bombardment of Fisher, under cover of which about 10,000 U.S. soldiers, sailors, and marines came ashore in an amphibious landing, digging in north of the fort. The garrison endured two days of the awesome naval shelling, which one Southern historian described as "by the side of which all previous artillery fighting in the world's history was child's play."[3]

Unable to persuade Bragg to send reinforcements to Lamb, Whiting went by boat from Wilmington to the fort, arriving during some of the heaviest of the shelling. "The fire of the fleet is beyond description," Whiting would later write on his deathbed. "No language can describe that terrific bombardment." Greeting Lamb, he said, "I have come to share your fate, my boy. You are to be sacrificed."[4]

Porter's guns finally fell silent about 2:30 P.M. on Sunday, January 15, as Terry and Porter prepared for a two-pronged assault against the bastion. A naval brigade composed of sailors and marines would rush the fort from the beachside. At the same time the XXIV Corps division of Brig. Gen. Adelbert Ames would launch the main attack against Fisher's landside defenses along the river and the Wilmington Road.

From the fort, Whiting sent repeated messages to Bragg for reinforcements, his tone growing harsher with each dispatch through the afternoon. He also ignored an order from Bragg to return to Wilmington. Bragg was angered by Whiting's insolence and suspected that Whiting had been drinking, harking back to earlier innuendo about his conduct. Bragg sent Brig. Gen. Alfred Colquitt to take command of the fort, even though Lamb, not Whiting, was the commander, but Colquitt would not arrive until after the battle was decided.

When the Union assaults came about 3:30 P.M., the 1,900 Rebel defenders blazed away with cannons and musketry. The attacking naval brigade was soon crushed, its survivors reeling down the beach, leaving the strand strewn with blue-clad bodies.

Whiting was among the cheering Confederates on the fort's northeast bastion as they watched the Union seamen retreat. Their jubilation was short-lived, however, as they soon saw Federal guidons and other flags fluttering atop the riverside batteries where Ames's regiments had broken through against outnumbered Rebels in that sector. Incensed by the enemy banners and the sight of bluecoats piling into the fort, Whiting shouted for the Confederates around him to counterattack, telling them to pull down the flags.

The yelling Rebels, about 500 in all, plunged off the works, Whiting leading them, as other gray artillerists scrambled from their posts to join the attack. Blue and gray meshed in a bloody collage, the fighting point-blank and brutal among the cannon positions and parapets, men falling in a blur of stabbing, clawing, and shooting.

Whiting was in the forefront and climbed atop a traverse to grab one of the enemy banners. He was instantly assailed by several Federals who shouted for him to surrender. "Go to hell, you Yankee bastards!" he roared in reply. The Northeners answered with ragged gunfire, two bullets dropping Whiting. He was hit twice in the right leg, the most severe being a round that tore into his hip.[5]

Seeing him fall, some of Whiting's men dragged him off the parapet to temporary safety. Whiting continued to give orders before he was taken to a field hospital at the Pulpit Battery, his attack running out of steam.

Shortly afterward, Lamb was wounded in the hip and brought to the hospital where he was laid next to Whiting. Despite their pain, the officers conferred and agreed to continue resisting, and Whiting dispatched another plea to Bragg for more troops. Bragg had a veteran division in place to attack Terry from the rear, but he withheld it, apparently believing in Fort Fisher's invincibility. With no help forthcoming, Fisher's remaining defenders tried to hang on as Terry poured fresh troops into the combat inside the fort. The fighting swept from bombproof to bunker to trenches, winding into the night, as the Confederates were killed or overpowered.

With the Yankees closing in about 10 P.M., Whiting and Lamb were evacuated on litters to Battery Buchanan, a strong earthwork just to the south. The Federals gained control of Fisher shortly afterward, the battle ending after some six hours. Terry found Whiting lying on a litter at Battery Buchanan after midnight. Gazing up at the victorious general, Whiting said, "I surrender, sir, to you the forces under my command, I care not what becomes of myself."[6]

The casualty totals for Fort Fisher vary Union losses of 700 to almost 1,000 were reported, while Confederate losses, in addition to the captured garrison, being about 500. Yet numbered there was no dispute: the fort's demise allowed Porter's squadron to cork Wilmington, effectively cutting the Confederacy's last lifeline to the outside world.

In the next few days while the Federals buried the dead and prepared to ship their prisoners north, Whiting dictated a detailed report of the battle while he was in the Fort Fisher hospital. The report was intended for General Lee and blamed Bragg for the defeat. But Whiting was unable to send the report before he and other officers were transferred to the prison compound at Fort Columbus on Governors Island in New York harbor, arriving on the night of January 25.

Whiting was attended by surgeon Spiers Singleton, also among the prisoners, but the week-long voyage left him weak and unable to move about in bed. Singleton's first task upon arrival at Fort Columbus was to act on Whiting's written request to be assigned indefinitely to the prison hospital. "At present, I am completely helpless and unable to turn in bed," Whiting wrote in the letter Singleton presented to Union authorities. "I have been seven days on a transport ship in heavy weather and really must rest." The Federals complied.[7]

From the hospital, he compiled another report on February 19, also condemning Bragg for the fort's capture. "I charge him with this loss; with neglect of duty," he said of Bragg. "I demand, in justice to the country, to the army and to myself, that the course of this officer be investigated."[8]

Criticism of Bragg was widespread, but with the Confederacy all but dead there would be no investigation. While in the prison infirmary Whiting received a February 22 letter from Butler who wanted information about Fort Fisher's defense in Butler's failed December operation. Butler had earlier sent a staff officer to Fort Columbus and the officer had found Whiting in a weakened condition. "I had not heard before of the severity of your wound and the critical condition of your health, or I would not have troubled you," Butler wrote. His letter contained more than twenty questions about the battle. Whiting sent Butler a reply with detailed answers to his inquiry, again castigating Bragg.[9]

The first days of March saw a number of Rebel officers, including Dr. Singleton, transferred from Fort Columbus to City Point, Virginia, where they were freed in one of the war's last prisoner exchanges. By this time, Whiting had gradually strengthened and his wounds were healing well. Singleton left him in the care of the post's medical staff. But diarrhea set in unexpectedly, possibly preceded by dysentery, and by March 9, Whiting was too drained to finish or sign a letter.[10]

Whiting died on Friday, March 10, twelve days short of his forty-first birthday. It was his lot to die in a dank prison fortress, viewed by many as a traitor to his nation, only a few miles from West Point where he had begun his soldiering career two decades earlier with such high scholastic accolades. The post chaplain described Whiting's decline: "I have seldom stood by a death-bed where there was so gratifying a manifestation of humble Christian faith. I asked him if he would like to see some of the religious papers. He said: 'No that they were so bitter in their tone, he preferred the Bible alone; that was enough for him.' He partook of the holy communion, at his own request, in private, on the Sunday afternoon before his death." The chaplain added that Whiting's death "was very sudden to all here, but it was a Christian's death, the death of the trustful, hopeful soul."[11]

The fort's provost-marshal, Bvt. Capt. William West, noted Whiting's passing in a brief message that day to Brig. Gen. William Hoffman, the Army's commissary-general of prisoners: "I have the honor to report that Major-General Whiting, C.S. Army, prisoner of war at this post, died in the hospital of this post this morning."[12]

Whiting's funeral was held on March 11 at New York City's Trinity Episcopal Church; among those attending were his mother and two sisters from Hartford, Connecticut, and a brother who lived in New York. Whiting's rosewood casket was borne by several Union officers and Confederate brigadier general W. N. R. Beall, the New York–based supply liaison for Rebel prisoners. "A very large concourse of people was present, and the profoundest respect was paid to the deceased and his sorrowing relatives and friends," one observer wrote.[13]

After the service a hearse with the general's camellia-draped coffin and followed by carriages of mourners made its way down Broadway to Greenwood Cemetery in Brooklyn where Whiting was buried. In January 1900, Whiting's remains were returned to Wilmington to be reinterred next to his wife, Katherine, at Oakdale Cemetery. In his postwar history of the Confederacy, Jefferson Davis described Whiting as "heroic and highly gifted."[14]

Years after the war, Blanton Duncan, who had been a close friend of Whiting's as well as an important Kentucky Confederate, received a letter that Whiting had been unable to finish on his deathbed. The letter had been found by a Union surgeon attending Whiting and who had finally forwarded it to Duncan. Even from his prison "bed of suffering," Whiting still smoldered over Bragg. "That I am here, and that Wilmington and Fisher are gone, is due wholly and solely to the incompetency, the imbecility and the pusillanimity of Braxton Bragg. . . . He could have taken every one of the enemy, but he was afraid."[15]

CONFEDERATE BRIGADIER GENERAL JOHN PEGRAM
Hatcher's Run, Virginia, February 6, 1865

When he was married less than three weeks before his death, the ceremony for Brig. Gen. John Pegram and his bride was beset by ill omens that alarmed many in the congregation. The same church would be the scene of his funeral.

Pegram, thirty-three, was a Petersburg native and an 1854 West Point graduate. He had fought and was captured in the Rich Mountain Campaign and, upon his exchange, had served on the staffs of Braxton Bragg, P. G. T. Beauregard, and Kirby Smith. Promoted brigadier as of November 1862, he was in action with cavalry commands at Stones River and Chickamauga before being transferred to the Army of Northern Virginia to lead an infantry brigade. Pegram was seriously wounded in the leg at the Wilderness but also fought in the Shenandoah Valley. After Robert Rodes's death at Winchester, he was given division command in Gen. John Gordon's 2nd Corps.

Pegram had relished a major milestone in his life on January 19, 1865, when he married his fiancée of more than two years, the beautiful Hetty Cary of Baltimore. The couple was married at St. Paul's Church in Richmond, and the new bride and her mother accompanied Pegram back to his command after a brief honeymoon in the capital. "One of the handsomest and most lovable men I ever knew wed to the handsomest woman in the Southland," recalled Maj. Henry Kyd Douglas, Pegram's adjutant.[16]

The wedding had not been without incident however. President and Mrs. Jefferson Davis had sent their private carriage to convey the bride and groom to St. Paul's, but the horses were unsettled and became unruly. Reaching the church, Hetty's gown was ripped as she entered the sanctuary, and "the veil was nearly torn from her face as she approached the altar," Douglas wrote. "A superstitious murmur passed through the immense congregation, but they went on to their fate."[17]

Pegram was unable to leave his command for a honeymoon, so the couple spent their wedding night in a farmhouse in Dinwiddie County that was serving as the general's headquarters. On February 2, Gordon held a review of Pegram's division, an occasion for Robert E. Lee and other generals to meet the new bride. After this grand honor, Mrs. Pegram, accompanied by Douglas, rode past her husband's soldiers returning to their camps as she was "sitting [on] her horse like the Maid of France and smiling upon them with her marvelous beauty." No one could have foreseen that she would be a widow four days later.[18]

On the night of February 5, Pegram talked deep into the night with his friend, John Esten Cooke, who wrote after the war that the young general seemed to feel that he was about to fight his last battle. Pegram was immersed in the fighting at Hatcher's Run on February 6, opposing the Union V Corps. He and Hetty had breakfasted together that morning before he rode off to join the fighting, which had already begun. Pegram was spurring on his troops near Dabney's Sawmill, the fierce combat in this sector centered on a large pile of sawdust as Pegram prepared to make a charge. His last order was to Capt. Samuel Buck of the 13th Virginia on the skirmish line, telling Buck to have his riflemen "conform to his movement." A Federal sharpshooter's bullet suddenly found Pegram. Wounded in the chest near his heart, he crumpled in the saddle. Douglas was near the stricken general at the time. "I jumped from my horse and caught him as he fell and with assistance took him from his horse," he recalled. "He died in my arms, almost as soon as he touched the ground."[19]

Major John H. New, a staff officer, remembered Pegram's last words as "I am badly—take me off the field." Gordon related that, "In one of General Grant's efforts to break through my lines, General John Pegram, one of my most accomplished commanders, fell, his blood reddening the white snow that carpeted the field."[20]

The body was placed on a blanket and soldiers carried it to an ambulance in the rear. Hetty, meanwhile, had gone into Petersburg to spend the day with her mother. She learned that her husband was unharmed in the early stages of the fray and she and her mother took a wagon back to Pegram's headquarters that night.

With the battle now over and night fallen, Pegram's comrades tried to decide who should have the unenviable task of informing the general's wife of his death. Douglas gave this version of the conversation:

"You must do it, Douglas," said General Gordon.

"Heavens! General—I'll lead a forlorn hope—do anything that is war—but not that.

"Send Major New. He's married and knows women; I don't."

Douglas had Pegram's body taken to his room at headquarters.

"An hour after, as the General lay, dead, on my bed, I heard the ambulance pass just outside the window, taking Mrs. Pegram back to their quarters. New had not seen her yet and she did not know; but her mother was with her. A fiancée of three years, a bride of three weeks, now a widow!"[21]

It is unknown whether New actually bore the news to Hetty. Her mother later wrote that Hetty did not learn of her husband's death until the following morning. As arrangements were made for Pegram's funeral at St. Paul's, Richmond's newspapers joined in mourning him. "Though unsuccessful early in the war, General Pegram had latterly established an enviable reputation as a gallant soldier and an able and efficient officer," the *Richmond Whig* stated on February 8.[22]

The *Richmond Dispatch* added that Pegram "fell nobly at the head of his men. . . . He had been in the army since the opening of the war, and had borne a distinguished part in many hard-fought fields. He was a man of the most unflinching gallantry and a high order of intellect."[23]

Lee and his wife both sent notes of condolence to Mrs. Pegram, and Custis Lee accompanied her at the funeral. Like so many other Confederates of every rank, Pegram was buried in Richmond's Hollywood Cemetery where he would not be alone very long. His brother and artillerist Col. William J. Pegram, was mortally wounded at Five Forks on April 1. In the fading echoes of the guns, the brothers rested together in peace.

CHAPTER 24

"You Have Killed
General A. P. Hill . . ."

CONFEDERATE LIEUTENANT GENERAL
AMBROSE POWELL HILL
Petersburg, April 2, 1865

The Rebel siege lines ringing Petersburg were falling apart under an all-out Union attack on the early morning of April 2, 1865, and one of the most illustrious generals in the Confederate pantheon would pay the ultimate price for the collapse.

Ambrose Powell Hill, he of the famed red battle shirt and Light Division that had been Robert E. Lee's broadsword at Antietam, who was scarred but survived two earlier wars and some of the hardest fighting of this conflict, met his end in an encounter with two lost Pennsylvania soldiers. Even with his army disintegrating and the losses of Petersburg and Richmond imminent that day, the blow of Hill's death would bring tears to Lee's eyes.

The slight, thirty-nine-year-old lieutenant general was a native of Culpeper, Virginia, and graduated fifteenth in the West Point class of 1847. A veteran of the Mexican and Seminole Wars, he entered Confederate service as colonel of the 13th Virginia Infantry. Commissioned brigadier in February 1862, his combat performance at Williamsburg and in the Peninsular Campaign earned him promotion to major general in May 1862. Hill was a stalwart in the Seven Days battles and at Cedar Mountain, and the arrival of his Light Division at Antietam likely saved Lee's army from destruction. Wounded at Chancellorsville, Hill was promoted lieutenant general in May 1863, and given command of the newly established III Corps, which he fought at Gettysburg and in the Wilderness.[1]

*Confederate lieutenant general
A. P. Hill.*
LIBRARY OF CONGRESS

Considered a top-notch combat officer, Hill was unsettled and erratic as a corps commander. His impetuous attack at Bristoe Station cost him some 1,400 casualties and angered Lee, but his courage was beyond question, although his frequent health problems raised concerns about his command capacity. Some historians contend that Hill's contraction of gonorrhea while at West Point contributed to his illnesses in later life. Hill's wife, Dolly, was a sister of Gen. John Hunt Morgan, and Hill was also a brother-in-law of Gen. Basil Duke. Dolly would be seven months pregnant when she was widowed.[2]

Hill had been ill for weeks by early spring 1865, much of his time spent in Richmond on sick leave, and had just returned to the Petersburg lines where he was in the saddle almost without respite. On April 1 he was with his troops in the trenches from before sunup until after dark. The day had been a crushing disaster for the Rebel army: the Federals had captured the critical road junction at Five Forks and were now menacing the South Side Railroad, Lee's last rail link out of Petersburg.

The Confederates had been in their siege lines around Richmond and Petersburg for almost ten months, but the loss of Five Forks threatened to topple their fortunes like bloody dominos. With the day's losses on his mind, Hill retired to the Venable Cottage where Dolly and their two young daughters, Russie and Lucy, were staying only a few yards from his headquarters. There would be little rest for anyone that evening. An enemy bombardment that began at twilight intensified during the night in preparation for what would be an all-out, predawn assault by four Union corps, the Federal VI Corps of Maj. Gen. Horatio G. Wright assailing Hill's sector.

Worried by the increased tempo of the cannonade, Hill left the cottage in the early morning hours of Sunday, April 2, and walked to his headquarters. After talking with members of his staff and apparently determining that an enemy attack was underway, he decided to ride to Lee's headquarters, directing courier Sgt. George Tucker and two other messengers to follow him as soon as possible. Mounted on Champ, his favorite gray, Hill went to Lee's bivouac at the Turnbull House about a mile and a half to the west on the Cox Road. Arriving at Turnbull's about 5:30 A.M., he was conferring with Lee when a staff officer burst in with the news that the Confederate line had been broken along the right flank.

Hill quickly ordered one of his couriers to return to his headquarters and have his staff rally the troops on the right. He, Tucker, and the other courier, William Jenkins, then set out for the danger point. The three rode south across Cattail Run and then west when two enemy soldiers suddenly appeared in their path. Tucker and Jenkins demanded their surrender and the Federals dropped their muskets. Hill ordered Jenkins to take the prisoners to Lee while he and Tucker continued on to the southwest, Hill wanting to reach Maj. Gen. Henry Heth who commanded a division of his corps. As they rode, they saw groups of Federals in the woods and fields in the distance. Realizing their danger, Hill said to Tucker, "Sergeant, should anything happen to me you must go back to General Lee and report it."[3]

Crossing the Boydton Plank Road they approached a field less than half a mile from Heth's headquarters, but saw Yankees on the road ahead of them. Trying to avoid the enemy, Hill and Tucker skirted some woods paralleling the plank road, but about 6:30 A.M., they encountered two other bluecoats who scurried to cover behind a large oak tree when they saw the Confederates.

These Federals were Cpl. John W. Mauk and Pvt. Daniel Wolford of Company F, 138th Pennsylvania Infantry. The 138th was a part of the 2nd Brigade, 3rd Division of the U.S. VI Corps, and a portion of the brigade had been separated in the corps' attack that morning. Mauk, from Bedford County, Pennsylvania, had been promoted to corporal a month earlier. With the lines intermingled and broken in the predawn combat, Mauk and Wolford soon found themselves isolated and trying to rejoin their regiment. They had trudged into a swamp when they saw two riders who appeared to be officers approaching them. Mauk recalled that the horsemen "advanced with cocked revolvers in their hands, which were leveled at us."[4]

From behind the tree the Yankees drew a bead on the approaching Rebels. Tucker recalled that when the Federals sought cover, he turned to see how Hill wanted to handle the situation. "We must take them," Hill said, drawing his Colt Navy revolver. "Stay there, I'll take them," Tucker replied. "By this time we were within twenty yards of the two behind the tree and getting closer every moment. I shouted: 'If you fire, you'll be swept to hell! Our men are here—surrender!'"[5]

Hill then rode up on Tucker's right side, also calling on them to surrender, both now about ten yards from the bluecoats. The Yankees were on the same side of the tree, Wolford aiming at Tucker while above him Mauk had his musket trained on Hill. Mauk made a snap decision to fight rather than fold. "I cannot see it," he whispered to Wolford regarding the surrender demand. "Let us shoot them."[6]

"The lower soldier let the stock of his gun down from his shoulder, but recovered quickly as his comrade spoke to him (I only saw his lips move) and both fired," remembered Tucker.[7]

Their muskets blazed in the gloom and Wolford's ball whizzed by the sergeant. Mauk's round, however, tore into Hill. The .58-caliber bullet severed Hill's left thumb in the gauntlet before penetrating his chest and heart and exiting his back. "We immediately raised our guns and fired, I bringing my man from his saddle," Mauk recalled.[8]

Hill slumped and fell off his horse, landing face down on the ground. In seconds, Tucker grabbed Champ's bridle and, wheeling to his left, spurred to safety, glancing to see "my General on the ground, with his limbs extended, motionless."[9]

Tucker galloped into the woods and soon switched mounts, taking the fresher and stronger Champ to report to Lee as Hill had instructed. Avoiding knots of Union infantrymen and their scattered fire, Tucker soon encountered Gen. James Longstreet and his officers as well as members of Hill's staff, including his chief of staff Col. William H. Palmer. All were shocked to hear the terrible news.

Palmer and Tucker then rode for Lee's headquarters, finding the general astride his horse on the Cox Road. Palmer broke down in telling Lee of Hill's fate, and Tucker had to finish the awful news. Lee was thunderstruck, tears brimming in his eyes as Tucker spoke. "He is now at rest, and we who are left are the ones to suffer," the general said in a trembling voice. Lee told Palmer to find and inform Dolly Hill of the tragedy, adding, "Colonel, break the news to her as gently as possible."[10]

Dolly was awake and singing while doing household chores when Palmer arrived at the cottage and knocked on the door. Seeing him, Dolly sensed immediately what had happened. In a paroxym of anguish she threw up her arms and cried, "The General is dead! You would not be here if he had not been killed!"[11]

Palmer tried to soothe her, saying that he didn't know for certain that Hill was dead. The worst was confirmed shortly afterward when soldiers of the 5th Alabama Battalion brought in the general's body, "still slightly warm, with nothing about it disturbed," Tucker remembered.[12]

As soldiers gently removed the body from the horse that had carried it, the distraught Mrs. Hill noted the wedding ring still on her husband's mutilated left hand.

Mauk and Wolford, meanwhile, had found their regiment, but later in the morning were summoned to brigade and corps headquarters. In the presence of General Wright, Mauk gave a statement about the encounter with the Rebel horsemen. "General Wright then asked me if I knew whom I had killed," Mauk related. "I told him that I did not. He said: "You have killed General A. P. Hill of the Confederate army."[13]

There would be no grand state funeral for Hill. The Confederacy was comatose and Lee evacuated Richmond and Petersburg that Sunday night. Amid this chaos, a rickety army wagon started for Richmond bearing Dolly, the children and Hill's body, his cape covering the general's face. The wagon was accompanied by Capt. Frank Hill, who was the general's nephew, and courier Jenkins. Roads jammed with soldiers and fleeing civilians prevented the little party from reaching the capital until early Monday morning. G. P. Hill and Henry Hill, both cousins of the general, took charge of the body after meeting the wagon near Richmond, but with the Rebels' collapse, found it impossible to make burial arrangements at Hollywood Cemetery.

Mrs. Hill decided to take the girls to G. P. Hill's family home near Chesterfield, Virginia, until events calmed. The Hill cousins, meanwhile, found a simple pine casket, and washed the remains while deciding what to do next. The family wanted Hill buried in his hometown of Culpeper if he could not be interred at Hollywood. Before dawn, the Hill cousins and a driver set out with the body, bound for Chesterfield. They hoped to reunite with Dolly there and then make a decision whether to proceed to Culpeper. When they arrived hours later, however, the immediate family was not there and a decision had to be made. Culpeper was more than one hundred miles away and the body was deteriorating rapidly in the spring heat. With little choice, the general was buried without ceremony in the old Winston family cemetery in Chesterfield on the afternoon of April 4.

On June 6, Dolly gave birth to her fourth child. (First daughter Netty had died in 1862, still a toddler.) She had hoped for a son, to name him after her late husband, but a baby girl came instead. The infant, Ann Powell Hill, was soon nicknamed A. P., but did not have long to carry on her father's memory, dying before she was three years old.[14]

In 1867, Hill's remains were finally moved to Hollywood Cemetery, and in 1892 reinterred under his statue at Hermitage and Laburnum avenues in Richmond. Jefferson Davis wrote in his memoir that Hill, who "had so often passed unscathed through storms of shot and shell, yielded up the life he had, in the beginning of the war, consecrated to the Confederate cause; and his comrades, while mourning his loss, have drawn consolation from the fact that he died before our flag was furled in defeat."[15]

CHAPTER 25

Last Blood

CONFEDERATE BRIGADIER GENERAL JAMES DEARING
High Bridge, Virginia, April 6, 1865

The blood of more than a million American soldiers—blue and gray—was on the land when the last Confederate general to die of battle wounds fell during combat with an enemy officer.

In the first week of April 1865, the Army of Northern Virginia was in exhaustive, headlong retreat after evacuating Richmond and Petersburg. Marching day and night with scant rations and Federal troops in close pursuit, the Rebels plodded west across Virginia, Robert E. Lee holding to the forlorn hope of linking with Joe Johnston's army in North Carolina and continuing the fight. Lee's columns stalled at Sailor's Creek near Farmville on the morning of April 6, as U.S. cavalry poured into a gap in their line of march, cutting off three of Lee's four corps and forcing these Rebels to make a stand.

Even as this battle unfolded, the Confederates were dealing with another threat. Union raiders ahead of the army were apparently intent on destroying the massive High Bridge over the Appomattox River. If they succeeded, the Confederate escape route would be cut. Rebel lieutenant general James Longstreet, commanding Lee's lead corps, guessed correctly that this enemy force was aimed at High Bridge and dispatched Gen. Thomas Rosser's cavalry division to stop it.

With Rosser was Brig. Gen. James Dearing, who led Rosser's old Laurel Brigade. Dearing was a twenty-four-year-old Virginian who resigned from West Point in 1861, before his graduation, to become a Confederate lieutenant in the Washington Artillery of New Orleans. He served in the artillery until after Gettysburg when he was transferred to the cavalry and promoted to colonel. Commissioned a brigadier in April 1864, Dearing and his brigade had shone in the Petersburg Campaign and in Richmond's evacuation.[1]

Col. Thomas Munford's cavalry was soon sent to aid Rosser, giving the Confederates a force of about 1,200. The bluecoat marauders—about 800 infantry and less than one hundred cavalry—were from Maj. Gen. E. O. C. Ord's Army of the James and commanded by Col. Francis Washburn of the 4th Massachusetts Cavalry. When Ord learned late in the morning that his expedition might meet enemy horsemen, he sent his chief of staff, Col. Theodore Read, to warn Washburn and take command of the column. (Read and Washburn both were brevet brigadier generals but never appointed to full rank.)

The Federals were nearing High Bridge and had driven off a detachment of Rebel home guards shortly after noon when the gray cavalry caught up to them. Washburn's few horsemen charged, and the fighting became hand-to-hand with swords, pistols, and carbines.

At this point Dearing and Washburn, who had known each other as cadets at the Military Academy, became engaged in a bloody reunion. They engaged in a brief personal duel on horseback, their sabers crossing as they wheeled. In the melee a Rebel trooper shot Washburn in the face and he pitched from his saddle. Stunned and bloodied, Washburn was then slashed across the head and fatally wounded by another Confederate.

Dearing then galloped after Read. The former was in the act of firing his revolver at Read when he was hit and gravely wounded, some accounts stating that he was accidentally shot by his own men in the mayhem.[2]

Whether from Dearing's pistol or another Rebel's weapon fired at close range, Read was also shot dead, the Yankees leaving his body on the battlefield. The Confederates made short work of the outnumbered Federal cavalry, shooting, sabering or capturing the bluecoats before turning their attention to the bluecoat infantrymen, who had made no effort to assist Washburn and Read. A Rebel charge pushed these Ohioans and Pennsylvanians off a hilltop position, and they quickly surrendered after offering weak resistance. The fifteen-minute battle was over, and the bridgeburners had been thwarted.

The total haul for the Rebels was almost 800 prisoners, six colors, and a brass band; but their losses, while light overall, were severe among officers, including Dearing, Col. Reuben Boston, Maj. John Knott, and Maj. James W. Thomason.

Shot through the lungs, Dearing was taken to a nearby farmhouse where Rosser and Col. Elijah White of the 35th Virginia Cavalry Battalion came to his bedside. White had led a flank attack that had earlier helped capture the enemy infantry. Dearing was especially close to Rosser since he commanded the Laurel Brigade, but also had much admiration for White. He clutched White's hand and with his other touched the general's stars on his own tunic. "Unable to speak above a whisper," Dearing told Rosser, "I want these to be put on his coat."[3]

High Bridge remained open for the Rebels, but disaster shrouded the Confederates a few miles away at Sailor's Creek where Lee lost almost 8,000 men before the day was over. The wrecked remains of his army limped away with literally only hours to live.

Dearing lingered for two weeks after Lee's surrender at Appomattox Court House on April 9. Taken to Lynchburg, Virginia, he was treated at the Ladies Relief Hospital, located in the old City Hotel. With him, Dearing had a letter from Lee, stating that papers for his promotion to major general were with the Secretary of War, "a promotion too long delayed by reason of my inability to fill your present command of the Laurel Brigade."[4]

Dearing died in Lynchburg on April 22 (some accounts state April 23), the last Confederate general to die of war wounds.[5] Shortly before his death, Dearing was visited and paroled by Union brigadier general Ranald S. Makenzie, who commanded U.S. troops in the town. Dearing was buried in Lynchburg's Spring Hill Cemetery.

Writing weeks after the surrender, Gen. Fitzhugh Lee, commander of the Confederate cavalry corps, recognized the minor victory at High Bridge, stating "the success was indeed dearly bought" in the deaths of Dearing and the others. Of Dearing, Boston, and Thomason, Lee wrote, "The splendid gallantry of these three officers had been tested on many fields, and their conspicuous valor was universally known."[6]

Even as Dearing lay on his deathbed, however, another Rebel general would become the last to actually die in battle, falling hundreds of miles away in Georgia.

UNION MAJOR GENERAL THOMAS A. SMYTH
Farmville, Virginia, April 7, 1865
Even as Lee prepared to surrender at Appomattox Court House on April 9, 1865, the last Union general to die of battle wounds in the war had succumbed a few miles away, unaware of the historic events of this day.

*Union major general
Thomas A. Smyth.*
LIBRARY OF CONGRESS

Brig. Gen. Thomas A. Smyth, thirty-two, had been shot in the face two days earlier in combat outside Farmville, a short distance from where Dearing fell. An Irishman from County Cork, he had come to the United States in 1854, becoming a soldier of fortune and later a coachmaker in Wilmington, Delaware. A militiaman as well, he served in an all-Irish regiment early in the war before it was dissolved, and later was appointed major of the 1st Delaware Infantry. Smyth was in battle at Antietam, Fredericksburg, Chancellorsville, and Gettysburg, by now having risen to colonel of the regiment. Promoted brigadier general of volunteers in October 1864, Smyth had been active in the Petersburg Campaign and in the western pursuit of Lee's army after the Confederates evacuated Richmond and Petersburg on April 3. Smyth commanded the 3rd Brigade of Brig. Gen. Francis Barlow's 2nd Division in the U.S. II Corps.[7]

About noon on April 7, he was riding along his skirmish line, as his troops pressed Confederates retreating toward Farmville. He and his men had seen little action the day before when the bulk of Lee's army had been trapped and routed at Sailor's Creek, but now they were in the hottest of the fighting.

Smyth was only about fifty yards from Rebels of John Gordon's corps when he was shot, tumbling off his horse. The sharpshooter's bullet struck him just above the mouth, tearing into his neck and splintering a cervical vertebra. Paralyzed, the general was placed on a stretcher and carried to the II Corps hospital on the Brooks Farm while Col. Daniel Woodall of the 1st Delaware took brigade command and continued the advance.[8]

On the morning of April 8, Smyth was taken by ambulance to Union medical facilities set up at Burke's Station about twelve miles away. At his request, he was carried into the home of Col. Samuel D. Burke for whom the little settlement was named. Smyth was weakening and asked his physicians about his chances of survival, adding, "Don't hesitate, Doctor, but speak candidly, for I am no coward and not afraid to die!"[9]

During his final hours, Smyth also thanked the Burke family for their compassionate care. His end came about 4 A.M. on April 9, a few hours before Lee's surrender. He would be the last Federal general to be killed in the war.

"Such brilliant successes have not been gained without severe loss, though comparatively small in number," reported Maj. Gen. A. A. Humphreys, the II Corps commander. "Among those who fell are Brigadier-General Smyth, in whom the service has lost a noble, gallant, and experienced soldier."[10]

Smyth's death drew two brief notices in the April 14th *New York Times*, including one stating that he was survived by a wife and child. Within hours, however, the newspaper and the rest of the nation would forget about the general amid the horror of President Lincoln's assassination. Smyth was laid to rest at the Wilmington and Brandywine Cemetery in Wilmington, posthumously promoted to major general to rank from the date of his wound. He had been a Mason less than a month, but more than one hundred members of the fraternal organization journeyed from five states to attend his funeral.[11]

CONFEDERATE BRIGADIER GENERAL ROBERT C. TYLER
West Point, Georgia, April 16, 1865

The one-legged Confederate general watching the advancing Union cavalrymen had the look of a Prussian officer with his long, waxed mustache and soldierly bearing. The date was April 16, 1865, a week after Lee's surrender, and Rebel brigadier general Robert C. Tyler was intent on keeping these Yankees from crossing the Chattahoochee River at West Point, Georgia.

The enemy he saw coming toward him and his handful of defenders were elements of U.S. major general James H. Wilson's cavalry, which had cut a destructive swath across central Alabama in a raid begun about three weeks earlier. Wilson and his 13,500 troopers intended to carry this devastation into Georgia, but they would have to cross the rain-swollen Chattahoochee, which here formed the border between the states. Wilson needed to seize an intact bridge to make his crossing. Otherwise, he would have to call up engineers to lay pontoons, delaying his progress. The Yankees learned that spans were standing at Columbus, Georgia, and thirty-five miles above it at West Point. Wilson targeted both towns. He sent Col. Oscar La Grange's brigade to capture the West Point bridge while the rest of his column spurred for Columbus.

Standing in La Grange's way was Tyler's patchwork force of about 120 Rebels, most of whom were Georgia militia, Louisiana and South Carolina artillerymen, and a few furloughed soldiers whom the war's fortunes had placed in West Point this particular day. The key to Tyler's defense was a small redoubt west of town and on the Alabama side of the river. Named Fort Tyler in the general's honor, this earthwork was thirty-five yards square and brandishing three cannons. A wide, deep ditch and inadequate abatis surrounded the fort.

Tyler had never fully recovered from a wound suffered at Missionary Ridge in November 1863 that necessitated the amputation of a leg. During his recuperation, he was promoted to brigadier, but apparently did not return to the main army. Little is known of his prewar life, although he was supposedly a native of Baltimore. He joined the Confederate service as a twenty-eight-year-old private in the 15th Tennessee Infantry in 1861 and saw rapid promotion. After serving as regimental quartermaster, Tyler had risen to lieutenant colonel by the time he led the Tennesseans in combat at Belmont and Shiloh, where he was wounded. He later was elected colonel of the regiment and commanded it until he was incapacitated at Missionary Ridge. Tyler had been on duty at West Point for most of the winter of 1864–65 and into the spring.[12]

Fort Tyler was not especially impressive to one Rebel officer who inspected the position with its commander, who limped about on a crutch. "Why, General, this is a slaughter pen!" the officer said. Tyler replied, "I know it, but we must man and try to hold it."[13]

La Grange's full brigade arrived near West Point about 10 A.M. Tyler's pickets were pushed back and Union artillery soon began drumming the Rebel stronghold. By early afternoon the Federals were ready to attack. Detachments of dismounted Wisconsin, Indiana, and Kentucky cavalrymen engaged the fort while other bluecoats secured the bridge. La Grange now focused on taking the bastion. Riflemen picked off any Rebel who showed himself, while other Yankees tore boards from nearby buildings for makeshift walkways over the fort's ditch.

It was during this time that Tyler was mortally wounded by a Union sharpshooter firing from a group of houses. Tyler had not ordered these homes torn down because of the hardship it would cause their residents.

"General Tyler while recklessly exposing himself at the portcullis, viewing the enemy through his field glasses, was shot," wrote S. F. Power, the Rebels' West Point quartermaster. Tyler had no sooner been hit then a second shot clipped his crutch in two and he tumbled to the ground. One account states that the sniper was posted in an upper story window in the home of Dr. A. W. Griggs.[14]

His men gently laid the dying Tyler at the foot of the fort's flagstaff. Overhead flew a silk Confederate banner presented to him by women from the West Point area and which Tyler had sworn to defend. He died about an hour later.

With Tyler gone, the final attack came near sunset. The cavalrymen quickly swarmed over the fort, taking it after a brief but furious fight. Tyler's second in command, a Capt. C. Gonzales, also was mortally wounded in the battle. La Grange suffered 36 dead or wounded while reporting Confederate losses of 18 killed, 28 wounded, and more than 200 captured.

The Union troopers were pushing in to West Point the next day when some of their skirmishers came under musket fire. The Federals soon discovered that the daughter of a Mrs. Potts had fired two shots, both missing, from near her family's house. La Grange issued orders to burn the home, but rescinded them when he learned that the bodies of Tyler and Gonzales were in the house. "Were it not for the honored dead that lie in that house, I would teach the female sharpshooter a lesson," La Grange remarked, based on Power's account.[15]

The enigmatic Tyler was buried at first in the Reese family cemetery and later reinterred at Pinewood Cemetery, not far from the scene of his final command.

CHAPTER 26

Short Stories and Loose Ends

A STONEWALL BRIGADE CURSE?

Only one general who commanded the Stonewall Brigade survived the war—Brig. Gen. James A. Walker. Four others—Stonewall Jackson, Charles S. Winder, Elisha F. Paxton, and Richard B. Garnett—were killed in combat or mortally wounded, as were three colonels who temporarily led the legendary brigade. After the brigade was destroyed at Spotsylvania, Brig. Gen. William Terry was given command of a consolidated brigade composed of the remnants of the Stonewall Brigade and two others. Terry drowned in 1888 while trying to ford a flooded creek near his home.[1]

MORE STONEWALL JACKSON

Jackson has the distinction of having *two* marked graves some 100 miles apart. While the general rests in a Lexington, Virginia, cemetery, his left arm, amputated early on the morning of May 3, 1863, is buried on the Chancellorsville battlefield where Jackson fell.

After the surgery, which occurred at a Confederate field hospital, the limb was solemnly interred at the family plot of Maj. J. H. Lacy's family at their estate, Ellwood. Lacy was the brother of Jackson's chaplain, B. Tucker Lacy.

A marker denoting the location was dedicated in 1903 by Jackson's friends. In 1921, U.S. Marine Corps major general Smedley D. Butler dug up the arm, and had it reburied there in a metal box, the ceremony being attended by President Warren G. Harding.[2]

MISTAKEN IDENTITY AT ANTIETAM

An intriguing item written by a Union officer in the May 1910 issue of *Confederate Veteran* described how Rebel brigadier general George B. Anderson died on the Antietam battlefield and was buried by a Federal soldier identified as Sgt. John M. Atwood of the 29th Massachusetts.

Atwood removed a gold ring from the general's hand and supposedly spent years trying to locate any of Anderson's relatives and return the ring to them. In truth, Anderson was not killed at Antietam, but died of his wound almost a month later in North Carolina, a fact that an elderly Rebel noted in a later issue of the *Confederate Veteran*. It is not known whom Atwood buried or whose ring he recovered.[3]

MORE ZOLLICOFFER CONTROVERSY

The most bizarre story regarding the death of Confederate general Felix Zollicoffer is the account of a Kentucky civilian who claimed to have killed the general with his squirrel rifle during the battle of Mill Springs in 1862.

The account of James Chrisman, a resident of Wayne County, first surfaced publically in 1885 in the *Birmingham (Alabama) Weekly Iron Age* newspaper. Chrisman claimed that on the day of the battle he was returning from a store in the vicinity and became trapped between the two armies. Chrisman stated that a "German regiment" of Federals charged and that he moved with them.

Chrisman continued: "At this moment Gen. Zollicoffer made a charge to meet them. He advanced in front, firing his pistol, and had killed ten men near me. I thought I would be the next man, and I raised my rifle and fired at him. He fell without a groan. . . . I have heard that soon after the battle . . . Colonel Frye was receiving honors for having killed Zollicoffer. Would to God he had instead of me; for the act has haunted me to this day. I cannot sleep. And yet I did it to save my life. I did not know the man."[4]

Based on official reports and other eyewitness accounts, Chrisman's story is unlikely.

ARMISTEAD'S SWORD

When Brig. Gen. Lewis Armistead fell at Gettysburg, his cherished 1850 sword was retrieved by Sgt. Michael Specht of the 72nd Pennsylvania Infantry. Specht carried the sword through the rest of the war. He was unable to attend the 1906 reunion of his Philadelphia Brigade and Pickett's division, but sent the sword to be presented to Mrs. George Pickett in a formal ceremony. The sword was later donated to the Museum of the Confederacy in Richmond.[5]

WHAT ABOUT . . . ????

Union brigadier general Alexander S. Asboth was badly wounded in the left cheek and left arm at Marianna, Florida, in September 1864. He survived the war and was appointed U.S. minister to Argentina and Uruguay. His facial wound never fully healed, however, and he died on January 21, 1868, in Buenos Aires, likely due to its effects.[6]

Edward D. Baker is sometimes described as being a Union general when he was killed at the battle of Ball's Bluff on October 21, 1861. Baker, a U.S. senator from Oregon, had indeed been appointed a major general of volunteers a few weeks before his death. But as historian Ezra Warner points out, Baker was required by law to resign from the Senate before he could accept the commission. He had neither accepted nor declined the generalship when he died and was leading his brigade as a colonel.[7]

Baker was riddled by six bullets, either while leading his men in a charge or helping some soldiers push a cannon to the front, according to various accounts. He had been a close friend and former law colleague of President Lincoln, and his death greatly saddened the first family. (The Lincolns' second son, Edward Baker Lincoln, had been named for him but died in 1850 at age three.)

On January 24, 1864, **Union brigadier general Stephen G. Champlin** lay dying, more than a year and a half after a Rebel bullet found him at the battle of Seven Pines. Champlin, thirty-six, was a native New Yorker who had attended Rhinebeck Academy and practiced law in Albany. He had moved to Grand Rapids, Michigan, in 1853, and had been a recorder's court judge and prosecutor. He had been mustered into service as major of the 3rd Michigan in June 1861 and commissioned colonel of the regiment in October. In the Peninsular Campaign, Champlin's regiment belonged to Hiram Berry's brigade of Brig. Gen. Phil Kearny's III Corps division.[8]

On the afternoon of May 31, 1862, Champlin's regiment was ordered into action along the Williamsburg road in the fighting at Seven Pines (also known as Fair Oaks). Sometime after 2 P.M., Champlin suffered "a severe wound in the hip, which prevented him from taking further part in the action," reported Lt. Col. Ambrose Stevens, Champlin's second-in-command. Berry wrote that Champlin's injury was "considered not dangerous, though severe."[9]

Champlin returned to his regiment in time to fight at Second Bull Run, but he had not allowed nearly enough time for his wound to heal. The 3rd Michigan sustained heavy casualties in the campaign and Champlin was among the fallen after the fighting on August 29.

In General Berry's absence due to illness, Col. Orlando Poe commanded the brigade and recognized Champlin in his battle report:

> I would particularly mention Colonel Champlin, of the 3rd Michigan, who was severely wounded at Fair Oaks, but who joined his regiment and led it into the fight on the 29th, although his wounds were far from being healed—indeed, so far that his wounds broke out afresh on the field owing to over-exertion, and he is now completely prostrated.[10]

Kearny described Champlin as "again disabled" in an August 31 action report. Before he could sign the document, Kearny was killed at Chantilly the next day, but the report was filed by Kearny's replacement, Brig. Gen. David B. Birney.[11]

Champlin recovered enough to be placed in charge of the Grand Rapids recruiting office and was promoted brigadier general of volunteers to rank from November 1862. On January 24, 1864, he died from the effects of his wounds, and was buried in the city's Fulton Street Cemetery.

Union major general George L. Hartsuff was seriously wounded in the Third Seminole War and during the Civil War, but lived until 1874 when he finally succumbed to complications from his injuries. Could a Seminole warrior or Confederate take credit for his demise? As a young officer, Hartsuff suffered two severe wounds in a skirmish with the Seminoles near Fort Drane, Florida, in 1855. He survived to serve in the Civil War, but was shot at Antietam. His latest injuries incapacitated him on and off for the rest of the conflict. Hartsuff continued his Army service after the war, retiring in June 1871 due to disabilities from his wounds. He died of pneumonia at his New York City home. An autopsy showed the infection was caused by a scar on his lung from his Florida wound.[12]

One day before the first anniversary of his wounding at Wilson's Creek, **Union brigadier general Joseph B. Plummer** drew his last breath in a Union camp near Corinth, Mississippi. Plummer, forty-five, had recovered sufficiently from his injuries to see action at Cape Girardeau, New Madrid and in action around Corinth before he succumbed on August 9, 1862. His cause of death was described as "Of Wound And Exposure In The Active Field."[13]

Union brigadier general Thomas E. G. Ransom was seriously wounded at Mansfield (also known as Sabine Crossroads), Louisiana, in April 1864, his fourth wound of the war. Less than four months later, Ransom, twenty-nine, was back in action, leading a division and, for a time, the XVI Corps in the Atlanta Campaign. After the city fell, he commanded the XVII Corps pursuit of Rebel forces into Alabama and led the corps on its return into northern Georgia. His partially healed wound, however, combined with illness and campaign rigors, resulted in his death near Rome, Georgia, on October 29, 1864. Ransom was brevetted a major general to rank as of September 1, 1864. Ransom carried on the tradition of sacrifice begun by his father, who was a colonel killed in the Mexican War.[14]

Maj. Gen. O. O. Howard described Ransom as "a young man, so full of promise, so enthusiastic in his country's cause, so untiring in his exertions to thwart the wicked men who have raised their hands against us."[15]

Bvt. Brig. Gen. James S. Morton had been the chief engineer of Union major general Ambrose Burnside's IX Corps for little more than a month when he was killed at Petersburg on June 17, 1864.

Elements of the IX Corps were to be involved in an assault on the Confederate defenses that day, and the division of Brig. Gen. Orlando Willcox would be the sword point. The brigade of Brig. Gen. John Hartranft was Willcox's lead. Willcox was aimed at Rebel breastworks across an open field and Morton, compass in hand, accompanied Hartranft to make sure they were assailing the correct location. With the Union troops waiting to advance from the edge of the field, Morton rode into the sights of a Rebel sniper. A bullet plunged into the left side of his chest, killing him instantly, and exiting the right side of his back.

"Major Morton exposed himself to the unerring shot of one of the enemy's sharpshooters," reported Maj. Nathaniel Michler of the Engineer Corps. "His great desire to excel in his profession, added to an energetic and impulsive nature, had led him on several previous occasions to greatly expose himself." Willcox's attack, meanwhile, went forward and was repelled with heavy casualties. "Among the killed was the gallant Morton," Willcox stated.[16]

Later that day, Burnside sent a dispatch to Maj. Gen. George Meade regarding Morton: "Major Morton was killed in the assault this afternoon leading the advance brigade. Cannot his body be sent home? It is now at my headquarters." Meade responded to Burnside in a 10 P.M. message: "I mourn the loss of the gallant Major Morton, who had attracted my notice by his activity and zeal. His body can be sent in an ambulance to City Point, where it can be forwarded to Philadelphia. . . . I regret the glorious exploits of the Ninth to-day should be dampened by such sad attending events."[17]

Morton was posthumously promoted brevet brigadier general. He was buried at Laurel Hill Cemetery in Philadelphia. Michler offered a fitting epitaph: "He laid down on the battle-field a useful, active, and brave life in the cause of his country, and deeply has the army (especially the corps to which he had been so long and ably attached) been called to grieve his sudden death."[18]

THE REBEL WHO KILLED TWO GENERALS?
Growing up in Bossier Parish, Louisiana, William "Billy" Singleton became a crack rifle shot who could drop a running deer or a wild turkey on the fly. Some Confederates believed, at least in postwar accounts, that Singleton, who combined dead-eye talent with luck of being in the right place at the right time, not only killed Phil Kearny at Chantilly but also John Reynolds at Gettysburg. Even more incredibly, Singleton was credited with capturing Reynolds a year before the general's death.

The unbelievable story of Singleton's supposed exploits was published in the November 1906 issue of *Confederate Veteran* and written by R. J. Hancock, who had been captain of Singleton's Company D, 9th Louisiana Regiment, which fought in Virginia.

Hancock claimed that during the Peninsular Campaign in June 1862, Singleton told his commanding officer that he had never been over a battlefield after a fight and wanted to do so. The officer agreed to his request. Singleton passed through a field strewn with the red-trousered bodies of New York Zouaves. From some bushes, the Rebel was hailed by a Union general who identified himself as Reynolds. The general told Singleton that he had been cut off from his command in the fighting and wanted to surrender for fear that some Confederates might shoot him. Singleton escorted him back to his brigade headquarters as a prisoner of war.

After the battle of Second Bull Run weeks later, Singleton happened upon a piece of light gum oilcloth and packed it to keep him dry in rainy weather. He needed it almost immediately in the combat at Chantilly where a thunderstorm drenched both sides. Wearing the makeshift poncho, Singleton was deployed as a skirmisher and in a narrow field surrounded by woods found himself face-to-face with Phil Kearny. Hancock gave this account: "Evidently he [Kearny] mistook Singleton for a Federal soldier. Singleton saw that it was a Northern officer from the uniform. They both advanced until within a few yards of each other, when Kearney [*sic*] asked in a brusque way: 'To what regiment do you belong?'"[19]

Singleton's answer was to raise his musket, identify himself and tell Kearny that he must surrender or be shot, based on Hancock's account. He continued: "Kearney dropped his head for a moment as if in a deep study, said nothing, and then, wheeling his horse, threw himself upon the horse's neck and started to run. Singleton fired, and Kearney fell dead. Singleton notified the ambulance corps that he had killed a Yankee officer, and went on skirmishing." Singleton was making coffee at a campfire later in the night "when a comrade passing by said that someone had killed a Northern officer without ever touching him. Singleton asked if the officer was a one armed man. The comrade replying in the affirmative, Singleton said that he had shot the officer, and told where the wound could be found. He was correct. The bullet had penetrated within, along the spinal column and lodged at the base of the skull. It may be well to state that Singleton was the only man who fired at Kearney, and it was done before sunset."[20]

Based on Hancock's account, Singleton fought in all of the battles waged by the Army of Northern Virginia, and at Gettysburg on July 1, 1863, he was deployed as a skirmisher in the 9th Louisiana in Brig. Gen. Harry Hays's brigade of Ewell's corps.

> Singleton saw a Federal officer [who] had his field glasses and was evidently watching the Confederates who were coming up in the distance. . . . There was a hedge of evergreen on the side of the pike, and Singleton, taking advantage of it, ran up within easy range of the officer, fired, and killed him. When Singleton went up to him, he found it was Reynolds, the very man he had captured at Cold Harbor the year before. Singleton expressed himself afterwards on several occasions that it was with sincere regret that it was Reynolds and not some other Northern officer who had been killed.

The fact that Ewell's corps was not in position to attack until hours after Reynolds's death and that Ewell was well north of Gettysburg, some distance from where the general fell, are fatal blows to Singleton's saga. But the passing years and dreams of lost glory didn't diminish this tall tale which endured into the next century. Singleton survived the war and died near Monroe, Louisiana, about 1902, Hancock stated, "no man to toast of anything he ever did."[21]

THE UNION BREVET BRIGADIERS

These officers were brevetted as brigadier generals during the war but had not been promoted to full rank at the time of their deaths.

Col. Thornton F. Brodhead of the 1st Michigan Cavalry was mortally wounded during the Second Bull Run Campaign. Brodhead's injuries occurred on August 30, 1862, during hand-to-hand combat with Confederate lieutenant Lewis Harman of the 12th Virginia Cavalry. He was captured and died on September 2.

Col. A. Van Horn Ellis of the 124th New York Volunteers was shot in the head and killed on July 2, 1863, at Gettysburg. Ellis "was one of those dashing and chivalrous spirits that we frequently read of, but seldom encounter in real life," wrote his commander, Brig. Gen. J. H. Ward. "He fell while gallantly leading his men in a charge."[22]

Col. George H. Ward of the 15th Massachusetts Volunteers was fatally wounded at Gettysburg on July 2, 1863, while vainly trying to repel a Confederate assault along the Emmitsburg Pike.

Col. Paul Joseph Revere of the 20th Massachusetts Volunteers was a grandson of the legendary patriot Paul Revere of the American Revolution. On July 2, 1863, the colonel, who had been ill, was lying in his tent behind Cemetery Hill, his command being held in reserve. Confederate artillery bombarded the position, however, and a shell fragment hit Revere in the chest. He died on July 5. Revere's brother, Edward, was an assistant surgeon in the 20th and had been killed at Antietam.

Col. Louis R. Francine of the 7th New Jersey Volunteers was mortally wounded at Gettysburg on the afternoon of July 2, 1863 in fighting near the Peach Orchard. He died on July 16.

Col. Lewis Benedict of the 162nd New York Volunteers was killed April 9, 1864, while leading his brigade at Pleasant Hill, Louisiana, in the Red River Campaign. Posted on the Union left, Benedict was wounded early in the fight, but refused to leave the field. Late in the battle, he was hit again and killed. Despite his first wound, Benedict "bore up until the fatal shot deprived him of life," related Maj. Gen. Nathaniel Banks, the Union expedition's commander.[23]

In Benedict's brigade was **Lt. Col. William N. Green** of the 173rd New York Volunteers who was severely wounded in the arm at Pleasant Hill the same day. Green refused to have the limb amputated and in the days that followed seemed to improve somewhat before gangrene set in. The arm eventually was removed, but it was too late to save Green, who died on May 14.

Maj. Henry H. Giesy of the 46th Ohio Volunteers was killed May 28, 1864, in fighting at Dallas, Georgia, near Atlanta. Giesy was a "brave and efficient" officer who fell "during the heat of the engagement, while at the front encouraging" his men, wrote his brigade commander, Col. Charles Walcutt.[24]

Col. John McConihe of the 169th New York Volunteers was killed on June 1, 1864, at Cold Harbor, Virginia. McConihe was leading his command in an assault when he was shot in or near the heart and died shortly afterward.

Col. Arthur H. Dutton of the 21st Connecticut Volunteers was mortally wounded at Bermuda Hundred, Virginia, on May 26, 1864, while on his brigade's skirmish line. He died in Baltimore on June 5. Dutton was an 1861 West Point graduate and a classmate of Union generals George Custer and Judson Kilpatrick. "Bold and chivalrous, with a nice sense of honor, a judgment quick and decisive, an unwavering zeal in his chosen profession, he was in every respect a thorough soldier," wrote Maj. Hiram Crosby of the 21st. "By his companions in arms he will never be forgotten, and to them his last resting place will be as a shrine commemorating the friendships which neither the rude shock of war nor lapse of time can blight or destroy."[25]

Col. Thomas W. Humphrey of the 95th Illinois Volunteers was mortally wounded at Brices Cross Roads (also known as the battle of Guntown), Mississippi, on June 10, 1864.

Col. William H. Sackett of the 9th New York Cavalry was mortally wounded at Trevilian Station, Virginia, on June 11, 1864. Captured, he died three days later in a Confederate hospital.

Col. George L. Prescott of the 32nd Massachusetts was mortally wounded on June 18, 1864, near Petersburg. Prescott was leading his men over an open plain in an assault along the Norfolk & Petersburg Railroad when he fell. He died the next day.

Col. William Blaisdell of the 11th Massachusetts Volunteers, was killed June 23, 1864, near Petersburg, Virginia. He was supervising his brigade on the picket line when he was fatally wounded.

Col. George A. Cobham Jr. of the 111th Pennsylvania Volunteers was killed July 20, 1864, at Atlanta. Described as a "model gentleman and commander," Cobham had seen action at Gettysburg, Lookout Mountain, Missionary Ridge, and Resaca before his death in the fighting along Peachtree Creek.[26]

Col. James A. Mulligan of the 23rd Illinois Volunteers was wounded three times and captured at Kernstown, Virginia, on July 24, 1864. He died two days later.

Col. Griffin A. Stedman of the 11th Connecticut Volunteers was mortally wounded by a canister shot near Petersburg on August 5, 1864. His appointment to the brevet of brigadier general was being processed when he died the next morning. Since he was a bachelor, the paperwork was sent to his grieving mother in New Haven, Connecticut.

Lt. Col. George E. Elstner of the 50th Ohio Volunteers was killed August 8, 1864, while leading a charge on Rebel rifle pits near Atlanta.

Maj. Henry Lyman Patten of the 20th Massachusetts Volunteers was was mortally wounded at Deep Bottom, Virginia, on August 17, 1864, and died on September 10, 1864.

Col. Alexander Gardiner of the 14th New Hampshire Volunteers, lost a leg at Winchester, Virginia, on September 19, 1864, and died on Oct. 7.

Lt. Col. Willoughby Babcock of the 75th New York Volunteers, mortally wounded by a grapeshot to the leg at Winchester, Virginia, on September 19, 1864. The leg was amputated, but he died on October 6.

Lt. Col. Frank H. Peck of the 12th Connecticut Volunteers died Sept. 30, 1864, at Chapin's Farm, Virginia. Peck was forming his line to attack when he was fatally wounded by a shell fragment. He "received his death wound in the saddle," reported Capt. S. E. Clark of the 12th. "His death is a severe and irreparable loss to the regiment." Peck's commander, Brig. Gen. James McMillan, added that Peck was "a gallant officer and a polished gentleman. . . . I deeply sympathize with his many friends in their distress for his loss."[27]

Col. George D. Wells of the 34th Massachusetts Volunteers was killed October 13, 1864, during reconnaissance against enemy positions at Fisher's Hill in the Shenandoah Valley. Wells died within the hour, another Union officer writing of him, "A more gallant, accomplished, and unflinching soldier would be hard to find."[28]

Col. J. Howard Kitching of the 6th New York Volunteer Artillery was mortally wounded at Cedar Creek on October 19, 1864. Kitching and Brig. Gen. James Ricketts were among wounded who arrived at Martinsburg, Virginia, two days later. Union brigadier general W. H. Seward reported that "both appear to be doing well." Kitching, however, died on January 10, 1865, while Ricketts' chest wound disabled him for the rest of his life.[29]

Col. Sylvester G. Hill of the 35th Iowa Volunteers was killed December 15, 1864, while leading his brigade in an assault at Nashville. Hill had just reached a Rebel earthwork when a musket ball struck him in the forehead, killing him almost immediately. Hill's superior, Maj. Gen. Andrew J. Smith commander of the Union XVI Corps, wrote of his loss: "Long with the command, he has endeared himself to every member of it; brave and courteous, the service has lost a gallant officer and society a gentleman by his untimely death."[30]

Col. Frederick Winthrop of the 5th New York Veteran Volunteers was killed April 1, 1865, in a charge at Five Forks near Petersburg. "His countrymen have lost no one of their soldiers who more deserves a lasting place in their memory," wrote Maj. Gen. G. K. Warren of the V Corps.

Brig. Gen. R. B. Ayres, Winthrop's division commander, added that Winthrop "in the moment of triumph freely laid down his life for his country. His dying thoughts were for his comrades, and his last anxious inquiries were concerning the fate of the day."[31]

Col. George W. Gowan of the 48th Pennsylvania Volunteers died on April 2, 1865, while leading his command against Fort Mahone in the Petersburg defenses. "It pains me to announce . . . the death of Colonel Gowan," Maj. Gen. John G. Parke of the IX Corps, Gowan's commander, wrote a few hours after his death. "He was instantly killed while gallantly leading his regiment in a charge upon the enemy's works this A.M."[32]

Col. Theodore Read, chief of staff to Maj. Gen. E. O. C. Ord, was killed April 6, 1865, at High Bridge, Virginia. Read was shot during a cavalry fight in which he was personally dueling with Confederate brigadier general James Dearing and other Rebel cavalrymen. Dearing was also killed.

Col. Francis Washburn of the 4th Massachusetts Cavalry was mortally wounded at High Bridge in the same battle. Washburn also engaged in a personal fight with Dearing, a West Point comrade, before Washburn was shot in the face by another Confederate. Unhorsed, he was sabered across the head by another Rebel trooper. Washburn lingered until April 22, 1865.

APPENDIX I:
THE GALLANT DEAD GENERALS

KEY:

U	=	Union
C	=	Confederate
MW	=	Mortally Wounded

Name	Allegiance	Rank	Battle/Date	Circumstances
Adams, John	C	Brigadier General	Franklin, 11/30/64	Killed in Hood's assault
Anderson, George B.	C	Brigadier General	Antietam, 9/17/62	Foot wound; died on 10/16
Armistead, Lewis A.	C	Brigadier General	Gettysburg, 7/3/63	MW in great charge; died on 7/5
Ashby, Turner	C	Brigadier General	Harrisonburg, 6/6/62	Shot in the side during rearguard action
Barksdale, William	C	Brigadier General	Gettysburg, 7/2/63	Shot and captured; died on 7/3
Bayard, George D.	U	Brigadier General	Fredericksburg, 12/13/62	MW in leg by artillery round
Bee, Barnard E.	C	Brigadier General	First Bull Run, 7/21/61	MW in stomach during a charge
Berry, Hiram G.	U	Major General	Chancellorsville, 5/3/63	Killed by a sharpshooter
Benton, Samuel	C	Brigadier General	Atlanta, 7/22/64	Chest and foot wounds; died on 7/28
Bidwell, Daniel D.	U	Brigadier General	Cedar Creek, 10/19/64	MW in chest and shoulder by a shell

Name	Allegiance	Rank	Battle/Date	Circumstances
Bohlen, Henry	U	Brigadier General	Freeman's Ford, 8/22/62	Bullet to the head during retreat
Branch, Lawrence O.	C	Brigadier General	Antietam, 9/17/62	Killed by a sharpshooter
Burnham, Hiram	U	Brigadier General	Ft. Harrison, 9/29/64	Abdomen wound in assault
Carter, John C.	C	Brigadier General	Franklin, 11/30/64	MW in attack; died on 12/10
Chambliss, John R. Jr.	C	Brigadier General	2nd Deep Bottom, 8/16/64	Shot in the body during cavalry action
Chapin, Edward P.	U	Brigadier General	Port Hudson, 5/27/63	Shot in the head
Cleburne, Patrick R.	C	Major General	Franklin, 11/30/64	Fell in Hood's assault
Cobb, Thomas R. R.	C	Brigadier General	Fredericksburg, 12/13/62	MW in leg; bled to death
Daniel, Junius	C	Brigadier General	Spotsylvania, 5/12/64	MW in the stomach; died the next day
Dearing, James	C	Brigadier General	High Bridge, 4/6/65	MW in the chest, died on 4/23
Deshler, James	C	Brigadier General	Chickamauga, 9/20/63	Killed by a shell through the chest
Doles, George P.	C	Brigadier General	Bethesda Church, 6/2/64	Sniper shot in the chest
Dunovant, John	C	Brigadier General	McDowell's Farm, 10/1/64	Gunshot to the chest
Farnsworth, Elon J.	U	Brigadier General	Gettysburg, 7/3/63	Death in reckless charge
Garland, Samuel Jr.	C	Brigadier General	South Mountain, 9/14/62	Musket round in the back while directing his men
Garnett, Richard B.	C	Brigadier General	Gettysburg, 7/3/63	Killed in great charge; body never identified
Garnett, Robert S.	C	Brigadier General	Corrick's Ford, 7/13/61	Shot in the body; first Rebel general to die
Garrott, Isham W.	C	Brigadier General	Vicksburg, 6/17/63	Killed by a bullet to the chest while in the trenches

Name	Allegiance	Rank	Battle/Date	Circumstances
Girardey, V. J. B.	C	Brigadier General	Second Deep Bottom, 8/16/64	Gunshot to the head
Gist, States Rights	C	Brigadier General	Franklin, 11/30/64	Shot in chest during Hood's assault
Gladden, Adley H.	C	Brigadier General	Shiloh, 4/6/62	MW by cannonball to the arm; died on 4/12
Godwin, Archibald C.	C	Brigadier General	Winchester, 9/19/64	Head wounds from exploding shell
Gordon, James B.	C	Brigadier General	Meadow Bridge, 5/12/64	MW in arm; died on 4/18
Gracie, Archibald Jr.	C	Brigadier General	Petersburg, 12/2/64	Neck and shoulder injuries from shell blast
Granbury, Hiram B.	C	Brigadier General	Franklin, 11/30/64	Musket shot to the face in Hood's assault
Green, Martin E.	C	Brigadier General	Vicksburg, 6/27/63	Shot by a sharpshooter
Green, Thomas	C	Brigadier General	Blair's Landing, 4/12/64	Shell wound to the head
Gregg, John	C	Brigadier General	Richmond, 10/7/64	Musket ball to the upper body
Gregg, Maxcy	C	Brigadier General	Fredericksburg, 12/13/62	Shot in the back
Griffith, Richard	C	Brigadier General	Savage Station, 6/29/62	MW by shell fragment to the thigh
Hackleman, Pleasant A.	U	Brigadier General	Corinth, 10/3/62	MW in the neck
Hanson, Roger W.	C	Brigadier General	Stones River, 1/2/63	MW in leg by a shell fragment
Harker, Charles G.	U	Brigadier General	Kennesaw Mt., 6/27/64	MW in the arm and chest
Hatton, Robert H.	C	Brigadier General	Fair Oaks Station, 5/31/62	Shot from his horse during assault
Hays, Alexander	U	Brigadier General	Wilderness, 5/5/64	Musket ball to the head
Helm, Benjamin H.	C	Brigadier General	Chickamauga, 9/20/63	MW in the body

Name	Allegiance	Rank	Battle/Date	Circumstances
Hill, Ambrose P.	C	Lieutenant General	Petersburg, 4/2/65	Musket round to the chest
Jackson, Conrad F.	U	Brigadier General	Fredericksburg, 12/13/62	Gunshot to the head
Jackson, James S.	U	Brigadier General	Perryville, 10/8/62	Two musket rounds in the chest
Jackson, Thomas J.	C	Lieutenant General	Chancellorsville, 5/2/63	Died of complications from left arm wounds and pneumonia
Jenkins, Albert G.	C	Brigadier General	Cloyd's Mt., 5/9/64	MW in the arm
Jenkins, Micah	C	Brigadier General	Wilderness, 5/6/64	MW in the head; friendly fire
Johnston, Albert S.	C	General	Shiloh, 4/6/62	MW in the leg; bled to death
Jones, John M.	C	Brigadier General	Wilderness, 5/5/64	Killed in opening of the battle
Jones, William E.	C	Brigadier General	Piedmont, 6/5/64	Shot in the head
Kearny, Philip	U	Major General	Chantilly, 9/1/62	Shot in the body
Kelly, John H.	C	Brigadier General	Franklin, 9/2/64	MW in the chest
Kirby, Edmund	U	Brigadier General	Chancellorsville, 5/3/63	MW by shell fragment to the leg
Kirk, Edward N.	U	Brigadier General	Stones River, 12/31/62	MW in the hip
Little, Lewis H.	C	Brigadier General	Iuka, 9/19/62	Musket round to the forehead
Lowell, Charles R.	U	Brigadier General	Cedar Creek, 10/19/64	MW in the body
Lyon, Nathaniel	U	Brigadier General	Wilson's Creek, 8/10/61	MW in the chest
Lytle, William H.	U	Brigadier General	Chickamauga, 9/20/63	Hit simultaneously by three bullets
McCook, Daniel Jr.	U	Brigadier General	Kennesaw Mt., 6/27/64	MW in charge
McCook, Robert L.	U	Brigadier General	Decherd, TN, 8/5/62	MW in stomach

Name	Allegiance	Rank	Battle/Date	Circumstances
McCulloch, Ben	C	Brigadier General	Pea Ridge, 3/7/62	Gunshot to the chest
McIntosh, James M.	C	Brigadier General	Pea Ridge, 3/7/62	Wounded in the body
McPherson, James B.	U	Major General	Atlanta, 7/22/64	Musket wound to the body
Mansfield, J. K. F.	U	Brigadier General	Antietam, 9/17/62	MW in the chest
Morgan, John H.	C	Brigadier General	Greeneville, Tennessee, 9/4/64	Shot in chest during ambush
Mouton, J. J. A. A.	C	Brigadier General	Mansfield, 4/8/64	Shot in the body while leading a charge
Paxton, Elisha F.	C	Brigadier General	Chancellorsville, 5/3/63	Gunshot to the chest
Pegram, John	C	Brigadier General	Hatcher's Run, 2/6/65	Shot near the heart
Pender, William D.	C	Major General	Gettysburg, 7/2/63	MW in the leg
Perrin, Abner M.	C	Brigadier General	Spotsylvania, 5/12/64	Seven bullets to the body
Pettigrew, James J.	C	Brigadier General	Falling Waters, 7/14/63	MW by pistol shot to the abdomen
Polk, Leonidas	C	Lieutenant General	Pine Mountain, 6/14/64	Hit by artillery round
Posey, Carnot	C	Brigadier General	Bristoe Station, 10/14/63	Complications from leg wound
Rains, James E.	C	Brigadier General	Stones River, 12/31/62	Bullet to the chest
Ramseur, Stephen D.	C	Major General	Cedar Creek, 10/19/64	MW in the lungs
Randal, Horace	C	Brigadier General	Jenkins' Ferry, 4/30/64	MW in a charge
Reno, Jesse L.	U	Major General	South Mountain, 9/14/62	Shot in the body
Reynolds, John F.	U	Major General	Gettysburg, 7/1/63	Bullet to the head or neck
Rice, James C.	U	Brigadier General	Spotsylvania, 5/10/64	MW in the leg
Rice, Samuel A.	U	Brigadier General	Jenkins' Ferry, 4/30/64	Ankle wound; died on 7/6

Name	Allegiance	Rank	Battle/Date	Circumstances
Richardson, Israel B.	U	Major General	Antietam, 9/17/62	MW by a cannon; died on 11/3
Rodes, Robert E.	C	Major General	Winchester, 9/19/64	Shell fragment to the head
Rodman, Isaac P.	U	Brigadier General	Antietam, 9/17/62	Bullet to the chest
Russell, David A.	U	Brigadier General	Winchester, 9/19/64	Shell fragment to the chest
Sanders, John C. C.	C	Brigadier General	Weldon Railroad 8/24/64	MW in both thighs
Sanders, William P.	U	Brigadier General	Knoxville, 11/18/63	MW in a holding action
Scurry, William R.	C	Brigadier General	Jenkins' Ferry, 4/30/64	Bled to death on the field
Sedgwick, John	U	Major General	Spotsylvania, 5/9/64	Musket shot to the face
Semmes, Paul J.	C	Brigadier General	Gettysburg, 7/2/63	MW in the thigh
Sill, Joshua W.	U	Brigadier General	Stones River, 12/31/62	Gunshot to the face
Slack, William Y.	C	Brigadier General	Pea Ridge, 3/7/62	MW in the thigh
Smith, Preston	C	Brigadier General	Chickamauga, 9/19/63	MW in the chest
Smyth, Thomas A.	U	Major General	Farmville, 4/7/65	Shot in the face
Stafford, Leroy A.	C	Brigadier General	Wilderness, 5/5/64	MW in the spine
Starke, William E.	C	Brigadier General	Antietam, 9/17/62	Three gunshots to the body
Stevens, Clement H.	C	Brigadier General	Atlanta, 7/20/64	MW in the head
Stevens, Isaac I.	U	Major General	Chantilly, 9/1/62	Shot in the temple
Stevenson, Thomas G.	U	Brigadier General	Ny River, 5/10/64	Killed by a sharpshooter
Strahl, Otho F.	C	Brigadier General	Franklin, 11/30/64	MW in the head
Strong, George C.	U	Brigadier General	Fort Wagner, 7/18/63	MW in the thigh
Stuart, J. E. B.	C	Major General	Yellow Tavern, 5/11/64	MW by pistol shot to the abdomen

Name	Allegiance	Rank	Battle/Date	Circumstances
Taylor, George W.	U	Brigadier General	Manassas Junction 8/27/62	MW in the leg
Terrill, James B.	C	Brigadier General	Bethesda Church, 5/30/64	Body buried by Union troops
Terrill, William R.	U	Brigadier General	Perryville, 10/8/62	MW in side by a shell fragment
Tilghman, Lloyd	C	Brigadier General	Champion Hill, 5/16/63	Shrapnel in the chest
Tracy, Edward D.	C	Brigadier General	Port Gibson, 5/1/63	Bullet to the chest
Tyler, Robert C.	C	Brigadier General	West Point, 4/16/65	Killed by a sharpshooter
Vincent, Strong	U	Brigadier General	Gettysburg, 7/2/63	MW in the leg
Wadsworth, James S.	U	Brigadier General	Wilderness, 5/6/64	MW in the head
Walker, W. H. T.	C	Major General	Atlanta, 7/22/64	Shot in the chest
Wallace, William H. L.	U	Brigadier General	Shiloh, 4/6/62	MW in the head
Weed, Stephen H.	U	Brigadier General	Gettysburg, 7/2/63	MW in the chest and arm
Whipple, Amiel W.	U	Major General	Chancellorsville, 5/4/63	Bullet to the stomach
Whiting, W. H. C.	C	Major General	Fort Fisher, 1/15/65	Two leg wounds and imprisonment killed him
Williams, Thomas	U	Brigadier General	Baton Rouge, 8/5/62	Shot in the chest
Winder, Charles S.	C	Brigadier General	Cedar Mountain, 8/9/62	MW by a cannon shell
Zook, Samuel K.	U	Brigadier General	Gettysburg, 7/2/63	MW in the abdomen
Zollicoffer, Felix K.	C	Brigadier General	Mill Springs, 1/19/62	Killed by volley fire

APPENDIX II:
WARTIME DEATHS FROM OTHER CAUSES

Confederate brigadier general James J. Archer died of natural causes in Richmond on October 24, 1864. His already fragile health had taken a fatal turn during a year of Union imprisonment after his capture and wounding on Gettysburg's first day. Exchanged in the summer of 1864, he returned to active duty command for a short time before his demise at age forty-six.

Confederate brigadier general William E. Baldwin died on February 19, 1864, in a horse-riding mishap near Dog River Factory, Alabama. Baldwin, thirty-six, had twice endured capture by the Federals, and was exchanged both times. A broken stirrup resulted in a fatal fall from his mount.

Confederate brigadier general John S. Bowen, thirty-two, was among the Rebel garrison surrendered when Vicksburg fell. Weakened by dysentery from which he had suffered during the siege, he died near Raymond, Mississippi, on July 13 after being paroled.

Confederate brigadier general Philip St. George Cocke, fifty-two, led a brigade at First Bull Run but his failing health forced him back to his home in Powhatan County, Virginia. Despondent over his illnesses and not being able to serve, he committed suicide on December 26, 1861. Family members found him in the yard, a temple wound inflicted with a pistol found next to his body.

Union brigadier general Michael Corcoran, thirty-six, was killed on December 22, 1863, near Fairfax, Virginia, when his horse fell. Corcoran was riding with Brig. Gen. Thomas Meagher at the time.

Confederate major general Daniel S. Donelson, sixty-one, was promoted from brigadier on April 22, 1863, but there was a slight problem. The Richmond government was unaware that Donelson, a nephew of President Andrew Jackson, had died of natural causes five days earlier in Tennessee.

Confederate brigadier general John B. Grayson was a veteran of the Mexican and Seminole wars with more than thirty years in the U.S. Army before he sided with the South. Commanding Rebel forces in middle and eastern Florida, health problems killed him on October 21, 1861, three days after his fifty-fifth birthday.

Confederate brigadier general Joseph L. Hogg, fifty-five, contracted dysentery shortly after arriving with his Texans at Corinth, Mississippi, after the battle of Shiloh. He died on May 16, 1862.

Union colonel Joshua B. Howell, who was posthumously promoted to brigadier general, died in a horse accident. Howell led a X Corps brigade. On September 12, 1864, the day after his fifty-eighth birthday, he was severely injured when he and his mount fell. Howell died two days later.

Confederate major general David R. "Neighbor" Jones distinguished himself in the campaigns of Second Bull Run and Antietam, but could not overcome heart problems. He was thirty-seven when he died in Richmond on January 20, 1863.

Union brigadier general Ormsby M. Mitchel was better known for being an American astronomy pioneer than for his exploits as a Union officer. He was instrumental in establishing several prominent observatories and also was a classmate of Robert E. Lee in the West Point class of 1829. Nicknamed "Old Stars" due to his passion, Mitchel's war career was less than shining. Serving on the South Carolina coast, he was seized by yellow fever and died at Beaufort on October 30, 1862, at age fifty-three.

Confederate brigadier general Allison Nelson, forty, had been in command of an infantry division in the Trans-Mississippi Department for ten days when he succumbed to a fever on October 7, 1862. Nelson's colorful career included serving as mayor of Atlanta and later as a legislator in Georgia and Texas, leading Cuban freedom fighters, and battling against the frontier Indians as well as in the Kansas border bloodshed.

Union major general William Nelson, thirty-eight, was shot and killed by Brig. Gen. Jefferson C. Davis in the lobby of the Galt House hotel in Louisville, Kentucky, on September 29, 1862. Davis felt that Nelson had unfairly reprimanded him on a previous occasion. In the hotel confrontation, the brigadier crumpled a card and hurled it into Nelson's face. Nelson then struck Davis, who left, but returned shortly with a revolver. Davis then shot Nelson, the latter dying within minutes. Davis was arrested, but restored to command in a few days and was never brought to trial for the slaying.

Union brigadier general Francis E. Patterson, forty-one, was the son of Pennsylvania Maj. Gen. Robert Patterson. The brigadier died on November 22, 1862, from a pistol wound he sustained while in his tent in bivouac near Fairfax, Virginia. The shooting was ruled accidental.

Union major general Charles F. Smith was a stalwart warrior whose Civil War accomplishments were cut short by his death in a freak accident. Smith shone while leading a division at Fort Donelson's capture in February 1862. A few weeks later, however, he scraped his shin while boarding a rowboat. The wound became infected and, aggravated by dysentery, caused his death on April 25, 1862, the day after his fifty-fifth birthday.

Confederate brigadier general William D. Smith's fame and career were on the rise in the high command at Charleston, South Carolina, in late summer 1862, including a stellar performance at the June battle of Secessionville. The thirty-seven-year-old Georgian's life was cut short, however, by yellow fever on October 4, 1862.

Confederate major general David E. Twiggs, when he died at age seventy-two, had fought in the War of 1812 and the Mexican War in more than four decades of service in the U.S. Army before joining the Confederacy. His age and declining health, however, prevented him from active duty in the Southern armies and he died on July 15, 1862.

Confederate major general Earl Van Dorn was murdered on May 7, 1863, at his headquarters in Spring Hill, Tennessee. Van Dorn, forty-two, sustained a pistol wound to the back of the head, his assailant being a retired physician named George Peters who lived in the vicinity. Jealousy over the general's supposed relations with Peters's wife, Jessie, is the most commonly stated motive, but some Confederate accounts at the time claimed that Peters was inspired by pro-Union sympathies. Peters was never brought to trial.

Confederate brigadier general John B. Villepigue, thirty-two, had seen combat in Florida, Alabama, Tennessee, and Mississippi, but succumbed to a fever apparently related to pneumonia at Port Hudson, Louisiana, on November 9, 1862.

Confederate brigadier general Lucius M. Walker was mortally wounded in a duel with fellow brigadier John S. Marmaduke. The feud stemmed from Marmaduke questioning Walker's courage and combat performance at the Arkansas battles of Helena and Reed's Bridge in the summer of 1863. The sunrise duel at Little Rock on September 6, 1863, resulted in Walker, thirty-three, being hit by a revolver round. He died the next night. Marmaduke never faced charges.

Confederate major general John A. Wharton was killed in an April 6, 1865, dispute with Col. George W. Baylor of the 2nd Texas Cavalry. The confrontation occurred at a Houston hotel where the officers' disagreement over "military matters" escalated. Baylor later claimed that Wharton, thirty-six, slapped his face and called him a liar. Baylor then shot Wharton, fatally wounding him beneath the ribs. Wharton was found to be unarmed.

Confederate brigadier general Claudius C. Wilson, thirty-two, died of a fever at Ringgold, Georgia, on November 27, 1863. His promotion to brigadier was posthumously confirmed by the Confederate Senate the following February.

Confederate brigadier general John H. Winder dropped dead of an apparent heart attack on February 7, 1865, two weeks shy of his sixty-fifth birthday. Winder, commissary general of prisoners east of the Mississippi River, was inspecting the prison stockade at Florence, South Carolina, when he was stricken.

NOTES

CHAPTER 1

1. *New York Times* (hereafter cited as *NYT*), July 16, 1861.
2. Ibid.
3. Ezra J. Warner, *Generals in Gray: Lives of the Confederate Commanders* (Baton Rouge: Louisiana State University Press, 1959), 100.
4. Jack Waugh, "Long Distance Victory," *Civil War Times Illustrated* (hereafter cited as *CWTI*) 22, no. 7 (November 1983): 14.
5. Ibid.
6. Warner, *Generals in Gray*, 374–75. Warner points out that while most accounts of the battle refer to the location as "Carrick's," the ford was named after the family of William Corrick who lived in the area.
7. Clement A. Evans, ed., *Confederate Military History* (Atlanta: Confederate Publishing Company, 1899), 3:55.
8. Douglas Southall Freeman, *Lee's Lieutenants: A Study in Command*, abridged by Stephen W. Sears (New York: Simon & Shuster, 2001), 65.
9. U.S. War Department, *The War of the Rebellion: A Compilation of the Official Records of the Union and Confederate Armies* (Washington, DC: Government Printing Office, 1880–1901) (hereafter cited as *OR*), pt. 1, 287.
10. Dr. Henry Price, "Rich Mountain in 1861—An Account of That Memorable Campaign and How General Garnett Was Killed," *Southern Historical Society Papers* (hereafter cited as *SHSP*) 27 (1899): 41.
11. *OR*, pt. 1, 204.
12. Ibid., pt. 1, 251.
13. *NYT*, July 16, 1861.
14. Warner, *Generals in Gray*, 375.
15. Evans, ed., *Confederate Military History*, 2:21.
16. Clarence C. Buel and Robert V. Johnson, *Battles and Leaders of the Civil War: Being for the Most Part Contributions by Union and Confederate Authors* (New York: Century Co., 1887), 1:232.
17. *Charleston Mercury*, July 25, 1861.
18. D. B. Conrad, "History of the First Battle of Manassas and the Organization of the Stonewall Brigade," *SHSP* 19 (1891): 89.

19. Henry Kyd Douglas, *I Rode With Stonewall* (Chapel Hill, N.C.: University of North Carolina Press, 1940), 21.

20. Conrad, "First Battle of Manassas," 90.

21. *OR*, pt. 1, 481.

22. William M. Robins, "The Sobriquet 'Stonewall'—How It Was Acquired," *SHSP* 19 (1891): 166.

23. Thomas L. Preston, "General Hill's Article on Stonewall Jackson," *The Century* 48, no. 1 (May 1894): 155–56.

24. Ibid.

25. William C. Davis, *Battle at Bull Run: A History of the First Major Campaign of the Civil War* (Baton Rouge: Louisiana State University Press, 1977), 198.

26. Douglas, *I Rode with Stonewall*, 21.

27. Buel and Johnson, *Battles and Leaders,* 1:210; Mary Chesnut, *A Diary From Dixie* (Cambridge, Mass.: Harvard University Press, 1980), 89; *Charleston Mercury*, July 25, 1861; and D. H. Hill, "The Real Stonewall Jackson," *The Century* 47, no. 4 (February 1894): 623. Years after the war, Jackson's brother-in-law, Gen. Daniel Harvey Hill, claimed that Bee's "stone wall" comment was nothing more than "a very pretty story" without truth. "Not only was the tale a sheer fabrication, but the name was the least suited to Jackson, who was ever in motion, swooping like an eagle on his prey," Hill wrote. "But the name spread like wild-fire, and has reached the uttermost limits of the globe." Hill was not present at Bull Run, and the number of witnesses who claimed to have heard Bee's remark seem to invalidate his claim.

28. Jefferson Davis, *The Rise and Fall of the Confederate Government* (New York: D. Appleton and Company, 1881), 1:357.

29. Buel and Johnson, *Battles and Leaders*, 1:237.

30. Douglas Southall Freeman, *Lee's Lieutenants: A Study in Command* (New York: Charles Scribner's Sons, 1942), 1:733–34.

31. *OR*, pt. 1, 499.

32. Jefferson Davis, *Rise and Fall*, 1:356–57.

33. Ezra J. Warner, *Generals in Blue: Lives of the Union Commanders* (Baton Rouge: Louisiana State University Press, 1964), 286.

34. *New York Herald* (hereafter cited as *NYH*), July 8, 1861.

35. Ibid., August 19, 1861.

36. Buel and Johnson, *Battles and Leaders*, 1:295.

37. Albert Castel, *General Sterling Price and the Civil War in the West* (Baton Rouge: Louisiana State University Press, 1968), 45.

38. *OR*, pt. 1, 61–62.

39. Ibid., pt. 1, 74.

40. Ibid., pt. 1, 77.

41. *NYH*, August 19, 1861

42. Buel and Johnson, *Battles and Leaders*, 1:295.

43. *NYH*, August 15, 1861; *OR*, pt. 1, 62.

44. Buel and Johnson, *Battles and Leaders*, 1:295; *OR*, pt. 1, 83.

45. *Confederate Veteran* 7: 169.

46. *Confederate Veteran* 19: 284–85.

47. *NYH*, August 19, 1861.

48. *Confederate Veteran* 19: 9; *Confederate Veteran* 17: 502.

49. Buel and Johnson, *Battles and Leaders*, 1:303.

50. *NYT*, August 15, 1861; *NYH*, August 15, 1861.

51. *OR*, pt. 1, 69, 92.

52. Ibid., pt. 1, 67, 93.

CHAPTER 2

1. Warner, *Generals in Gray*, 349–50.

2. *OR*, pt. 1, 107.

3. J. H. Battle, W. H. Perrin, and G. C. Kniffin, *Kentucky: A History of the State* (Louisville, Ky.: F. A. Battey, 1885), 393.

4. Ibid.

5. Evans, ed., *Confederate Military History*, 8:348.

6. *Louisville Daily Courier*, March 1, 1862.

7. *Confederate Veteran* 18: 163.

8. *OR*, pt. 1, 86.

9. *Confederate Veteran* 18: 574.

10. *OR*, pt. 1, 104–108.

11. Evans, ed., *Confederate Military History*, 8:348.

12. *Confederate Veteran* 18: 163.

13. Warner, *Generals in Gray*, 200–201.

14. Ibid., 202–3.

15. *Confederate Veteran* 13: 551.

16. *Confederate Veteran* 14: 61–62.

17. *OR*, pt. 1, 218.

18. *Confederate Veteran* 13: 551.

19. *OR*, pt. 1, 218.

20. *Confederate Veteran* 11: 552.

21. *Confederate Veteran* 14: 61–62.

22. *Confederate Veteran* 12: 18. From a January 1904 account of a speech given by Joseph M. Hill at the dedication of a Confederate monument in Fort Smith.

23. *OR*, pt. 1, 285.

24. Ibid.

25. Ibid.

26. Dabney H. Maury, "Recollections of the Elkhorn Campaign," *SHSP* 2 (1896): 189.

27. *Confederate Veteran* 19: 10.

28. *OR*, pt. 1, 199.

29. Warner, *Generals in Gray*, 278.

30. *Confederate Veteran* 14, 62.

31. *OR*, pt. 1, 285.

32. Buel and Johnson, *Battles and Leaders*, 1:277.

33. Warner, *Generals in Gray*, 278; *OR*, pt. 1, 305.

34. *Confederate Veteran* 14: 497.

CHAPTER 3

1. *Confederate Veteran* 9: 21.

2. Warner, *Generals in Gray*, 159–60.

3. Ibid.

4. *OR*, pt. 1, 538.

5. Ibid., pt. 1, 540.

6. Ibid., pt. 1, 389.

7. Buel and Johnson, *Battles and Leaders*, 1:587.

8. *Confederate Veteran* 5: 610.

9. *Confederate Veteran* 5: 613.

10. William Preston Johnston, "Albert Sidney Johnston and the Shiloh Campaign," *The Century* 29, no. 4 (February 1885): 626.

11. Ibid.

12. Ibid., 626–27.

13. Ibid.

14. *OR*, pt. 1, 404–5.

15. *Confederate Veteran* 5: 611.

16. Johnston, "Albert Sidney Johnston," 626–27.

17. *Confederate Veteran* 5: 611.
18. Albert Castel, "Dead on Arrival—The Life and Sudden Death of General Albert Sidney Johnston," *CWTI* 36, no. 1 (March 1997): 37.
19. *Confederate Veteran* 5: 612–13; Johnston, "Albert Sidney Johnston," 626–27.
20. Ibid.
21. *OR*, pt. 1, 569.
22. Ibid., pt. 1, 409.
23. Ibid., pt. 1, 384.
24. Ibid., pt. 1, 387.
25. Johnston, "Albert Sidney Johnston," 627.
26. *Confederate Veteran* 9: 21–22.
27. Buel and Johnson, *Battles and Leaders*, 1:18.
28. Castel, "Dead on Arrival," 37.
29. *New Orleans Picayune*, January 23, 1898.
30. James D. Richardson, ed., *A Compilation of the Messages and Papers of the Confederacy, including the Diplomatic Correspondence, 1861–1865* (Nashville: United States Publishing Co., 1906), 1:208–9.
31. *OR*, pt. 1, 117.
32. Jefferson Davis, *Rise and Fall*, 2:67.
33. Buel and Johnson, *Battles and Leaders*, 1:483–84.
34. Ibid.
35. *OR*, pt. 1, 408–9.
36. Chesnut, *A Diary from Dixie*, 156.
37. Ibid.
38. Warner, *Generals in Blue*, 536–37
39. James Lee McDonough, *Shiloh—in Hell before Night* (Knoxville: University of Tennessee Press, 1977), 95.

CHAPTER 4
1. Warner, *Generals in Gray*, 128.
2. *Confederate Veteran* 7: 553.
3. Ibid.
4. Ibid.
5. *Confederate Veteran* 8: 112.
6. *Confederate Veteran* 15: 507.
7. *Confederate Veteran* 7: 553.
8. *Confederate Veteran* 8: 112.
9. *Confederate Veteran* 1: 15.
10. *Confederate Veteran* 15: 507.
11. Evans, ed., *Confederate Military History*, 5:186.
12. Douglas, *I Rode with Stonewall*, 84.
13. Ibid., 88.
14. Warner, *Generals in Gray*, 13–14.
15. Evans, ed., *Confederate Military History*, 3:254–55.
16. Darrell Cochran, "First of the Cavaliers," *CWTI* 25, no. 10 (February 1987): 28.
17. Jack D. Welsh, *Medical Histories of Confederate Generals* (Kent, Ohio: Kent State University Press, 1996), 11.
18. Douglas, *I Rode with Stonewall*, 86–87.
19. Ibid., 87.
20. Ibid.
21. James H. Wood, *The War: "Stonewall" Jackson, His Campaigns and Battles, the Regiment as I Saw Them* (Cumberland, Md.: The Eddy Press Corp., 1911), 58.
22. Douglas, *I Rode with Stonewall*, 88.
23. Cochran, "First of the Cavaliers," 28.

24. Douglas, *I Rode with Stonewall*, 88.

25. Evans, ed., *Confederate Military History*, 3:579.

26. Ibid.; Jefferson Davis, *Rise and Fall*, 2:112.

27. Evans, ed., *Confederate Military History*, 3:255.

28. E. V. Clemens, "Lines On General Turner Ashby," *The Old Guard* 4, no. 3 (March 1866): 182.

29. Warner, *Generals in Gray*, 120.

30. *OR*, pt. 1, 750; Welsh, *Medical Histories of Confederate Generals*, 89.

31. *Confederate Veteran* 9: 20.

32. *OR*, pt. 1, 664.

33. *Confederate Veteran* 1: 206.

34. Evans, ed., *Confederate Military History*, 12:257–58; *OR*, pt. 1, 748.

35. Jefferson Davis, *Rise and Fall*, 2:141.

36. Ibid., 2:318–19; Warner, *Generals in Gray*, 339–40.

37. Douglas, *I Rode with Stonewall*, 129.

38. J. William Jones, "Reminiscences of the Army of Northern Virginia—Cedar Run," *SHSP* 10 (1882): 86–87.

39. James I. Robertson Jr., *The Stonewall Brigade* (Baton Rouge: Louisiana State University Press, 1963), 129–30.

40. Ibid., 134.

41. Ibid., 130.

42. Freeman, *Lee's Lieutenants*, 299.

43. Ibid.

44. Ibid, 299–300; Douglas, *I Rode with Stonewall*, 128.

45. *OR*, pt. 1, 172.

46. Ibid., pt. 1, 185–86.

47. Ibid., pt. 1, 178.

48. Evans, ed., *Confederate Military History*, 4:167.

49. *OR*, pt. 1, 191.

50. Jefferson Davis, *Rise and Fall*, 2:319.

CHAPTER 5

1. Warner, *Generals in Blue*, 563–64.

2. Buel and Johnson, *Battles and Leaders*, 1:639.

3. *OR*, pt. 1, 70.

4. Ibid., pt. 1, 57.

5. Ibid., pt. 1, 52.

6. Ibid., pt. 1, 41.

7. Ibid.

8. Norman Delaney, "General Thomas Williams," *CWTI* 14, no. 4 (July 1975): 46. The *New York Times* also reported, apparently erroneously, in an August 18, 1862, article that a cannonball killed Williams.

9. Delaney, "General Thomas Williams," 47.

10. *NYT*, August 25, 1862, and Buel and Johnson, *Battles and Leaders*, 3:584.

11. Warner, *Generals in Blue*, 297.

12. *OR*, pt. 1, 840.

13. Ibid.

14. *NYT*, August 9, 1862. This report appears to be fabricated, since there were no Federals, or reporters for that matter, present when McCook died.

15. Warner, *Generals in Blue*, 297.

16. *OR*, pt. 1, 839.

17. Ibid.; *NYH*, August 9, 1862; *NYT*, August 9, 1862.

18. *OR*, pt. 1, 840–41.

19. *NYH*, August 9, 1862; *NYT*, August 9, 1862.

20. *OR*, pt. 1, 773.
21. Ibid., pt. 1, 771.
22. John W. Rowell, "General McCook's Murderer," *CWTI* 17, no. 8 (May 1978): 16.
23. *OR*, pt. 1, 898.
24. Warner, *Generals in Blue*, 38–39.
25. Evans, ed., *Confederate Military History*, 1:96.
26. *NYT*, August 26, 1862; *Philadelphia Press*, August 25, 1862.
27. *OR*, pt. 1, 552–53. Hood estimated Federal casualties at 200 to 300.
28. *NYT*, August 26, 1862; *Philadelphia Press*, August 25, 1862.
29. Warner, *Generals in Blue*, 493–94.
30. *OR*, pt. 1, 408.
31. Ibid., pt. 1, 406–407.
32. Ibid., pt. 1, 734–35.
33. Ibid., pt. 1, 643–44.
34. Jack D. Welsh, *Medical Histories of Union Generals* (Kent, Ohio: Kent State University Press, 1996), 332.
35. Pindell, "Phil Kearny: One-Armed Devil," *CWTI* 27, no. 3 (May 1988): 46.
36. Buel and Johnson, *Battles and Leaders*, 2:492–93.
37. Warner, *Generals in Blue*, 475–76.
38. Henry Steele Commager, ed., *The Blue and the Gray: The Story of the Civil War as Told by Participants* (New York: The Bobbs-Merrill Company, 1950), 1, 191–92.
39. Buel and Johnson, *Battles and Leaders*, 2:493.
40. Pindell, "Phil Kearny," 46.
41. Warner, *Generals in Blue*, 258–59.
42. Commager, *The Blue and the Gray*, 1:191–92.
43. Ibid.
44. Buel and Johnson, *Battles and Leaders*, 2:521–22.
45. Ibid., 537.
46. Ibid., 536–37; *OR*, pt. 1, 418.
47. W. W. Blackford, *War Years with Jeb Stuart* (New York: Charles Scribner's Sons, 1945), 137.
48. Alexander Hunter, "A High Private's Account of the Battle of Sharpsburg," *SHSP* 10 (January–February 1882): 506.
49. Buel and Johnson, *Battles and Leaders*, 2:536–37.
50. Douglas, *I Rode with Stonewall*, 146.
51. *NYT*, September 3, 1862.
52. *OR*, pt. 1, 414.
53. *Philadelphia Press*, September 2, 1862, and *NYT*, September 4, 1862.
54. Buel and Johnson, *Battles and Leaders*, 2:492–93; *OR*, pt. 1, 45–48.
55. *NYT*, September 4, 1862.
56. *OR*, pt. 1, 811.
57. George E. Pickett, *The Heart of a Soldier, As revealed in the Intimate Letters of Genl. George E. Pickett, C.S.A.* (New York: Seth Moyle, Inc., 1913), 53.
58. *NYT*, September 7, 1862.
59. Buel and Johnson, *Battles and Leaders*, 2:492.

CHAPTER 6
1. Buel and Johnson, *Battles and Leaders*, 2:562.
2. Warner, *Generals in Gray*, 98–99.
3. Buel and Johnson, *Battles and Leaders*, 2:563.
4. Daniel Harvey Hill, "The Battle of South Mountain, or Boonsboro," *The Century* 32, no. 1 (May 1886): 140.
5. D. P. Halsey Jr., "Sketch of Capt. Don P. Halsey—A Gallant Officer, Accomplished Scholar and Able Lawyer," *SHSP* 31 (1903): 199.

6. Buel and Johnson, *Battles and Leaders*, 2:572.
7. Rev. Alexander D. Betts, *Experience of a Confederate Chaplain—1861–1865* (Greenville, S.C.: n.p., n.d.), 16.
8. Buel and Johnson, *Battles and Leaders*, 2:589.
9. Warner, *Generals in Blue*, 394–95.
10. *NYT*, September 22, 1862.
11. Buel and Johnson, *Battles and Leaders*, 2:589.
12. Stephen W. Sears, *Landscape Turned Red: The Battle of Antietam* (New York: Ticknor & Fields, 1983), 140.
13. *NYT*, September 22, 1862.
14. *OR*, pt. 1, 26, 50.
15. Ibid., pt. 1, 418.
16. Ibid., pt. 1, 1020, 1041.
17. Ibid., pt. 1, 210; *NYH*, September 17, 1862.
18. *OR*, pt. 1, 1020, 1026.
19. Buel and Johnson, *Battles and Leaders*, 2:562.
20. Warner, *Generals in Blue*, 395; *NYT*, September 22, 1862.
21. Terry L. Jones, *Lee's Tigers: The Louisiana Infantry in the Army of Northern Virginia* (Baton Rouge: Louisiana State University Press, 1987), 127–28.
22. *OR*, pt. 1, 1008.
23. Ibid., pt. 1, 1012, 1017.
24. Sears, *Landscape Turned Red*, 203; Warner, *Generals in Blue*, 309.
25. Sears, Landscape Turned Red, 205–6.
26. *NYH*, September 21, 1862.
27. Evans, ed., *Confederate Military History*, 4:289.
28. Ibid., 4:289–90.
29. A. M. Waddell, "General George Burgwyn Anderson," *SHSP* 14 (1886): 395.
30. *NYT*, November 6, 1862; *NYH*, November 5, 1862.
31. Warner, *Generals in Blue*, 402–3.
32. *OR*, pt. 1, 343–44.
33. Ibid., pt. 1, 60, 302.
34. *NYT*, September 20, 1862; *NYH*, September 21, 1862.
35. James V. Murfin, *The Gleam of Bayonets: The Battle of Antietam and the Maryland Campaign of 1862* (Baton Rouge: Louisiana State University Press, 1965), 262.
36. Warner, *Generals in Gray*, 31.
37. Evans, ed., *Confederate Military History*, 4:324–25.
38. *OR*, pt. 1, 981; James I. Robertson Jr., *General A. P. Hill: The Story of a Confederate Warrior* (New York: Vintage Books, 1987), 146–47.
39. Warner, *Generals in Blue*, 409–10.
40. *OR*, pt. 1, 29, 275.
41. Waddell, "General George Burgwyn Anderson," 395.
42. *OR*, pt. 1, 1026.
43. Henry Woodhead, *Voices of the Civil War—Antietam* (Alexandria, Va.: Time-Life Books, 1996), 150–51.
44. Warner, *Generals in Blue*, 410; *NYT*, October 5, 1862.
45. *NYH*, October 7, 1862.
46. *OR*, pt. 1, 423.
47. *NYT*, September 22, 1862.
48. *OR*, pt. 1, 85.
49. Welsh, *Medical Histories of Union Generals*, 278.
50. *NYH*, November 5, 1862.
51. *NYT*, November 6, 1862.
52. Ibid.; *NYH*, November 5, 1862.

CHAPTER 7

1. Warner, *Generals in Gray*, 188–89.
2. Welsh, *Medical Histories of Confederate Generals*, 141.
3. *Confederate Veteran* 4: 353; Frank Von Phul, "General Little's Burial," *SHSP* 29 (1901): 213.
4. Buel and Johnson, *Battles and Leaders*, 2:733.
5. *OR*, pt. 1, 123–24.
6. Ibid., 124–27.
7. Von Phul, "General Little's Burial," 214.
8. Ibid., 215.
9. Ibid.
10. Evans, ed., *Confederate Military History*, 9:89.
11. Jefferson Davis, *Rise and Fall*, 2:387.
12. Evans, ed., *Confederate Military History*, 2:170; Von Phul, "General Little's Burial," 214.
13. Von Phul, "General Little's Burial," 215.
14. Warner, *Generals in Blue*, 194–195.
15. *OR*, pt. 1, 256.
16. *Ibid.*, pt. 1, 257; *NYT*, October 11, 1862.
17. *OR*, pt. 1, 155.
18. Ibid., pt. 1, 160, 282.
19. Buel and Johnson, *Battles and Leaders*, 3:57.
20. Warner, *Generals in Blue*, 247–48.
21. Ibid., 496–97.
22. Buel and Johnson, *Battles and Leaders*, 3:57.
23. James Lee McDonough, *War in Kentucky: From Shiloh to Perryville* (Knoxville: University of Tennessee Press, 1994), 252.
24. *OR*, pt. 1, 1060; McDonough, *War in Kentucky*, 252.
25. *NYH*, October 15, 1862.
26. *OR*, pt. 1, 1060, 1121.
27. McDonough, *War in Kentucky*, 279.
28. Buel and Johnson, *Battles and Leaders*, 3:57.
29. Ibid., 17; Sam R. Watkins, *"Co. Aytch"—A Sideshow of the Big Show* (New York: Macmillan Publishing Co., 1962), 64.
30. *NYH*, October 15, 1862.
31. *OR*, pt. 1, 1044; Philip H. Sheridan, *Civil War Memoirs*, ed. Paul Andrew Hutton (New York: Bantam Domain Books, 1991), 52.
32. *OR*, pt. 1, 111, 1032.
33. *NYT*, October 11, 1862.
34. James M. Hillard, "'You Are Strangely Deluded': General William Terrill," *CWTI* 13, no. 10 (February 1975): 18.

CHAPTER 8

1. Warner, *Generals in Gray*, 56; Jim Miles, *Civil War Sites in Georgia* (Nashville: Rutledge Hill Press, 1996), 103.
2. Thomas R. R. Cobb, "Thomas R. R. Cobb—Extracts From Letters To His Wife, February 3, 1861–December 10, 1862," *SHSP* 28 (1900): 300–301.
3. Ibid.
4. Commager, *The Blue and the Gray*, 1:237.
5. Letter from R. K. Porter to Brig. Gen. Howell Cobb, *Confederate Veteran* 7: 309.
6. Cobb, "Extracts from Letters to His Wife," 301; Miles, *Civil War Sites*, 103.
7. *OR*, pt. 1, 590.
8. E. P. Alexander, "The Battle of Fredericksburg," *SHSP* 10 (1882): 450–51.
9. *Confederate Veteran* 7: 309.
10. *OR*, pt. 1, 571.

11. Ibid., pt. 1, 582.
12. Robertson, *General A. P. Hill*, 160.
13. Dr. Hunter McGuire, "Career and Character of General T. J. Jackson," *SHSP* 25 (1897): 107.
14. *OR*, pt. 1, 646.
15. Warner, *Generals in Blue*, 246–47.
16. *Philadelphia Inquirer*, December 25, 1862; *NYH*, December 17, 1862.
17. *OR*, pt. 1, 522.
18. Robertson, *General A. P. Hill*, 166.
19. *OR*, pt. 1, 522.
20. Freeman, *Lee's Lieutenants*, abridged by Stephen W. Sears, 415.
21. Warner, *Generals in Blue*, 26.
22. *NYH*, December 17, 1862.
23. Ibid.
24. Ibid.
25. James P. Smith, "With Stonewall Jackson," *SHSP* 43 (August 1920): 30.
26. Dr. Hunter McGuire, "General Thomas J. Jackson," *SHSP* 19 (1891): 309.
27. James P. Smith, "With Stonewall Jackson," 33–34.
28. Douglas, *I Rode with Stonewall*, 201; Warner, *Generals in Gray*, 119–20.
29. *NYH*, December 17, 1862; Buel and Johnson, *Battles and Leaders*, 3:136–37.
30. *NYT*, December 15, 1862; *NYH*, December 15, 1862.
31. *OR*, pt. 1, 643.
32. Ibid., pt. 1, 451.
33. Ibid., pt. 1, 1067–68.
34. Ibid.
35. Ibid., 556.
36. *Confederate Veteran* 7: 309.
37. Ibid.
38. *Confederate Veteran* 20: 281.

CHAPTER 9
1. *OR*, pt. 1, 255.
2. Warner, *Generals in Blue*, 271.
3. *OR*, pt. 1, 255.
4. Ibid., pt. 1, 301, 305.
5. *Confederate Veteran* 3: 162.
6. *OR*, pt. 1, 301, 323.
7. *NYH*, January 9, 1863.
8. Warner, *Generals in Blue*, 448–449. Some of Sill's men participated in the "Great Locomotive Raid" in Georgia, one of the more famous exploits of the war.
9. Sheridan, *Civil War Memoirs*, 68.
10. *OR*, pt. 1, 353, 357.
11. Warner, *Generals in Gray*, 250–51.
12. *Confederate Veteran* 16: 210.
13. Ibid., 391.
14. *OR*, pt. 1, 938.
15. Warner, *Generals in Gray*, 251; *Confederate Veteran* 16: 391.
16. *OR*, pt. 1, 913, 938.
17. Ibid., pt. 1, 775, 940.
18. Ibid., pt. 1, 320.
19. Ibid., pt. 1, 307.
20. *Confederate Veteran* 16: 391.
21. *OR*, pt. 1, 88.
22. Ibid., pt. 1, 857, 862, 914.

23. Ibid., pt. 1, 666.
24. McDonough, "Cold Day in Hell: The Battle of Stones River, Tennessee," *CWTI* 25, no. 4 (June 1986): 41; Warner, *Generals in Gray*, 123–24
25. William C. Davis, *The Orphan Brigade: The Kentucky Confederates Who Couldn't Go Home* (Baton Rouge: Louisiana State University Press, 1983), 155.
26. *Confederate Veteran* 16: 453; *OR*, pt. 1, 798.
27. Ibid., pt. 1, 454.
28. Evans, ed., *Confederate Military History*, 9:166–67.
29. William C. Davis, *The Orphan Brigade*, 157.
30. Ibid., 157–58; Evans, ed., *Confederate Military History*, 9:166–67.
31. William C. Davis, *The Orphan Brigade*, 160.
32. Lot D. Young, *Reminiscences of a Soldier of the Orphan Brigade* (Louisville, Ky.: Courier-Journal Job Printing Company, 1918), 58. Young added that he visited the house during a tour of the battlefield in 1912.
33. *OR*, pt. 1, 787, 828.
34. *Diary of a Confederate Soldier: John S. Jackman of the Orphan Brigade*, ed. William C. Davis (Columbia: University of South Carolina Press, 1990), 63; *Confederate Veteran* 16: 454.
35. *OR*, pt. 1, 186, 548.
36. Young, *Reminiscences*, 51.
37. *OR*, pt. 1, 670.
38. Ibid., pt. 1, 358.
39. McDonough, "Cold Day in Hell," 21.
40. *OR*, pt. 1, 258.
41. *NYH*, January 9, 1863.
42. Sheridan, *Civil War Memoirs*, 58.
43. Warner, *Generals in Blue*, 272, 637. Warner relates that other accounts list the date of Kirk's death as July 23 and July 29. His gravestone and cemetery records, however, indicate July 21.
44. Warner, *Generals in Gray*, 308–9.
45. *OR*, pt. 1, 679.
46. Ibid. Garrott himself was killed about six weeks later, unaware of his promotion to brigadier general.
47. *OR*, pt. 1, 258, 667.

CHAPTER 10

1. Warner, *Generals in Gray*, 151–52.
2. *Confederate Veteran* 13: 229–30.
3. R. E. Wilbourn, "The Wounding of Stonewall Jackson—Letter from Captain Wilbourn of Jackson's Staff," *SHSP* 6 (1878): 269.
4. Ibid.
5. Ibid.
6. Ibid., 270.
7. Ibid.
8. Ibid., 271.
9. Freeman, *Lee's Lieutenants*, abridged by Stephen W. Sears, 483. Morrison, Smith, Leigh, and Wilbourn offer conflicting versions of what happened in the confusion and shock that night. Leigh's account, however, is from a May 12, 1863, letter, and since it appears to be accurate, is the most current with the event, and is the only narrative of the four not written years after the war, it is considered the most reliable in this work.
10. James P. Smith, "Stonewall Jackson's Last Battle," *The Century*, 32 (October 1886): 925; and Benjamin Watkins Leigh, "The Wounding of Stonewall Jackson—Extract From A Letter of Major Benjamin Watkins Leigh," *SHSP* 6 (1878): 234.
11. James P. Smith, "Stonewall Jackson's Last Battle," 925.
12. Dr. Hunter McGuire, "Death of Stonewall Jackson," *SHSP* 14 (1886): 155–56.

13. Freeman, *Lee's Lieutenants*, abridged by Stephen W. Sears, 484.

14. *OR*, pt. 1, 1010.

15. McGuire, "Death of Stonewall Jackson," 157.

16. Ibid. Some accounts state that the hand wound could have been inflicted when Jackson's entourage first encountered enemy fire in the woods.

17. Mark Grimsley, "Jackson: The Wrath of God," *CWTI* 23, no. 1 (March 1984): 19.

18. Wilbourn, "Wounding of Stonewall Jackson," 273.

19. *OR*, pt. 1, 769.

20. James P. Smith, "Stonewall Jackson's Last Battle," 926.

21. Warner, *Generals in Gray*, 229–30.

22. Douglas, *I Rode with Stonewall*, 217.

23. Ibid., 218.

24. John G. Paxton, *Memoir and Memorials: Elisha Franklin Paxton, Brigadier-General, C.S.A.: Composed of his Letters from Camp and Field While an Officer in the Confederate Army, with an Introductory and Connecting Narrative Collected by his Son, John Gallatin Paxton* (New York: The Neale Publishing Company, 1907), 101.

25. Douglas, *I Rode with Stonewall*, 218.

26. Paxton, *Memoir and Memorials*, 107. Barton wrote to John Paxton on Sept. 14, 1885.

27. Ibid., 107–108.

28. *OR*, pt. 1, 1013.

29. Evans, ed., *Confederate Military History*, 645.

30. Douglas, *I Rode with Stonewall*, 219–20.

31. Paxton, *Memoir and Memorials*, 102–3.

32. Ibid.; *OR*, pt. 1, 803.

33. Douglas, *I Rode with Stonewall*, 219–20.

34. McGuire, "Death of Stonewall Jackson," 158.

35. Ibid., 159.

36. Ibid.

37. Ibid., 160.

38. *Richmond Enquirer*, May 7, 1863.

39. McGuire, "Death of Stonewall Jackson," 161.

40. James P. Smith, "Stonewall Jackson's Last Battle," 926.

41. Evans, ed., *Confederate Military History*, 3:393.

42. Douglas Southall Freeman, *Lee*, abridged by Richard Harwell (New York: Charles Scribner's Sons, 1961), 301–2.

43. McGuire, "Death of Stonewall Jackson," 162.

44. Ibid., 161.

45. Freeman, *Lee's Lieutenants*, abridged by Stephen W. Sears, 520.

46. McGuire, "Death of Stonewall Jackson," 162.

47. Ibid.

48. Ibid.

49. Ibid.

50. Douglas, *I Rode with Stonewall*, 221.

51. McGuire, "Death of Stonewall Jackson," 162–63.

52. *OR*, pt. 1, 791.

53. Douglas, *I Rode with Stonewall*, 221.

54. *Richmond Dispatch*, May 12, 1863.

55. Douglas, *I Rode with Stonewall*, 155.

56. *OR*, pt. 1, 791.

57. Douglas, *I Rode with Stonewall*, 221.

58. *Richmond Dispatch*, May 12, 1863.

59. *Richmond Enquirer*, May 12, 1863.

60. *Richmond Dispatch*, May 12, 1863.

61. Ibid., May 13, 1863.
62. Douglas, *I Rode with Stonewall*, 222.
63. *Richmond Dispatch*, May 13, 1863.
64. Ibid.
65. Ibid., May 14, 1863.
66. *OR*, pt. 1, 433–34.
67. Ibid., 473.
68. Ibid., 458.
69. Ibid., 394.
70. Ibid., 803.
71. Jefferson Davis, *Rise and Fall*, 2:364–65.
72. Warner, *Generals in Blue*, 31–32.
73. *NYH*, May 8, 1863; and Stephen W. Sears, *Chancellorsville* (New York: Mariner Books, 1996), 323.
74. Henry Woodhead, *Voices of the Civil War—Chancellorsville* (Alexandria, Va.: Time-Life Books, Inc., 1996), 116; *OR*, pt. 1, 447.
75. Warner, *Generals in Blue*, 396; Woodhead, *Voices of the Civil War—Chancellorsville*, 116.
76. Warner, *Generals in Blue*, 270–71.
77. Buel and Johnson, *Battles and Leaders*, 3:167–68.
78. Warner, *Generals in Blue*, 271.
79. *NYT*, May 30, 1863.
80. Warner, *Generals in Blue*, 554.
81. *NYT*, May 10, 1863.
82. *NYH*, May 8, 1863.
83. Ibid.; *NYT*, May 10, 1863; Warner, *Generals in Blue*, 554. A May 8 *Times* report stated erroneously that Whipple was sitting in his tent near the front lines when he was hit "by a chance ball from a rebel sharpshooter."
84. *OR*, pt. 1, 393–94.
85. Ibid., pt. 1, 394–95; Woodhead, *Voices of the Civil War—Chancellorsville*, 116.

CHAPTER 11
1. Warner, *Generals in Gray*, 306; *OR*, pt. 1, 80.
2. Francis H. Kennedy, *The Civil War Battlefield Guide* (Boston: Houghton-Mifflin Co., 1990), 130.
3. *Confederate Veteran* 1: 296.
4. Ibid.
5. Ibid.
6. *OR*, pt. 1, 265.
7. Warner, *Generals in Gray*, 306.
8. *OR*, pt. 1, 77.
9. Ibid., 85.
10. Ibid., 80.
11. Warner, *Generals in Blue*, 79.
12. Buel and Johnson, *Battles and Leaders*, 3:594.
13. Warner, *Generals in Blue*, 80.
14. Warner, *Generals in Gray*, 100–101.
15. Evans, ed., *Confederate Military History*, 7:412.
16. *OR*, pt. 1, 351, 412.
17. Warner, *Generals in Gray*, 116–17, and Welsh, *Medical Histories of Confederate Generals*, 87.
18. *OR*, pt. 1, 420–21.
19. *Confederate Veteran*, 12:447.
20. *OR*, pt. 1, 413.
21. *Charleston Mercury*, July 23, 1863.
22. *OR*, pt. 1, 295.
23. Warner, *Generals in Blue*, 483–84.

24. Luis F. Emilio, *A Brave Black Regiment*, edited by Paul Andrew Hutton (New York: Bantam Domain Books, 1991), 84.

25. Buel and Johnson, *Battles and Leaders*, 4:59.

26. Emilio, *A Brave Black Regiment*, 92; *NYT*, July 31, 1863.

27. Buel and Johnson, *Battles and Leaders*, 4:59–60.

28. *NYT*, July 31, 1863.

29. Buel and Johnson, *Battles and Leaders*, 4:59–60.

30. Warner, *Generals in Blue*, 484.

CHAPTER 12

1. Edward G. Longacre, "John F. Reynolds, General," *CWTI* 11, no. 5 (August 1972): 42.

2. Warner, *Generals in Blue*, 396–97.

3. *NYH*, July 4, 1863.

4. Commager, *The Blue and the Gray*, 2:601. Gettysburg historians refer to Reynolds's death site as Herbst Woods rather than the popular but inaccurate "Reynolds Woods," or "McPherson Woods."

5. Ibid., 2:602.

6. Paul Steiner, *Medical-Military Portraits of Union and Confederate Generals* (Philadelphia: Whitmore Publishing Co., 1968), 246.

7. *NYH*, July 4, 1863.

8. *OR*, pt. 1, 245.

9. Commager, *The Blue and the Gray*, 2:602; *Confederate Veteran* 9:85.

10. Longacre, "John F. Reynolds," 43.

11. Ibid.

12. *OR*, pt. 1, 705; Buel and Johnson, *Battles and Leaders*, 3:277.

13. *OR*, pt. 1, 273.

14. Ibid., pt. 1, 637, 677.

15. C. R. Fleet, "The Fredericksburg Artillery, Captain Edward S. Marye, In the Three Days' Battle of Gettysburg, July 1863," *SHSP* 32 (1904): 240–41.

16. *NYH*, July 3, 1863.

17. Longacre, "John F. Reynolds," 43.

18. Warner, *Generals in Gray*, 272–73.

19. *Charleston Mercury*, July 23, 1863.

20. Ibid.; Evans, ed., *Confederate Military History*, 6:436.

21. Warner, *Generals in Blue*, 576–77.

22. *OR*, pt. 1, 132–33; *NYH*, March 12, 1864.

23. Ibid.

24. Harry W. Pfanz, *Gettysburg: The Second Day* (Chapel Hill, N.C.: University of North Carolina Press, 1987), 277.

25. Warner, *Generals in Gray*, 16.

26. Evans, ed., *Confederate Military History*, 12:180.

27. *Confederate Veteran* 17: 229.

28. Glenn Tucker, *High Tide at Gettysburg* (Dayton, Ohio: Morningside House, Inc., 1983), 280.

29. *Confederate Veteran* 14: 216.

30. *Confederate Veteran* 19: 286.

31. Evans, ed., *Confederate Military History*, 12:180.

32. Tucker, *High Tide at Gettysburg*, 281.

33. *Charleston Mercury*, July 23, 1863.

34. Tucker, *High Tide at Gettysburg*, 424.

35. Warner, *Generals in Blue*, 527–28.

36. Ibid., 547–48.

37. *OR*, pt. 1, 603.

38. *NYH*, July 6, 1863.

39. *OR*, pt. 1, 652.
40. Pfanz, *Gettysburg: The Second Day*, 240.
41. Ibid.; Tucker, *High Tide at Gettysburg*, 264.
42. *NYH*, July 6, 1863.
43. *OR*, pt. 1, 593, 635.
44. Warner, *Generals in Gray*, 233.
45. Freeman, *Lee's Lieutenants*, abridged by Stephen W. Sears, 607.
46. Wayne E. Motts, *"Trust in God and Fear Nothing": Gen. Lewis A. Armistead, CSA* (Gettysburg, Pa.: Farnsworth House Military Impressions, 1994), 37.
47. Pickett, *Heart of a Soldier*, 93.
48. Gerard Patterson, *Rebels from West Point* (New York: Doubleday, 1987), 77.
49. Warner, *Generals in Gray*, 99.
50. Col. Winfield Peters, "The Lost Sword of Gen. Richard B. Garnett, Who Fell At Gettysburg," *SHSP* 33 (December 1905), 26–31.
51. *Confederate Veteran* 2: 271.
52. *Confederate Veteran* 10: 263.
53. Peters, "The Lost Sword of Gen. Richard B. Garnett," 26–31.
54. Buel and Johnson, *Battles and Leaders*, 3:365.
55. Ibid.
56. *OR*, pt. 1, 1000.
57. Peters, "The Lost Sword of Gen. Richard B. Garnett," 26–31.
58. Tucker, *High Tide at Gettysburg*, 364.
59. Peters, "The Lost Sword of Gen. Richard B. Garnett," 26–31.
60. *OR*, pt. 1, 387.
61. Evans, ed., *Confederate Military History*, 3:418.
62. *OR*, pt. 1, 428.
63. Ibid., pt. 1, 1000.
64. Motts, *"Trust in God and Fear Nothing,"* 46.
65. Ibid., 48.
66. Ibid.
67. Ibid., 49.
68. *OR*, pt. 1, 298.
69. Pickett, 107–8.
70. Warner, *Generals in Blue*, 148–49.
71. Ibid.
72. Buel and Johnson, *Battles and Leaders*, 3:394.
73. Ibid.
74. Ibid., 3:395.
75. William C. Oates, "Gettysburg—The Battle on the Right," *SHSP* 6 (July–December 1878), 182.
76. Buel and Johnson, *Battles and Leaders*, 3:329.
77. Oates, "Gettysburg," 182.
78. *Confederate Veteran* 8: 168.
79. *OR*, pt. 1, 1005, 1013.
80. *Confederate Veteran* 8: 240; *Confederate Veteran* 16, 119.
81. H. L. Benning, "Explanatory Notes by General Benning," *SHSP* 4 (1877): 177.
82. Buel and Johnson, *Battles and Leaders*, 3:396.
83. Ibid.
84. *OR*, pt. 1, 993.
85. J. H. Kidd, *A Cavalryman with Custer*, edited by Paul Andrew Hutton (New York: Bantam Domain Books, 1991), 92–93.
86. *OR*, pt. 1, 916.
87. Buel and Johnson, *Battles and Leaders*, 3:396.
88. *OR*, pt. 1, 74, 260.

89. *Confederate Veteran* 1: 206.

90. Pfanz, *Gettysburg: The Second Day*, 277; Warner, *Generals in Blue*, 577. Some accounts state that Zook died just after midnight on July 3, which is inaccurate.

91. *OR*, pt. 1, 380.

92. Buel and Johnson, *Battles and Leaders*, 3:424.

93. Ibid.

94. Welsh, *Medical Histories of Confederate Generals*, 167; *OR*, pt. 1, 608.

95. *OR*, pt. 1, 658; and Robertson, *General A. P. Hill*, 229.

96. Evans, ed., *Confederate Military History*, 6:436; *Charleston Mercury*, July 23, 1863.

97. *OR*, pt. 1, 1041.

98. Ibid., pt. 1, 620.

99. Ibid., pt. 1, 594, 603–4.

100. Buel and Johnson, *Battles and Leaders*, 3:309; *NYH*, July 6, 1863.

101. Kidd, p. 93 and Buel and Johnson, *Battles and Leaders*, vol. 3, 396.

102. Warner, Generals in Gray, pp. 237–38.

103. Wilson, "'The Most Promising Young Man of the South': James J. Pettigrew," CWTI, vol. 11, no. 10, 22–23.

104. Kidd, *A Cavalryman with Custer*, 110.

105. *OR*, pt. 1, 644.

106. *Confederate Veteran* 18: 462; Tucker, *High Tide at Gettysburg*, 388.

107. *Confederate Veteran* 18: 462; Evans, ed., *Confederate Military History*, 4:196.

108. Evans, ed., *Confederate Military History*, 4:196; *OR*, pt. 1, 641.

109. Kidd, *A Cavalryman with Custer*, 112.

110. *OR*, pt. 1, 94.

111. Wilson, "Most Promising Young Man," 23; Freeman, *Lee's Lieutenants*, abridged by Stephen W. Sears, 606.

112. Wilson, "Most Promising Young Man," 23.

113. *OR*, pt. 1, 648; Robertson, *General A. P. Hill*, 229.

114. *OR*, pt. 1, 310–11.

115. Ibid.

116. Ibid, pt. 1, 325.

117. Evans, ed., *Confederate Military History*, 4:336–37.

CHAPTER 13

1. Warner, *Generals in Gray*, 283–84.

2. Maj. W. W. Carnes, "Chickamauga," *SHSP* 14 (1886): 400.

3. John B. Gordon, *Reminiscences of the Civil War* (New York: Charles Scribner's Sons, 1903), 204.

4. Evans, ed., *Confederate Military History*, 8:101.

5. *Confederate Veteran* 6: 517.

6. Warner, *Generals in Gray*, 132–33.

7. Jackman, *Diary of a Confederate Soldier*, 88.

8. William C. Davis, *The Orphan Brigade*, 182.

9. Glenn Tucker, *Chickamauga: Bloody Battle in the West* (Dayton, Ohio: Morningside House, Inc., 1984), 242.

10. Warner, *Generals in Gray*, 71–72.

11. Evans, ed., *Confederate Military History*, 7:404.

12. Ibid., 6:175–76.

13. *OR*, pt. 1, 156; Evans, ed., *Confederate Military History*, 7:405.

14. Warner, *Generals in Blue*, 287.

15. Ibid., 288.

16. Roy Morris, "I Am Dying, Egypt, Dying," *CWTI* 25, no. 6 (October 1986): 30.

17. Ibid.

18. Ibid.

19. Douglas West, "'I Am Dying, Egypt, Dying!'—Touching Account of the Death of Its Gallant Author, Gen. W. H. Lytle," *SHSP* 23 (1895): 85.

20. Ibid.

21. Morris, "I Am Dying, Egypt, Dying," 31.

22. West, "'I Am Dying, Egype, Dying,'" 86–87.

23. William C. Davis, *The Orphan Brigade*, 191.

24. Tucker, *Chickamauga*, 239–40.

25. *OR*, pt. 1, 811.

26. Ibid., pt. 1, 22.

27. Ibid., pt. 1, 35.

28. William C. Davis, *The Orphan Brigade*, 191.

29. West, "'I Am Dying, Egypt, Dying,'" 87.

30. Morris, "'I Am Dying, Egypt, Dying,'" 31.

31. West, "'I Am Dying, Egypt, Dying,'" 87.

32. *OR*, pt. 1, 330; *New Orleans Picayune*, December 1, 1895.

33. *Cincinnati Commercial*, September 28, 1863.

34. *OR*, pt. 1, 583.

35. Ibid., 581.

36. Buell and Johnson, *Battles and Leaders*, 3:665.

37. Morris, "'I Am Dying, Egypt, Dying,'" 31.

38. Ibid.

39. *OR*, pt. 1, 583.

40. Warner, *Generals in Blue*, 419–20.

41. Buel and Johnson, *Battles and Leaders*, 3:737.

42. Ibid., 747.

43. Ibid., 737–38.

44. *OR*, pt. 1, 274–75.

45. Buel and Johnson, *Battles and Leaders*, 3:747.

46. *OR*, pt. 1, 296.

47. Buel and Johnson, *Battles and Leaders*, 3:738.

48. Warner, *Generals in Blue*, 420; *OR*, pt. 1, 269.

49. *OR*, pt. 1, 241.

50. Robertson, *General A. P. Hill*, 239.

51. Warner, *Generals in Gray*, 244–45.

52. *OR*, pt. 1, 427; *Charleston Mercury*, October 23, 1863.

53. Welsh, *Medical Histories of Confederate Generals*, 176; Warner, *Generals in Gray*, 245. Davis was a professor of anatomy at the University of Virginia.

54. *NYH*, November 30, 1863.

55. Evans, ed., *Confederate Military History*, 12:266.

CHAPTER 14

1. Warner, *Generals in Gray*, 222–23; Evans, ed., *Confederate Military History*, 10:139.

2. *OR*, pt. 1, 564.

3. Evans, ed., *Confederate Military History*, 10:139–40.

4. Ibid.

5. *Confederate Veteran* 8: 103.

6. Bruce S. Allardice, *More General in Gray* (Baton Rouge: Louisiana State University Press, 1995), 192–93.

7. Warner, *Generals in Gray*, 117–18.

8. *OR*, pt. 1, 453.

9. Ibid., 571.

10. *Confederate Veteran* 8: 103.

11. *OR*, pt. 1, 204–5.

12. Ibid., 382, 409.

13. Ibid., 266.

14. Allardice, *More Generals in Gray*, 193.

15. Warner, *Generals in Gray*, 270–71.

16. Ibid., 271.

17. Warner, *Generals in Blue*, 401–2.

18. *OR*, pt. 1, 77.

19. Ibid., 691.

20. Ibid., 671.

21. Warner, *Generals in Blue*, 402; Welsh, *Medical Histories of Union Generals*, 278.

22. *OR*, pt. 1, 818.

23. Ibid., 550. Some accounts list Hiram L. Grinstead, commander of the 33rd Arkansas Infantry, as a third Confederate general killed at Jenkins' Ferry. Grinstead, however, was a colonel and was not promoted before his death.

24. Samuel T. Gill, "The Pain of Pyrrhic Victory," *CWTI* 23, no. 3 (May 1984): 43.

CHAPTER 15

1. Warner, *Generals in Gray*, 164–65.

2. *OR*, pt. 1, 1070.

3. Patterson, *Rebels from West Point*, 54.

4. Warner, *Generals in Gray*, 287–88.

5. Terry L. Jones, *Lee's Tigers*, 197.

6. Warner, *Generals in Blue*, 223–24.

7. Horace Porter, *Campaigning with Grant* (New York: The Century Co., 1897), 52.

8. *OR*, pt. 1, 1028.

9. Warner, *Generals in Blue*, 532–33.

10. *OR*, pt. 1, 540.

11. Buel and Johnson, *Battles and Leaders*, 4:160.

12. *OR*, pt. 1, 540; *NYT*, May 19, 1864.

13. John R. Turner, "The Battle of the Wilderness—The Part Taken by Mahone's Brigade," *SHSP* 20 (1892): 73, 86.

14. Clifford Dowdey, *Lee's Last Campaign* (New York: Bonanza Books, Crown Publishers, Inc., 1960), 158.

15. Turner, "The Battle of the Wilderness," 84; Welsh, *Medical Histories of Union Generals*, 355.

16. Warner, *Generals in Gray*, 155.

17. Dowdey, *Lee's Last Campaign*, 165–66.

18. *OR*, pt. 1, 1062.

19. C. W. Field, "Campaigns of 1864 and 1865," *SHSP* 14 (1886): 545.

20. Warner, *Generals in Gray*, 155; Freeman, *Lee's Lieutenants*, abridged by Stephen W. Sears, 669.

21. Charles R. McAlpine, "Sketch of Company I, Sixty-first Virginia Infantry, Mahone's Brigade, C.S.A.," *SHSP* 24 (1896): 101.

22. *OR*, pt. 1, 452.

23. Ibid., 190, 480.

24. Welsh, *Medical Histories of Union Generals*, 355.

25. *OR*, pt. 1, 1028; *Richmond Whig*, May 9, 1864.

26. Warner, *Generals in Gray*, 287; *OR*, pt. 1, 1074. At least one account states that Stafford died at the Spotswood Hotel, which does not appear to be the case.

27. *Charleston Mercury*, May 9 and 12, 1864.

28. *OR*, pt. 1, 1074.

29. *NYH*, May 9 and 14, 1864; *NYT*, May 10, 1864.

30. *OR*, pt. 1, 64.

31. Ibid., 67, 554.

32. Ibid., 654.

33. *NYT*, May 11, 1864.
34. Ibid., May 13 and 14, 1864.
35. *NYH*, May 15, 1864.
36. *OR*, pt. 1, 783, 841.
37. *NYT*, May 19, 1864.
38. *OR, pt. 1, 326.*
39. Warner, *Generals in Blue*, 224, 533.

CHAPTER 16
1. Warner, *Generals in Blue*, 430–31.
2. Ibid.
3. *OR*, pt. 1, 574.
4. Porter, *Campaigning with Grant*, 89.
5. Buel and Johnson, *Battles and Leaders*, 4:175.
6. Ibid.
7. Ibid.
8. *OR*, pt. 1, 228.
9. Buel and Johnson, *Battles and Leaders*, 4:175.
10. Porter, *Campaigning with Grant*, 89.
11. Ibid., 90.
12. *OR*, pt. 1, 297.
13. *NYT*, May 12, 1864.
14. Ibid., May 11, 1864.
15. Porter, *Campaigning with Grant*, 90.
16. Warner, *Generals in Blue*, 477–78. Stevenson's earlier appointment to brigadier, in December 1862, was not confirmed by the Senate.
17. *OR*, pt. 1, 613.
18. Ibid., 908–909.
19. *NYT*, May 13, 1864.
20. Ibid., May 17, 1864.
21. Warner, *Generals in Blue*, 400–401; *NYT*, May 13, 1864.
22. Welsh, *Medical Histories of Union Generals*, 277.
23. *OR*, pt. 1, 191, 625. Some sources wrongly state that Rice died on May 11.
24. *NYT*, May 13, 1864.
25. Ibid., May 14, 1864.
26. Ibid., May 13, 1864.
27. Ibid., May 16, 1864.
28. *Confederate Veteran* 16: 347.
29. Ibid.
30. Warner, *Generals in Gray*, 66–67.
31. Ibid., 235.
32. *OR*, pt. 1, 1030.
33. P. T. Bennett, "General Junius Daniel," *SHSP* 18 (1890): 346–47.
34. Evans, ed., *Confederate Military History*, 4:307.
35. *OR*, pt. 1, 1074; John B. Gordon, *Reminiscences of the Civil War*, 273.
36. Louis Leon, *Diary of a Tar Heel Confederate Soldier* (Charlotte, N.C.: Stone Publishing Co., 1913), 63–64.
37. Bryan Grimes, *Extracts of Letters of Major-Gen'l Bryan Grimes To His Wife, Written While in Active Service in the Army of Northern Virginia—Together with Some Personal Recollections of the War, Written by Him after Its Close* (Raleigh, N.C.: Edwards, Broughton & Co., 1883), 54.
38. Warner, *Generals in Gray*, 154–55.
39. *OR*, pt. 1, 10.
40. Ibid., 11.

41. Ibid.
42. Welsh, *Medical Histories of Confederate Generals*, 115.
43. Warner, *Generals in Gray*, 301–302.
44. *Confederate Veteran* 10: 34–35.
45. James Hillard, "'You Are Strangely Deluded': General William Terrill," *CWTI* 13, no. 10 (February 1975): 18.
46. Welsh, *Medical Histories of Confederate Generals*, 55.
47. Warner, *Generals in Gray*, 74.
48. *Richmond Dispatch*, June 4, 1864.
49. Evans, ed., *Confederate Military History*, 6:413–14.

CHAPTER 17
1. Warner, *Generals in Gray*, 296–97.
2. G. W. Dorsey, "Fatal Wounding of General J.E.B. Stuart," *SHSP* 30 (1902): 237.
3. Ibid.
4. Patterson, *Rebels from West Point*, 100.
5. McClellan, *I Rode with Jeb Stuart*, 415.
6. W. B. Poindexter, "A Midnight Charge and the Death of General J.E.B. Stuart," *SHSP* 22 (1904): 120–21.
7. Jefferson Davis, *The Rise and Fall*, 2:510.
8. McClellan, *I Rode with Jeb Stuart*, 409–17.
9. *Richmond Examiner*, May 14, 1864; McClellan, *I Rode with Jeb Stuart*, 409–17.
10. Jefferson Davis, *The Rise and Fall*, 2:510.
11. *Richmond Examiner*, May 14, 1864.
12. Ibid.
13. W. Gordon McCabe, "Major Andrew Reid Venable, Jr.," *SHSP* 37 (1909): 68; Jon Guttman, "Jeb Stuart's Last Ride," *America's Civil War* 7, no. 2 (May 1994): 79.
14. *Richmond Examiner*, May 14, 1864.
15. Sheridan, *Civil War Memoirs*, 168.
16. Kidd, *A Cavalryman with Custer*, 211–12.
17. Douglas, *I Rode with Stonewall*, 269.
18. John B. Gordon, *Reminiscences of the Civil War*, 273.
19. *Richmond Examiner*, May 14, 1864.
20. Warner, *Generals in Gray*, 110.
21. Chris Hartley, "Personality: James B. Gordon," *America's Civil War* 7, no. 6 (January 1995): 85.
22. *Richmond Examiner*, May 20, 1864.
23. *OR*, pt. 1, 780, 819.
24. *Confederate Veteran* 6: 216; Hartley, "Personality: James B. Gordon," 85.
25. *Charlotte Observer*, January 3, 1902.
26. Douglas, *I Rode with Stonewall*, 156; Warner, *Generals in Gray*, 166–67.
27. *Confederate Veteran* 32: 18.
28. Ibid.
29. Ibid.
30. Ibid.
31. *OR*, pt. 1, 118.
32. Ibid.
33. Ibid., 95.
34. Warner, *Generals in Gray*, 167.

CHAPTER 18
1. Evans, ed., *Confederate Military History*, 10:193; Young, *Reminiscences*, 78.
2. Warner, *Generals in Gray*, 242–43.
3. Young, *Reminiscences*, 78.

4. *Confederate Veteran* 8: 532.
5. *Confederate Veteran* 7: 220.
6. *Confederate Veteran* 3: 88.
7. Stephen Elliott, *Funeral Services at the Burial of the Right Rev. Leonidas Polk, D.D., Together with the Sermon Delivered in St. Paul's Church, Augusta, Ga., on June 29, 1864: Being the Feast of St. Peter the Apostle* (Columbia, S.C.: Evans & Cogswell, 1864), 5.
8. Ibid., 5–6.
9. Evans, ed., *Confederate Military History*, 6:314.
10. Ibid., 1:665.
11. William T. Sherman, *Sherman's Civil War* (New York: Crowell-Collier Publishing Co., 1962), 244.
12. Ibid.
13. Young, *Reminiscences*, 78.
14. Elliott, *Funeral Services*, 6.
15. Ibid.
16. *Confederate Veteran* 5: 520; Watkins, *"Co. Aytch,"* 154.
17. *OR*, pt. 1, 480.
18. Ibid., 481.
19. Elliott, *Funeral Services*, 12.
20. Jefferson Davis, *The Rise and Fall*, 2:554–55.
21. Warner, *Generals in Blue*, 207.
22. Ibid., 295.
23. Buel and Johnson, *Battles and Leaders*, 4:31.
24. *OR*, pt. 1, 357, 361.
25. Ibid., 710–11; Watkins, *"Co. Aytch,"* 158.
26. *OR*, pt. 1, 611.
27. Ibid., 69, 91, 168.
28. Ibid., 445–46. Sherman letter to William Harker, August 9, 1864.
29. Warner, *Generals in Gray*, 291–92.
30. *OR*, pt. 1, 213.
31. Welsh, *Medical Histories of Confederate Generals*, 205.
32. Arthur James Lyon Fremantle, *Three Months in the Southern States: April–June 1863* (Mobile, Ala.: S. H. Goetzel, 1864), 61; Warner, *Generals in Gray*, 323–24.
33. Mosser, "I Shall Make Him Remember This Insult," *CWTI* 32, no. 1 (March/April 1993): 54.
34. *Confederate Veteran* 10: 406.
35. Russell K. Brown, *"To The Manner Born": The Life of General William H. T. Walker* (Athens, Ga.: University of Georgia Press, 1994), 274–75.
36. *OR*, pt. 1, 476.
37. Warner, *Generals in Blue*, 307.
38. *OR*, pt. 1, 73.
39. Ibid.
40. Official Souvenir, McPherson County, Kansas, July 4, 1917, 21–25.
41. Ibid.
42. *OR*, pt. 1, 394–95.
43. Ibid., 82.
44. Ibid., 122.
45. *Confederate Veteran* 11: 118–19.
46. Ibid.
47. Ibid.
48. *OR*, pt. 1, 546.
49. Ibid., 476.
50. *NYT*, July 26, 1864.
51. *Confederate Veteran* 11: 119.
52. *OR*, pt. 1, 54; Steiner, *Medical-Military Portraits*, 202.

53. *OR*, pt. 1, 75.

54. *NYT*, July 27, 1864; Bruce Catton, *This Hallowed Ground: The Story of the Union Side of the Civil War* (Garden City, N.Y.: Doubleday & Co., 1956), 345.

55. Albert D. Richardson, *A Personal History of Ulysses S. Grant* (Hartford, Conn.: American Publishing Co., 1868), 420.

56. *OR*, pt. 1, 550.

57. Ibid., 486.

58. *NYT*, July 25, 1864; *OR*, pt. 1, 28.

59. Buel and Johnson, *Battles and Leaders*, 4:317.

60. Catton, *This Hallowed Ground*, 345.

61. Steiner, *Medical-Military Portraits*, 202–3.

62. Albert D. Richardson, *Personal History of Ulysses S. Grant*, 420–21.

63. Ibid.

64. John B. Hood, *Advance and Retreat* (Secaucus, N.J.: Blue and Gray Press, 1985), 182.

65. *OR*, pt. 1, 88.

66. Jefferson Davis, *The Rise and Fall*, 2:562; Hood, *Advance and Retreat*, 181.

67. Brown, *"To the Manner Born,"* 283.

68. Evans, ed., *Confederate Military History*, 7:242. Some accounts, including Hooker's, erroneously state that Benton was mortally wounded on July 28.

69. Warner, *Generals in Gray*, 26–27.

70. John W. DuBose, *General Joseph Wheeler and the Army of Tennessee* (New York: Neale Publishing Co., 1912), 386.

71. *OR*, pt. 1, 88, 911.

72. Maud M. Kelly, "John Herbert Kelly—The Boy General of the Confederacy," *Alabama Historical Quarterly* 9, no. 1 (spring 1947), 109.

73. *OR*, pt. 1, 799–800, 961.

74. Maud M. Kelly, "John Herbert Kelly," 109–10; *Mobile (Ala.) Register & Advertiser*, March 17, 1866. Some sources, including Kelly, list General Kelly's last battle date as August 20, which is incorrect.

CHAPTER 19

1. *Confederate Veteran* 16: 269; Jeffry D. Wert, *From Winchester to Cedar Creek: The Shenandoah Campaign of 1864* (Carlisle, Pa.: South Mountain Press, 1987), 66.

2. William R. Cox, "Major General Stephen D. Ramseur: His Life and Character," *SHSP* 18 (1890): 248.

3. John B. Gordon, *Reminiscences*, 321–22.

4. Ibid.

5. Robert E. Park, "Diary of Captain Robert E. Park, Twelfth Alabama Regiment," *SHSP* 2 (July–December 1876): 26.

6. *OR*, pt. 1, 555; Jubal Early, *Autobiographical Sketch and Narrative of the War between the States* (Philadelphia: J. B. Lippincott Company, 1912), 423.

7. Douglas, *I Rode with Stonewall*, 297; Evans, ed., *Confederate Military History*, 4:258.

8. Warner, *Generals in Blue*, 416–17.

9. *NYH*, September 22, 1864; Wert, *From Winchester to Cedar Creek*, 67.

10. *OR*, pt. 1, 164.

11. Clarence R. Hatton, "The Great Battle at Cedar Creek—Early's Thin Gray Line," *SHSP* 34 (1906): 194.

12. *Confederate Veteran* 28: 136; Hatton, "Great Battle at Cedar Creek," 195–97.

13. Ibid.

14. Buel and Johnson, *Battles and Leaders*, 4:510; Park, "Diary," 29.

15. *OR*, pt. 1, 574.

16. Ibid., 552.

17. Ibid., 54, 110, 151.

18. Ibid., 165.

19. *NYH*, September 22, 1864.
20. Park, "Diary," 26; *Confederate Veteran* 16: 269.
21. Commager, *The Blue and the Gray*, 2:1049.
22. John B. Gordon, *Reminiscences*, 63.
23. Ibid., 64; Douglas, *I Rode with Stonewall*, 303–4.
24. Cox, "Major General Stephen D. Ramseur," 257.
25. Patterson, *Rebels from West Point*, 110.
26. Warner, *Generals in Blue*, 32–33.
27. Wert, *From Winchester to Cedar Creek*, 209.
28. Kidd, *Cavalryman with Custer*, 303.
29. Warner, *Generals in Blue*, 284–85.
30. Wert, *From Winchester to Cedar Creek*, 235.
31. *OR*, pt. 1, 450–51.
32. Kidd, *Cavalryman with Custer*, 307.
33. Cox, "Major General Stephen D. Ramseur," 257.
34. Ibid., 257–58.
35. Buel and Johnson, *Battles and Leaders*, 4:520.
36. Cox, "Major General Stephen D. Ramseur," 256–57.
37. *OR*, pt. 1, 450.
38. Ibid., 434; Kidd, *Cavalryman with Custer*, 307.
39. *OR*, pt. 1, 451.
40. *NYT*, October 23, 1864.
41. Ibid., October 31, 1864.
42. *OR*, pt. 1, 211, 217.
43. Ibid., 196.
44. Early, *Autobiographical Sketch and Narrative*, 450–51.
45. John B. Gordon, *Reminiscences*, 64.

CHAPTER 20
1. *OR*, pt. 1, 242.
2. Warner, *Generals in Gray*, 46–47.
3. *OR*, pt. 1, 204.
4. *NYH*, August 19, 1864.
5. *OR*, pt. 1, 215.
6. *NYH*, August 19, 1864.
7. *OR*, pt. 1, 216, 228.
8. *NYH*, August 19, 1864.
9. Warner, *Generals in Gray*, 105–106; Freeman, *Lee's Lieutenants*, abridged by Stephen W. Sears, 734.
10. *OR*, pt. 1, 688.
11. Ibid., 688, 696.
12. Ibid., 210, 229.
13. Ibid., 253.
14. Ibid., 1189.
15. Evans, ed., *Confederate Military History*, 6:421.
16. Warner, *Generals in Gray*, 268.
17. Evans, ed., *Confederate Military History*, 12:444; *OR*, pt. 1, 393.
18. Ibid., 441.
19. *Confederate Veteran* 10: 169, 17: 381.
20. *Charleston Mercury*, August 26, 1864.
21. Evans, ed., *Confederate Military History*, 12:444.
22. Warner, *Generals in Blue*, 55–56.
23. *NYH*, October 2, 1864.
24. *OR*, pt. 1, 799.

25. *NYT*, October 2, 1864.

26. Ibid.

27. *OR*, pt. 1, 799.

28. Evans, ed., *Confederate Military History*, 8:99; Warner, *Generals in Gray*, 118–19.

29. Field, "Campaigns of 1864 and 1865," 558.

30. *Confederate Veteran* 17: 269, 20: 112.

31. Warner, *Generals in Gray*, 78–79.

32. *Confederate Veteran* 16: 184; *OR*, pt. 1, 635.

33. *Confederate Veteran* 16: 184.

34. U. R. Brooks, *Butler and His Cavalry in the War of Secession—1861–1865* (Oxford, Miss.: Guild Bindery Press, 1989), 331–32.

35. *OR*, pt. 1, 635–36.

36. Ibid., 948, 1133.

37. *Confederate Veteran* 16: 184.

38. Warner, *Generals in Gray*, 113–14.

39. *Confederate Veteran* 5: 429–32. Frances O. Ticknor later described the incident in the poem, "Gracie of Alabama."

40. Welsh, *Medical Histories of Confederate Generals*, 86.

41. *Confederate Veteran* 15: 127; *OR*, pt. 1, 794.

42. *Confederate Veteran* 5: 429.

43. Ibid., 430.

44. Ibid., 431.

CHAPTER 21

1. Warner, *Generals in Gray*, 220–21.

2. *Confederate Veteran* 15: 237.

3. *OR*, pt. 1, 489–90.

4. John W. Scully, "General John Hunt Morgan—An Account of His Death," *SHSP* 31 (1903): 126.

5. William J. Stier, "Morgan's Last Battle," *CWTI* 35, no. 6 (December 1996): 84.

6. *OR*, pt. 1, 491.

7. Ibid.

8. Stier, "Morgan's Last Battle," 87.

9. Scully, "General John Hunt Morgan," 126; Stier, "Morgan's Last Battle," 87.

10. Stier, "Morgan's Last Battle," 87.

11. Ibid., 89.

12. Ibid.

13. Ibid., 90.

14. Scully, "General John Hunt Morgan," 127.

15. *OR*, pt. 1, 489–90.

16. *Confederate Veteran* 18: 112; *Charleston Mercury*, October 22, 1864.

17. Scully, "General John Hunt Morgan," 128.

18. *OR*, pt. 1, 491.

19. Ibid.

20. Ibid.

21. Jefferson Davis, *The Rise and Fall*, 2:684.

22. Scully, "General John Hunt Morgan," 127; *New Orleans Picayune*, July 5, 1903.

23. Ibid.

24. Ibid.

25. *Louisville Daily Courier*, April 18, 1868.

26. *Confederate Veteran* 19: 571.

CHAPTER 22

1. Watkins, *"Co. Aytch,"* 233.
2. Bruce Catton, *Never Call Retreat* (New York: Pocket Books, 1965), 391.
3. Warner, *Generals in Gray*, 53–54.
4. Ibid.
5. *Confederate Veteran* 20: 358.
6. *OR*, pt. 1, 737.
7. *Confederate Veteran* 11: 166.
8. *Confederate Veteran* 1: 31.
9. William J. Hardee, "Biographical Sketch of Major-General Patrick R. Cleburne," *SHSP* 21 (1903): 156.
10. *Confederate Veteran* 5: 300.
11. Evans, ed., *Confederate Military History*, 10:374.
12. Watkins, *"Co. Aytch,"* 234.
13. *Kennesaw (Ga.) Gazette*, June 15, 1887. Cleburne and Mangum were law partners in Helena, Arkansas, before the war.
14. Evans, ed., *Confederate Military History*, 10:374.
15. G. W. Gordon, "General P. R. Cleburne," *SHSP* 18 (1890): 267–68.
16. *Kennesaw (Ga.) Gazette*, June 15, 1887.
17. Welsh, *Medical Histories of Confederate Generals*, 41.
18. *Confederate Veteran* 1: 31.
19. Ibid.
20. *Confederate Veteran* 9: 149.
21. *OR*, pt. 1, 737.
22. *Kennesaw (Ga.) Gazette*, June 15, 1887.
23. *Confederate Veteran*, 5: 299.
24. Ibid., 300–301.
25. Buel and Johnson, *Battles and Leaders*, 4:439.
26. *Confederate Veteran* 5: 300–301.
27. *Confederate Veteran* 11: 166–67.
28. *Confederate Veteran* 1: 208.
29. *OR*, pt. 1, 353.
30. *Confederate Veteran* 5: 301.
31. *Confederate Veteran* 1: 264.
32. *Confederate Veteran* 12: 482.
33. *OR*, pt. 1, 643–44.
34. *Kennesaw (Ga.) Gazette*, June 15, 1887.
35. *Confederate Veteran* 7: 272.
36. Ibid.
37. Hardee, "Biographical Sketch," 163.
38. *Confederate Veteran* 12: 175.
39. *OR*, pt. 1, 614.
40. Virginia McDaniel Bowman, *Historic Williamson County: Old Homes and Sites* (n.p., n.d.), 157–58.
41. Chesnut, *A Diary from Dixie*, 339.
42. Michael J. Klinger, "Gallant Charge Repulsed," *America's Civil War* 1, no. 5 (January 1989): 30–31.
43. Evans, ed., *Confederate Military History*, 10:375.
44. Jefferson Davis, *The Rise and Fall*, 2:577.
45. *Confederate Veteran* 11: 167.

CHAPTER 23

1. Warner, *Generals in Gray*, 334–35. Whiting's academic achievements at West Point were unequaled until Douglas MacArthur scored higher grades some sixty years later.
2. Ibid.
3. Evans, ed., *Confederate Military History*, 4:354.
4. C. B. Denson, "William Henry Chase Whiting," *SHSP* 26 (1898): 174.
5. Rod Gragg, *Confederate Goliath: The Battle of Fort Fisher* (New York: HarperCollins Publishers, 1991), 192.
6. Ibid., 228.
7. Ibid., 250–51.
8. Denson, "William Henry Chase Whiting," 170–73.
9. *OR*, pt. 1, 977.
10. Welsh, *Medical Histories of Confederate Generals*, 234.
11. Denson, "William Henry Chase Whiting," 174–75.
12. *OR*, Correspondence, etc.—Union and Confederate, 375.
13. Denson, "William Henry Chase Whiting," 175.
14. Jefferson Davis, *The Rise and Fall*, 2:646.
15. Denson, "William Henry Chase Whiting," 173–74.
16. Douglas, *I Rode with Stonewall*, 311.
17. Ibid.
18. Ibid.
19. Ibid., 312.
20. John B. Gordon, *Reminiscences*, 377–78.
21. Douglas, *I Rode with Stonewall*, 312.
22. *Richmond Whig*, February 8, 1865.
23. *Richmond Dispatch*, February 9, 1865.

CHAPTER 24

1. Warner, *Generals in Gray*, 134–35.
2. Welsh, *Medical Histories of Confederate Generals*, 99–100; Warner, *Generals in Gray*, 135.
3. George Tucker, "Death of General A. P. Hill," *SHSP* 11 (1883): 564–69.
4. John W. Mauk, "The Man Who Shot General A. P. Hill," *SHSP* 20 (1892): 349–50.
5. George Tucker, "Death of General A. P. Hill," 564–69.
6. Mauk, "The Man Who Shot General A. P. Hill," 349–50.
7. George Tucker, "Death of General A. P. Hill," 564–69.
8. Mauk, "The Man Who Shot General A. P. Hill," 349–50.
9. George Tucker, "Death of General A. P. Hill," 564–69.
10. Robertson, *General A. P. Hill*, 318–19.
11. Ibid.
12. George Tucker, "Death of General A. P. Hill," 564–69.
13. Mauk, "The Man Who Shot General A. P. Hill," 349–50.
14. Robertson, *General A. P. Hill*, 321–22.
15. Jefferson Davis, *The Rise and Fall*, 2:655.

CHAPTER 25

1. Warner, *Generals in Gray*, 69–70.
2. Chris M. Calkins, *The Appomattox Campaign* (Conshohocken, Pa.: Combined Books, Inc., 1997), 143.
3. Frank M. Myers, *The Comanches: A History of White's Battalion, Virginia Cavalry, Laurel Brigade, Hampton Division, Army of Northern Virginia* (Baltimore: Kelly, Piet & Company, 1871), 380.
4. Calkins, *Appomattox Campaign*, 143.
5. Ibid.; Welsh, *Medical Histories of Confederate Generals*, 53.
6. *OR*, pt. 1, 1302–3.

7. Warner, *Generals in Blue*, 465–66.
8. Calkins, *Appomattox Campaign*, 128.
9. Ibid., 141.
10. *OR*, pt. 1, 685.
11. Warner, *Generals in Blue*, 466.
12. Ibid.; *Generals in Gray*, 312–13.
13. Noah Andre Trudeau, *Out of the Storm: The End of the Civil War, April–June 1865* (Baton Rouge: Louisiana State University Press, 1994), 253.
14. *Confederate Veteran* 15: 237, 18: 28.
15. *Confederate Veteran* 18: 29.

CHAPTER 26
1. Warner, *Generals in Gray*, 302.
2. William Hassler, "Stonewall's Other Grave," *CWTI* 23, no. 1 (March 1984): 18.
3. *Confederate Veteran* 18: 252, 19: 75.
4. Rebecca Hunt Moulder, "'Remorse and Repentance': The Death of General Felix K. Zollicoffer," *Tennessee Historical Quarterly* 37, no. 2 (summer 1978): 170–74; *Birmingham Weekly Iron Age*, April 30, 1885.
5. Motts, *"Trust in God and Fear Nothing"*, 50.
6. Warner, *Generals in Blue*, 11.
7. Ibid., 16.
8. Ibid., 78–79.
9. *OR*, pt. 1, 865–68.
10. Ibid., 435–36.
11. Ibid., 417.
12. Warner, *Generals in Blue*, 212–13.
13. Ibid., 374–75.
14. Ibid., 389–90.
15. *OR*, pt. 1, 734.
16. Ibid., 290, 571.
17. Ibid., 138.
18. Ibid., 290; Warner, *Generals in Blue*, 337.
19. *Confederate Veteran* 14: 498–99.
20. Ibid.
21. Ibid.
22. *OR*, pt. 1, 494.
23. Ibid., 184.
24. Ibid., 317.
25. Ibid., 145.
26. Ibid., 141.
27. Ibid., 314-16.
28. Ibid., 372.
29. Ibid., 441.
30. Ibid., 437.
31. Ibid., 836, 870.
32. Ibid., 487.

BIBLIOGRAPHY

Agnew, James B. "General Barnard Bee." *Civil War Times Illustrated* 14, no. 8 (December 1975).

Alexander, Gen. E. P. "The Battle of Fredericksburg." *Southern Historical Society Papers* 10 (1882).

Allardice, Bruce S. *More Generals in Gray*. Baton Rouge: Louisiana State University Press, 1995.

Avirett, James B. "Life Of General Turner Ashby." *The Old Guard* 5, no. 4 (April 1867).

Battle, J. H., W. H. Perrin, and G. C. Kniffin. *Kentucky: A History of the State*. Louisville, Ky.: F. A. Battey, 1885.

Bennett, P. T. "General Junius Daniel." *Southern Historical Society Papers* 18 (1890).

Benning, H. L. "Explanatory Notes by General Benning." *Southern Historical Society Papers* 4 (1877).

Bergeron, Arthur W., Jr. "Three-Day Tussle at Hatcher's Run." *America's Civil War* 16, no. 1 (March 2003).

Betts, Rev. Alexander D. *Experience of a Confederate Chaplain, 1861–1865*. Greenville, S.C.: n.p., n.d.

Blackford, Lt. Col. W. W. *War Years with Jeb Stuart*. New York: Charles Scribner's Sons, 1945.

Boatner, Mark M., III. *The Civil War Dictionary*. Rev. ed. New York: David McKay Company, Inc., 1987.

Bowman, Virginia McDaniel. *Historic Williamson County—Old Homes and Sites*. N.p., n.d.

Buel, Clarence C., and Robert V. Johnson. *Battles and Leaders of the Civil War: Being for the Most Part Contributions by Union and Confederate Authors*. 4 vols. New York: Century Co., 1887.

Brooks, U. R. *Butler and His Cavalry in the War of Secession, 1861–1865*. Oxford, Miss.: The Guild Bindery Press, 1989.

Brown, Russell K. *To the Manner Born: The Life of General William H. T. Walker*. Athens, Ga.: The University of Georgia Press, 1994.

Calkins, Chris M. *The Appomattox Campaign*. Conshohocken, Pa.: Combined Books, Inc., 1997.

Carnes, Maj. W. W. "Chickamauga," *Southern Historical Society Papers* 14 (1886).

Castel, Albert. "Dead on Arrival: The Life and Sudden Death of General Albert Sidney Johnston." *Civil War Times Illustrated* 36, no. 1 (March 1997).

———. *General Sterling Price and the Civil War in the West*. Baton Rouge: Louisiana State University Press, 1968.

Catton, Bruce. *Never Call Retreat*. New York: Pocket Books, 1965.

———. *The Army of the Potomac: Mr. Lincoln's Army*. Garden City, N.Y.: Doubleday & Company, Inc., 1962.

———. *This Hallowed Ground: The Story of the Union Side of the Civil War*. Garden City, N.Y.: Doubleday & Company, Inc., 1956.

Chesnut, Mary Boykin. *A Diary From Dixie*. Cambridge, Mass.: Harvard University Press, 1980.

Clemens, E. V. "Lines On General Turner Ashby." *The Old Guard* 4, no. 3 (March 1866).

Cobb, Brig. Gen. Thomas R. R. "Thomas R.R. Cobb—Extracts From Letters To His Wife, February 3, 1861–December 10, 1862," *Southern Historical Society Papers* 28 (1900).

Cochran, Darrell. "First of the Cavaliers," *Civil War Times Illustrated* 25, no. 10 (February 1987).

Commager, Henry Steele, ed. *The Blue and the Gray: The Story of the Civil War as Told by Participants*. 2 vols. New York: The Bobbs-Merrill Company, Inc., 1950.

Conrad, D. B. "History of the First Battle of Manassas and the Organization of the Stonewall Brigade." *Southern Historical Society Papers* 19 (1891).

Cox, William R. "Major General Stephen D. Ramseur: His Life and Character." *Southern Historical Society Papers* 18 (1890).

Davis, Jefferson. *The Rise and Fall of the Confederate Government*. 2 vols. New York: D. Appleton and Company, 1881.

Davis, William C. *Battle at Bull Run: A History of the First Major Campaign of the Civil War*. Baton Rouge: Louisiana State University Press, 1977.

———. *The Orphan Brigade: The Kentucky Confederates Who Couldn't Go Home*. Baton Rouge: Louisiana State University Press, 1983.

Delaney, Norman C. "General Thomas Williams." *Civil War Times Illustrated* 14, no. 4 (July 1975).

Denson, C. B. "William Henry Chase Whiting." *Southern Historical Society Papers* 26 (1898).

Dorsey, Col. G. W. "Fatal Wounding of General J.E.B. Stuart." *Southern Historical Society Papers* 30 (1902).

Douglas, Henry Kyd. *I Rode with Stonewall*. Chapel Hill: The University of North Carolina Press, 1940.

Dowdey, Clifford. *Lee's Last Campaign*. New York: Bonanza Books, Crown Publishers, Inc., 1960.

DuBose, John Witherspoon. *General Joseph Wheeler and the Army of Tennessee*. New York: The Neale Publishing Co., 1912.

Early, Lt. Gen. Jubal Anderson. *Autobiographical Sketch and Narrative of the War between the States*. Philadelphia: J. B. Lippincott Company, 1912.

Elliott, Stephen. *Funeral Services at the Burial of the Right Rev. Leonidas Polk, D.D., Together with the Sermon Delivered in St. Paul's Church, Augusta, Ga., on June 29, 1864: Being the Feast of St. Peter the Apostle*. Columbia, S.C.: Evans & Cogswell, 1864.

Emilio, Luis F. *A Brave Black Regiment: History of the Fifty-Fourth Regiment of Massachusetts Volunteer Infantry, 1863–1865*. Edited by Paul Andrew Hutton. New York: Bantam Domain Books, 1991.

Evans, Clement A., ed. *Confederate Military History*. 12 vols. Atlanta: Confederate Publishing Company, 1899.

Evans, David. "The Atlanta Campaign." *Civil War Times Illustrated* 28, no. 4 (summer 1989).

Field, Gen. C. W. "Campaigns of 1864 and 1865." *Southern Historical Society Papers* 14 (1886).

Fleet, C. R. "The Fredericksburg Artillery, Captain Edward S. Marye, In the Three Days' Battle at Gettysburg, July 1863." *Southern Historical Society Papers* 32 (1904).

Freeman, Douglas Southall. *Lee's Lieutenants: A Study in Command*. Abridged by Stephen W. Sears. New York: Simon & Shuster, 2001.

———. *Lee's Lieutenants: A Study in Command*. Vol. 1. New York: Charles Scribner's Sons, 1942.

Fremantle, Lt. Col. Arthur James Lyon. *Three Months in the Southern States: April-June 1863*. Mobile, Ala.: S. H. Goetzel, 1864.

Gill, Samuel T. "The Pain of Pyrrhic Victory." *Civil War Times Illustrated* 23, no. 3 (May 1984).

Gordon, Gen. G. W. "General P.R. Cleburne," *Southern Historical Society Papers* 18 (1890).

Gordon, Gen. John B. *Reminiscences of the Civil War*. New York: Charles Scribner's Sons, 1903.

Gragg, Rod. *Confederate Goliath: The Battle of Fort Fisher*. New York: HarperCollins Publishers, 1991.

Grimes, Bryan. *Extracts of Letters of Major-Gen'l Bryan Grimes To His Wife, Written While In Active Service In The Army Of Northern Virginia—Together With Some Personal Recollections Of The War, Written By Him After Its Close, Etc.* Raleigh, N.C.: Edwards, Broughton & Co., Steam Printers and Binders, 1883.

Grimsley, Mark. "Jackson: The Wrath of God." *Civil War Times Illustrated* 23, no. 1 (March 1984).

Guttman, Jon. "Jeb Stuart's Last Ride." *America's Civil War* 7, no. 2 (May 1994).

Halsey, D. P., Jr. "Sketch of Capt. Don P. Halsey—A Gallant Officer, Accomplished Scholar and Able Lawyer." *Southern Historical Society Papers* 31 (1903).

Hardee, General William J. "Biographical Sketch of Major-General Patrick R. Cleburne." *Southern Historical Society Papers* 21 (1903).

Hartley, Chris. "Personality: James B. Gordon." *America's Civil War* 7, no. 6 (January 1995).

Freeman, Douglas Southall. *Lee.* Abridged by Richard Harwell. New York: Charles Scribner's Sons, 1961.

Hassler, William. "Stonewall's Other Grave." *Civil War Times Illustrated* 23, no. 1 (March 1984).

Hatton, Clarence R. "The Great Battle At Cedar Creek—Early's Thin Gray Line," *Southern Historical Society Papers* 34 (1906).

Hill, General Daniel H. "The Battle of South Mountain, or Boonsboro." *The Century* 32, no. 1 (May 1886).

Hill, Gen. Daniel H. "The Real Stonewall Jackson." *The Century* 47, no. 4 (February 1894).

———. "'You Are Strangely Deluded': General William Terrill." *Civil War Times Illustrated* 13, no. 10 (February 1975).

Hood, Lt. Gen. John B. *Advance and Retreat.* Secaucus, N.J.: Blue and Gray Press, 1985.

Hunter, Alexander. "A High Private's Account of the Battle of Sharpsburg." *Southern Historical Society Papers* 10 (January–February, 1882).

Jackman, John S. *Diary of a Confederate Soldier: John S. Jackman of the Orphan Brigade.* Edited by William C. Davis. Columbia: University of South Carolina Press, 1990.

Johnston, William Preston. "Albert Sidney Johnston and the Shiloh Campaign." *The Century* 29, no. 4 (February 1885).

Jones, J. William. "Reminiscences of the Army of Northern Virginia-Cedar Run." *Southern Historical Society Papers* 10 (1882).

Jones, Terry L. *Lee's Tigers: The Louisiana Infantry in the Army of Northern Virginia.* Baton Rouge: Louisiana State University Press, 1987.

Katcher, Philip. *The Army of Robert E. Lee.* New York: Arms and Armour Press, Sterling Publishing Company, Inc., 1994.

Kelly, Dennis. "Second Manassas: The Battle and Campaign." *Civil War Times Illustrated* 22, no. 3 (May 1983).

Kelly, Maud McLure. "John Herbert Kelly: The Boy General of the Confederacy." *Alabama Historical Quarterly* 9, no. 1 (spring 1947).

Kennedy, Francis H., ed. *The Civil War Battlefield Guide.* Boston: Houghton-Mifflin Co., 1990.

Kidd, J. H. *A Cavalryman with Custer.* Edited by Paul Andrew Hutton. New York: Bantam Domain Books, 1991.

Klinger, Michael J. "Gallant Charge Repulsed." *America's Civil War* 1, no. 5 (January 1989).

Lane, Bryan. "The Familiar Road: The Life of Confederate Brigadier General John Adams." *Civil War Times Illustrated* 35, no. 5 (October 1996).

Lange, James E. T., and Katherine De Witt Jr. "Was Stonewall Jackson Fragged?" *North & South* 2, no. 4 (April 1999).

Leigh, Benjamin Watkins. "The Wounding of Stonewall Jackson—Extract From A Letter of Major Benjamin Watkins Leigh." *Southern Historical Society Papers* 6 (1878).

Leon, Louis. *Diary of a Tar Heel Confederate Soldier.* Charlotte, N.C.: Stone Publishing Co., 1913.

Longacre, Edward G. "John F. Reynolds, General." *Civil War Times Illustrated* 11, no. 5 (August 1972).

Longstreet, James. *From Manassas to Appomattox: Memoirs of the Civil War in America.* Philadelphia: J. B. Lippincott Company, 1896.

Martin, David G. *The Shiloh Campaign, March-April 1862.* New York: Fairfax Press, 1987.

Mauk, John W. "The Man Who Shot General A. P. Hill." *Southern Historical Society Papers* 20 (1892).

Maury, Gen. Dabney H. "Recollections of the Elkhorn Campaign," *Southern Historical Society Papers* 2 (1876).

McAlpine, Maj. Charles R. "Sketch of Company I, Sixty-first Virginia Infantry, Mahone's Brigade, C.S.A." *Southern Historical Society Papers* 24 (1896).

McCabe, W. Gordon. "Major Andrew Reid Venable, Jr." *Southern Historical Society Papers* 37 (1909).

McClellan, Henry B. *I Rode with Jeb Stuart: The Life and Campaigns of Major General J.E.B. Stuart.* Bloomington: Indiana University Press, 1958.

McDonough, James Lee. "Cold Day in Hell: The Battle of Stones River Tennessee." *Civil War Times Illustrated* 25, no. 4 (June 1986).

———. *Shiloh: In Hell before Night.* Knoxville: University of Tennessee Press, 1977.

———. *War in Kentucky: From Shiloh to Perryville.* Knoxville: University of Tennessee Press, 1994.

McGuire, Dr. Hunter. "Career and Character of General T. J. Jackson." *Southern Historical Society Papers* 25 (1897).

———. "Death of Stonewall Jackson." *Southern Historical Society Papers* 14 (1886).

———. "General Thomas J. Jackson." *Southern Historical Society Papers* 19 (1891).

McManus, Howard R. "Cloyd's Mountain." *Civil War Times Illustrated* 18, no. 10 (February 1980).

Miles, Jim. *Civil War Sites in Georgia.* Nashville: Rutledge Hill Press, 1996.

Morris, Roy, Jr. "I Am Dying, Egypt, Dying." *Civil War Times Illustrated* 25, no. 6 (October 1986).

Mosser, Jeffrey. "I Shall Make Him Remember This Insult." *Civil War Times Illustrated* 32, no. 1 (March/April 1993).

Motts, Wayne E. *"Trust in God and Fear Nothing": Gen. Lewis A. Armistead, CSA.* Gettysburg, Pa.: Farnsworth House Military Impressions, 1994.

Moulder, Rebecca Hunt. "'Remorse and Repentance': The Death of General Felix K. Zollicoffer." *Tennessee Historical Quarterly* 37, no. 2 (summer 1978).

Murfin, James V. *The Gleam of Bayonets: The Battle of Antietam and the Maryland Campaign of 1862.* Baton Rouge: Louisiana State University Press, 1965.

Myers, Frank M. *The Comanches: A History of White's Battalion, Virginia Cavalry, Laurel Brigade, Hampton Division, Army of Northern Virginia.* Baltimore: Kelly, Piet & Company, 1871.

Myers, J. Jay. "Who Will Follow Me?" *Civil War Times Illustrated* 32, no. 3 (July/August 1993).

Neville, H. Clay. "Battle of Wilson's Creek, or Oak Hills; Monument of Those Who Fell There." *Southern Historical Society Papers* 38 (1910).

Oates, William C. "Gettysburg: The Battle on the Right." *Southern Historical Society Papers* 6 (July–December 1878).

Official Souvenir, McPherson County (Kansas), July 4, 1917. McPherson, Kansas: n.p. 1917.)On the occasion of the unveiling of the Gen. James B. McPherson monument.)

Park, Robert E. "Diary of Captain Robert E. Park, Twelfth Alabama Regiment." *Southern Historical Society Papers* 2 (July–December 1876).

Patterson, Gerard A. *Rebels From West Point.* New York: Doubleday, Inc., 1987.

Paxton, John G. *Memoir and Memorials: Elisha Franklin Paxton, Brigadier-General, C.S.A.; Composed of his Letters from Camp and Field While an Officer in the Confederate Army, with an Introductory and Connecting Narrative Collected and Arranged by his Son, John Gallatin Paxton.* New York: The Neale Publishing Company, 1907.

Peters, Col. Winfield. "The Lost Sword of Gen. Richard B. Garnett, Who Fell At Gettysburg." *Southern Historical Society Papers* 33 (1905).

Pfanz, Harry W. *Gettysburg: The Second Day.* Chapel Hill: The University of North Carolina Press, 1987.

Pickett, George E. *The Heart of a Soldier, As revealed in the Intimate Letters of Genl. George E. Pickett C.S.A.* New York: Seth Moyle, Inc., 1913.

Pindell, Richard. "Phil Kearny: One-Armed Devil" *Civil War Times Illustrated* 27, no. 3 (May 1988).

Poindexter, W. B. "A Midnight Charge and the Death of General J.E.B. Stuart." *Southern Historical Society Papers* 22 (1904).

Porter, Gen. Horace. *Campaigning with Grant.* New York: The Century Co., 1897.

Preston, Thomas L. "General Hill's Article on Stonewall Jackson." *The Century* 48, no. 1 (May 1894).

Price, Dr. Henry. "Rich Mountain in 1861—An Account of That Memorable Campaign and How General Garnett Was Killed." vol. 27, *Southern Historical Society Papers* 27 (1899).

Rhea, Gordon C. "Phil Sheridan and his Cavalry Come of Age at the Battle of Meadow Bridge," *North & South* 2, no. 3 (March 1999).

Richardson, Albert D. *A Personal History of Ulysses S. Grant.* Hartford, Conn.: American Publishing Co., 1868.

Richardson, James D., ed. *A Compilation of the Messages and Papers of the Confederacy, including the Diplomatic Correspondence, 1861–1865.* 2 vols. Nashville: United States Publishing Co., 1906.

Robins, William M. "The Sobriquet 'Stonewall'—How It Was Acquired," *Southern Historical Society Papers* 19 (1891).

Robertson, James I. Jr. *General A. P. Hill: The Story of a Confederate Warrior*. New York: Vintage Books, 1987.

———. *The Stonewall Brigade*. Baton Rouge: Louisiana State University Press, 1963.

Rowell, John W. "General McCook's Murderer," *Civil War Times Illustrated* 17, no. 8 (May 1978).

Scully, Col. John W. "General John H. Morgan—An Account of his Death." *Southern Historical Society Papers* 31 (1903).

Sears, Stephen W. *Chancellorsville*. Boston: Mariner Books, 1996.

———. *Landscape Turned Red: The Battle of Antietam*. New York: Ticknor & Fields, 1983.

Sheridan, Gen. Philip H. *Civil War Memoirs*. Edited by Paul Andrew Hutton. New York: Bantam Domain Books, 1991.

———. *Personal Memoirs of P. H. Sheridan, General, United States Army*. 2 vols. New York: Charles L. Webster & Company, 1888.

Sherman, William T. *Sherman's Civil War*. New York: Crowell-Collier Publishing Co., 1962.

Skoch, George. "Stonewall Jackson's Last March." *Civil War Times Illustrated* 28, no. 3 (May 1980).

Smith, Derek. *Civil War Savannah*. Savannah, Ga.: Frederic C. Beil, Publisher, Inc., 1997.

Smith, James Power. "With Stonewall Jackson." *Southern Historical Society Papers* 43, no. 5 (August 1920).

———. "Stonewall Jackson's Last Battle." *The Century* 32, no. 6 (October 1886).

Starr, Stephen Z. *The Union Cavalry in the Civil War*. 3 vols. Baton Rouge: Louisiana State University Press, 1985.

Steiner, Paul E. *Medical-Military Portraits of Union and Confederate Generals*. Philadelphia: Whitmore Publishing Co., 1968.

Stier, William J. "Morgan's Last Battle." *Civil War Times Illustrated* 35, no. 6 (December 1996).

Suderow, Bryce. "Only A Miracle Can Save Us." *North & South* 4, no. 2 (January 2001).

Trudeau, Noah Andre. *The Last Citadel: Petersburg, Virginia, June 1864–April 1865*. Baton Rouge: Louisiana State University Press, 1991.

———. *Out of the Storm: The End of the Civil War, April–June 1865*. Baton Rouge: Louisiana State University Press, 1994.

Tucker, George. "Death of General A. P. Hill." *Southern Historical Society Papers* 11 (1883).

Tucker, Glenn. *Chickamauga: Bloody Battle in the West*. Dayton, Ohio: Morningside House, Inc., 1984.

———. *High Tide at Gettysburg*. Dayton, Ohio: Morningside House, Inc., 1983.

Turner, John R. "The Battle of the Wilderness—The Part Taken By Mahone's Brigade." *Southern Historical Society Papers* 20 (1892).

U.S. War Department. *The War of the Rebellion: A Compilation of the Official Records of the Union and Confederate Armies*. 128 vols. Washington, D.C.: U.S. Government Printing Office, 1880–1901.

Von Phul, Frank. "General Little's Burial." *Southern Historical Society Papers* 29 (1901).

Waddell, A. M. "General George Burgwyn Anderson." *Southern Historical Society Papers* 14 (1886).

Warner, Ezra J. *Generals in Blue: Lives of the Union Commanders*. Baton Rouge: Louisiana State University Press, 1964.

———. *Generals in Gray: Lives of the Confederate Commanders*. Baton Rouge: Louisiana State University Press, 1959.

Watkins, Sam R. *"Co. Aytch": A Side Show of the Big Show*. New York: Macmillan Publishing Co., 1962.

Waugh, Jack. "Long Distance Victory: McClellan's First Battles." *Civil War Times Illustrated* 22, no. 7 (November 1983).

Welsh, Jack D. *Medical Histories of Confederate Generals*. Kent, Ohio: The Kent State University Press, 1995.

———. *Medical Histories of Union Generals*. Kent, Ohio.: The Kent State University Press, 1996.

Wert, Jeffry D. *From Winchester to Cedar Creek: The Shenandoah Campaign of 1864*. Carlisle, Pa.: South Mountain Press, 1987.

———. "Stephen D. Ramseur." *Civil War Times Illustrated* 12, no. 2 (May 1973).

West, Col. Douglas. "'I Am Dying, Egypt, Dying!' Touching Account of the Death of Its Gallant Author, Gen. W. H. Lytle." *Southern Historical Society Papers* 23 (1895).

Wilbourn, R. E. "The Wounding of Stonewall Jackson—Letter from Captain Wilbourn of Jackson's Staff." *Southern Historical Society Papers* 6 (1878).

Wilson, Clyde N., Jr. "'The Most Promising Young Man of the South': James J. Pettigrew." *Civil War Times Illustrated* 11, no. 10 (February 1973).

Wise, Col. J. C. "The Boy Gunners of Lee." *Southern Historical Society Papers* 42 (September 1917).

Wood, James H. *The War; "Stonewall" Jackson, His Campaigns, and Battles, the Regiment as I Saw Them.* Cumberland, Md.: The Eddy Press Corp., 1911.

Woodhead, Henry, and the Editors of Time-Life Books. *Voices of the Civil War: Antietam.* Alexandria, Va.: Time-Life Books, Inc., 1996.

———. *Voices of the Civil War: Chancellorsville.* Alexandria, Va.: Time-Life Books, Inc., 1996.

Young, Lt. Lot D. *Reminiscences of a Soldier of the Orphan Brigade.* Louisville, Ky: Courier-Journal Job Printing Company, 1918.

NEWSPAPERS

Birmingham (Ala.) Weekly Iron Age
Charleston (S.C.) Mercury
Charlotte Observer
Cincinnati Commercial
Confederate Veteran
Kennesaw (Ga.) Gazette
Louisville Daily Courier
Mobile (Ala.) Register & Advertiser
New Orleans (La.) Picayune
New York Herald
New York Times
Philadelphia Inquirer
Philadelphia Press
Richmond Dispatch
Richmond Enquirer
Richmond Examiner
Richmond Whig

INDEX

Page number in italics indicate illustrations.